Engineering for Human-Computer Interaction

IFIP - The International Federation for Information Processing

IFIP was founded in 1960 under the auspices of UNESCO, following the First World Computer Congress held in Paris the previous year. An umbrella organization for societies working in information processing, IFIP's aim is two-fold: to support information processing within its member countries and to encourage technology transfer to developing nations. As its mission statement clearly states,

IFIP's mission is to be the leading, truly international, apolitical organization which encourages and assists in the development, exploitation and application of information technology for the benefit of all people.

IFIP is a non-profitmaking organization, run almost solely by 2500 volunteers. It operates through a number of technical committees, which organize events and publications. IFIP's events range from an international congress to local seminars, but the most important are:

- The IFIP World Computer Congress, held every second year;
- open conferences;
- working conferences.

The flagship event is the IFIP World Computer Congress, at which both invited and contributed papers are presented. Contributed papers are rigorously refereed and the rejection rate is high.

As with the Congress, participation in the open conferences is open to all and papers may be invited or submitted. Again, submitted papers are stringently refereed.

The working conferences are structured differently. They are usually run by a working group and attendance is small and by invitation only. Their purpose is to create an atmosphere conducive to innovation and development. Refereeing is less rigorous and papers are subjected to extensive group discussion.

Publications arising from IFIP events vary. The papers presented at the IFIP World Computer Congress and at open conferences are published as conference proceedings, while the results of the working conferences are often published as collections of selected and edited papers.

Any national society whose primary activity is in information may apply to become a full member of IFIP, although full membership is restricted to one society per country. Full members are entitled to vote at the annual General Assembly, National societies preferring a less committed involvement may apply for associate or corresponding membership. Associate members enjoy the same benefits as full members, but without voting rights. Corresponding members are not represented in IFIP bodies. Affiliated membership is open to non-national societies, and individual and honorary membership schemes are also offered.

Engineering for Human-Computer Interaction

IFIP TC2/TC13 WG2.7/WG13.4
Seventh Working Conference on
Engineering for Human-Computer Interaction
September 14-18, 1998, Heraklion, Crete, Greece

Edited by

Stéphane Chatty
Centre d'Études de la Navigation Aérienne
France

Prasun Dewan
University of North Carolina at Chapel Hill
USA

KLUWER ACADEMIC PUBLISHERS
BOSTON / DORDRECHT / LONDON

Distributors for North, Central and South America:
Kluwer Academic Publishers
101 Philip Drive
Assinippi Park
Norwell, Massachusetts 02061 USA
Telephone (781) 871-6600
Fax (781) 871-6528
E-Mail < kluwer@wkap.com >

Distributors for all other countries:
Kluwer Academic Publishers Group
Distribution Centre
Post Office Box 322
3300 AH Dordrecht, THE NETHERLANDS
Telephone 31 78 6392 392
Fax 31 78 6546 474
E-Mail < services@wkap.nl >

 Electronic Services < http://www.wkap.nl >

Library of Congress Cataloging-in-Publication Data

IFIP TC 2/WG 2.7 Working Conference on Engineering for Human-Computer Interaction
(7th : 1998 : Heraklion, Crete, Greece)
  Engineering for human-computer interaction : Seventh Working Conference on
Engineering for Human-Computer Interaction, September 14-18, 1998, Heraklion, Crete,
Greece / edited by Stéphane Chatty, Prasun Dewan.
     p.   cm.   — (International Federation for Information Processing ; 22)
  Includes bibliographical references.
  ISBN 0-412-83520-7
  1. Human-computer interaction Congresses. I. Chatty, Stéphane. II. Dewan, Prasun.
III. Title. IV. Series: International Federation for Information Processing (Series) ; 22.
QA76.9.H85I35   1998
004'.019—dc21   99-16593
                                                                                   CIP

Printed on acid-free paper.

Printed in the United States of America.

CONTENTS

SESSION 10: Workshops

Preface

The aim of IFIP Working Group 2.7 (13.4) for User Interface Engineering is to investigate the nature, concepts and construction of user interfaces for software systems. The group's scope is:

- developing user interfaces based on knowledge of system and user behaviour;
- developing frameworks for reasoning about interactive systems; and
- developing engineering models for user interfaces.

Every three years, the group holds a "working conference" on these issues. The conference mixes elements of a regular conference and a workshop. As in a regular conference, the papers describe relatively mature work and are thoroughly reviewed. As in a workshop, the audience is kept small, to enable in-depth discussions. The conference is held over 5-days (instead of the usual 3-days) to allow such discussions.

Each paper is discussed after it is presented. A transcript of the discussion is found at the end of each paper in these proceedings, giving important insights about the paper. Each session was assigned a "notes taker", whose responsibility was to collect/transcribe the questions and answers during the session. After the conference, the original transcripts were distributed (via the Web) to the attendees and modifications that clarified the discussions were accepted.

Another distinguishing feature of the conference is the wide variety of topics covered in it, ranging from traditional topics such as formal specification, user-interface management systems, task models, and help facilities to the more contemporary ones such as embodied user-interfaces, components, multimedia, the Web and groupware. Since attracting a large audience is not a goal of this conference, it can afford to take more risks in the paper selection and cover unfashionable topics.

The conference also included three parallel workshops:

- Technical Feasibility of a Virtual University system (moderated by Gilbert Cockton)
- Information Visualization (moderated by Robert Spence).
- Requirements of Groupware Development Tools (moderated by Nicholas Graham).

Intermediate and final plenary sessions were used to inform the whole group about the discussion in each workshop. Reports on the workshop topics appear at the end of the proceedings.

Len Bass was the conference chair. Laurence Nigay and Rick Kazman chaired the programme committee, which consisted of WG2.7 members. 39 papers were received, and their authors came from Austria, Brazil, Canada, Denmark, France, Germany, Greece, Italy, Spain, Switzerland, The Netherlands, UK, South Africa, Japan, New Zealand, Australia, USA. Each paper was reviewed by at least three referees from members and observers of WG2.7. Four of these papers were submitted by members of WG2.7. For these papers, one extra review was solicited from an external reviewer not associated with the working group. Eighteen papers were selected for presentation, and their authors come from 10 countries.

IFIP WG2.7 wishes to thank many individuals who contributed to the conference and the proceedings. Constantine Stephanidis made the local arrangements and organised activities for the conference participants, providing an extremely enjoyable environment throughout the week. The referees provided thorough reviews of the papers. Marie Tarjan provided invaluable help in collecting the papers, formatting the book, and creating the keyword index.

Prasun Dewan

Stéphane Chatty

Reviewers

Gregory Abowd	Balachander Krishnamurthy
Len Bass	Jim Larson
Rémi Bastide	Reed Little
Michel Beaudouin-Lafon	Wendy Mackay
Stéphane Chatty	Ian Newman
Yih-Farn Chen	Stephen North
Gilbert Cockton	Philippe Palanque
Joëlle Coutaz	Fabio Paternò
Prasun Dewan	John Patterson
Alan Dix	Chris Roast
Nicholas Graham	Helmut Stiegler
Christian Gram	Pedro Szekely
Morten Harning	Jacob Ukelson
Keith Hopper	Claus Unger

Conference Participants

Len Bass[+][*]
Rémi Bastide
Stéphane Chatty[+][*]
Henrik Baerbak Christensen
Gilbert Cockton[+][*]
Joëlle Coutaz[*]
Bertrand David
Prasun Dewan[+][*]
Ken Fishkin
Michael Freed
Federico Garcia
Patrick Girard
Nick Graham[+][*]
Christian Gram[*]
Dimitris Grammenos
John Grundy
Morten Borup Harning

Lorraine Johnston
Nicole de Koning
Shijian Lu
Roberto Moriyon
Jocelyne Nanard
Laurence Nigay[+]
Ricardo Orosco
Philippe Palanque[+][*]
Fabio Paternò[+]
Xiangshi Ren
Chris Roast
Jean Scholtz
Robert Spence
Constantine Stephanidis
Helmut Stiegler[+]
Franck Tarpin-Bernard
Claus Unger[*]

[+]*Discussion transcriber*
* Session chair

Embodied User Interfaces: Towards Invisible User Interfaces

Kenneth P. Fishkin, Thomas P. Moran & Beverly L. Harrison
Xerox PARC, 3333 Coyote Hill Road, Palo Alto, CA 94304, USA. {fishkin, moran, beverly}@parc.xerox.com

Abstract: There have been several recent examples of user interface techniques in which the user uses a computational device by physically manipulating the device. This paper proposes that these form an interesting new paradigm for user interface design, *Embodied User Interfaces*. This paper presents and defines this paradigm, and places it in the evolution of user interface paradigms leading towards the ideal of an invisible user interface. This paper outlines the space of design possibilities in this paradigm, presents a design framework for embodied user interface design, and articulates a set of design principles to guide design.

Key words: gestures, physical manipulation, user interfaces, tactile ui, tangible computing, kinaesthetics, design principles.

1.   THE EVOLUTION OF INTERFACE PARADIGMS

There have been a number of recent explorations of emerging user interface paradigms in which the user interacts with a computing device by means of direct physical manipulation. In one paradigm, termed the *Tangible User Interface* by Ishii and Ullmer (1997), the user interacts with a physical object that then controls an "attached" virtual representation. Examples of this paradigm include the "bricks" of Fitzmaurice et al. (1995), the "doll's head" of Hinckley et al. (1994), the "meta-desk" and "phicons" of Ishii and Ullmer (1997), and the "marbles" of Bishop (in Smith, 1995). Alternatively, the user can interact with the computational device itself (usually a handheld device) by tilting it, translating it, rotating it, etc., in which case the manipulation and the virtual representation are integrated within the same object, a paradigm which we term *Embodied User Interfaces*. Examples of this include scrolling a menu by tilting a device (Rekimoto, 1996), zooming text by pushing/pulling a device (Small and Ishii, 1997), navigating a list by tilting and squeezing a device (Harrison et al., 1998), and changing device behaviour by carrying it to another locale (Fitzmaurice, 1993; Want et al., 1995). These provocative user interface techniques present compelling examples of innovation that attempt to minimise the cognitive distance between a task goal and the human actions needed to accomplish that task. We believe these interaction paradigms are on an evolutionary path towards an ideal of the invisible user interface, as shown in Figure 1.

Keyboard UI —>
  Graphical UI (GUI) —>
    Gestural UI —>
      Tangible UI —>
        Embodied UI —>
          ... *invisible user interface*

Figure 1. Evolution of Computer User Interfaces

As user interface paradigms evolve, new features are added that make the interfaces more direct and more invisible. Figure 2 is a brief look at a few example techniques in the various user interface paradigms and the new features they exemplify.

Paradigm	Example Techniques	New Features
Keyboard	Unix shell	general command language
Graphical	mouse/window/desktop	"direct manipulation" on displayed objects; real-world metaphor
	light pen on display	direct contact with displayed objects
Handles	bricks	multiple generic handles; bi-manual; more degrees of freedom in manipulation
Tangible	MIT dome phicon	specific, tightly coupled input metaphor
	doll's head	3-D manipulations
	LCD lens over meta-desk	feedback in device itself
Embodied	page-turning tablet	embodied task; tightly coupled input and output metaphors.

Figure 2. Perceptual-Motor Features of Evolving User Interface Paradigms.

From this figure, we see the emergence of metaphoric representations of real-world objects on displays and the ability to "directly manipulate" these displayed objects. Then, more general control "handles" are introduced providing greater manipulatory freedom of expression. Then "tangible" objects representing the objects of work are introduced; physically manipulating these produces effects on a display and, in one case, on the device itself. There tends to be a progression towards tighter embodiments, more directness in manipulating the intended object, and more coincidence between input and output. We believe that this reflects a progression towards a more real-world interaction style, where there is no perceived mediation, i.e., an invisible user interface. However, computational systems must mediate (sense and interpret) the actions of the user. In order to provide interaction experiences that are more akin to real world experiences and that leverage everyday skills, we therefore attempt to design these mediators to become as transparent as possible.

In this paper we focus on the Embodied User Interface paradigm, the distinguishing features of which are:

− the *task is embodied* in a device .
− there is *coincidence of input and output* in the device.
− the device *provides highly specific and familiar affordances* for particular kinds of actions.

In essence, *all* aspects of the interaction are embodied in the device. At this point in the paper, we are only considering the perceptual-motor dimension of UIs, in which they are regarded as a means to manipulate objects. There is another dimension of UIs in which they are regarded as a means of communication between the user and the system. Even the most "invisible" UIs have a communication aspect to them, because systems must "know" (by sensing and interpreting) when and how the user is communicating with them. This aspect will arise later in this paper in the Design Principles section, where some communicative principles appropriate to Gestural, Tangible, and Embodied interfaces are presented.

Early user interface paradigms such as GUIs have been systematically and extensively studied, and design principles and evaluative criteria have been derived and documented (e.g. Preece et al., 1994). However, the recent paradigms, such as Tangible and Embodied User Interfaces, have thus far only been studied via isolated exploratory design probes into a potentially large and complex design space. Indeed, until very recently there has been no notion of Tangible and Embodied User Interfaces *existing* as coherent classes. This paper attempts to remedy this lack of analysis of the paradigm of Embodied User Interfaces by presenting, in Section 2, a framework for designing Embodied UIs and illustrating it with two examples of Embodied UIs. In Section 3, we show that the space of manipulations on Embedded UIs is enormous, which raises a multitude of design issues to be dealt with. In Section 4, we present a set of design principles for Embedded UIs, many of which are applicable to other UI paradigms. It is our hope that this framework and these principles will inspire a more systematic and principled investigation of novel and emerging user interface techniques and contribute to a more solid foundation for pursuing the invisible interfaces of the future.

2.   A FRAMEWORK FOR DESIGNING EMBODIED USER INTERFACES

The design features presented above imply that the user's task environment should be *embodied* within a physical/computational device, and that this embodied task should be linked to an analogous *real-world* task. The stronger this coupling, the more natural and pervasive the metaphor(s) involved, the more naturalistic and transparent the interaction becomes. Ideally, these invisible interfaces reflect high

3

degrees of embodiment, coincidence, and appropriate manipulations, and thus enhance the richness and intuitiveness of the interaction experience.

Real-World Task	Device-Embodied Task
Physical objects	Physical device
Real properties of objects	Represented objects & properties
Manipulations on objects	Manipulations on device *sensors on device* *input grammar and* *interpretation*
Feedback from objects	Feedback from device and representation

Figure 3. Design Framework for Embodied Uis.

In the real world, we wish to perform some task using a given physical object. That object has a set of real physical properties. These properties include the physical affordances (some manipulations are more natural to perform than others), the expected effects of certain manipulations, the atomicity of the object, and so forth. Some set of physical manipulations of the target object is performed to perform the task. We expect feedback, in a variety of forms, during and after the manipulation. Several items not required in real world interactions are necessary in the device interactions: sensors, a grammar, and an interpretation. These reflect the fact that a mediating agent of some sort must detect manipulations, form a command sequence based on these, and then interpret that command sequence.

We now illustrate this framework, and ground our presentation, by presenting two examples of Embodied interfaces from our own recent work (Harrison et al., 1998). We then proceed from the specific back to the general, analysing each component of the framework and presenting design principles appropriate to each.

Example 1. Navigation Within a Document or Book

In the first example, the Embodied Task consists of page-by-page navigation through a multi-page document, only one page of which can be displayed on the screen of a pen or tablet computer at a time. A book was chosen as the most appropriate physical object to map to this device object. While a tablet computer isn't a perfect match for a book, it does share a number of object properties: a flat surface for displaying text, a sequential organization of displayed pages, obvious start/end points, and the user expectation that the device is often used for displaying and navigating text.

To turn to the next page in a book, users flick on the upper right corner from right to left (Figure 4a). To turn to the previous page, they flick on the upper left corner from left to right. To keep the interface embodied, coincident, and afforded by real-world expectations, our implementation therefore supported both of these manipulations (Figure 4b) on the device.

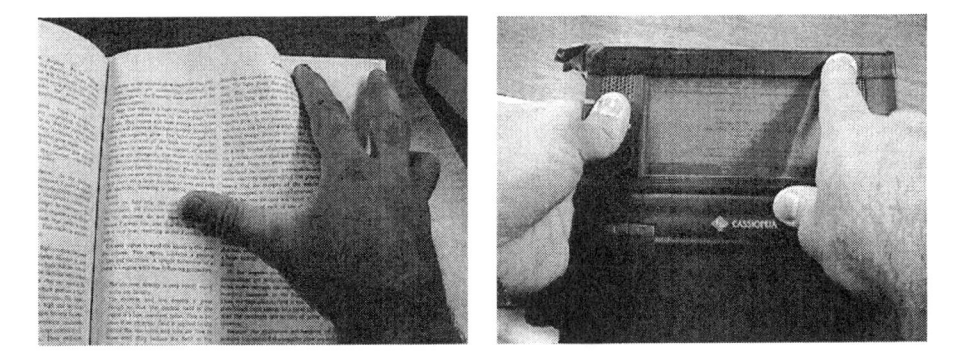

Figure 4. (a) Page-by-page navigation, real world and (b) virtual embodiment.

As a page turns in a book, feedback is provided visually (pages move, the new destination page shows, a new relative location shows), aurally (the sound of pages turning), and kinaesthetically (tactile pressure on finger or thumb, tactile feedback of pages moving or sliding). In our implementation, therefore, visual feedback mimicked real world feedback; pages changed with animation, and after a page turning manipulation, both the page number and the contents changed to reflect the new page. A "page-turning" audio cue, similar to the real-world sound, was also provided. However, no kinaesthetic feedback was provided.

The framework therefore guides the linkage between the real world task and an embodied task, modified by the constraints imposed from particular device choices, manipulations, and feedback from the user interface. Implementation constraints and sensor constraints are introduced as a result of having to use a mediating agent. This embodied manipulation requires that the left and right upper corners detect a finger press, the direction of a stroke, and a release of pressure. This was implemented by attaching pressure sensors to the surface of the device. This allowed us to "retro-fit" pressure-sensing technology onto a normally pressure-insensitive device, while also maintaining the "book" metaphor – the book stroke gesture is typically made on a corner, hence also in our implementation.

The interface was therefore specific to the task at hand – each manipulation corresponded to a specific command within one specific application.

Example 2. Navigation Through Sequential Lists

In our second example, the Embodied Task was to scroll through a sequential list displayed on a small handheld computer, a Palm Pilot™. A Rolodex was chosen as the physical target object which would best map to this target object. In this case, then, the real world task representation assumes physically manipulable items or cards, a circular sequential organisation, and a knob that controls the Rolodex (see Figure 5a). While it was impractical for us to glue a knob onto the side of the computer, our implementation did support circular sequential organisation, and displayed virtually manipulable cards of roughly the same size and shape as in the physical Rolodex.

5

In this real-world task, physical manipulations include turning the knob (with a rate parameter), and stopping at a desired location. The direction of turn determines the direction of list traversal. Our embodied task manipulations were similar. We used card items with visual tabs arranged in a sequence (Figure 5b). Turning the circular list towards the user would begin flipping from A towards Z (assuming an alphabetised list) and vice-versa. On a physical Rolodex, users turn the knob rotationally (at some rate of speed) (Figure 5a), tilting the wrist. Similarly, on the Pilot™, the user manipulation was a wrist tilt movement away from a neutral resting position. Extent or degree of tilt corresponded to rate or speed of turning. Turning harder moves faster through the list, similar to (Rekimoto, 1996). To stop at a particular item, the user either ceases to tilt (i.e., maintains the list container in a neutral position), or squeezes the device, (roughly akin to grasping the Rolodex card).

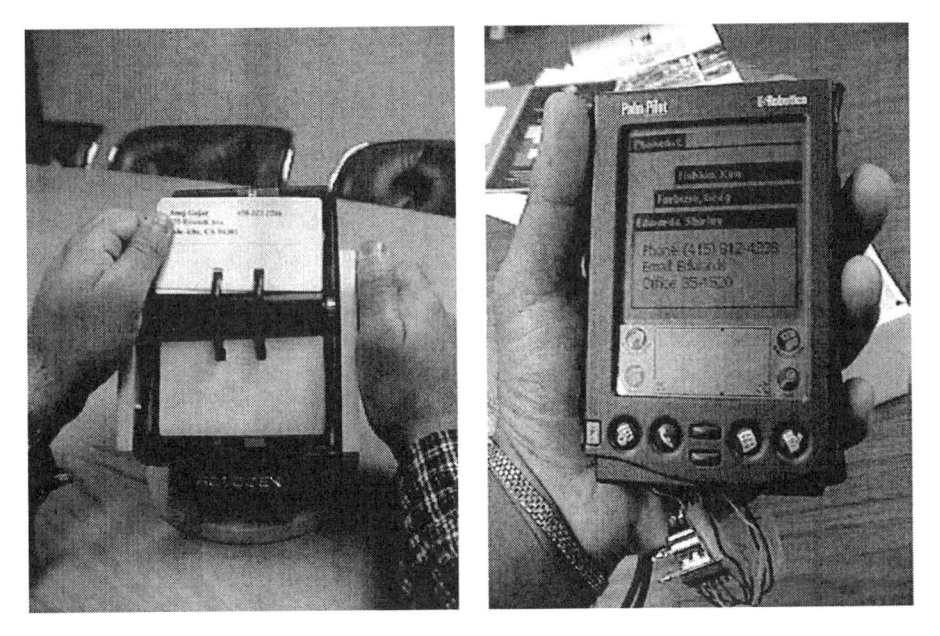

Figure 5. (a) list navigation, real-world, (b) virtual embodiment.

In the real-world task, visual feedback includes the flipping of cards, and the display of the new card. Auditory feedback is the sound of the cards flipping. Kinaesthetic cues include finger pressure, extent of rotational movement, and direction of rotation. Due to time constraints, our implementation contained only some visual feedback – users often commented that this lack of feedback affected the "naturalness" of the interface, which we regard as more evidence in favour of this as a design component.

The mediating agent used to implement the tilting manipulation was a tilt sensor, attached to the top of the Pilot, parallel to the plane of the display. As the device is angled towards or away from either plate, the amount of fluid in contact with the plate varies and impedance varies accordingly. We were therefore able to use the sensor readings as a crude measure of the computer's orientation relative to gravity.

In the real world, the rotation manipulation is sufficiently gross (a significant wrist action), and the penalty for a "false positive" is sufficiently small, that no "safety" or "clutch" is necessary to protect against flipping a Rolodex past the target. However, in our embodied task, this was not the case — the manipulation was rather small, and the penalty for scrolling when the user did not wish to scroll was significant. Accordingly, the implementation required a second manipulation, signalling an enabling/disabling of the scrolling feature. In our case, we decided to use an initial squeeze of the device to indicate the desire to navigate through the list, followed by a second squeeze to "grasp" the desired item, thereby ending the navigation task. To avoid muscle stress, users did not have to maintain the squeezing pressure during navigation. The device was padded with foam to further suggest squeezing capability. By mismatching the kinaesthetic motion scales, therefore, we had to backtrack from invisibility in other aspects of the design.

3.   DESIGN ISSUES IN THE SPACE OF MANIPULATIONS

These two sample application developments illustrate the essential features of an embodied user interface: embodiment, coincidence of input and output, and the use of specific metaphorically appropriate manipulations. We believe they also illustrate the need for a more disciplined design process and the creation of a set of articulated design principles appropriate for this space. The design space is enormous, and confronts us with a host of subtle design issues. To illustrate the size of the design space, consider the number of design parameters that may vary for each manipulation:

— Type of manipulation. Manipulations may be spatial (the device is translated, rotated, tossed, spun, shaken, flipped, etc.,), structural (the device is squeezed, folded, curled, etc.), or environmental (the device is heated, lit, etc.). Many manipulations exist, each with their own affordances, user expectations, and kinaesthetic profiles.

— Portion of device affected. The manipulation may affect the entire device, or can be restricted to any arbitrarily small portion or portions of the device. For example, conventional keyboards, by looking at the portion of the device affected (which keyboard button is spatially depressed), map each button to a different semantic effect.

— Body part(s) employed. While we envision most manipulations as being performed by one or both hands, many other possibilities exist. Not only may other body parts (elbow, arm, feet) be employed, but portions of said body parts (e.g. fingers) could also be employed, and semantics can differ depending on which portions of which body part(s) are employed. For example, Harrison et al. (1998) shows a handwriting device that alters its display depending on which hand is used. Furthermore, implements other than the body, such as pens, rods, etc can perform the manipulation.

− Magnitude. The manipulations may be gross in nature (e.g. carrying a device across a room), but in general the magnitude of the manipulation can be arbitrarily small, a barely perceptible nudge or a tiny increase in pressure.
− Simultaneity. A manipulation can take place either singly (a device is tilted), in temporally simultaneous groups (a device is tilted while squeezing), or sequentially (a device is shaken, then tilted, then brought to eye level).
− Direction. Each manipulation has other parameters, corresponding to the physical nature of the manipulation: the vector of a translation, the angle of a rotation, the displacement vector of a depression, and so forth. All of these parameters can be mapped to varying semantic effects.

In general, how are designers to choose which subset of this great space of manipulations should be employed? How does one choose the real world task upon which the embodied task is based? When is specificity useful (versus generality)? If a device is to support a range of operations, and a range of manipulations, what inter-manipulation principles apply? Tangible and Embodied designs have thus far answered these questions by inspiration and intuition on a case-by-case basis. To attempt to redress this, we now discuss specific design principles that address some of these issues.

4.   DETAILED DESIGN PRINCIPLES

Returning to the framework of Figure 3, we now analyse each component for a more detailed set of design principles to guide the design and assessment of interfaces that strive towards invisibility. While these design principles are targeted at Embodied interfaces, some are also applicable to neighbouring paradigms from the spectrum presented in Figure 1.

4.1   Embodiment Principle

The notion of mapping has often been used in user interface design theory, with principles presented to guide the mapping from real world tasks to internal representations of the tasks within the system (Moran, 1983). In physically manipulable interfaces, the mappings are more specific, relying on the physicality of the device and the user's handling of it. In most real-world situations, manipulation of an object produces changes in the same object. Therefore, for the most consistent mapping, the elements of the embodied task should be represented by parts of the device's hardware or on the device's displays (which can be visual, auditory kinaesthetic, etc.).

The various states of the task need to be embodied in the device, so the user can perceive the states of the task and, further, can think of the task as physical transformations of the parts of the device representing elements of the task. The user can then affect the physical transformations by directly physically manipulating all or part of that same device. The adherence to the Embodiment principle is precisely what distinguishes Embodied from Tangible interfaces.

8

4.2   Physical Effects Principle

Given a particular embodied task, the designer has a choice of many manipulations for the user to effect the task. HCI theory has argued for a consistent mapping from task to action (e.g., Moran, 1981; Payne and Greene, 1986) for user interfaces. Studies on human gestural systems (Skelly, 1979) stress the importance of direct physical pantomime in making these mappings natural to use and remember. As the Tangible and Embodied interface paradigms employ such physical manipulations, we propose that the best manipulations can be conceptualised as physically transforming the device in a way that accomplishes the physical transformation of the embodied task. The expected physical effects of the manipulation account for the task accomplished. We term this the **Physical Effects Principle**.

For example, consider an Embodied Task of telling a computer to compress a file. In the physical world, one way things are compressed is by squeezing them. In this task, the file is embodied on the display, so the Physical Effects Principle suggests that the device's case should be squeezed to signal the act "compress". The logic of the design is that the casing surrounds the display, and squeezing the casing causes the device, and its contents, to be compressed.

The Physical Effects Principle applies to tasks that extend beyond the boundaries of the device. For example, consider the task of sending email. The email message is embodied on the display of a wireless device. In the physical world one way things are sent off a surface to which they are attached is by flicking. Therefore, since the message is embodied as an entity on the surface of the display, "send" could be signalled by flicking the device, thereby flicking the embodied object into the air. If there are various nearby devices that could serve as the destination of the message, then the direction of the flick could indicate which device is to receive the message.

4.3   Metaphor

There are times when obvious appropriate direct physical motions don't apply. In this case, user interfaces have traditionally relied on the power of metaphor. For example, in GUI interfaces, the user manipulates windows, but they are only "metaphorical" windows. They aren't made of glass; they can be dynamically resized, and so forth. However, they still appeal to an underlying physical real-world metaphor, that of "windows" into different virtual worlds. We therefore extend the Physical Effects Principle: when there are no direct physical interpretations for manipulations to do a task, then the next best manipulations are those that appeal to a metaphor.

For example, consider a computer that can compile C++ files. There is no obvious direct real-world physical manipulation that causes things to be compiled. However, there are metaphors to encompass this. For example, we can think of compiling as a process in which "raw material" is transformed into a more "digestible" state, like a meat grinder with a rotary handle on its side. By tightly orbiting the device around some external point, "turning the crank", the embodied task is signalled metaphorically.

There will be times where no natural physical or metaphorical analogy obtains. For example, suppose our compiler can compile from a number of languages: C++ is only one of many. The manipulatory sequence must now include a manipulation that symbolises "C++". There is no obvious physical or metaphorical analogy to this word: some arbitrary manipulation must be assigned. However, we believe that in practice this will rarely be the case. For example, sign languages routinely use both physical and metaphorical analogies in their mappings and rarely resort to truly abstract mappings. Furthermore, this worst case is no worse then the average case of existing user interfaces. For example, the interface can have two buttons, one marked "C" and another marked "+" (others are possible...), and the manipulation for "C++" can be depression of a portion of the device (the "C" button), followed by two sequential depressions of another portion of the device (the "+" button).

Sets of related tasks should be considered together during design, so that metaphors can be shared across tasks to avoid confusion between them. For example, consider the task of randomising a list of items. The items are embodied on the device display as a vertical list. A manipulation for randomising the list might be to shake the device back and forth, the logic being that the physical transformation is to mix the items on the display. Now consider the additional task of sorting the list in ascending or descending order. A natural manipulation for this task might also be a shaking action. However, ambiguity then exists between the "randomise" and "sort" operations. A single shared metaphor can be achieved by decomposing the tasks into two parts: moving the items, and arranging them in a certain order. A shaking manipulation is appropriate to indicate the first part. Tilting can specify the ordering: an upward tilt for an ascending sort, a downward tilt for a descending sort, and no tilt for randomisation. The metaphor is that the "heavier" items will sink to the bottom.

4.4   Kinaesthetic Manipulation Principles

Embodied interfaces, like all interfaces, signal device operations via a set of kinaesthetic motions on the part of the user. Various aspects of good kinaesthetic design have been well studied. Their lessons are particularly germane to Gestural, Tangible, and Embodied interfaces, as the possible range of kinaesthetic motions and muscles used is so great. Some principles from these studies that apply here are:

Comfort: The best manipulations are the ones that can be comfortably performed. The range of comfortable physical movements is determined by established guidelines in anthropometry and physiology (e.g. avoid movements that stress joints such as putting both hands behind the back). Furthermore, the sequence of manipulations should be designed such that they comfortably flow into each other. Sturman (1992) discusses this for the specific case of kinaesthetic sequences involving the hand.

Comfort applies to a single manipulation, a manipulation sequence, and also to the entire sequence performed throughout the course of a day – carpal tunnel, tendonitis, and other woes of the modern era must be avoided. By restricting the device areas manipulated, and the magnitude of said manipulations, we can hopefully create user interaction sequences no worse than, and potentially better than (due to the increased degrees of freedom) existing user work practices.

Appropriate Modifiers. These manipulations can be parameterised in many ways: the speed, strength, force, and area of their affect, for example. These modifiers may have varying precision, degrees-of-freedom, and temporal duration. The corresponding modifications to the kinaesthetic motion should be a good match. For example, a modifier with a fine precision (e.g. the amount by which to resize an image) shouldn't be bound to a coarse motion such as wrist motion (Sturman, 1992). The list-navigation interaction described earlier in this paper suffered from lack of attention to this design principle: a modifier with a coarse precision (move to next element in list) was bound to a very fine motion (a slight wrist tilt).

Roles of the Hands. Humans use both hands working in parallel to express a single concept at a time. This is done either by having both hands perform the same action, or with the non-dominant hand setting the context for the dominant hand, as described by Guiard and Ferrand (1995) and applied by Buxton and Myers (1986). While interfaces could be designed in which the two hands operated in parallel to express multiple concepts (one per hand), such use simply does not seem to be natural for human users, whether in explicit communicative systems or in spontaneous gestures accompanying speech (McNeill, 1992). Therefore, an interface should not be designed to support, let alone require, this type of operation.

Socio-Cultural Factors. Given the context for our application domain, i.e., the design and use of portable computational devices, we must be aware of the limitations of the physical environment. For example, such devices may be used in locales where expansive gestures or manipulations that might be intrusive or embarrassing must be eliminated. The expansiveness of a gesture can be limited to the range of space that limits one's personal zone, as determined by proxemics (Hall, 1966). Potentially embarrassing or culturally problematic gestures or manipulations can be based on current cultural anthropology norms (Morris, 1977). These are more difficult to address since the cultural meaning of a gesture varies with location.

4.5   Sensing Principles

The best-designed manipulation is worthless if it can't be properly sensed. There are a number of constraints introduced by the sensing technology and the user's conception of that sensing technology. In an ideal setting, the sensing technology will exist completely transparently, such that users are unaware of how and when sensors activate. However, realistically this is not generally the case, for it takes a great deal of care to implement natural-feeling gestures.

4.6   Communication Principles

The design principles presented thus far have focused on the Perceptual-Motor features of user interface design. There is another axis of analysis, however, in which user interfaces are regarded as mediating agents for communicative dialogues. As Card et al. (1991) put it, "the design of human-machine dialogues is, at least in part, the design of artificial languages for this communication." We now consider manipulations on devices as a communicative language designed to impart a command sequence to a device, and we seek to apply some principles from communications theory and linguistics to further aid interface design.

This gestural command language, as sensed by the computer, is a sentence consisting of gestural units, each unit representing a single word (noun, verb, adverb, etc.) in a command sequence, each unit derived from a set of manipulations. As discussed earlier, we may assume that such words don't temporally overlap (manipulations overlap, gestures don't). The sentence may start with a 'START' symbol, and end with a 'STOP' symbol.

While design principles for user interfaces conveying information via text or speech have been well studied, we are unaware of literature analysing interfaces such as these in which information is conveyed via manipulation. However, there is a great body of literature from other disciplines that analyse gestural systems created to communicate information kinaesthetically. While none of these systems are exactly equivalent to manipulative systems, there may be lessons we can learn from them by extracting principles that hold in common across various kinaesthetic systems. Such systems include:

Spoken Language-Based Sign Languages. Gestural languages have been developed in which arbitrary messages may be formed. The syntax and grammar of these languages is borrowed, in part or whole, from a spoken language known to the gesturers. Examples of these languages are American Sign Language (ASL) (Butterworth and Flodin, 1991), and the sign languages of Australian Aborigines (Umiker-Sebeok and Sebeok, 1978), and Cistercian monks (Barakat, 1975).

Home Systems. When deaf or deaf-mute children are not taught a sign language, they develop their own gestural systems, called home systems. These systems are totally free from any spoken language, as the children know none. While each child develops their language in isolation, studies have shown (Feldman, 1975; Goldin-Meadow, 1975; Goldin-Meadow, 1979) a high level of similarity in the languages they develop.

Plains Sign Language. The most sophisticated and successful gestural language is the American Indian Sign Language, or Plains Sign Language (PSL), which has received significant study (Clark, 1959; Mallery, 1972; Skelly, 1979; Taylor, 1975; Tomkins, 1969; Umiker-Sebeok and Sebeok, 1978). PSL is at least 500 years old, and at its peak was used by hundreds of thousands of users, who spoke over 500 spoken languages from over 70 linguistic families. The language does not owe its grammar to any particular spoken language. Indeed, it evolved in order to facilitate communication amongst tribes with no common language.

Start Signal. In all of these systems, people send signals that they are about to communicate. However, these are *extra*-linguistic cues such as body stance, eye gaze, and social context. In the case of an Embodied interface, the need to detect a start symbol is particularly acute, just as it is in computerised systems with audio input, as there is no restricted location that must be used for the communication. Computers aren't as good at detecting extra-linguistic cues as humans. Therefore, if an explicit linguistic start symbol is employed, it should try to inherit the desirable properties of the extra-linguistic cues. Namely, the gesture for the start symbol should flow easily into, yet be distinct from, the gesture space used for other symbols, something like the wrist-flick suggested by Sturman et al. (1989), or the squeeze used by Harrison et al. (1998).

12

Stop Signal. In all of these systems, an explicit stop signal is rarely employed: there is no analogue to the "over" used by simplex communication protocols. Instead, a temporal pause indicates that a sentence is complete. In the rare cases when an explicit stop symbol is used, it's simply to provide emphasis (Mallery, 1972). We propose, therefore, that interfaces that support multi-gesture sequences should also use this protocol: a sentence should be considered complete after a temporal pause. This implies that an interface should not act immediately upon receipt of a gesture, but rather delay to make sure the sequence is complete. In this case the device must give continual feedback so the user knows which parameters have been received. This is particularly significant in light of the preferred gestural sequencing (see below), in which the user may optionally transmit modifiers by successive gestures.

Appropriate Linguistic Units. Earlier, we proposed that each gesture in an interface should represent known linguistic units such as nouns, verbs, adverbs, and adjectives. One can imagine systems in which this is not the case, in which the gestural units support some other structuring. However, even in home systems, where the children don't know any spoken language, individual gestures still represent linguistic units of these types. It appears that there is something deeply natural about conceptualisation at this level. Therefore, we propose that an interface also be structured to support this level of conceptualisation.

Gestural Sequencing. A complicated command can be given by arranging its component gestures in a temporal sequence. We now discuss design principles for the ordering of this sequence. Consider the home systems and PSL, in which grammars have evolved from scratch. Perhaps the dominant "meta-rule" of these grammars is to transmit a sentence in the fewest gestures possible. Specifically, they are structured such that the most significant information is transmitted first, with successive gestures progressively refining the sentence into finer and finer detail. The sentence is ended whenever a sufficient amount of detail has been transmitted. The literature refers to this as a "taxonomic" (Taylor, 1975) or "telegraphic" (Skelly, 1979) protocol. To computer scientists, this is recognisable as a "big-endian" communications protocol, in which the most significant bits are transmitted first.

If we consider a gestural sentence as indicating that an operation *op*, plus its parameters, affect an embodied virtual object *affectee*, then home systems have the basic grammar (paraphrasing Goldin-Meadow, 1975):

$$[\textit{affectee}]\ [\textit{op}]\ [\text{param}_1]\ [\text{param}_2]\ ...\ [\text{param}_n]\ \text{STOP}$$

Every element in this grammar is optional. Gestural systems make heavy use of defaults, only expressing the information that is necessary. This suggests that an embodied interface should be similarly structured.

Each parameter consists of one noun phrase. In both home systems and PSL, the modifiers to a noun phrase occur after the noun, in accordance with the "big-endian" principle: "big house" is transmitted as "house big".

Putting these implications together, consider an interface that is used to manipulate graphical images. The command "using a Gaussian filter of width 3 (the default), scale image A about the x-axis by 120%" should be transmitted as: image-A scale 120 X-axis gaussian. The affectee "A" comes first, then the operation

13

"scale," then the parameters. Each parameter transmits itself in increasing level of detail. The gestural sequence could end at any point.

5. CONCLUSIONS

This paper has proposed that recent user interface designs have represented isolated probes into a rich, largely unexplored paradigm for user interface design: that of Embodied Interfaces. Furthermore, we feel that this paradigm can be placed on a continuum with other paradigms, and that this points the way towards future paradigms whose goal will be making the user interface more and more invisible. We believe that it is important to begin to try to understand the paradigm to lay the groundwork for more disciplined design. We have presented a conceptual framework in which to place the various aspects of design in this direction, and then attempted to enumerate a set of design principles within that framework. From this investigation, we have come to appreciate that different theoretical viewpoints are needed to encompass the range of issues confronting designers.

This is only the first step in understanding the design of directly manipulable computational artefacts. We will continue to explore the design space by implementing and testing more devices to gain experience in designing, using, and assessing new user designs within this space.

At the same time, we want to broaden and deepen our analysis and understanding of the nature of the design paradigm. For example: just how important is specificity of technique, as opposed to generality? How are multimodal interaction techniques (Oviatt and Wahlster, 1997) best integrated? The answers to these can only be found by proposing different theoretical formulations.

This paper attempts to identify and understand this new user interface design paradigm. We hope that it provokes others to think systematically about where current research in user interface design is taking us, and what the design principles might be.

ACKNOWLEDGMENTS

The breadth of the Bibliography reflects the debt the authors owe to Lisa Alfke and Maia Pindar of the PARC information center, whose tireless scouring of the nation's libraries is appreciated greatly. We thank the members of the PARC Personal Document Reader effort, led by Polle Zellweger, and the "eXtreme team" (Roy Want, Anuj Gujar, and Carlos Mochon) for their support. Thanks also to Rob Burtzlaff, PARC patent attorney, for his help in clearing this paper for release.

REFERENCES

Barakat, R.A. "The Cistercian Language: A Study in Non-verbal communication". Cistercian Publications. Kalamazoo MI, 1975.

Butterworth, R. and Flodin, M. "The Perigee Visual Dictionary of Signing", Perigee, New York, 1991.

Buxton, B. and Myers, B. "A Study in two-handed input", Proceedings of CHI '86, pp. 321-326.

Card, S.K., Mackinlay, J.D., and Robertson, G.G. "A Morphological Analysis of the Design Space of Input Devices". ACM Transactions on Information Systems, (2), April 1991, pp. 99-122.

Card, S.K., Moran, T.P., and Newell, A. "The Psychology of Human-Computer Interaction". Erlbaum Associates, 1983.

Clark, W.P., "The Indian Sign Language". Hammersly, Philadelphia, 1885. Reprinted 1959 by Rosicrucian Press, San Jose.

Feldman, H., "The Development of a Lexicon by deaf children of hearing parents, or, there's more to language than meets the ear". PhD. thesis, University of Pennsylvania, 1975.

Fitzmaurice, G. "Situated Information Spaces and Spatially Aware Palmtop Computers", CACM, Vol. 36, 7, July 1993, pp.38-49.

Fitzmaurice, G., Ishii, H., and Buxton, W. "Bricks: Laying the Foundations for Graspable User Interfaces", Proceedings of CHI'95, pp. 442-449.

Goldin-Meadow, S., "Structure in a manual communication system developed without a conventional language model: Language without a helping hand". In H. Whitaker & H. A. Whitaker (Eds), Studies in Neurolinguistics, Vol. 4, New York, Academic Press, 1979, pp. 125-209.

Goldin-Meadow, S., "The Representation of Semantic Relations in a Manual Language Created by Deaf Children of Hearing Parents: A Language you can't dismiss out of hand". PhD. Thesis, University of Pennsylvania, 1975.

Guiard, Y. and Ferrand, T. "Asymmetry in Bimannual Skills", in "Manual Asymmetries in Motor Performance", Elliot & Roy (eds), CRC Press, Boca Raton FL, 1995, pp. 176-195.

Hall, E.T. "The Hidden Dimension". Doubleday, 1966.

Harrison, B.L., Fishkin, K.P., Want, R. Gujar, A., and Mochon, C.. "Suqeeze Me, Hold Me, Tilt Me! An Exploration of Manipulative User Interfaces". Proceedings of SIGCHI '98 (to appear).

Hinckley, K., Pausch, R., Goble, J.C., and Kassell, N.F. "Passive Real-World Interface Props for Neurosurgical Visualization", Proceedings of CHI'94, pp. 452-458.

Ishii, H. and Ulmer, B. "Tangible Bits: Towards Seamless Interfaces between People, Bits, and Atoms". Proceedings of CHI'97, pp. 234-241.

Mallery, G. "Sign Language Among North American Indians, compared with that among other peoples and deaf-mutes". Mouton, 1972 (reprint).

McNeill, D. "Hand and Mind: What Gestures Reveal about Thought". University of Chicago Press. 1992.

Moran, T.P. "The Command Language Grammar: a representation for the user interface of interactive computer systems". International Journal of Man-Machine Studies, 1981, 15, 3-50.

Moran, T.P, "Getting into a system: external-internal task mapping analysis". Proceedings of SIGCHI '83.

Morris, D., "Manwatching: A field guide to human behavior". Harry N. Abrams, New York, 1977.

Oviatt, S. and Wahlster, W., eds. Special Issue on Multimodal Interfaces, Human-Computer Interaction, 1997, vol. 12, nos. 1-2, pp. 1-226.

Payne, S. and Green, T. "Task-Action Grammars: A Model of the Mental Representation of Task Languages." Human-Computer Interaction, 1986, vol. 2, no. 2, pp. 93-133.

Preece, J., Rogers, Y., Sharp, H., Benyon, D., Holland, S., and Carey, T. (1994). Human-computer interaction. New York: Addison-Wesley.

Rekimoto, J. "Tilting Operations for Small Screen Interfaces". Proceedings of UIST '96, pp.167-168.

Skelly, M. "Amer-Ind Gestural Code Based on Universal American Indian Hand Talk". Elsevier, 1979.

Small, D. and Ishii, H. "Design of Spatially Aware Graspable Displays". Extended Abstracts of CHI'97, pp. 367-368.

Smith, G.C. "The Hand that Rocks the Cradle". *I.D..*, May/June 1995, pp. 60-65.

Sturman, D., Zeltzer, D., and Pieper, S. "Hands on Interaction with Virtual Environments". Proceedings of UIST'89, pp. 19-24.

Sturman, D. "Whole-hand input". PhD Thesis, MIT, 1992.

Taylor, A.R. "Nonverbal Communications Systems in Native North America", Semiotica, 1975, 13, 4, pp. 329-374.

Tomkins, W. "Indian Sign Language", Dover, New York, 1969. Reprint of 1931 edition.

Umiker-Sebeok, D.J. and Sebeok, T.A. introduction to "Aboriginal Sign Languages of the Americas and Australia", Plenum Press, New York, 1978. 2 volumes.

Want, R., Schilit, B.N., Adams, N.I., Gold, R., Petersen, K., Goldberg, D., Ellis, J.R. and Weiser, M. "An Overview of the ParcTab Ubiquitous Computing Experiment". IEEE Personal Communications, December 1995, pp. 28-43

BIOGRAPHY

Kenneth P. Fishkin is a research scientist at Xerox PARC. Since joining PARC in 1991, his research interests have included colour, 2D computer graphics, the Magic Lens user interface, and augmented reality. He holds BS degrees in Mathematics and Computer Science from the University of Wisconsin-Madison, and an MS degree in Computer Science from the University of California-Berkeley.

Thomas P. Moran is Principal Scientist and Manager of the Collaborative Systems Area at Xerox PARC. He was the first Director of the Rank Xerox EuroPARC laboratory in Cambridge. He is the founding and current Editor of the journal *Human-Computer Interaction*. His research with Card and Newell on the theoretical foundations of HCI resulted in the seminal book, *The Psychology of Human-Computer Interaction* in 1983. He has developed analysis tools and theoretical frameworks for HCI (e.g. CLG and QOC), innovative interactive systems (e.g. NoteCards and Tivoli), and collaborative multimedia systems (e.g. RAVE and meeting capture tools).

Beverly L. Harrison is a research scientist at Xerox PARC. Her research interests include augmented reality, the design/evaluation of physical-virtual interfaces, and the design of media technologies. Prior to joining PARC, she worked in product and UI design for Bell-Northern Research and has done extensive consulting in UI design and usability. She holds a Ph.D. and M.A.Sc. in Industrial Engineering (Human Factors Engineering, U. Toronto) and a B.Mathematics (Computer Science, U. Waterloo).

Discussion

Prasun Dewan: The spectrum you presented may have flaws. For example, if I type the Unix command: rm filename; ls (the output) is not coupled to the action. In direct manipulation of the directory, input and output are coupled. In tangible, again we have de-coupling, but in embodied we regain it. So embodied is to tangible, what direct manipulation was to command languages. Instead of a linear spectrum, we have a 2-D space.

Ken Fishkin: Good point.

Prasun Dewan: Will embodied interfaces reduce the chances of getting tendonitis?

Ken Fishkin: Yes. Over the last 50 years, we have been forcing people to work within a very narrow kinaesthetic pipeline. This has placed great demands on certain parts of the body, while leaving the rest "disembodied." This ignores the wide study of the operation of machinery. By widening the range of possible operations, we can reduce the load on any one part of the body.

Henrik Christensen: According to design principle #2, we should build on gestures from the "real world". I'm 35, and have never used a rolodex, only the virtual equivalent. Can we usefully adopt the metaphors of real-world artifacts that we have never used?

Ken Fishkin: There is a wide range of possible metaphors for any given task. Each has advantages and disadvantages. For example, in steering a car, the metaphor adopted in early vehicles was the tiller. I.e., you would move the tiller to the right to make the car go to the left. The steering wheel metaphor (adapted from the wheel on a ship) turned out to be more natural.

Henrik Christensen: How can you parameterize embodied interfaces? Is it necessary that embodied interfaces are less general?

Ken Fishkin: There's a trade-off between specializing an interface and generality. For example, if you put every possible function on a remote control, people no longer use them.

Claus Unger: You defined UI design as the design of a language. Doesn't UI design mean the design of a protocol based upon a language? A poor protocol based upon a great language may lead to a poor UI.

Ken Fishkin: Is a set of manipulations a language? Or is the grammar describing possible sets of manipulations the language? According to Card, Moran and Newell, a protocol *is* the grammar of the language.

Michael Freed: What about expert users?

Ken Fishkin: Generally, losing generality implies improving usability for naive users. Widening kinaesthetic range does not necessarily limit generality.

Michael Freed: But how about power of the user interface?

Ken Fishkin: Embodied interfaces can make dangerous actions safe.

Len Bass: Did you go back to exisiting embodied UI's and try to explain them in terms of your principles? Did you attempt to evaluate existing UI's?

Ken Fishkin: No, but it would be a good idea.

Morten Harning: It seems that you say that direct manipulation is for naive users. It should also be applicable for expert users.

Ken Fishkin: Direct manipulation is not just for naive users. Direct manipulation does not necessarily sacrifice generality. Direct manipulation is normally supported in frameworks where there is less generality.

Morten Harning: Transferring physical gestures associated with existing physical objects might prevent the designer from revolutionizing how a task is carried out.

Ken Fishkin: Yes, but associating the gesture with something that makes sense to the user will be better than selecting a random gesture.

Joelle Coutaz: Have you conducted comparative user studies between the scroll bar of the palm pilot and the squeeze/tilt palm pilot version for the specific task of scrolling lists?

Ken Fishkin: We want to, next year.

Helmut Stiegler: To what extent do you expect new paradigms -- not based on examples referring to the physical world -- to emerge?

Ken Fishkin: I don't know. It will be interesting to find out. It is interesting for small devices, international devices, and devices for naive users, e.g., pagers, remote controls. For example, of three commercial electronic books, two use variants of the page turning gesture.

Efficient strategies for selecting small targets on pen-based systems: an evaluation experiment for selection strategies and strategy classifications

Xiangshi Ren and Shinji Moriya
Department of Information and Communication Engineering, Tokyo Denki University, 2-2
Kanda-Nishikicho, Chiyoda-ku, Tokyo 101-8457, Japan
Tel: +81-3-5280-3335, Fax: +81-3-5280-3564
ren @c.dendai.ac.jp, moriya@c.dendai.ac.jp

Abstract: This paper describes six strategies for selecting small targets on pen-based systems. We have classified the strategies into strategy groups according to their characteristics. An experiment was conducted comparing selection time, error rate and user preference ratings for the six selection strategies. We focused our attention on the three variables associated with pen-based selection: size, direction and distance to target. Three target sizes, eight pen-movement-directions and three pen-movement-distances were applied to all six strategies. Experimental results show that the best strategy was the "Land-on2" strategy when the strategies were evaluated individually, and the best strategy group was the "In-Out" strategy group when evaluated in groups. Analyses also showed that differences between strategies were influenced by variations in target size, however, they were not influenced by pen-movement-distance and pen-movement-direction. Analyses of grouped strategies produced the same results. Ideas for future research are also presented.

Key words: mobile computing, pen-based input interfaces, selection strategies, classifications of selection strategies, small targets, differences between selection strategies.

1. INTRODUCTION

The advent of mobile computing has meant that pen-based computers have created a large niche in the computer market. Pen-based input is well suited to jotting down text and accessing information in mobile computing situations.

However, not enough empirical tests have been performed to measure how we can improve its usage.

We pay attention to the problems as follows: (1) In small pen-based systems, attempts are more often made to access information than to input information. Access includes the selection of menus, data (one character of the text or graphic segment, etc.), ranges etc., or the selection of a software keyboard displayed on a screen (Soukoreff and Mackenzie 1995). Data input includes handwriting input for both recognition and non-recognition applications. (2) As the amount of information displayed on the screen increases, users have to select smaller targets. This tendency is especially obvious in mobile products, such as personal digital assistants (PDAs), personal information managers (PIMs), and other mobile pen-based applications. The trade-off between the accessibility of targets and the amount of information presented is a fundamental problem in human-computer design. In order to solve the problem, some leading studies have developed a variety of relatively efficient selection strategies for the touchscreen (Potter, Weldon, and Shneiderman, 1988; Sear, Plaisant, and Shneiderman, 1992), the mouse (Brewster, et al., 1995; Kabbash and Buxton, 1995; Worden et al., 1997), and 3D input systems (Zhai, Buxton, and Milgram, 1994).

However, current target selection strategies for pen-based systems are mostly only imitations of selection techniques for mouse and touch-screen devices. Our previous papers have addressed the problem and described an experiment which compared strategies on a pen-based system (e.g. Ren and Moriya, 1997a). However, studies that identify and quantify the influential factors that make strategies more or less efficient remained a challenge. This paper addresses this issue. The work reported here is part of a project that looks at selection strategy problems in interface design (Ren, 1996; Ren and Moriya, 1997a, 1997b, 1998).

In section 2, we describe the six strategies and their classification. In section 3, we describe the experiment, the procedure, the design, and the aims. In section 4, we show the results of the analyses. In section 5, we identify the best strategies from the six individual strategies and from the strategy groups. We also evaluate the influence of the variables on the differences between the strategies and the strategy groups. In section 6, we present ideas for future research.

2.   THE SIX STRATEGIES AND THEIR CLASSIFICATION

2.1   Tablet structure and the six strategies

An electromagnetic tablet was used in the experiment. When the pen-tip is within a given height above the tablet surface (1 cm), the computer can recognise the co-ordinates (x, y) of the pen-tip. Thus, even though the menu on the screen is 2 dimensional (2D), it can be highlighted or selected when the pen is above the tablet surface (within 1cm). This means that the menu can be expressed as a 3 dimensional (3D) target.

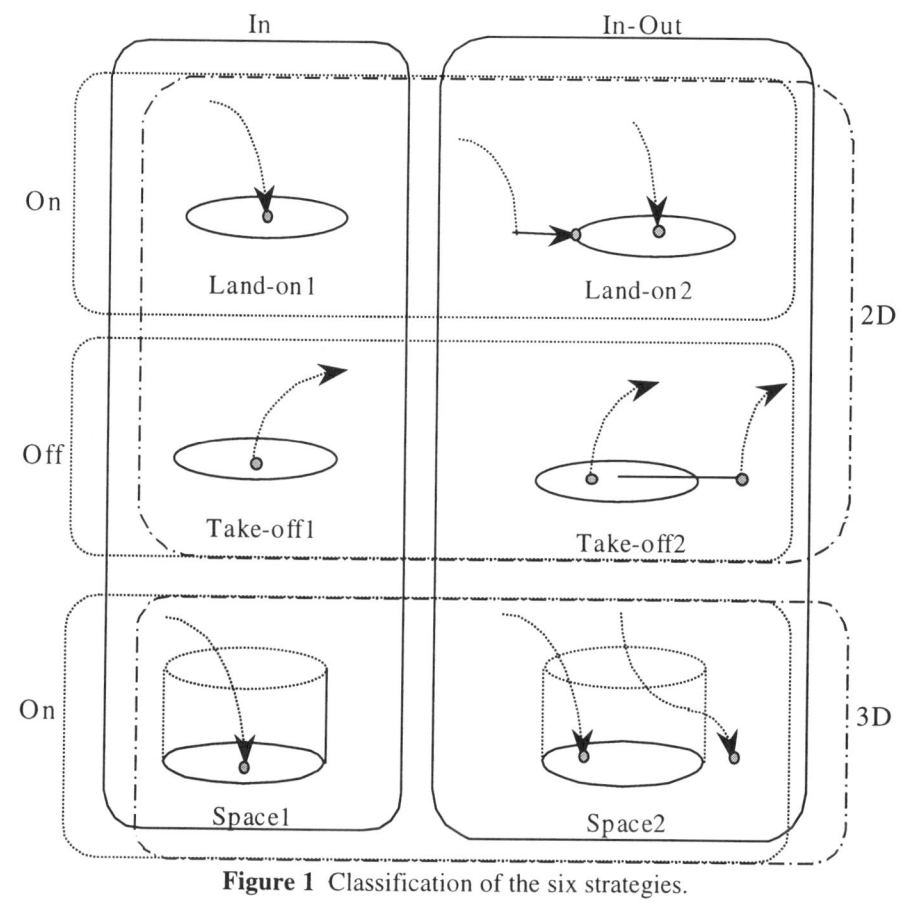

Figure 1 Classification of the six strategies.

The six strategies are illustrated in Figure 1. The ellipse and the cylinder shown in Figure 1 illustrate targets on the screen. The ellipse represents a 2D circular target. The cylinder represents a 3D target. That is, the circle with a solid line is at the bottom of the 3D target. Some responses will take place when the pen is in the cylinder. It is important to note that although the illustration in Figure 1 shows circular targets, the shape of the target has no definitive bearing on this discussion. The arrow shows the movement of the pen-tip. A dashed line arrow means the pen-tip is above the screen and a solid line arrow shows that the pen-tip is on the screen. The point (small dark circle) shows where the target selection is made by the pen.

The six strategies for selecting a target in the experiment are as follows:

- Land-on1 strategy: the pen approaches from above. The target is selected only momentarily at the time the pen makes contact with the screen in the target area.
- Land-on2 strategy is an extension of the Land-on1 strategy. Here also the target is selected when the pen touches it for the first time, but in this case the pen lands outside the target area before moving into it.
- Take-off1 strategy: the target is highlighted only while the pen is touching it. The selection is made at the moment the pen is taken off the target.

21

- Take-off2 strategy is an extension of the Take-off1 strategy. The target is highlighted only while the pen is in contact with it, however the selection is made when the pen is removed from any point on the screen either inside or outside the target area.
- Space1 strategy: the pen approaches from above. The target is highlighted while the pen is within the 1 cm high cylinder above the target. Selection is made at the moment the pen makes contact with the target area (i.e. inside the bottom circle).
- Space2 strategy is an extension of the Space1 strategy. The target is highlighted while the pen is within the 1 cm high cylinder above the target. After highlighting, the selection is made when the pen makes contact with any point on the screen either inside or outside the target area.

The Land-on1 and Take-off1 strategies are already in common use. The Land-on2 strategy corresponds to the first-contact strategy (Potter, Weldon, and Shneiderman, 1988). The Take-off2, Space1 and Space2 strategies were new strategies designed by Ren and Moriya (1997a).

2.2 Characteristics of the Six Strategies and their Classification

What characteristics do these various strategies have? What criteria were used to select the six strategies? Regarding the above questions, we concentrated on the six conditions created by the pen parameters (Ren and Moriya, 1995). They are: contact with the screen, removal from the screen, contact inside the target, contact outside the target, target highlighted and target not highlighted.

Figure 1 shows classification of the six strategies according to their characteristics.

- 2D and 3D strategies: Targets exist both as planes (2D) and as solid bodies (3D). Here, the 2D strategies are the Land-on1, Land-on2, Take-off1 and Take-off2 strategies. The 3D strategies are the Space1 and Space2 strategies.
- On and Off strategies: Contact and removal of the pen were considered as movements between the 2D plane and 3D space. Pen contact involves a movement from 3D to 2D, while removal involves a movement from 2D to 3D. These interactions were considered to be suitable conditions for the subject to recognise and confirm the moment of target selection. The strategies in which selection was made by contact with the screen (Land-on1, Land-on2, Space1 and Space2 strategies) were named On strategies. The strategies in which selection was made by removal from the screen (Take-off1 and Take-off2 strategies) were named Off strategies. Where the target existed on the 2D plane, both the On and Off strategies were deployed. Where the target oriented in 3D space, only the On strategies were used, assuming that the pen was approaching the target from above.
- In and In-Out strategies: We considered the movement of the pen into and out of the target from the perspective of the user's eyes and ears. When the pen moved into or out of the target, users could confirm whether or not the target was highlighted. Those strategies in which selection was made by contact

within the target area were named In strategies (the Land-on1, Take-off1 and Space1 strategies). On the other hand, those strategies in which selection was made by contact or removal either inside or outside the target were named In-Out strategies (Land-on2, Take-off2 and Space2 strategies).

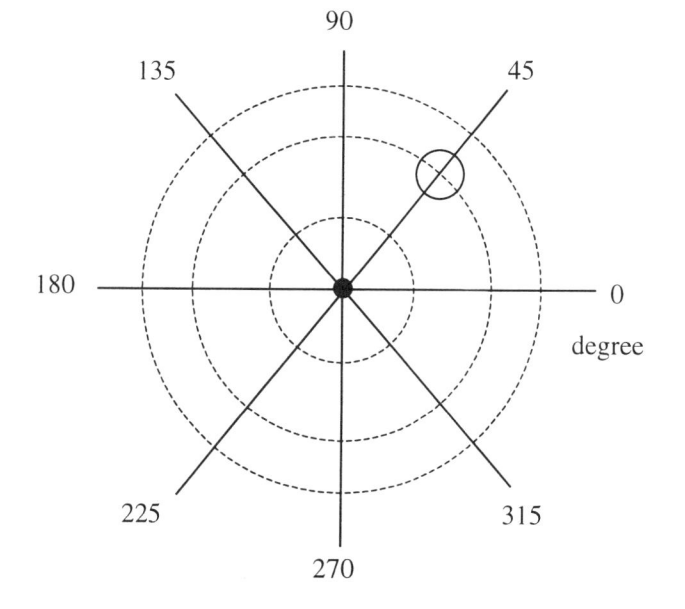

Figure 2 An example of the display of a target. The black dot is the initial position. The small circle shows one of the twenty-four possible positions for the display of a target. The dotted line shows the pen-movement-distances from the initial position to the target. The solid line indicates the pen-movement directions to the target from the initial position.

3.   THE EXPERIMENT

3.1   Subjects

Twenty-one subjects (17 male, 4 female; all right-handed, university students), were tested for the experiment. Their ages ranged from twenty-one to twenty-three years. Ten had had previous experience with pen-input systems, while the others had had no experience.

3.2   Apparatus

The hardware used in this experiment was: an electromagnetic tablet-cum-display (HD-640A, WACOM Corp.), a stylus pen (SP-200A, WACOM Corp.), and a personal computer (PC9801-DA, NEC Corp.). The space resolution of the tablet input was 0.05 mm per point. The height of the liquid crystal screen was 144.0 mm and the width was 230.4 mm. The liquid crystal display resolution was 600 x 400 pixels. 1 pixel was about 0.36 mm. The pen/screen contact area was 1.40 mm in diameter.

3.3   Procedure

First the experiment was explained to each subject. Each of them had 20 practice trials immediately before the experiment started. The message "Select a target as quickly and accurately as possible using the strategy" was displayed on the screen of the experimental tool when the experiment started.

When a target was being selected using any one of the strategies, the steps were as follows (Figure 2): (a) initial position: a circular initial position was displayed at the centre of the screen. The initial position was the place where the pen was pointed immediately before beginning the selection procedure. The subject had been told which strategy he/she was to use and how many trails he/she had to do. (b) Touching at the initial position: the subject touched the initial position with the pen. (c) Display of a target: the target was displayed with size and position changed at random by the computer. Targets of a particular size were never displayed in the same position twice. The distances between the initial position and the target were 39, 131 or 160 pixels, randomly selected by the computer. (d) Target selection: the subject received a message on the screen to indicate whether he/she had made a successful selection or not. (e) The subject then repeated (a) and (d) above. (f) End of test: a message indicating the end of the test was displayed when the subject had completed the task.

After they finished testing each strategy, the subjects were asked to fill in a questionnaire. The first question was: "For the strategy tested just now, when selecting T, how do you rate P? Please answer on a 1-to-5 scale (1 2 3 4 5)". Here, 1 = lowest preference, and 5 = highest preference. "T" means large or small targets as tested in the particular trial. "P" consisted of the six sub-questions regarding selection accuracy, selection speed, selection ease, learning ease, satisfaction and desire to use⬜ The questions (P) were asked of both large and small target sizes in each strategy. The second question was: "Which positions (i.e. direction and distances) were most comfortable for selecting the targets in the strategy?" The subject marked his/her preferences on Figure 2.

The strategies were not mixed. In a given trial each subject used only one strategy. The data for each strategy were recorded automatically as follows:
(1) Presence or absence of error when a target was selected. One selection was a continuous operation from the moment the pen touched the initial position until the removal of the pen from the tablet surface. Feedback to the subject indicated

whether the selection was successful or not. In either case, the subject could not cancel the selection.

(2) Position and size of the target displayed.

(3) The time lapsed between display of the target and the moment when the pen contacted the screen.

(4) The time lapsed between contact with the target and removal from the screen.

(5) The time lapsed between contact with the screen and contact with the target.

These times were measured to an accuracy of 10 ms using a special program.

Data as defined in item (3) was recorded for the Land-on1, Space1 and Space2 strategies. Data as defined in item (5) above was recorded for the Land-on2 strategy. Data as defined in item (4) above was recorded for the Take-off1 and Take-off2 strategies.

3.4   Design

The experiment used a mixed factorial design. (1) Size of target: To examine the relationship between target size and strategy, three target sizes of 3, 5 and 9 pixels (1.1 mm, 1.8 mm, and 3.2 mm diameter circles) were used in all trials. All the targets for the experiment were circular. Circular targets were used so that the distance between the initial position and the edge of all targets on each radius remained constant in all directions. (2) Pen-movement-distance: the distance to the target was the radius of a circle in which the centre point was the initial position (Figure 2). To examine the relationship between distance and strategy, the distances of 39, 131 and 160 pixels (14.0, 47.2 and 57.6 mm) were determined by a preliminary experiment. (Distances of 39 pixels and 131 pixels were the average values used by ten subjects in a preliminary experiment. When their wrists were in a fixed condition, 39 pixels was the radius of the arc which could be drawn by the subjects; 131 pixels was the radius of the circular arc which was the maximum finger-movement-distance. The outside circle radius of 160 pixels was determined according to the size limitations (height) of the tablet screen. It was also a distance by which the wrist could be moved.). (3) Pen-movement-direction : eight directions were used. They were at 0, 45, 90, 135, 180, 225, 270 and 315 degrees from the initial position (Figure 2).

The subject had a total of 92 trials for each strategy. These consisted of 20 practice trials and 72 test trials (= 3 target sizes x 3 distances x 8 directions).

A break was taken at the end of each strategy trial. Whenever the subject felt tired he/she was allowed to take a rest. Each subject completed 432 test trials (= 6 strategies x 72). In each strategy 1512 test trials (= 21 subjects x 72) were completed. The order for the six strategies was different for each of the twenty-one subjects.

4.   RESULTS

An ANOVA (analysis of variance) with repeated measures was performed to determine which strategies and strategy groups were the most efficient. We measured these strategies and strategy groups in terms of selection time, error rate, and subjective preference. Moreover, we evaluated the influence of the variables (size, distance, and direction) on the performance differences between these strategies and strategy groups. Error rates were determined by dividing the number of errors by the total number of selection attempts. Selection time was the time required to select the target correctly.

4.1   Selection Times

4.1.1   Comparison of selection times by strategy groups

Figure 3 shows the selection time for six strategy groups. There was a significant difference between the strategy groups in selection time, $F(5,120) = 2.63$, $p < 0.05$. The In-Out strategies were faster (mean $=1.39$ s) than others. However, there were no significant differences between the On and Off strategies, $F(1,40) = 6.01$, $p < 0.01$, between the 2D and 3D strategies, $F(1,40) = 3.66$, $p < 0.01$, and between the In and In-Out strategies, $F(1,40) = 3.37$, $p < 0.01$.

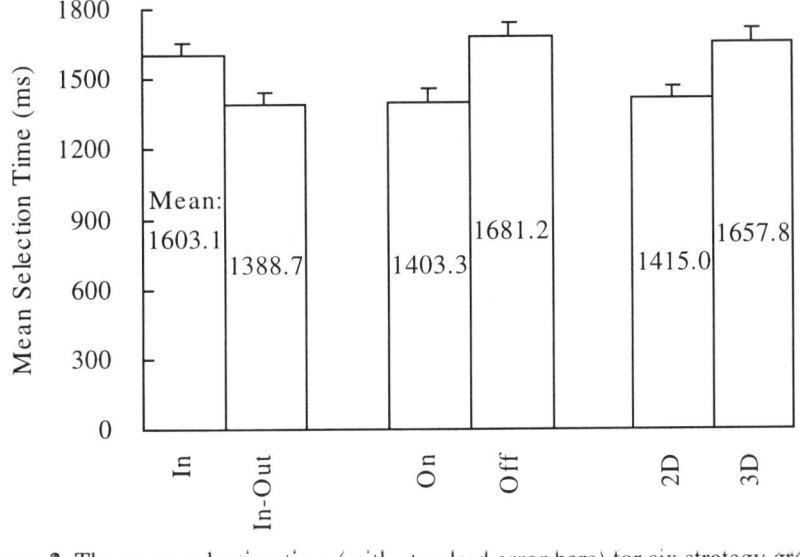

Figure 3 The mean selection time (with standard error bars) for six strategy groups

4.1.2   Comparison of selection times by individual strategies

There was a significant interaction between the six strategies in selection time, $F(5,120) = 10.8$, $p < 0.0001$. From this we have concluded that the selection time was influenced by the particular strategy, i.e. selection time changed according to the strategy being applied. The Land-on2 strategy was the fastest among the six strategies (mean = 0.98 s).

Significant interaction was also found between the Land-on2, Take-off2 and Space2 strategies, $F(2, 60) = 19.8$, $p < 0.0001$. Analyses were also conducted to determine the significant difference between the six strategies in terms of target size, pen-movement-distance and pen-movement-direction.

- Target size: There were significant differences between the six strategies for each target size, 3, 5, and 9 pixels in selection time, $F(5,120) = 9.75$, 6.85, and 5.22, $p < 0.001$. This means that significant differences between the six strategies in selection time did not change even when the target size was changed.
- Pen-movement-distance: There were significant differences between the six strategies for each distance, 39, 131, and 160 pixels in selection time, $F(5,120) = 7.33$, 10.3, and 10.1, $p < 0.0001$.
- Pen-movement-direction: Significant differences in selection time were observed between the six strategies in all directions 0, 45, 90, 135, 225, 270 degrees ($p < 0.0001$, in case of 180 degrees, $p < 0.001$).

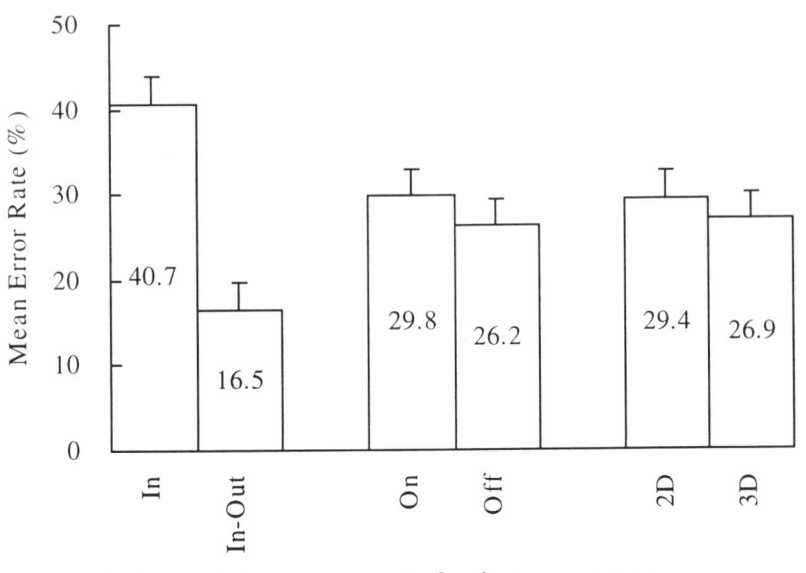

Figure 4 The mean error rate for six strategy groups.

4.2   Error Rates

4.2.1   Comparison of error rates by strategy groups

Figure 4 shows the error rate for six strategy groups. There was a significant difference among the strategy groups in error rates, $F(5,120) = 6.91$, $p < 0.001$. The In-Out strategies had the lowest error rates (16.5%) and the In strategies had the most error rates (40.7%) among the strategy groups (In, In-Out, On, Off, 2D, and 3D). Moreover, a significant difference was found between the In and In-Out strategies, $F(1,40) = 34.2$, $p < 0.01$, however, significant differences were not seen between the On and Off strategies, $F(1,40) = 0.7$, and between the 2D and 3D strategies, $F(1,40) = 0.4$.

To investigate the reasons for this, analyses were conducted to determine the significant difference between the In and In-Out strategies in terms of target size, pen-movement-distance and pen-movement-direction.

- Target size: significant differences were found between the In and In-Out strategies for each of the target sizes of 3 and 5 pixels in error rates, $F(1,40) = 52.3$, 18.0, $p < 0.01$. On the other hand, there was no significant difference for the target size 9 pixels in error rates, $F(1,40) = 1.2$, $p < 0.01$.

- Pen-movement-distance: there were significant differences between the In and In-Out strategies for each distance, 39, 131, and 160 pixels, in error rates, $F(1,40) = 30.2$, 34.7, and 33.3, $p < 0.01$.

- Pen-movement-direction: there were significant differences between the In and In-Out strategies for all eight directions, in error rates, $p < 0.01$.

4.2.2 Comparison of error rates by individual strategies

There was a significant difference between the six strategies in error rates, $F(5,120) = 17.8$, $p < .0001$. This means that the error rate was influenced by the differences between the strategies. The Land-on2, Take-off2 and Space2 strategies had lower error rates (16.6%, 17.4% and 15.5%) than the other three (Land-on1, Take-off1 and Space1). There was no significant difference between the three (the Land-on2, Take-off2 and Space2 strategies) in error rates, $F(2, 60) = 0.08$.

Analyses were also conducted to determine the significant difference between the six strategies in terms of target size, pen-movement-distance and pen-movement-direction.

- Target size: between the six strategies there were significant differences for each of the target sizes of 3 and 5 pixels in error rates, $F(5,120) = 24.7$, 9.99 $p < 0.0001$. On the other hand, there was no significant difference for the target size 9 pixels on error rates, $F(5,120) = 0.65$.
- Pen-movement-distance: there were significant differences between the six strategies for each distance, 39, 131 and 160 pixels, in error rates, $F(5,120) = 15.2$, 16.3, and 15.5, $p < 0.0001$.
- Pen-movement-direction: there were significant differences between the six strategies for all eight directions in error rates, all at the $p < 0.0001$ level.

4.3 Subject preferences

Significant main effects were seen between the six strategies with regard to target size (large targets, $F(5,30) = 14.8$, $p < 0.0001$, and small targets, $F(5,30) = 58.1$, $p < 0.0001$. The Land-on2 and Take-off2 strategies were rated highly for both large targets and small targets. When selecting a small target, the Land-on2 strategy was the most preferred (mean = 3.08).

Figure 5 shows the subject ratings for six strategy groups. Significant differences among the strategy groups were found (large targets, $F(5,30) = 7.01$, $p < 0.001$, and small targets, $F(5,30) = 45.3$, $p < 0.0001$. They were based on the average value of the answers given to the twelve questions by the subjects. The In-Out strategy was rated highly for both large targets (mean = 4.68) and small targets (mean = 2.81).

From the marks left in Figure 2 by all subjects, we determined that the smallest radius (39 pixels) and the medium radius (131 pixels) were the most popular pen-movement-distances. These radii were determined by a preliminary experiment. Though they were radii in which the movements of the hand were few, nevertheless significant differences in the six strategies were observed. There was also a significant difference between the six strategies at the maximum outside radius of 160 pixels. Furthermore, 135, 180, and 225 degrees of pen-movement-direction could be comfortably accommodated.

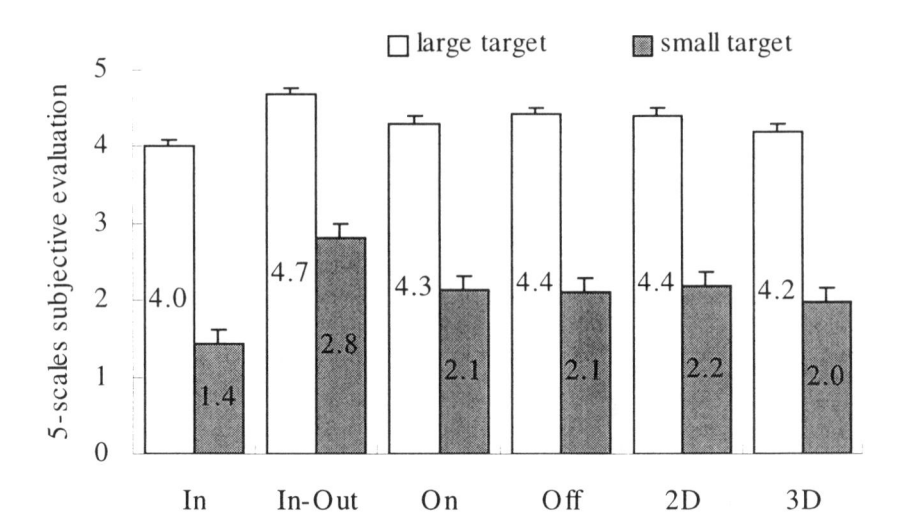

Figure 5 The mean subject ratings for six strategy groups and target sizes (5 = highest preference; 1 = lowest preference).

5.   DISCUSSION

5.1   The Land-on2 strategy and the In-Out strategy group

Based on analyses (see 4.) of selection times, error rates and the subjective evaluations, the Land-on2 strategy was the best strategy of the six. This result is the same as the result obtained in another experimental study (Ren and Moriya, 1997a, 1997b). We have verified again that the Land-on2 strategy is the most effective of the six strategies for selecting a small target. Furthermore, the In-Out strategy group was the best among the six strategy groups (In, In-Out, On, Off, 2D and 3D), based on analyses of selection times, error rates, and in particular, the subject preferences (mean = 4.7 on large targets, 2.8 on small targets in 5 scale rating).

The experimental results show that In-Out strategies (including the Land-on2 strategy) were more efficient than the others. This particularly applies in situations where other targets do not exist near the target, or in situations where they are not too close together, or where other targets do not exist near one side of the target (e.g. the upper part). Sears and Shneiderman (1991) also cite this point with reference to touchscreen situations. For instance, in the Land-on2 strategy, contact with the target may be affected after landing on the screen outside the target area. However, in the Land-on2 strategy, selection is affected on contact with the target area. Since the first target contacted will be selected, prior visual confirmation may be difficult

30

to achieve. In this situation, the Take-off2 strategy can be used because selection does not depend on the point of removal from the screen. Therefore the pen may pass through the target which will not be selected until the pen is removed from any point on the screen.

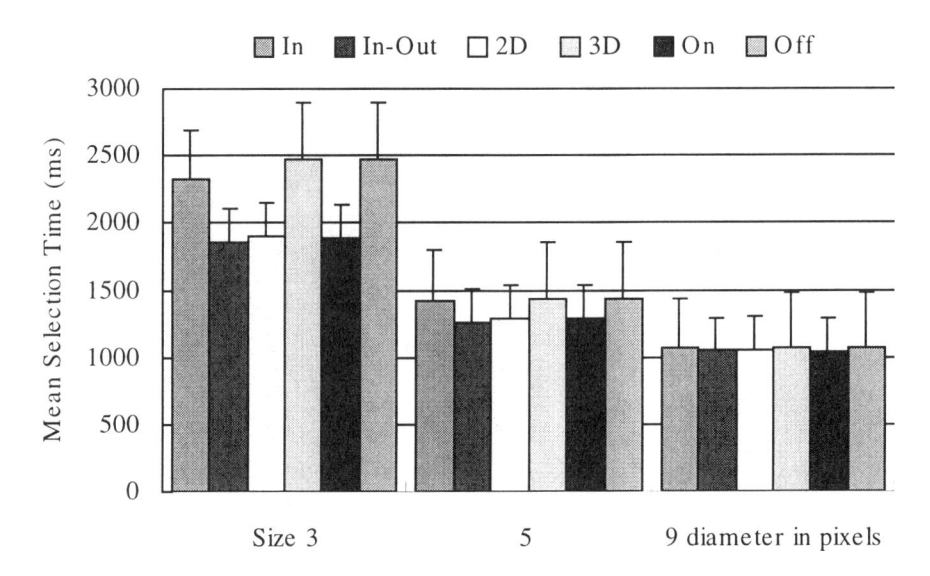

Figure 6 The mean selection time for each strategy group according to target size.

On the other hand, In-Out strategies would not be efficient in the selection of targets in dense displays. Thus, the Land-on1 and Take-off1 strategies (In strategies) can be used when the screen is a 2D surface. For instance, the Take-off1 strategy is the same as the familiar mouse technique. Here the selection is made when the pen contacts the surface of the screen and is moved into the target area after visual confirmation. However, hand/eye coordination is essential when using the Land-on1 and Take-off1 strategies. For the Take-off1 strategy the pen must be within the target (that is, "catching" the target) when the pen is removed from the screen. In the Land-on1 strategy the pen approaches the screen and target area and it is in the target area only momentarily.

When using an electromagnetic tablet, a target on the screen can be designed as a 3D target. Thus the Space1 and Space2 strategies may be used in the same situation. In the Space1 and Space2 strategies the pen can affect the target before it makes contact with the screen.

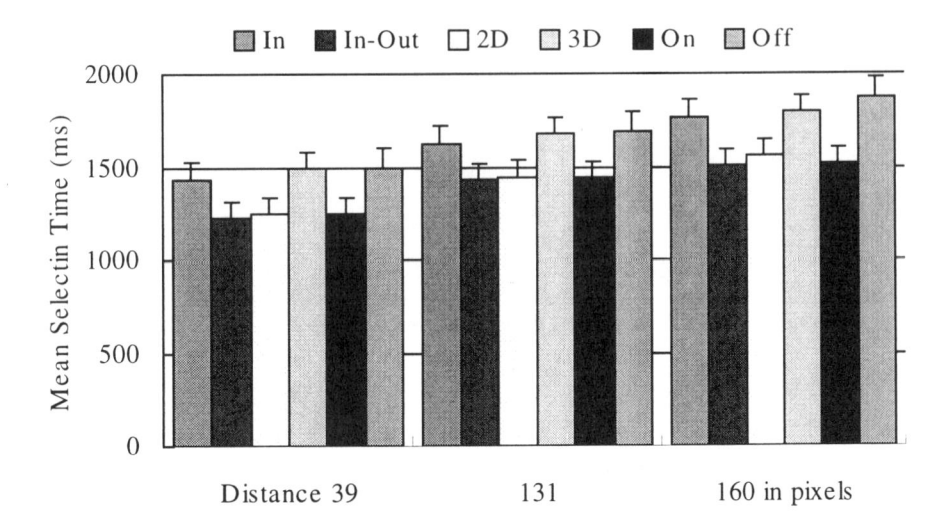

Figure 7 The mean selection time for each strategy group according to distance.

5.2 Factors influencing the differences between the strategies

Target size: Regarding target size, there were significant differences between the six strategies in terms of both selection time and error rates for target sizes of 3 pixels and 5 pixels. On the other hand, in the case of the target size of 9 pixels, no significant difference in error rate between the six strategies was observed. The analyses between the In and In-Out strategy groups show the same results. The significant differences between selection strategies were changed by changing the target size. In other words, the error rates were influenced by the selection strategies when the targets were small. These results are important factors in the design of strategies for selecting small targets in pen-based systems.

Pen-movement-distance and pen-movement-direction: It was shown that there were significant differences between the six strategies in both selection time and error rate caused by each of the pen-movement-distances and each of the pen-movement-directions. Significant differences in error rate between the In and In-Out strategy groups was also observed by each of the pen-movement-distances and each of the pen-movement-directions. This means that significant differences between selection strategies remained in all directions and all distances. Conversely, the differences between the strategies are not changed even when the pen-movement-distance or the pen-movement-direction are changed. These results offer some hints for the design of selection strategies. The influence of pen-movement-distance and pen-movement-direction on both error rate and selection time should be considered in pen input strategy design.

6.   FUTURE RESEARCH

Fitts' law (Fitts, 1954) states that the time taken to select a target is a function of the size of the target and the distance to the target. There are many variations of this formula. One common form is Movement time = a +bID, ID = log2 (Distance / Size +1), where, a and b are empirically determined constants, ID is an abbreviation of Index of Difficulty with regard to pointing/selecting.   This law has been demonstrated in numerous studies (MacKenzie, 1992). Figure 6 (target size) and Figure 7 (distance) show that selection time gets longer as the target size gets smaller and the distance greater.   However, to validate these results additional analyses to plot the selection time against the ID will be conducted. It is not clear that this law, in its original form, applies to all selection methods with all targets. New tasks paradigms presented by Accot and Zhai (1997) may be used to model the Land-on2, Take-off1, and Take-off2 strategies.

The In-Out strategies all allow the user to stray a little from the target and thus the user need not be so accurate.   Thus, for small targets, the In-Out strategies reduce selection times and error rates, as confirmed by our results.   Future experiments will investigate how far from the target users touch down (in the Land-on2 strategy) and how far from the target they take off (in the Take-off2 strategy). This may reveal an effectively larger virtual target.

Comparisons between the Land-on2 strategy and other interaction selecting/pointing techniques should also be conducted to improve the performance of small target acquisition tasks.

It has been reported that differences in target shapes influence the selection time (Sheikh and Hoffmann, 1994).   Various target shapes should be used to explore the effects on selection strategies. It is also necessary to investigate the relationships between strategies and target shapes, and to find strategies which are suitable for specific shapes (and vice versa).

7.   CONCLUSIONS

The paper proposed six strategies and classified the strategies into strategy groups according to their characteristics. It described the experiment in which we compared six strategies for pen-based systems. Experimental results show that the best strategy was the "Land-on2" strategy when the strategies were evaluated individually, and the best strategy group was the "In-Out" strategy group when evaluated in groups. Moreover, the differences between strategies are influenced by variations in target size, however, they are not affected by pen-movement-distance and pen-movement-direction.

We believe that these results will be helpful for designers in identifying and quantifying important factors, and for enhancing user efficiency on pen-based systems.   These results may also be useful in future studies to discover new and better strategies.   There remains further scope for additional research on the characteristics of pen-based input devices.

ACKNOWLEDGEMENTS

We wish to thank the three anonymous reviewers of EHCI'98 for their excellent comments on the draft paper. The TEPCO Research Foundation in Japan has provided the first author with generous financial support for presenting this paper. This support is gratefully appreciated.

REFERENCES

Accot, J. and Zhai, S. (1997). Beyond Fitts' Law: models for trajectory-based HCI Tasks. Proceedings of the CHI'97 Conference on Human Factors in Computing Systems, pp.295-302.

Brewster, S. A., Wright, P. C., Dix, A.J., and Edwards, A.D.N. (1995). The sonic enhancement of graphical buttons. Human-Computer Interaction -INTERACT '95, Lillehammer, pp.43-48.

Fitts, P.M. (1954). The information capacity of the human motor system in controlling amplitude of movement. Journal of Experimental Psychology, Vol.47, No.6, pp.381-391.

Kabbash, P. and Buxton, W. (1995). The "Prince" technique: Fitts' law and selection using area cursors. Proceedings of the CHI'95 Conference on Human Factors in Computing Systems, pp.273-279.

MacKenzie, I. S. (1992). Fitts' law as a research and design tool in human-computer interaction. Human-Computer Interaction. 7, pp.91-139.

Potter, R., Weldon, L. and Shneiderman, B. (1988). Improving the accuracy of touch screens: An experimental evaluation of three strategies. Proceedings of the CHI'88 Conference on Human Factors in Computing Systems, pp.27-32.

Ren, X. and Moriya, S. (1995). The concept of various pointing strategies on pen-based computers and their experimental evaluation. Proceedings of the Eleventh Symposium on Human Interface (in Japanese), pp.565-574.

Ren, X. (1996). Pen-based input interfaces for writing and selecting. PhD Thesis (in Japanese), Tokyo Denki University.

Ren, X. and Moriya, S. (1997a). The strategy for selecting a minute target and the minute maximum value on a pen-based computer. Extended Abstract of the CHI'97 Conference on Human Factors in Computing Systems, pp.369-370.

Ren, X. and Moriya, S. (1997b). The best among six strategies for selecting a minute target and the determination of the minute maximum size of the targets on a pen-based computer. Human-Computer Interaction -- INTERACT '97, Chapman & Hall, pp.85-92 .

Ren, X. and Moriya, S. (1998). The Influence of Target Size, Distance and Direction on the Design of Selection Strategies. Proceedings of HCI'98, Springer, pp.67-82.

Sears, A. and Shneiderman, B. (1991). High precision touchscreens: design strategies and comparisons with a mouse. International Journal of Man-Machine Studies, 34, pp.593-613.

Sears, A., Plaisant, C. and Shneiderman, B. (1992). A new era for high precision touchscreens. Advances in Human-Computer Interaction, Vol.30, Ablex, Norwood, NJ, pp.1-33.

Sheikh, I. and Hoffmann, E. (1994). Effect of target shape on movement time in a Fitts task. Ergonomics, Vol.37, No.9, pp.1533-1547.

Soukoreff, W., and Mackenzie, I. S. (1995). Theoretical upper and lower bounds on typing speed using a stylus and soft keyboard. Behaviour & Information Technology, vol.14, No.6, pp.370-379.

Worden, A., Walker, N., Bharat, K. and Hudson, S. (1997). Making computers easier for older adults to use: area cursors and sticky icons. Proceedings of the CHI'97 Conference on Human Factors in Computing Systems, pp.266-271.

Zhai, S., Buxton, W., and Milgram, P. (1994). The "silk cursor": Investigating transparency for 3D target acquisition. Proceedings of the CHI'94 Conference on Human Factors in Computing Systems, pp. 459-464.

BIOGRAPHY

Xiangshi Ren obtained his BS (1991), MS (1993) and Ph.D. (1996) degrees from Tokyo Denki University. He is currently an assistant lecturer in the Department of Information and Communication of Engineering at Tokyo Denki University. His research interests include all aspects of human-computer interaction, in particular, pen-based input interfaces and multimodal interfaces. He is a member of IPSJ, IEICE, and SIGHI of SICE in Japan, and of the British HCI group in UK.

Shinji Moriya received the Ph.D. degree from Tokyo Denki University in 1980. He was visiting associate professor in the State University of New York at Buffalo in 1981 and in the University of Illinois at Urbana-Shampaign in 1982, and visiting professor in the Yunnan Polytechnic University in China in 1994. He is currently professor of Tokyo Denki University. His research interests include pen-based user interactions, voice input user interfaces, and evaluation and modelling of human-computer interaction. He is a member of IEICE, IPSJ, SICE, Television Society of Japan, ACM and IEEE.

Discussion

Philippe Palanque: What about the variable "density of targets?" Usually when you have a small target it means that you have a lot of targets in a small space, thus a high density of possible targets. Have you studied that problem, as it looks like strategy two will lead to a great number of undesired selected targets?

Xiangshi Ren: No, we haven't studied that problem yet. Yes, the density of target displays on small screens is a problem, as you mentioned. Our approach is from the simple to the complex so that we are able to make fundamental comparisons. We feel that research into the complexities relating to multi-target displays with the increased possibility of undesired selection depends on this basic work. We recognize that there will be an infinite number of screen contexts that impact the choice of strategy. Our focus was therefore to discover, describe and measure the essential characteristics and parameters relating to selection strategies as distinct from targets, and target arrangements. We saw this as a necessary precursor to the matters your question raises.

Stefane Chatty: With land-on strategy two, what if I land on a neighbour and then move to the target?

Xiangshi Ren: In the Land-on2 strategy, the target is selected only momentarily at the time the pen makes contact in the target area. If the pen misses the target you can still move the pen to the target to be selected. But if your pen contacts a neighbouring target first an error will occur. By beginning with the simple display of one target, we now have some helpful results which better justify and prepare us for an examination of complex situations.

Ken Fishkin: I worry about relying on selection time as the sole measure of which strategy is best. There are actually two tasks users are performing: acquiring and selecting the target. I might argue that take-off is better, since there is an opportunity to abort. With land-on, there is no abort. Was this measured?

Xiangshi Ren: We measured selection times, error rates, and subjective preferences for six selection strategies in a simple display context. The range of possible solutions for problems relating to variables other than variables in strategy characteristics is potentially infinite. For example, abort functions may or may not be built into a single selection strategy. There are many variables that require examination in their simple form so that solutions to issues of complexity may be resolved on the basis of the results of such research.

Ken Fishkin: Do you have any intuition or experience as to what works best for double-clicking versus single-clicking?

Xiangshi Ren: No, not yet. Our research related only to pen-based devices and functions. The possibility of double tapping with a pen could be researched.

Stephane Chatty: The pen is already located on the screen, then you move to another target. What if the user's hand is not near the display?

Xiangshi Ren: We need an initial position in order to be able to time selection attempts. The range of possible starting points is perhaps infinite, e.g. hand on the desk, pen in hand, pen not in hand. Our experiment controlled the environment so that the action was measurable.

Jean Scholtz: You have specific distances, e.g., 39 pixels. Why were exactly these distances chosen?

Xiangshi Ren: We performed a preliminary experiment to determine the distances of 39 and 131 pixels. We have reported the details in the body of this paper (refer to Section 3.4). The largest distance (radius) of 160 pixels was determined according to the size limitations of the screen. It was also a distance by which the wrist could possibly be moved.

Utilising a Geographic Space Metaphor in a Software Development Environment

Henrik Bærbak Christensen

Centre for Experimental System Development, Department of Computer Science, University of Aarhus, DK-8000 Århus C, Denmark, hbc@daimi.au.dk

Abstract: Current software systems are growing ever larger and more complex. This increase in size and complexity is of course reflected in the data produced in the development process and overviewing and navigating the structure are becoming daunting tasks. This paper presents a model for visualising many important aspects of the complex, multi-dimensional, data in a software development project. The model is based on a *geographic space metaphor:* Entities in the software architecture are organised geographically in what becomes a design 'landscape'. Thereby overview and navigation is supported by tapping into humans fine spatial and visual perception. The landscape is shared in the project team, and mediates daily development activities thereby providing a common reference frame, and a framework for visualising aspects of the software. A prototype implementation of a software development environment, Ragnarok, based on this model is presented and some preliminary experiences outlined.

Keywords: Information Visualisation and Navigation, User Interface Design, Spatial Metaphors, Computer Supported Cooperative Work, Software Development Environments.

1. INTRODUCTION

One problem facing managers and developers alike in large software development projects is the complexity and sheer amount of data produced during the development process. As systems grow ever larger it becomes increasingly difficult to maintain overview and navigate in the many aspects and data of the system.

One of the possible causes of this difficulty was pointed out by Brooks in his famous article 'No Silver Bullet–Essence and Accidents of Software Engineering' where Brooks states *invisibility* as an inherent property of software (Frederick P. Brooks, Jr., 1987): The multi-dimensional nature of software does not easily lend itself to a single 2D or 3D diagrammatic form and thereby deprives us one of our most powerful conceptual tools: Our visual and spatial perception.

In this paper we try to show, however, that many interesting dimensions of software and data from the development process can still be visualised beneficially using a single metaphor: A geographic space metaphor (Kuhn and Blumenthal, 1996). Our proposal is to use the logical design structure (Lamb, 1996; Sommerville, 1992) of a software system as basis and organise it geographically in a two-dimensional space: The abstractions and hierarchy of a software design are represented by *landmarks* having stable positions, sizes, and appearances in a plane thereby creating a manifest 'design landscape'. These landmarks are directly manipulable: Daily development tasks are mediated through landmarks. Different dimensions (aspects) of the design entities like e.g. the source code files implementing it, documentation, staffing- and budget information, profiling information, version- and configuration control, etc., are visualised by processing the associated data appropriately and control the visual appearance of landmarks based on this processing; just like ordinary maps may show different aspects like vegetation, roads, elevation, or population density, of the same region of a country.

The approach has some inherent limitations. The data and aspects handled must have a one-to-one mapping to design abstractions/landmarks and a 2D visualisation must be natural. For instance, the planning phase of a project where tasks are best organised on a time line, cannot be handled well by this approach. Still enough interesting aspects exist to make the presented approach worth while.

The visual model is implemented in a prototype software development environment, Ragnarok, which currently supports basic handling and visualisation of a handful of aspects. Some preliminary experiences with Ragnarok will be reported.

The motivation for Ragnarok's visual model is described in section 2. In section 3, the Ragnarok model of a software architecture is briefly outlined followed by a description of the visual model in section 4. The Ragnarok prototype implementation is described in section 5. Section 6 discusses the benefits of using a geographic space metaphor in software development. Finally related work, future work, and conclusion are described in sections 7–9.

2. MOTIVATION

The problems that motivated the Ragnarok visual model are:

• *Overview and navigation:* Overviewing large software systems and finding the correct piece of code in the thousands of files and libraries, is becoming a daunting task even in systems with a sound logical design. Explaining the design to newcomers is also problematic (Bürkle et al., 1995). We believe the problem is not that the software structure is not sufficiently *logical* but that it is not sufficiently *physical*. The goal in Ragnarok is to make software tangible and manifest by associating software entities with stable positions.

• *Mediating, up-to-date, software design:* The majority of software systems are still implemented in terms of source code files–and files does not convey much information about the design of a software system. Though strong graphical design notations exists, like OMT and UML (Rumbaugh et al., 1991; Rational Rose, 1997), these are mainly used in the analysis, design, and initial implementation phase with a tendency that the diagrams becomes outdated in later implementation and maintenance phases. The goal is to use graphical notation to make a software design that is used *actively* to perform daily development tasks.

• *Collaboration:* Software development is a team effort today. Therefore a common understanding and reference frame is essential to allow the software design to be discussed, documented, and reused. The goal is to provide a shared landscape that provides a common reference frame and secondly let the landscape visualise development progress.

• *Visualisation framework:* Data in a software project is inherently multi-dimensional: One dimension is the source files; another the budgets, task-lists, and staffing information; yet another version control, etc. Traditionally these different dimensions are handled by different tools and organisational procedures and summary information presented in different formats: Lists, tables, graphs, etc. The goal is to provide a stable, unifying visualisation framework that allows diverse information to be visualised overlaid over the design landscape.

The means to achieve these goals is to organise the software design entities geographically using a geographic space metaphor. One distinguishes between *desktop- (small scale)* and *geographic (large scale) spaces* in spatial metaphors (Kuhn and Blumenthal, 1996; Egenhofer and Mark, 1995). The distinction comes from everyday experience: Objects in a desktop space have sizes comparable to the human body and can readily be moved and turned, whereas objects in geographic space are beyond the human body and have fixed positions over a long time-scale, like for instance buildings, trees, streets, and so forth.

Humans are apt at navigating in a well known physical environment: As Kuhn and Blumenthal notes: 'Perception, manipulation, and motion in space are largely subconscious activities that impose little cognitive load while offering powerful functionality' (Kuhn and Blumenthal, 1996). By providing a geographical layout of design abstractions, we believe that humans fine sense of locality can be utilised.

3. SOFTWARE ARCHITECTURE MODEL

Abstraction and hierarchy are key concepts in designing, building, testing, and managing large software systems. Large software systems are decomposed into a hierarchy of abstractions, where each entity in this hierarchy is an abstraction of the underlying parts. The resulting structure is often termed the software architecture (Lamb, 1996) or the logical design structure (Sommerville, 1992). Traditionally such abstractions are termed systems, subsystems, libraries, modules, classes, or class categories, depending on the type and granularity of the abstraction and its position in the hierarchy. In Figure 1, such a hierarchical decomposition is exemplified.

In the Ragnarok software architecture model, an abstraction in the software design is represented by an object denoted a **software component**. A software component contains **substance** which is a physical manifestation of the abstraction; currently implemented as a set of files. A typical example is the abstraction of a class which is represented by a software component whose substance is an interface- and implementation file for the class.

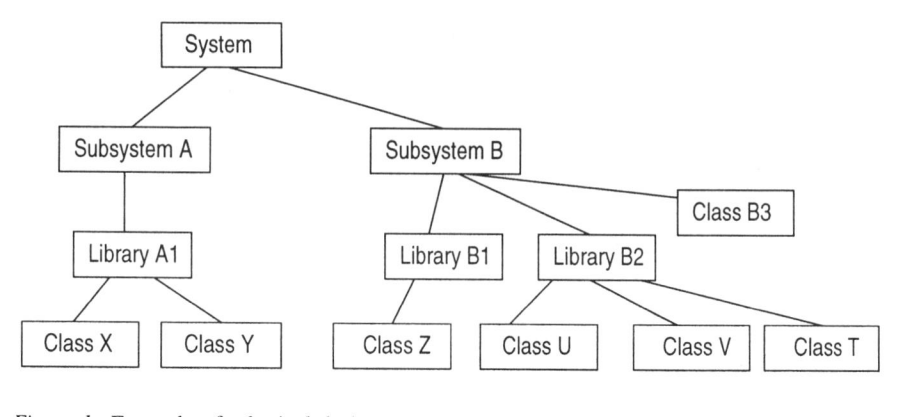

Figure 1: Example of a logical design structure. A box represents an abstraction/component and the lines between boxes are composition (part/whole) relationships.

An abstraction is often composed of other abstractions in the software architecture, for instance a library is a composition of individual modules. This is modelled in the software component by **composition relations** (part/whole) to other software components, like library B2 in Figure 1 that is composed of classes U, V, and T.

Finally a software component has a set of **annotations**. Each annotation contains structured data for a specific dimension/aspect of the component. Examples include: Managerial annotations (staffing: Who is responsible for implementing this component; budget: How many staff hours are budgeted for implementation, how many have been spent so far; estimated-time-to-complete etc.), quality assurance annotations (checklists to be gone through in release situation, regression test suits), progress logs (what bug-fixes/enhancements have been carried out, by whom and when), etc.

4. VISUAL MODEL

In this section the basic concepts in the Ragnarok visual model will be presented.

The **landscape** is an infinite two dimensional plane. The landscape serves as a space for geographically organising **landmarks** and **decorations**.

A landmark occupies a well defined region of the landscape and represents a software component (and thus an abstraction in the software design). The composition (part/whole) structure is visualised by *spatial containment* i.e. the landmarks associated with components that are part of a component A are positioned inside the landmark of A. In Figure 2 a legal layout for the design structure in Figure 1 is shown.

A decoration is simple graphics, like text, lines, polygons, images, etc., at a specific position in the landscape. Specifically the Ragnarok prototype provides basic support for UML notation, the unified modelling language (Rational Rose, 1997). Thereby the software design can be further documented by stating associations, multiplicity, roles, etc., as seen on Figure 3 in section 5.

The landscape is not directly accessible but viewed and manipulated through **maps**. A map visualises a region of the landscape on the computer display. The region displayed is determined by the map's *view-parameters*: (O, w, h, s, A). O is the position

42

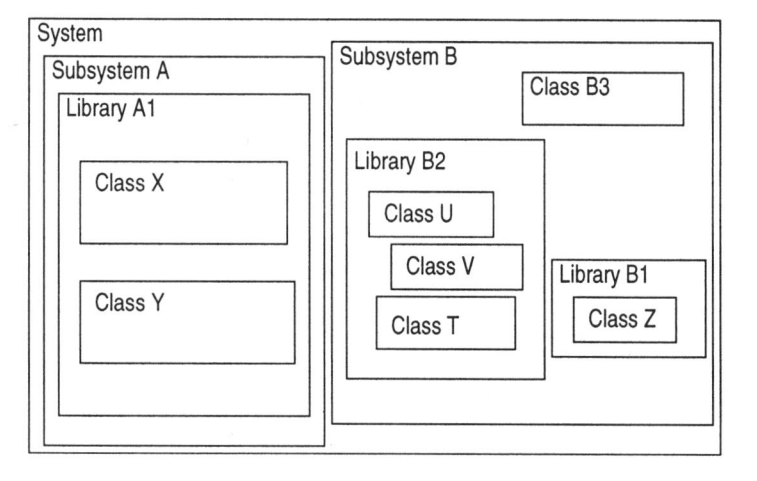

Figure 2: Example of legal landscape of landmarks for the components in Figure 1.

of the map's top left pixel projected onto the landscape, w and h the map's physical (pixel) width and height, s the map's scale, and A the map's aspect. Hence a map w pixels wide and h pixels tall will display region $(O.x, O.y, O.x + ws, O.y + hs)$ of the landscape. This is denoted the *displayed region*. The landmarks appearing in a map are denoted *visual landmarks* when we explicitly want to distinguish them from the landmarks in the landscape: There is only one landmark in the landscape for each component but there may be several maps displaying different visual landmarks for the same underlying landmark.

The **aspect** A determines the appearance of visual landmarks in the displayed region by (processing) a subset of the data in the associated software component. For instance, in a management aspect map the management annotation data of a component may be processed to yield a colour code for estimated-time-to-complete which is then used as the background colour for the visual landmark.

4.1 Global context

Any number of maps can be created showing regions of the landscape in various aspects. However, a large number of maps does not in itself provide overview nor global context: How are the displayed regions positioned relative to each other? Therefore the Ragnarok visual model introduces a **map outline**. A map outline is a projection of the displayed region of one map (**detail** map) onto another map dedicated for showing global context (**world** map). To distinguish outlines in the world map, a given outline and the frame of the corresponding detail map have identical colours. The outline and the displayed region in the corresponding map are synchronised so any change in either of them is immediately reflected in the other.

4.2   Interaction

The interaction model employed is *direct manipulation* (Shneiderman, 1983; Hutchins et al., 1986).

Landmarks can be moved and resized directly using the mouse. A move may reflect an architectural/design change; for instance if the landmark for class T in Figure 2 is moved from library B2 to B1.

Landmarks are created using the mouse; thus landscape (and thereby software design) creation and (re)design is an interactive process.

Landmarks also mediate actions from the user to the associated components. The set of actions available on any given component depends on the aspect of the map it is located in; e.g. in a version control map, landmarks mediate actions like check-in and check-out to the underlying components, in a management aspect map the user can edit task lists, log spent staff hours, etc.

The direct interaction also extends to outlines: Moving/resizing an outline will change the displayed region in the corresponding detail map. This is an intuitive way of moving in 2D space compared to the often seen use of a vertical and horizontal scrollbar.

4.3   Shared landscape

The landscape with landmarks and decorations as well as the data of the underlying components are shared among developers in the software project. Therefore modifications made by one developer to a landmark and/or to data in the underlying component are immediately reflected in all running Ragnarok instances.

5.   RAGNAROK PROTOTYPE

The Ragnarok visual model exists in a prototype implementation. Though the basic concepts of the model are implemented, the current prototype only provides a handful of different aspects. A subset of these aspects is described below.

A snapshot of the prototype, loaded with the Ragnarok project itself, is depicted in Figure 3. The Ragnarok window is divided into four part: In the upper left corner is the *world map* (1) with outlines (9) of open detail maps. The world map has a fixed position in the Ragnarok window for easy reference and overview. The lower left part contains the *log window* (2) which is essentially a running log of important operations, here a version control check-out operation. The bottom right corner contains the *status bar* (3), which displays warnings and status information. On the right is a large area (4) in which may reside multiple *detail maps* (5–7). Each detail map has its own frame colour identical to the colour of the corresponding outline in the world map. Visual landmarks are generally displayed as simple, coloured, rectangles containing component name and possible additional information. Clicking any visual landmark brings up a context-sensitive menu which lists available actions on the underlying component (8).

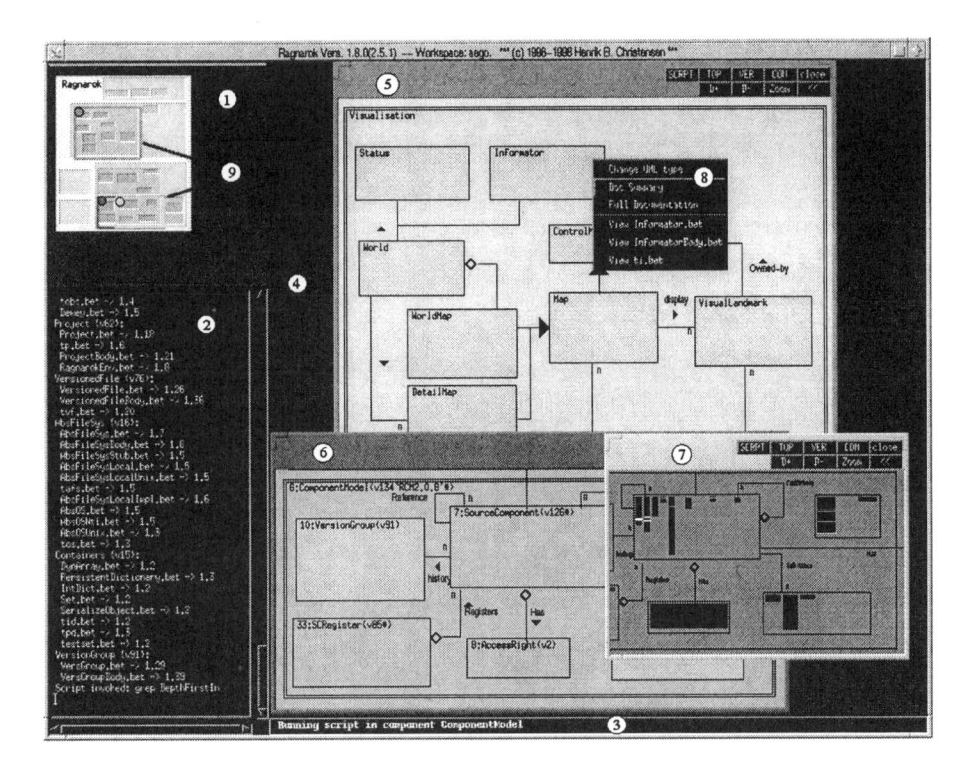

Figure 3: Overview over the Ragnarok prototype window. The numbered parts are explained in the text.

5.1 Prototype usage

Initially the prototype only displays the world map. To create new detail maps, the user defines the region to view by drag-selecting a rectangle ('rubber-banding') on the world map using the mouse. This results in the creation of a new detail map and the corresponding outline in the world map. Outlines can be dragged around the world map using the small circle in the upper left corner; when released the associated detail map is updated to display the new region.

Detail maps can be moved and resized. Two types of resize are possible: Normal (making the map bigger reveals a larger portion of the underlying landscape) or rubber-sheet (making the map bigger displays the same region but zoomed in, like if the landmarks were on a rubber sheet). To zoom in on a certain region one simply defines the region by drag-selecting it, using the mouse, directly in the detail map; the map then zooms in on the region while possibly resizing itself to keep the aspect ratio of the selected region. Aspects can be chosen using the buttons in the top right part or using pop-up menus on the map frame.

45

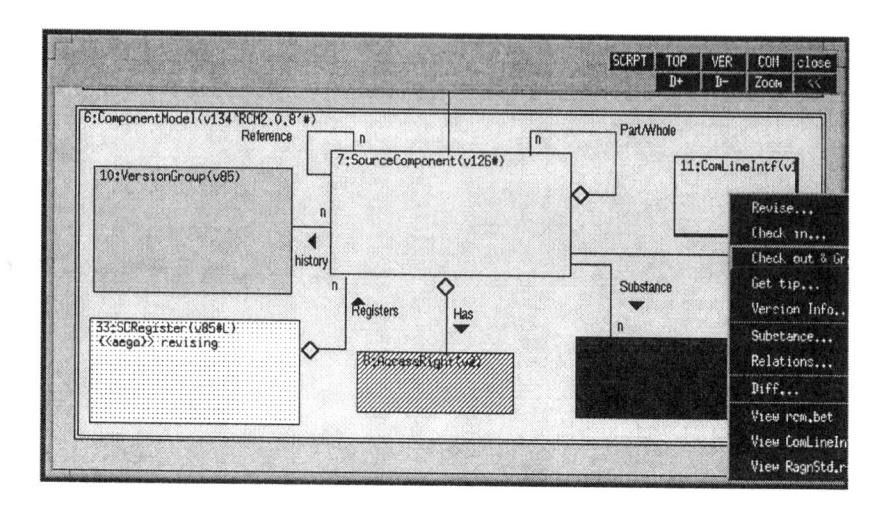

Figure 4: A map showing the version control aspect.

5.2 Version control

Software components in Ragnarok are under tight version- and configuration control (Christensen, 1998a; Christensen, 1997). An important collaboration aspect in source code version- and configuration management is to enable the individual developer to overview how his/her private copy of source code relates to the overall project code. The typical question is: 'Do I have the newest version of the project libraries?'

The version control aspect visualises this in a compact form. Colour coding of landmarks is used to show the state of the developers local copy. Referring to Figure 4 light red (medium gray on the figure) indicates components where newer versions exist. Gray (hatched) indicate that the local source code match the newest. The colours light green (dotted) and bright red (dark gray) are used to convey information about currently ongoing work: Light green indicates that the developer himself is currently editing source code in the component, bright red (warning) that some other, named, developer is working on it, and thus warns about potential conflicts if the developer decides to edit this component as well. Light yellow (light gray) indicate indirect changes because components depended upon have changed.

The context sensitive menu, half visible, allows version control commands, check-in and -out, display version graph, source code access, etc., to be issued to the individual components.

Progress is instantly reflected in all running Ragnarok instances and thus the evolution of the software system is visible on-line: For instance, if developer 'johan' checks in component 'VersionedFile' in Figure 4, the component will immediately turn light red in version control maps of all other developers, to indicate that a new version is available.

46

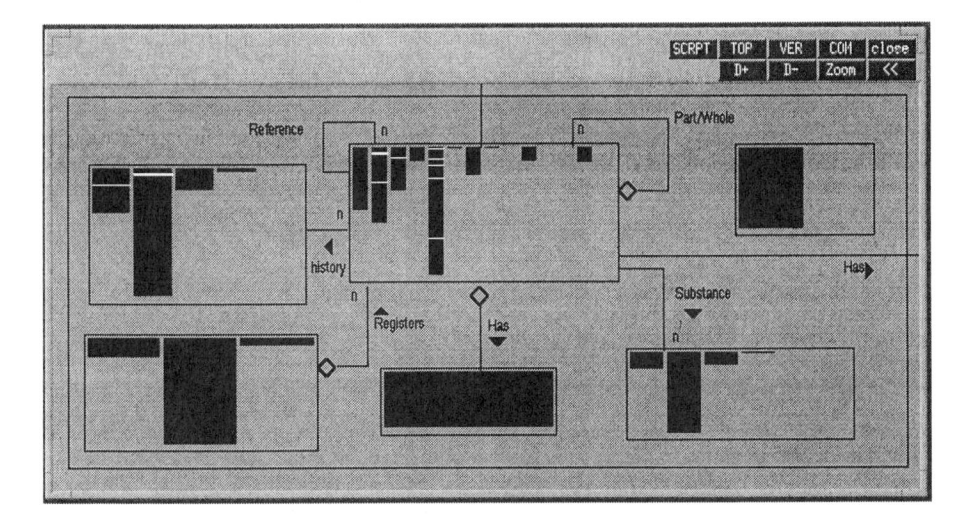

Figure 5: A map in visual scripting aspect, showing the result of a grep for the string 'Get-LockOwner'.

5.3 Topography

This aspect minimises the amount of information presented to provide a compact overview, refer to the world map (1) in Figure 3. Decorations are not shown, and landmarks are grayed according to their nesting levels and without text. The context-sensitive menu lists (source) files in the component and choosing one loads the file into an editor.

This aspect is the standard one for the world map providing convenient overview of the project landscape and a neutral background for outlines. An unanticipated but strong feature of the topography aspect world map is that in essence it is a compact and fast file browser: Any of the 160 source files in the Ragnarok project can be loaded into our emacs editor using *one* mouse-click in the world map (clicking the landmark brings up a pop-up menu listing all files, releasing the mouse button over the wanted file tells our editor to load it).

5.4 Visual script

This aspect allows users to run scripts, written in the interpreted language TCL (Ousterhout, 1994) on (parts of) the project and interpret the result spatially and visually. User actions like mouse clicks on landmarks or positions also result in user defined TCL functions being called. As an illustration the prototype has a visual grep facility, please refer to Figure 5. Here the user has requested for a grep in the source files with target string 'GetLockOwner' to be run in a part of a project (same part as in Figure 4).

In this aspect the interior of landmarks is filled with black bars. Each bar represents a single file in the component, the bar height is a relative measure of the file size measured in lines. Each red line (white on the figure) shows that the search string

47

occurs in the file at this relative position. Clicking and holding down the left mouse button near a red line pops up a text viewer displaying 20 lines around the position where the search string occurs in the file–releasing the mouse button again makes the text viewer disappear again. This way one can quickly browse the occurrences and their immediate context without polluting the screen with numerous new windows. Double clicking a red line automatically loads the file into the editor centred on the matching line.

This visualisation of a recursive grep is compact and provides better overview than traditional textual recursive greps. Furthermore the clustering, density, and distribution of red lines in itself give important information. For instance, grepping for a function or class name may show misuses ('Now why is there a call in the GUI library?') or high coupling ('Hey, look, this class pops up in every component in the system!') that are easily missed in a 300 line textual output.

By basing this aspects on user written, interpreted, scripts, Ragnarok provides a degree of tailorability to the context of a given project: Developers can write scripts that provide custom visualisations. The TCL language has strong support for file handling and invoking external programs and it is therefore relatively simple to parse files (as done in the grep case above), or invoke profilers, run regression tests, extract relevant data from a project database, etc., and visualise the results of such external processing. The ability to associate user written TCL scripts to mouse clicks makes these custom visualisation direct manipulable: Clicking a landmark that highlights an unsuccessful regression test run can load the test into an editor; clicking a landmark with project data can instruct the database to load the proper table/view, etc.

5.5   Preliminary experiences

The Ragnarok prototype has been used in the continued development of Ragnarok itself, as well as on a minor part of the Mjølner BETA System (Andersen et al., 93). It is currently being introduced in a medium-sized project (code size: 225KLOC), ConSys (ISA, 1996), where three developers are developing a control system for large scale equipment in experimental physics.

Preliminary results are encouraging. Some observations follow:

• Typically landmarks are created with sizes that allows about three to four levels of the design structure to be visible on a map.
• When designing a landscape, it is important to vary landmark sizes and arrange them in somewhat irregular patterns; otherwise the landscape becomes too uniform and identifying the right component based on its position and appearance becomes difficult.
• In software development there are often a number of core components that are constantly worked upon and a larger number of more stable components that are inspected less often. Not surprisingly developers can accurately locate the landmarks of core components without hesitation. Less often visited landmarks are located in an iterative manner, where a larger region around the expected location is examined and the sought landmark identified from its name.

6. DISCUSSION

Below we argue for the benefits of using a geographic space metaphor in a software development environment:

- *Overview and navigation:* In traditional systems the method for data and file access is name-based: You must remember the sequence of folder/directory names in order to find a file. The Ragnarok approach change the focus from name-based to location-based search: Developers know *where* the landmark containing the file is located. Because navigational and overview knowledge acquired performing one task can be carried on and remains valid performing the next, the design landscape (or the relevant part of it) quickly becomes well known. A company can define *positional semantics* by for instance require that GUI components are placed in the upper parts of the landscape, etc. Thereby the rough outlines of a project landscape will be known even for a new developer on a project.

- *Mediating, up-to-date, software design:* The software landscape becomes the focal point of daily activities: Many daily development activities are performed through interaction with the landscape. We believe this is a direct and intuitive way and that the pressure to ensure a correct, up-to-date, design landscape is strengthened. Newcomers on a project can be introduced to the software design directly in the daily software development environment.

- *Collaborative issues:* Members of the development team get well acquainted with the software landscape creating a common understanding and allows everyday language, like 'to the left', 'in the northern part', to be used. The same, spatially stable, layout can be used to visualise different aspects meaning that persons with different responsibilities, like managers, designers, programmers, testers, maintainers, etc., refer to the same layout. Secondly the landscape always provides a snapshot of the state of the project: One example was given in section 5.2, another is that when any developer log spent staff hours on a component this is immediately reflected visually on a management aspect map showing estimated-time-to-complete and/or budgeted versus actual spent time.

- *Visualisation framework:* Different aspects/data of the same component are visualised in the same geographical region of the landscape. The primary effect is stability of the visual appearance which is important for navigation. A second effect is that different aspects gets geographically correlated, which is a natural and strong way of comparing data: If a bug-report aspect map (displaying number of detected bugs) highlights certain landmarks, and the same landmarks are highlighted in a staffing aspect (displaying how components are staffed), one is instantly warned.

The aspects described in section 5 of course only serve as a sample of uses. Many other aspects can be envisioned: Defect reporting, possibly determined by automatically running regression test suits on modified components; profiling information to identify bottlenecks in a system; release control, based on passed tests on checklists for each component; different management aspects focusing on estimated-time-to-complete, actual- versus budget-cost estimates, etc.

The map aspect property is important because of the inherently multi-dimensional nature of software. Each dimension can be superimposed on the same landscape–just as different types of ordinary maps visualise different properties of the same region of a country: Vegetation, town names, elevation, or population density, etc.

Note that Ragnarok is not purely location-based: The files defining the substance of a component/landmark are not assigned a position (however, this can be simulated by having one component per file), therefore files are accessed from a traditional textual list of filenames in a context-sensitive menu. This design is deliberate because the focus is on design abstractions like classes, libraries, etc., and not on files; and usually such abstractions require several files (for example a .h and a .cpp file in C++ to implement a class).

Navigation using the presented visual model relies on a stable landscape that is well known to the developers: If the landscape is constantly modified, spatial knowledge is virtually non existing–compare the effort of driving home from the office every day with the effort of driving in an unknown city. Consequently, navigation will become easier as the design stabilises. During the initial analysis and design phases, ideas and abstractions are fostered and discarded rapidly meaning many changes in the landscape; in these phases, a more traditional, search-based, navigation mechanism is a beneficial supplement.

In 'different-place' software development teams, the design landscape can more actively mediate collaborative awareness: When a developer is working on a certain component, she is metaphorically speaking working in a certain place in the landscape. This can be shown in all running Ragnarok instance by for instance a special image/cursor identifying the developer. This indicator could be a link to the person for instance by opening a audio- or video link when clicked.

An important issue is scalability. As the Ragnarok software architecture- and visual models are inherently hierarchical Ragnarok should scale without problems. In the discussion so far the world map has been described as displaying the overall project but in a large project the typical situation would be that it displays only the part relevant for the team or individual–in essence defining their 'world'.

A final note is on software abstractions that are reused in different contexts. Consider a container class hierarchy defined in a library component that we want to document is used in, say, both a business- and graphics module. The Ragnarok visual model demands that a component is assigned a unique position and thus the same container classes cannot be displayed both in the library, business- and graphics regions of the design landscape. This problem has no easy solution; our current suggestion is to provide 'shadow' landmarks which through their appearance (grayed for instance) acts as hyperlinks to the real landmarks–actions are forwarded to the real landmark and a special action should be to initiate a zoom and pan travel to the real landmark.

7. RELATED WORK

CASE tools: Looking at e.g. map (5) in Figure 3 Ragnarok may resemble a traditional CASE tool or UML diagram editor. However, the focus of CASE tools and Ragnarok is different. CASE tools are generally analysis and design tools with code generation features i.e. with strong support and focus on the early phases of a project and the programming task. The emphasis in Ragnarok is foremost on making design abstractions manifest and manipulable by assigning a geographic location and secondly on documenting the design using some notation like UML; once this is done it is used as a visualisation framework for project data which CASE-tools traditionally do not address.

Pad++: Another interesting comparison is to Pad++(Bederson et al., 1996; Bederson and Hollan, 1994; Perlin and Fox, 1993). Pad++ is an innovative and powerful 2D visualisation system. In Pad++ the user manipulate objects on an infinitely zoomable 2D surface. The Pad++ system incorporates a very effective engine for panning and zooming. The objects on the surface are text, simple graphics, and images. The underlying visual model employed in Ragnarok is similar to Pad++. The difference is the objects handled. In Pad++ objects reside directly on the Pad surface; in contrast landmarks serve as visual *representations* of the complex, multi-dimensional, data of the underlying component; they *are* not the actual data. Therefore Ragnarok uses the *same* region to visualise *different* data in different aspect maps (e.g. grep matches or version information). Pad++ provides portals and lenses but these provide different visual representations of the *same* data, say a slider or textual representation of an integer object. The aspect property of Ragnarok is essential because of the multi-dimensional nature of software.

SeeSoft: The visual scripting facilities are inspired by the interesting work in the Bell Labs 'SeeSoft' systems (Ball and Eick, 1996; Baker and Eick, 1995). SeeSoft is a powerful tool for visualising properties of text files (source code) in a highly compact form. Individual lines in the source code are represented by colour coded text lines, pixel lines or even individual pixels. Compared to SeeSoft the Ragnarok visual layout is less compact due to the 'unused' space between the landmarks but on the other hand it carries valuable information in itself compared to SeeSoft which sorts files alphabetically. The stable layout is important in many contexts because it eases comparisons (like profiling information before and after an optimisation phase) and the distribution and density of 'hot spots' in itself provides valuable clues to system properties as mentioned in section 5.4.

MacFinder: No comparison is complete without contrasting the Ragnarok visual model to well-known desktop space metaphors like the Macintosh Finder. In Finder objects (files/directories) are represented by icons that when clicked expands into a window showing its contents (part objects). These only shows one level of the part/whole hierarchy and therefore navigation typically spawns many new windows. In contrast most Ragnarok aspects show 3-5 levels of the hierarchy thus showing context and avoiding intermediate maps during navigation. More important, however, is the underlying spatial model: In Ragnarok all landmarks have a specific relative position to all other landmarks–you can always answer the question: 'Does landmark A lie left of landmark B?' In contrast MacFinder objects only have a position relative to the window it is part of but not to objects in other windows: You cannot tell the position of MyMac:FolderA:Document1 relative to MyMac:FolderB:Document2 in general, only where they are relative to each other in your current, transient, layout of your desktop. Therefore the Finder spatial reference frame is weaker and more difficult to remember, share, and communicate in a team.

8. FUTURE WORK

Currently there are a number of lines along which Ragnarok evolves. A high priority is to get more experience with actual every-day use of the prototype. Ragnarok is build upon a software configuration management (SCM) subsystem that is currently used in two, real, medium-sized development projects (Christensen, 1998a). They use the SCM subsystem through a character- and command based interface and experiences from these projects show a substantial navigational overhead. The Ragnarok prototype is currently being introduced in one of these projects and the other will follow soon. We expect this will prove a significant decrease in navigational effort. Therefore a current effort is instrumentation of the prototype which allows the actual usage pattern to be logged for later analysis.

Tailorability of aspects and visualisations is another key issue. No two development projects are alike and visualisation needs will vary. Therefore it should be possible to create run-time specifications of new aspects and visualisations including: A) Define structure of an annotation B) Processing scheme defining the appearance of landmarks based on annotation data processing, and C) A set of context sensitive actions (tailorable pop-up menus and associated actions). The current visual scripting facility currently provides a limited version of B) only.

Pad++ introduced the concept of semantic zooming i.e. the appearance of an object varies according to the zoom level it is seen in. Ragnarok presently have limited support for this capability, but it is an beneficial extension: When landmarks appears physically small on the display they should only convey summary information as e.g. a colour coding; when zoomed in the landmark itself could begin to display more detailed information in its interior.

9. CONCLUSION

The main contribution of the present work is the proposal to use a geographic space metaphor to organise the multi-dimensional data produced in the software development process, centred on the logical software design; that the design landscape should mediate daily development activities; and the use of aspect maps to visualise the individual dimensions of the data, possibly in a processed way.

We have argued that this proposal provides a development team with a common reference frame for overviewing, navigating within, and documenting a large software structure by utilising humans fine spatial and visual perception. Furthermore it has the ability to visualise many, although not all, interesting aspects of the data associated with software and software development in a way that makes comparisons of different aspects easy.

The preliminary experiences support the strength of position-based navigation–once the landscape has become well-known the world map is a compact and fast browser of source files in a project: Faster and less tedious than traditional approaches like shell name-completion or other graphical hierarchical tools like MacFinder and Windows95 Explorer. The visual grep in the scripting aspect provides better overview and less confusion than traditional textual recursive greps. The ability to explain the software design to newcomers on a project directly in the daily development environment is valuable.

The Ragnarok prototype is freely available from the author. A overview and reference guide describing the prototype in detail is provided on the World-Wide-Web (Christensen, 1998b).

REFERENCES

Andersen, P., Bak, L., Brandt, S., Knudsen, J. L., Madsen, O. L., Møller, K. J., Nørgaard, C., and Sandvad, E. (93). The Mjølner BETA System. In *Object-Oriented Environments - The Mjølner Approach*, pages 24–35. Prentice-Hall.

Baker, M. J. and Eick, S. G. (1995). Space-filling Software Visualisation. *Journal of Visual Languages and Computing*, 6:119–133.

Ball, T. and Eick, S. G. (1996). Software Visualization in the Large. *IEEE Computer*, 29(4):33–43.

Bederson, B. B. and Hollan, J. D. (1994). Pad++: A Zooming Graphical Interface for Exploring Alternate Interface Physics. In *Proceedings of ACM UIST '94*. ACM Press.

Bederson, B. B., Hollan, J. D., Perlin, K., Meyer, J., Bacon, D., and Furnas, G. (1996). Pad++: A Zoomable Graphical Sketchpad for Exploring Alternate Interface Physics. *Journal of Visual Languages and Computing*, 7:3–31.

Bürkle, U., Gryczan, G., and Züllighoven, H. (1995). Object-Oriented System Development in a Banking Project: Methodology, Experience, and Conclusions. *Human-Computer Interaction*, 10:293–336.

Christensen, H. B. (1997). Context-Preserving Software Configuration Management. In Conradi, R., editor, *Supplementary Proceedings: 7th International Workshop, SCM7*, pages 14–24, Boston, USA.

Christensen, H. B. (1998a). Experiences with Architectural Software Configuration Management in Ragnarok. In Magnusson, B., editor, *System Configuration Management*, Lecture Notes in Computer Science 1439. ECOOP'98 SCM-8 Symposium, Springer Verlag.

Christensen, H. B. (1998b). *Ragnarok: Overview and Reference Guide*. Department of Computer Science, University of Aarhus. http://www.daimi.au.dk/~hbc/Ragnarok/ragn_doc.html.

Egenhofer, M. J. and Mark, D. M. (1995). Naive Geography. In Frank, A. U. and Kuhn, W., editors, *Spatial Information Theory / A Theoretical Basis for GIS*, pages 1–15. COSIT '95, Lecture Notes in Computer Science 988, Springer-Verlag.

Frederick P. Brooks, Jr. (1987). No Silver Bullet—Essence and Accidents of Software Engineering. *IEEE Computer*, 20:10–19.

Hutchins, E. L., Hollan, J. D., and Norman, D. A. (1986). Direct manipulation interfaces. In Norman, D. A. and Draper, S. W., editors, *User Centered System Design*, chapter 5. Lawrence Erlbaum.

ISA (1996). Consys. http://isals.dfi.aau.dk. ISA: Institute for Storage Ring Facilities, University of Aarhus.

Kuhn, W. and Blumenthal, B. (1996). *Spatialization: Spatial Metaphors for User Interfaces*. Geoinfo-Series, Department of Geoinformation, Technical University, Vienna. Reprinted tutorial notes from CHI'96.

Lamb, D. A. (1996). Introduction: Studies of Software Design. In Lamb, D. A., editor, *Studies of Software Design*, Lecture Notes in Computer Science 1078. ICSE'93 Workshop, Springer Verlag.

Ousterhout, J. K. (1994). *Tcl and the Tk Toolkit*. Addison-Wesley Professional Computing Series.

Perlin, K. and Fox, D. (1993). Pad - An Alternative Approach to the Computer Interface. In *Proceedings of ACM SIGGRAPH '93*. ACM Press.

Rational Rose (1997). Unified Modeling Language, version 1.0. Rational Software Corporation, Santa Clara/CA. URL:http://www.rational.com.

Rumbaugh, J., Blaha, M., Premerlani, W., Eddy, F., and Lorensen, W. (1991). *Object-Oriented Modeling and Design*. Prentice-Hall International Editions.

Shneiderman, B. (1983). Direct Manipulation: A Step Beyond Programming Languages. *IEEE Computer*, 16(8):56–69.

Sommerville, I. (1992). *Software Engineering*. Addison-Wesley Publishers Ltd., 4 edition.

Discussion

Ken Fishkin: Layout is a severely underconstrained problem, and the algorithm you choose can drastically affect user experience. How do you deal with this?

Henrik Bærbak Christensen: I agree. For that reason, we use no layout algorithm: layout is specified interactively by the user.

Helmut Steigler: How open or closed is your system e.g. with respect to include existing software or products?

Henrik Bærbak Christensen: The system is on top of and independent of the underlying development environment. In our case the interfacing to Visual C++ raised some difficult questions.

Stephane Chatty: You presented graphs more than landscapes actually, and I think that trigger different ways of thinking. So do you think that what is really important is properties like salient positions, or that a real landscape would bring even more?

Henrik Bærbak Christensen: I decided to use maps instead of a more true "real world" metaphor as they are easier to navigate in, and generally easier to use. For instance, travel in real space is more time-consuming than just clicking at some point on a map. Gilbert Cockton added to the answer: "There is no big difference between landscape and maps."

Nick Graham: Have you considered the social aspects of introducing this kind of tool where you may run into difficulties with stakeholders who are not enthusiastic about giving up their "power" of being the only one to understand the software architecture?

Henrik Bærbak Christensen: No, an interesting issue that I have not thought about.

Morten Harning: In what situations would you suggest the use of a geographic metaphor?

Henrik Bærbak Christensen: If you have a system with objects in a hierarchical structure, that is relatively stable over time, this metaphor has much to offer.

Shijian Lu: One of the important aspects of geographic space is that all locations are predefined therefore the layout of a map is dictated by location while in a software architecture diagram the layout is very much dictated by readability. How do you map a software architecture into a unique layout?

Henrik Bærbak Christensen: Yes and No; Yes, a complete rearranged landscape would make us loose sense of direction; but most rearrangements takes place at the detail level (adding few new classes, removing some), and not in the overall picture. Large architectures are prohibitively costly to do large restructurings on.

Shijian Lu: If there is no unique map from a software architecture into a fixed layout, in the fail of modification, the components' location will be changed, then the notion of fixed location of the software landscape will be lost. How can that improve easy navigation?

Henrik Bærbak Christensen: Yes and no. Yes, because we need stable structure for the layout, but No, as large architectures are costly to build and therefore in real situations it is unlikely that the whole architecture is rebuild.

Frank Tarpin-Bernard: Even if designers use creative processes, I am not sure that they design from scratch. Don't you think that reusable design patterns are a good way to improve design?

Henrik Bærbak Christensen: True, patterns and preexisting subarchitectures are very important. I think one should therefore import their landscape just as much as import the underlying architecture.

Prasun Dewan: Many programming environments typically impose a lot of overhead on you. To build a "hello world" Java program I have to create a class, a file, a project and a workspace. Now you want me to also create a landscape. Is this a reasonable overhead?

Henrik Bærbak Christensen: Good comment: A landscape may seems like an overhead but in Ragnarok drawing a landmark potentially constructs much of the framework you speak of: Source code framework, project management framework, etc. The vision is of course that the benefits should outweight the cost.

Christian Gram: Why are landmarks dull similar rectangles? Why not use triangles, circles, ...

Henrik Bærbak Christensen: We did that because it was easier.

Christian Gram: Why is the system called "Ragnarok" and not Paradise?

Henrik Bærbak Christensen: Ragnarok is the cataclysmic struggle between gods and giants where the old world is destroyed, according to nordic mythology. The Ragnarok name is kind of black humour—we hope to do better, and surely we have not promised too much :)

Early experience with the mediaspace CoMedi

J. Coutaz, F. Bérard, E. Carraux, J. Crowley
CLIPS-IMAG
BP 53, 38041 Grenoble Cedex 9
Tel. +33 04 76 41 91 57, fax +33 04 76 44 66 75,
email: {Joelle.coutaz,fberard,jlc}@imag.fr

Abstract: Mediaspaces have been designed to facilitate informal communication and support group awareness while assuring privacy protection. However, low bandwidth communication is a source of undesirable discontinuities in such systems, resulting in a loss of peripheral awareness. In addition, privacy is often implemented as an accessibility matrix coupled to an all-or-nothing exposure of personal state. In this article, we describe CoMedi, a mediaspace prototype that addresses the problem of discontinuity and privacy in an original way: computer vision and speech recognition are used in conjunction to minimize visual discontinuities while supporting free movements in a room. Publication filters maintain privacy at the desired level of transparency.

Key words: Computer mediated communication, mediaspace, privacy, group awareness, computer vision, face tracking, publication filter

1.   INTRODUCTION

The concept of «mediaspace» has been introduced in the early 90's as a means for facilitating informal communication and group awareness between spatially separated individuals. Informal communication denotes unplanned opportunistic encounters such as meeting someone by chance in the hall-way or glancing at someone through an opened door. Group awareness denotes a collective situated context for personal actions. It is grounded on the knowledge of the external world whether this knowledge is explicit, central and formal, or implicit, peripheral and informal, and whether it is useful now or in the future.

In typical mediaspace settings such as Cavecat (Mantei, 1991), Cruiser (Fish, 1992) and Montage (Tang, 1994), users can teleglance at a remote office, open a V-phone connection or maintain a permanent link with a distant shared location such as the commons. Although these services support informal communication and provide a global sense of a shared community (Dourish, 1992), they may also be used abusively and threaten privacy.

Access control to privacy may rely on social protocols as in the very first mediaspace developed at PARC (Stults, 1986) or it may use technical solutions as in Cruiser. Alternatively, access control may include a combination of both imperative and indicative controls as in Montage. Most solutions to disclosing privacy are two-fold: either the connection is permitted and an audio-video link is opened providing a full perceptual view on the distant location, or the connection is denied, and the distant visitor has no perceptual access to the remote site. Actually, the disclosure of private data is more complex than these simplistic binary solutions.

Another problem with mediaspaces is the restricted field of view on remote sites. As a result, peripheral awareness of distant people, objects, and events is lost. In addition, the static nature of the cameras induces extra articulatory tasks that interfere with the real world activity. For example, when V-phoning, users must keep their head within the field of the camera in order to be perceived by distant parties. Multiple views on remote sites improve the information bandwidth of a single static channel, but users have difficulties in linking the different views together (Gaver, 1993).

The mediaspace CoMedi has been developed as an answer to these concerns: group awareness and informal communication should be supported but privacy should be protected and sources of discontinuities should be avoided. In the next section, we describe CoMedi in details. Based on this early experience, we then present our research agenda for future development.

2.   COMEDI

CoMedi (Communication and Mediaspace) is a mediaspace prototype that allows users to perform the following communication tasks: glance at someone, tele-visit a location using multiple forms of camera remote control, V-phone with someone while moving around in the office using a video tracking system, and publish private state variables through publication filters. Users are able to control the system using speech when they can't reach the mouse and the keyboard: glancing, opening a V-phone connection, etc., can be performed using either speech or direct manipulation.

2.1   The overall structure of the CoMedi user interface

The graphical user interface of CoMedi is structured into three functional parts: a menu bar, a porthole, and a control panel (see Figures 1 and 2).

2.1.1 The menu bar

At the top of the screen, the menu bar groups together the least frequent tasks. These include setting the access rights and the publication of sensitive data. When opening the *accessibility matrix*, the user can express the types of connection each distant user is allowed to issue. For example, the user can authorize good friends to both tele-visit his site and call him through the V-phone facility. On the other hand, less privileged colleagues may not be allowed to tele-visit his place. Publication of sensitive data, which forms an original feature of CoMedi, is discussed in 2.2.

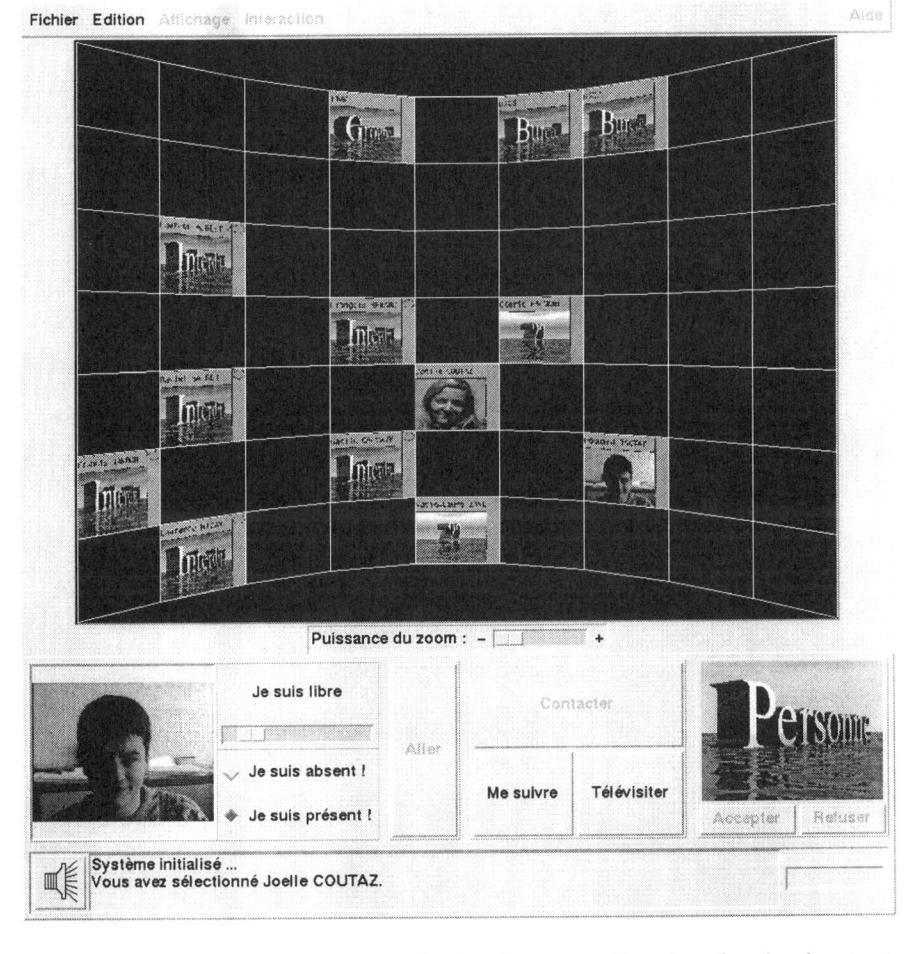

Figure 1: The graphical user interface of CoMedi is structured into three functional parts: at the top, a menu bar for non frequent tasks. In the center, a porthole that supports group awareness. At the bottom, a control panel for frequent tasks.

59

2.1.2 The fisheye porthole

In the center of the screen, a fisheye porthole supports group awareness. A slot in the porthole corresponds either to a remote user or to a group of users. An individual slot displays the personal information that the remote user has accepted to make observable through publication filters. When opening a collective slot, the current porthole is replaced with the porthole of the corresponding group.

As shown in Figure 1, the porthole may have the shape of an amphitheater where every slot is of equal size. When the fisheye feature is on, selecting a slot, using either the mouse or a spoken command, provokes an animated distortion of the porthole that brings the selected slot into the center with progressive enlargement. For example, in Figure 2, Eric has selected Joëlle after having tuned the zoom factor using the slider below the porthole.

The motivation for a fisheye porthole is three-fold: it supports lightweight glancing, it provides detailed rendition in context, and it promotes scalability.

- At the opposite of most mediaspaces, glancing does not require any explicit action from the user except looking at the porthole.
- A selected slot denotes the current focus of attention. It is enlarged in a way that details about the remote activity are revealed at the appropriate level of granularity. Meanwhile, the other slots, which denote peripheral attention, are shrinked but still observable to convey information about on going activities at remote sites.

The porthole technique can accommodate a large number of users or group of users (see the 63 slots in Figure 1). For an even larger number of users, the slots may be too small to be discernable. If so, the porthole could be augmented with holophrastic techniques. For example, a number of slots would be used to synthesize the activity of multiple slots and indicate relevant state changes at remote sites. When selected, an aggregate slot would expand in place and reveal details progressively about the slot parts

2.1.3 The control panel

At the bottom of the screen, a panel is dedicated to the most frequent control tasks: requesting or closing a remote connection, accepting or rejecting connection requests, checking personal sensitive data, and starting or stopping the tracking video system. Checking sensitive data is discussed in 2.2. The tracking system is presented in 2.3.

With regard to connection monitoring, CoMedi combines both imperative and indicative access controls: an authorized distant user can send a connection request using the Contact or the Tele-visit buttons (see the bottom right side of the control panel). This permission has been set up through the accessibility matrix discussed above. Looking at the porthole, the caller can also check whether the distant user is currently available. Although the connection is authorized, the user may postpone the call based on social cues.

When contacted, the receiver can see the image of the caller (in the right most part of the control panel) as well as a pop-up timing band. He can accept or reject the request on the fly or ignore it. When the time out has elapsed, the connection returns to the idle state.

In the next sections, we present the original contributions of CoMedi for supporting privacy and minimizing discontinuities.

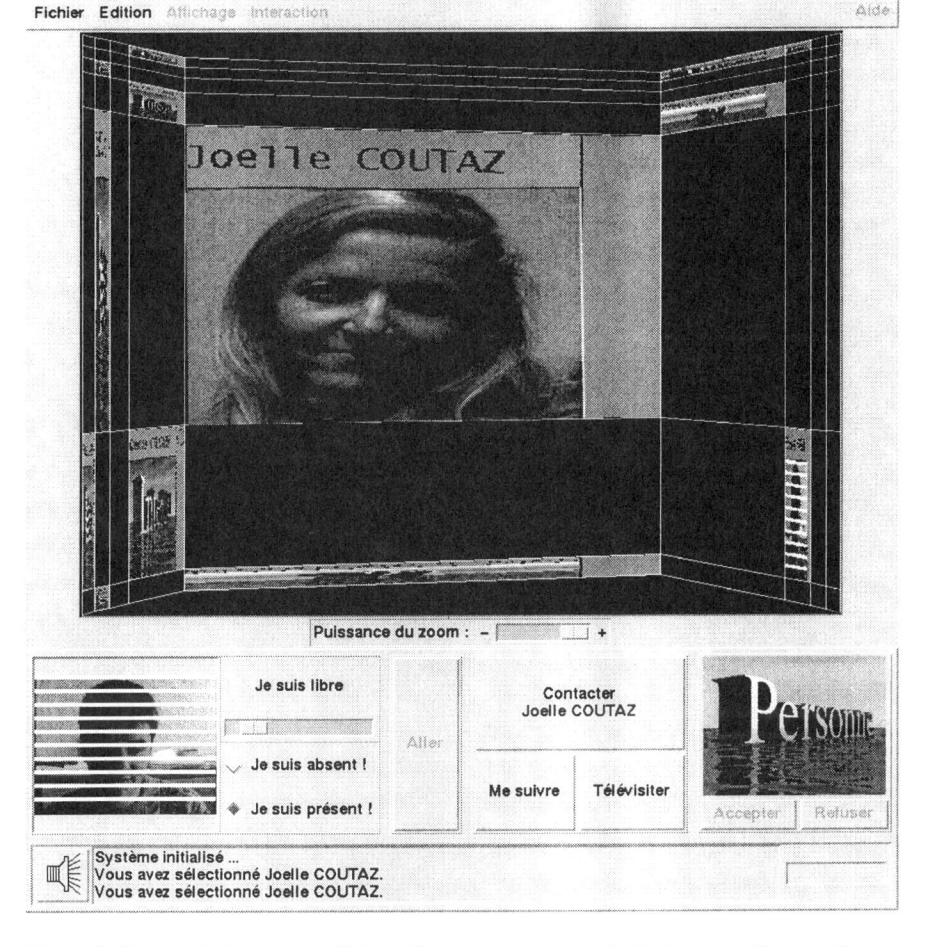

Figure 2: The porthole when the fisheye feature is activated. At the bottom left, according to the reflexivity property, the user can check and modify sensitive data. Here, Eric is using Venetian blinds to filter his private video scene.

2.2 Supporting privacy through publication filters

In CoMedi, personal data include a business card and sensitive data rendered through publication filters.

2.2.1 Sensitive data

Sensitive data model the private space, for example, the fact that the user is currently in his office reading E-mail. Clearly, the observability of sensitive data is relevant to group awareness but may conflict with privacy. Our concept of *published observability* allows designers to reason about this antagonism (Salber, 1995). Sensitive data is made observable only if its owner has authorized its publication.

In the current implementation of CoMedi, the types of sensitive data are the following:
- the absence or presence,
- the level of availability (available, busy, very busy, do not disturb),
- the audio scene (captured by the local microphone),
- the video scene (captured by the local camera).

Publication is set up for each type of sensitive data through the top level menu bar. At the opposite of the accessibility matrix used for access control, the publication matrix is the same for every remote user. This design choice is motivated by implementation simplification only. In the example of Figure 2, Joëlle has authorized the publication of her video scene, but not her presence nor her level of availability.

Exporting private sensitive data is one thing, remembering what is currently exported about oneself is a second thing.

2.2.2 Checking sensitive data: the reflexivity property

The capacity for the user to check the publication of his own sensitive data complies with the *reflexivity* property (Salber, 1995). The mirror image found in most tele-conferencing systems illustrates a simplistic case of reflexivity. CoMedi goes further: as shown at the bottom left of Figure 1, Eric can verify that he is currently publishing his private video scene as well as his presence and his level of availability. In addition, this portion of the control panel allows him to change the values of his sensitive data (for example, switching the level of availability from «busy» to «do not disturb»). The binary duality of publishing or hiding sensitive data does not however convey the subtlety of human social relations. We have introduced the concept of publication filter to satisfy this requirement (Salber, 1995).

2.2.3 Publication filter

A filter is a transformation function that applies to a set of published sensitive data. As shown in Figure 2, Eric is using a «Venitian blinds» filter that hides his private video space partially. Other filters such as posters are also available. In Figure 1, we observe that most users are hidden behind a poster. Setting a publication filter is performed through a pop-up menu that offers the list of available filters. The menu appears when clicking on the private video scene of the control panel.

Other techniques for filtering private video scenes have been developed recently: a low resolution image as in the Nynex Porthole (Lee, 1997), a ghost that denotes moving entities over time while blurring the entity itself (Hudson, 1996).

In (Coutaz, 1997), we present an innovative filter for video-based sensitive data using principal component analysis. Source images are coded as their coordinates in an N-dimensional orthogonal space: an eigen-space. This space is defined as the principal components computed from a set of representative publishable video images. The received image is rebuilt in real time on distant sites using a linear combination of the basis images. As a result, features in a source image that would not appear in the basis images are not reconstructed.

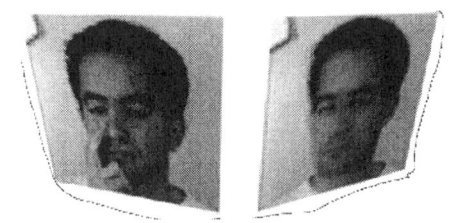

Figure 3: Eigen-space filtering for private video space. On the left, the source image; on the right the source image cleaned up through an eigen space filter.

For example, in Figure 3, the source image showing François picking his nose is cleaned up through an eigen-space filter to produce a socially acceptable picture. Similarly any person appearing in the background would not be published to distant observers if not present in the basis images.

2.3 Minimizing discontinuity

Discontinuity in Computer Mediated Communication (CMC) is an opened problem. It covers multiple forms of disruptions primarily due to low perceptual bandwidth (Sellen, 1995). In CoMedi, we have investigated several ways of minimizing discontinuities for the two most relevant tasks in CMC: tele-visit and audio-video communication with distant users. We have addressed the visual dimension of discontinuity using computer vision and image processing in conjunction with speech.

2.3.1 The computer vision tracker

The computer vision tracker developed for CoMedi uses a pan-tilt-zoom color camera. As shown in Figure 4, it is based on an architecture in which a supervisor activates and co-ordinates three visual complementary processes: eye blink, color histogram, and cross-correlation (Coutaz, 1996; Crowley, 1997).

Eye blink detection is based on the difference of successive images. If the eyes happened to be closed in one of the two images, two small roundish regions appear over the eyes where the difference is significant. Eye blink detection is computationally inexpensive and can handle a wide range of lightning conditions.

The head position estimation provided by eye blink detection is used to calibrate the color histogram from a region of the image (close to the eyes) that contains skin colored pixels. Color histogram is computationally cheap but sensitive to camera noise resulting in jittering. To achieve accuracy, correlation tracking is used.

Cross-correlation operates by comparing a reference template (e.g., piece of an eyebrow) to an image neighborhood at each position within a search region. Cross correlation is very accurate but it is unable to track head rotation. This problem is solved using the cooperation of the two other complementary detection techniques.

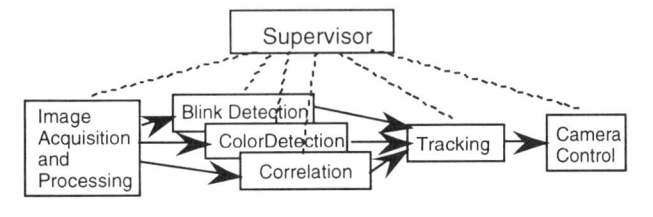

Figure 4: A Supervisory controller selects and controls the sequencing of visual processes. Dotted lines denote activation by the supervisor. Arrows express the main stream data flow.

In order to support cooperation, the output provided by each visual process is normalized and formalized: each process returns its estimation of the head position, a precision and a confidence factor. Figure 5 illustrates the cooperation of the three visual processes.

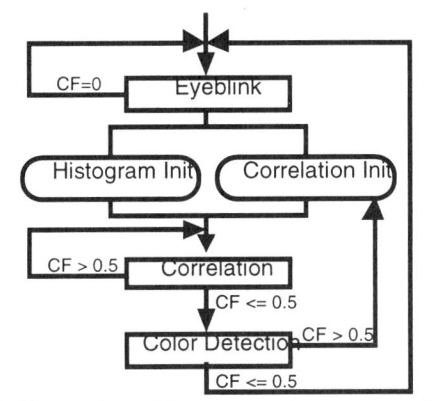

Figure 5: Cooperation of the perceptual processes techniques.

When tracking confidence is low, the supervisor runs blink detection to look for a face (eye blink is fast and does not need initialisation). When blink is detected, a color histogram is initialised, a correlation template is stored for each eye. As long as the tracking CF remains high, correlation is used to track the eyes (correlation is fast and precise). When a tracking CF with a low value is obtained, correlation tracking has failed, the color histogram is used to recover the face (histogram always returns a result). If the tracking CF is high again, the correlation template is re-initialised at an eye position estimated from the face position and the correlation is run again. If, on the other hand, the tracking CF drops below a threshold, the supervisor draws upon the eye blink detector.

2.3.2 Minimizing discontinuity with the computer vision tracker

In CoMedi, the computer vision tracker is used to control the movement of the local camera. It can also be used to control the field of view of a remote camera as in Gaver's virtual window (Gaver, 1995).

To start/stop the local tracker, the user can utter the sentence «follow me»/«stop following me» or click the «follow me» button in the control panel (in French: «me suivre»). Local tracking avoids users to check their location within the field of view of the camera. The migration to the system of counterproductive articulatory tasks minimizes discontinuities in the communication process.

In addition, local tracking opens the way to a new kind of interactive user: a user who is not wired to a terminal, a user free to move. Because the tracking system is based on multiple visual processes, it has the potential to smoothly shift from the head target (i.e., talking head mode) to the hand pointing at a new object of interest (e.g., the drawing on the blackboard the users are currently talking about). As users talk, it is possible for them to move around while the local camera adjusts the field of view dynamically.

To start/stop the virtual window, the user can utter the sentence «tele-visit»/«stop tele-visiting» or click the «tele-visit» button in the control panel (in French: «télévisiter»). As users talk, they can telecontrol the remote camera by moving their head and ajust the remote field of view according to their needs. Because users can explore distant sites under their own control just like they would do it in front of a physical window, Gaver has demonstrated a decrease in visual discontinuities. On the other hand, the virtual window technique offers one single view at a time. As observed by Gaver et al., «one [view] is not enough» (Gaver, 1993). We have developed Fovea, a technique based on image processing, to address this problem.

2.3.3 Minimizing discontinuity with Fovea

The motivation for Fovea is to avoid the visual discontinuity due to the split screen solution adopted in Extra-Eyes (Yamaashi, 1996). In Extra-eyes, a low resolution camera provides the observer with a wide angle view of the remote site. A detailed view of the focus of interest is obtained at a high resolution in a second window. Although a rectangle is drawn in the wide angle view to show the location of the detailed view, the user has to consolidate the visual discontinuity between the two views.

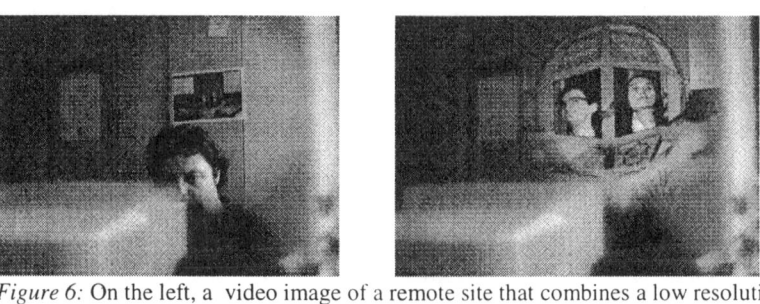

Figure 6: On the left, a video image of a remote site that combines a low resolution picture with a high resolution fovea . It is currently pointing at a picture on the wall. On the right, the video image when using a zoomed fovea.

Fovea fuses multiple views into a single image. It is inspired by foveal and peripheral architecture of the human visual system. As shown in Figure 6, the image received at a distance results from the combination of a low resolution image (the periphery) with a high resolution image (the fovea). In its current implementation, the location of the fovea in the remote scene is controlled with the mouse (but the head tracker described above could be used as well).

As the user explores the remote site, he may find something of interest, for example a postcard pinned on the wall. As shown on the right side of Figure 6, the zoom facility of the fovea can be used to obtain information at the right level of detail without loosing the context. From preliminary user studies where six users were asked to find random targets, users were more efficient with a rectangular fovea than with Extra-Eyes but they were more efficient with Extra-Eyes than with the circle shape fovea. On the other hand, all of them preferred the circular fovea. These preliminary results need additional experimentation to confirm our findings.

2.3.4 Minimizing discontinuity using speech

The motivation for speech is to support mobility: as the user moves away from the mouse and the keyboard, he can still control the mediaspace using speech.

Spoken control in the context of audio communications may generate confusions. In particular, the speech recognition system needs to identify whether the user is talking to a distant partner or uttering a system command. In general, speech systems can be used in a «push to talk» mode or in a continuous recognition mode. The push to talk approach increases system robustness but induces an extra articulatory task. The continuous mode is free from extra task but computationally more expensive and less robust.

In CoMedi, we use the speech system in the continuous recognition mode to eliminate the push button additional task but we prevent the system from listening by hiding the microphone: The HF receiver/transmitter is placed in the user's pocket while the microphone itself is clipped on the wristwatch (not on the shirt collar!). In general, users keep their non dominant hand far from the mouth. To talk to the system, the user makes the same gesture as for reading the watch. Although the naturalness of the setting has not been tested formally, early experience indicates easy acceptance.

3.   LESSONS LEARNED AND RESEARCH AGENDA

The lessons learned from our early experience with CoMedi are both technical and human centered.

3.1   Technical aspects: CoMedi is a concept demonstrator

CoMedi is implemented according to the PAC* architecture model (Calvary, 1997). Its functional core, which maintains the data base of users, is an active data structure implemented as a GroupKit environment (Roseman, 1992). The Interaction and the Presentation components host the modality interpreters: the speech recognition system (ViaVoice from IBM), the computer vision tracker, and the graphical abstract machine Tk.   These interpreters are all encapsulated in Tcl providing a uniform view to the Dialogue Component. The Dialogue Component is refined in terms of PAC agents according to the PAC style (see Coutaz, 1997b for a more detailed description of this CoMedi component).

For efficiency, modality interpreters are distributed over multiple processors: a PC runs the speech recognition system while a SGI Indy is dedicated to computer vision and a second one runs the rest of the local computations. As a result, every CoMedi user needs 3 workstations to be part of the mediaspace. Clearly, CoMedi is a concept demonstrator. Its computational cost is too prohibitive for an effective large scale use.

In addition, the absence of guaranteed bandwidth makes impossible tightly coupled interaction over the Ethernet. For example, the remote control of cameras as in Fovea or the virtual window, is difficult to achieve with unstable response times.

Figure 7: The graphical user interface of CoMedi Light.

Based on this early experience, we have developed a lightweight version of CoMedi for a realistic use in the IMAG community. So far, CoMedi Light does not include any computer vision tracker nor speech recognition. Interpersonal communication is limited to glances and Post-It messages. On the other hand, CoMedi Light is portable on standard platforms (MacOs, Irix and Windows NT) connected over the Ethernet; its efficient use of resources makes it possible non-stop background execution. Figure 7 shows the actual graphical user interface of CoMedi Light implemented in Java. It has been in use for one month only between 15 volunteers who daily meet face-to-face (publication filters have not been installed yet). Although it is too early to report on CoMedi Light as a social object, we have already observed interesting social phenomena

3.2 Human centered aspects

The technical limitations observed for both CoMedi and CoMedi Light add new items to our research agenda: balance of the equipment, camera full coverage, filter refinement, audio and video scenes analysis.

3.2.1 Balance of the equipment

The disparity between mediaspace workstations may have undesirable effects on social behavior. For example, 5 CoMedi Light users, who did not have a camera,

68

would not launch the mediaspace. They said they would see other people without being observed. In this case, the lack of reciprocity due to unbalanced equipment induced an undesirable sense of voyeurism. Unbalanced equipment, whose increase follows the advent of mobile and ubiquitous computing, is an important issue to address in order to guarantee social fairness in CMC.

3.2.2 Camera full coverage

Although Fovea and the virtual window support tele-exploration, it is still difficult for remote observers to identify which part of the distant place is currently seen by the camera. There are two reasons for this: a single camera is not enough to scan 360°; second, people take possession of their camera: they keep changing its location. As a result, users cannot develop a stable model of remote sites.

Camera full coverage can be addressed through the cooperation of multiple cameras. In addition, each camera should be able to dynamically compute its own location within the scene. With this information, it is then possible to provide users with an additional picture that makes concrete the current field of view of the camera within the remote scene.

3.2.3 A filter algebra

So far, filters work independently and use one single sensitive information at a time. For example, video filters apply to the whole scene as opposed to a patchwork composition. As an example of composition, a poster may hide the latest results written on the blackboard, the user's face may be cleaned up through an eigen-space filter, and the visitors may be blurred with a low resolution picture. As the user and the visitors move around, filters may overlap: what is the resulting image?

Fusing multiple sensitive data into a meaningful synthesized representation is also another way to go. For example, combining keystrokes, mouse actions, differences of audio and video images into a single level of activity. But the resulting combination of filters should not be reversible in order to prevent any form of maleficence.

We plan to develop a filter algebra to reason about publication filtering.

4.   CONCLUSION

In this article, we have described CoMedi, a prototype mediaspace, that addresses the problem of discontinuity and privacy in an original way. This heavy weight concept demonstrator has opened the way to the development of a portable version for effective use by a large community of users: Comedi Light. The services of CoMedi Light will be incrementally augmented along the lines of our research agenda.

ACKNOWLEDGMENT

This work is being supported by France Telecom-CNET.

REFERENCES

Calvary, G., Coutaz, J. and L. Nigay (1997) From Single-User Architectural Design to PAC*: a Generic Software Architecture Model for CSCW. In *Proceedings of CHI 97*, ACM publ., pp. 242-249.

Coutaz, J. , Crowley, J. L. and Bérard, F. (1996) Coordination of Perceptual Processes for Computer Mediated Communication, *in proceedings of the second International Conference on Automatic Face and Gesture Recognition*, IEEE Computer Society Press, pp. 106-111.

Coutaz, J., Crowley, J. and F. Bérard (1997) Eigen space Coding as a Means to Support Privacy in Computer Mediated Communication. *In Proceedings of INTERACT'97*, Chapman & Hall Publ.

Coutaz, J. (1997b) PAC-ing the Software Architecture of your User Interface. *DSV-IS'97, 4th Eurographics Workshop on Design, Specification and Verification of Interactive Systems*, 1997, Springer Verlag Publ., pp. 15-32.

Crowley, J. L. and F. Bérard (1997) Multi-Modal Tracking of Faces for Video Communications, *IEEE Conference on Computer Vision and Pattern Recognition CVPR '97*, Puerto Rico.

Dourish, P. and Bly, S.A. (1992) Portholes : Supporting Awareness in a Distributed Work Group, in *proceedings of the CHI'92 Conference on Human Factors in Computing Systems*, pp. 541-547.

Fish, R.S., Kraut, R.E., Root, R.W., and Rice R.E. (1992) Evaluating Video as a Technology for Informal Communications, in *proceedings of the CHI'92 Conference on Human Factors in Computing Systems*, pp. 37-47.

Gaver, W., Sellen, A., Heath, C. and P. Luff (1993) One is not Enough: Multiple Views on a Media Space, *Proc. INTERCHI'93*, ACM Publ., pp. 335-341.

Gaver, W., Smets, G. and K. Overbeeke (1995) A Virtual Window on a Media Space, *Proc. CHI'95*, ACM publ., pp. 257-264.

Hudson, S. & Smith, I. (1996) Techniques for Addressing Fundamental Privacy and Disruption Tradeoffs in Awareness Support Systems. In Proc. CSCW'96, ACM Press, pp. 248-257.

Lee, A., Girgensohn, A. and Schlueter K. (1997) NYNEX Portholes: Initial User Reactions and Redesign Implications. *In Proc. GROUP'97, International Conf. on Supporting Group work*, ACM Publ.

Mantei, M., Backer, R.M., Sellen, A., Buxton, W., Milligan, T. and Wellman B. (1991) Experiences in the use of a Media Space, in *proceedings of the CHI'91 Conference on Human Factors in Computing Systems*, pp. 203-208.

Roseman, M. and Greenberg, S. (1992) GROUPKIT: A groupware Toolkit for Building Real-Time Conferencing Applications, *in Proc. CSCW'92*, ACM Conference on CSCW, pp. 43-50.

Salber, D. (1995) *De l'interaction Homme-Machine individuelle aux systèmes multi-utilisateurs: l'exemple de la communication homme-homme médiatisée*, Thèse de doctorat de l'Université Joseph Fourier, Grenoble.

Sellen, A. (1995) Remote Conversations: The Effects of Mediating Talk with Technology, in *Human Computer Interaction*, Lawrence Erlbaum Publ., Vol. 10(4), pp. 401-444.

Stults, R. (1986) *MediaSpace*, rapport technique Xerox PARC.

Tang, J.C. and Rua, M. (1994) Montage: Providing Teleproximity for Distributed Groups, in *Proc. of the Conference on Computer Human Interaction (CHI'94)*, pp. 37-43.

Yamaashi, K., Cooperstock, J., Narine, T. and Buxton, W. (1996) Beating the limitations of Camera-Monitor Mediated Telepresence with Extra Eyes, In *proc. CHI'96*.

BIOGRAPHY

François Bérard is a Ph.D. student at the Université Joseph Fourier (Grenoble, France). His research interest is Computer Vision for HCI. Eric Carraux received his Masters degree in Software Engineering from Université Joseph Fourier, currently working as a visiting programmer at Carnegie Mellon University. James L. Crowley is professor at Institut National Polytechnique of Grenoble. He received his doctorate from Carnegie Mellon University in 1982. His research is in Computer vision and Mobile Robotics. Joëlle Coutaz is professor at Université Joseph Fourier. Her research interest covers the software aspects of HCI, software modelling architecture, and the design of new interaction techniques for Computer Mediated Communication.

Discussion

Prasun Dewan: Can the focus and peripheral cameras show objects on the same scale. It looked weird having the focus in larger scale.

Joelle Coutaz: Yes. You can zoom in and zoom out.

Ken Fishkin: Does your blink-detection algorithm work on people wearing glasses ?

Joelle Coutaz: Yes, unless they are severely nearsighted, in which case the magnification of the lenses is so severe that the camera can no longer see the user's eyes.

Ken Fishkin: I don't participate in video systems such as your describe because I don't like being under surveillance all day. How unusual am I ?

Joelle Coutaz: Of 14 people, 2 felt as you do.

Stephane Chatty: In your Eigen-value video system, I noticed that the eyes and the mouth of the final image are blurred. Is it a feature? And if you were to control a virtual clone or a cartoon rather than a video face, would that kind of problem remain?

Joelle Coutaz: It is not a feature. It is a design problem. Yes you can drive a robot or a cartoon character.

Morten Harming: Have you considered using a semi-trasparent fovea to make navigation easier on the low resolution image?

Joelle Coutaz: The usability study has not been done yet, but you can zoom out and vary the size of the overlayed image.

Stephane Chatty: I could see that you use a scrollbar to control your availability degree. What are the social consequences of your different levels ? For instance, as a boss, how do you feel when someone in your group is always available, and never busy ?

General laugh in the audience

Modelling Unwarranted Commitment in Information Artefacts

Chris Roast

School of Computing and Management Sciences, Sheffield Hallam University, Sheffield, UK.

Abstract: This paper extends an analytic framework based upon that of Cognitive Dimensions which provides formal definitions for assessing the suitability of interactive systems for particular tasks. Elsewhere we have demonstrated that interface design can benefit from interpreting cognitive dimensions as formal tools for assessing interface characteristics relevant to effective use. Our interpretation of these dimensions has the benefit of introducing a level of precision to the otherwise informal notion of cognitive dimension. In general developing a more precise interpretation of the dimensions is a necessary prerequisite for their employment within software engineering.

In this paper an interpretation of the cognitive dimension termed 'premature commitment' is examined and its relation the dimensions of 'viscosity' considered. We demonstrate the appropriateness of the measures developed as a means of assessing implicit bias in interface behaviour and the general results that their formalisation enables. The effectiveness of the proposed formal characterisations is illustrated with a small case study.

Keywords: Cognitive Dimensions, Evaluation, Formal Modelling, Premature Commitment

1. INTRODUCTION

Numerous conceptual tools have been proposed to alleviate the complexities of effective interface design. This paper develops one such conceptual tool, termed cognitive dimensions. Cognitive dimensions have been proposed by Green (Green, 1989) as providing broadbrush widely applicable usability metrics. These ideas have received considerable interest and are widely recognised as a promising aids to design and evaluation activities within the broad domain of information artefacts (Gilmore, 1997; Lavery et al., 1996; Yang et al., 1995; Green and Petre, 1996; Blandford and Green, 1997). The research described here is concerned with refining concepts drawn from cognitive dimensions to provide an analytic basis for understanding and applying them.

Employing formal models has a number of potential benefits: it provides a precise representation that can focus discussion and negotiation; tools and techniques can be employed to analyse a formal design prior to implementation and empirical evaluation; and design tools and techniques may directly feed off such representations. In this paper we are concerned with the first two of these benefits, with the aim of bridging the gap between usability, as a poorly expressed requirement, and precise design representations, as necessitated by the eventual system. In some cases this has involved developing enhanced system models that embody usability requirements (Dix, 1991; Roast and Siddiqi, 1997b; Roast, 1998), while in others explicit models of the user (or task) have been formally combined with system representations (Barnard and Harrison, 1992; Duke et al., 1995; Harrison et al., 1993; Palanque and Bastide, 1997).

An analytical framework incorporating formal interpretations of some of the cognitive dimensions has been developed and applied to systems ranging from individual dialogue boxes to programming environments (Roast and Siddiqi, 1996; Siddiqi and Roast, 1997).

The paper first introduces the particular dimensions examined and illustrates the approach to be taken by briefly reviewing viscosity. Formal interpretations of the dimension of 'premature commitment' are introduced and examined. Finally, the validity of the formalisation is considered using a small case study.

2. INTERPRETING COGNITIVE DIMENSIONS

Cognitive dimensions (Green, 1989) have been developed as psychologically motivated metrics for a wide range of devices that focus upon factors central to successful use. The dimensions suggest a valuable and informal evaluative space in which artefacts can be located and compared (Green and Petre, 1996). In particular the dimensions are intended to reflect general concepts which are familiar and yet not well understood, hence they support the articulation of a range of familiar interactive behaviours and interface characteristics in terms that are sufficiently general to enable diverse design problems, and their solutions, to be easily related. The dimensions ideally provide a framework available to both designers and users which supports both interface evaluation and design. The informal nature of cognitive dimensions is in some cases assumed to benefit to their broad application and adoption as an evaluative and. However their largely anecdotal nature is highly limiting when considering their uniform and consistent application, as demanded by an engineering context (Gilmore, 1997; Lavery et al., 1996; Yang et al., 1995). In addition, very few studies of the dimensions have focused upon understanding the characteristics of the underlying framework which they presuppose.

In this paper we concern ourselves primarily with the dimension termed premature commitment and identify its potential associations with dimensions of viscosity. For both premature commitment and viscosity the primary concern is how hard it is for users to reach or transform easily particular goal states.

Premature Commitment concerns the complexities associated with of attaining a specific goal state and the possible inappropriateness of the states encountered and the actions necessary to satisfy the primary goal. In particular, it involves the system engaging the user in making a decision which is not immediately relevant to achieving their primary goal. A simple example is that of a desktop publishing package which when starting a new document asks the user how many pages their document is to consist of. Clearly, for some uses the number of pages in a document may be a primary concern in which case the interface behaviour may not be problematic. However for many document preparation tasks, such as report writing, the number of pages is more commonly a secondary outcome of completing the document (the primary goal). If we take this example to be illustrative of premature commitment, we can observe that in attempting to achieve one primary goal: the user has to engage in achieving a secondary sub-goal; and, the secondary sub-goal is not essential for achieving the primary goal.

By contrast *viscosity* concerns the complexity of achieving changes in the medium offered by an interface. Two types of resistance to change have been examined: *repetitive viscosity* refers to modifications involving intensive, and often repetitive, user effort; *knock-on viscosity* refers to the need for corrective work following a conceptually simple modification.

2.1 Formalisation

The formal interpretation of cognitive dimensions serves a number of purposes. First, it provides a common framework in which the informal notions can be represented and related. In general this benefits interface engineering, supporting the general understanding of how factors influencing effective and appropriate interaction are inter-related. Second, the formal interpretation provides a framework in which the concepts underlying illustrative examples can be teased-out and refined, and their overall validity assessed.

The approach taken to modelling the dimensions in this research is that of employing a design representation as a means of expressing system characteristics and requirements in system objective terms (Jackson, 1997). This approach provides a focused perspective upon the artefact, treating factors such as the context of use, user tasks and psychological make-up as reflected within the artefact. System orientated modelling reflects the complexity of interface design in which system behaviours can only be defined in terms of the interaction history. The same approach has been employed elsewhere to investigate the implicit assumptions underlying interface design and the impact of user centred requirements upon system specification and architecture (Dix, 1991; Dearden and Harrison, 1997; Markopoulos et al., 1997; Roast, 1997).

To characterise cognitive dimensions it has been convenient to provide interpretations based upon: *the goals* (and sub-goals) which users may achieve, and *the user inputs* which enable users to satisfy different goals. This system framework is clearly not cognitive in nature and hence our interpretations are best viewed as comprises between the cognitive view and the practical demands of the system model.

2.2 Examining Viscosity

A previous investigation of the cognitive dimensions of viscosity has been conducted and used to illustrate inter-dependencies between *repetitive viscosity* and *knock-on viscosity* (Siddiqi and Roast, 1997).

Repetitive viscosity concerns the complexity of actions required to make modifications. We model these in terms of the user inputs which can implement a modification which is characterised by a pre-condition (*pre*) and a post-condition (*post*). The expression *pre* REP *post* is taken to denote the language of all possible input sequences which can satisfy *post* starting from a state in which *pre* is satisfied. The repetitive viscosity of changes are assessed in terms of the complexity of *pre* REP *post*. At present we have taken the length of the minimal elements within *pre* REP *post* as a simple and immediate measure of complexity.

This model can be illustrated using a simple example of editing an enumerated list (such as a reference list). We will assume use goals include: *enum* meaning the list is enumerated, and; *list(...)* indicating the list contents. The repetitive viscosity of adding an item (N) to the list is based upon the language:

$$list(I_1, ..., I_n) \text{ REP } list(I_1, ..., I_i, N, I_{i+1}, ..., I_n)$$

This language would include inputs which locate the point of insertion and enter the new item. The added complexity of modifying an enumerated list (without special tool support) can be illustrated when we consider adding an item *and* keeping the list enumerated:

$$(enum \land list(I_1, ..., I_n)) \text{ REP } (enum \land list(I_1, ..., I_i, N, I_{i+1}, ..., I_n))$$

This language will not only include the insertion of the new item, but also the necessary commands to keep the list enumerated.

By contrast, *knock-on viscosity* is characterised in terms of how a system makes the satisfaction of some goals unnecessarily interfere with others. One characterisation of this interference is where an input satisfies one user goal (p), and yet a second goal (q) is not satisfied — this relation is written p DIS q. In our examination of knock-on viscosity, the number of instances of DIS that can influence a modification is taken to be indicative of the degree of knock-on viscosity. For example, considering the modification of an enumerated list we have that. $list(I_1, ...I_n)$ DIS *enum* when inserting an item. That is, achieving a specific list content by inserting an item results in the list no longer being enumerated, thus the user may subsequently have to re-satisfy *enum*.

The distinctive nature of the two dimensions modelled can be illustrated by the considering the effect of modifying the list edit example to include an 'auto-enumerate' command. In this case the repetitive viscosity can be reduced since the work to enumerate a list is now far simpler using the 'auto-enumerate' command. However, despite the availability of the new command, the instance of DIS still holds, thus indicating the persistence of a more general level of resistance to change.

2.2.1 Composition

Assuming that these interpretations are reasonable characterisations, their formal definitions can be used to investigate general properties of the dimensions. Such general properties can be used to provided a predictive assessment of general classes of interfaces and identify legitimacy of particular design proposals (Roast, 1997). This can be illustrated by considering interface designs expressed in terms of the composition of interface elements.

Briefly, given two interfaces (A and B) which both enable access to the same functionality. If a design is proposed which combines the two interfaces ($A \oplus B$) enabling users to freely switch between A and B, then the viscosity of the combined interface can be inferred using the definitions. The repetitive viscosity of $A \oplus B$ will be the minimum of that of A and B; and, the knock-on viscosity of $A \oplus B$ will be summative, that is the knock-on viscosity of A and B combined. Hence, under this form of composition *repetitive viscosity* will be no worse than that of the individual elements composed, where as *knock-on viscosity* will be no better.

These observations illustrate one way in which a cognitive dimensional space can be investigated by virtue of relying on accurate definitions. In particular, such observations can be related back to the informal concepts as a means of clarifying their effective application.

3. PREMATURE COMMITMENT

This section develops a proposed formal characterisation of the system behaviours we would consider to be indicative of premature commitment. The notation used to represent the dimension formally is an action logic ACTL (Nicola et al., 1991). Temporal action logics have been utilised elsewhere in formally modelling interaction (Paterno, 1997). In this work atemporal propositions correspond to system state properties and the influence of user inputs is represented by temporal constructs.

Briefly, for any property p:

- $[op]p$ is true iff following the input op, property p is true;
- AG p is true iff following any sequence of inputs p is true;
- EF p is true iff there is some sequence of inputs that may lead to p being true;
- A p U q is true iff in all futures p is true until q is true.

When using ACTL we assume that all inputs, or operations, are user driven and that all user goals correspond to state properties.

In the introduction we employed the notion of a primary goal and a secondary (unforeseen) goal, and described premature commitment as the user having to satisfy the secondary goal prior to achieving the primary goal. In terms of the initial example, the primary goal would be to complete the document and the secondary goal would be to declare the size of the document in pages. To develop a formal estimation of premature commitment we focus upon three facets of the concept: (i) the characterisation of how the secondary goal is unavoidable; (ii) the relationship between the secondary and primary goals which indicates the inappropriateness of having to commit to the first, and; (iii) the initial conditions implicit in cases of premature commitment.

Imposed ordering For a secondary goal to be premature, it is not possible for the primary goal to be satisfied without the user having to explicitly encounter the secondary goal.

A special notation will be used to represent user actions which explicitly concern possible goal properties. The user action $assert_g$ will be used to represent an input by the user which confirms or inputs information asserting the goal property g.

In order to represent unavoidably encountering the secondary goal, we have all possible futures satisfying the primary goal (p) only after asserting the secondary goal (q):

$$A (\neg p) \cup [\text{assert}_q] q$$

Always not p until q has been asserted

It can be noted that this is a weak interpretation of the imposed ordering that has been attributed to some examples of premature commitment. In particular the above property does not demand that the secondary goal is satisfied strictly before the primary, since it is possible that the input $assert_q$ can satisfy it. Thus, a similar investigation of premature commitment could focus upon the stronger characterisation, such as:

$$A (\neg p) \cup [\text{assert}_q](q \wedge \neg p)$$

Contingency In addition to the imposed ordering the description of premature commitment suggests that the goals involved are r elated within the domain. Here, we consider the possible dependencies between the primary and secondary goals that systems can impose.

First, the secondary goal is often deemed unforeseen or inappropriate when focusing upon the primary goal. Hence, one view of the word processor example is that the size of the document in pages is independent of the goal of completing the document. Thus, in general the secondary goal is superfluous. One way of characterising this lack of dependency between the goals is to require that no logical alternative is intrinsically prevented:

$$AG (EF (p \wedge q) \wedge EF (\neg p \wedge q) \wedge EF (p \wedge \neg q) \wedge EF (\neg p \wedge \neg q))$$

No domain dependencies exist between p and q

Second, the account of premature commitment can be interpreted as focusing the users attention upon secondary details which would have to be answered at some point in order to achieve the primary goal. Hence, in the context of the example, this interpretation suggests that the number of pages is a facet of the users' primary goals, which they are required to declare earlier than they wish. In this case the relation between the primary and secondary goal, is that the secondary goal is entailed by the primary.

$$AG\ (p \Rightarrow q)$$

p entails q

Initial Conditions Examples of premature commitment describe behaviour starting from some situation initiating a period of interaction. Hence its formal characterisation should make explicit the initial condition for such a period. Formally, there is no simple way to characterise what is perceived as a period of use, but for it being the case that neither primary or secondary goals are met when the period starts. Hence, we propose a relatively weak initial condition: $\neg p \wedge \neg q$.

We combine these elements to obtain formal interpretation of *strong prematurity* and *weak prematurity*. Strong prematurity is distinguished by the primary goal not logically entailing the secondary goal.

Definition The goal q is said to be **strongly premature** to p (written q PREM p), iff:

$\neg p \wedge \neg q \wedge$
$A\ (\neg p)\ U\ [\text{assert}_q] q \wedge$
$AG\ \ (EF\ (p \wedge q) \wedge EF\ (\neg p \wedge q) \wedge EF\ (p \wedge \neg q) \wedge EF\ (\neg p \wedge \neg q))$

The two goals are domain independent, however it is not possible to satisfy p without first asserting q.

Definition The goal q is said to be **weakly premature** to p (written q prem p), iff:

$\neg p \wedge \neg q \wedge$
$A\ (\neg p)\ U\ [\text{assert}_q] q \wedge$
$AG\ p \Rightarrow q$

In general, p entails q within the domain, however it is not possible to satisfy p without first asserting q.

3.1 The Interpretation Applied

In this section we characterise three reported examples of premature commitment.

3.1.1 Programming By Example

Modugno et al. (Modugno et al., 1994) describe a GUI front end to an operating system which provides a 'programming by example' facility — the user demonstrates an operation and the system derives a script for performing the operation. Two examples, of high and low premature commitment are reported with this facility. First, if the user wishes to ensure a derived script is robust, they must engage in an activity of checking its behaviour for all possible classes of data object that it may encounter. Second, the derivation in itself makes assumptions about the generalisable characteristics of a demonstration, and the user does not have to speculate about specific details.

Both examples, depend upon distinguishing an operation which is properly defined to accommodate all contingencies (termed robust), from a derived operation which is adequate for many purposes but not necessarily all. The first is considered prematurely committing since the user has to check details which they may not have envisaged, and the second has low commitment since the user does not have to examine the generalisations made. For both cases we characterise an operation as a set of condition action pairs $(c_1, a_1), ..., (c_n, a_n)$ which identify the function performed. In the case of a derived operation ($drvd$) there will be conditions under which the operation does not function correctly, since the operation is mechanically 'guessed'. In the case of a robust operation ($robust$) which a user may wish to develop, all conditions will be accommodated.

The first case of premature commitment has the primary goal of $robust$ and recognises that some conditions action pairs have to be provided by the user in order to achieve the goal. The condition action pairs asserted are premature in the sense that the conditions will include unforeseen system configurations, hence: (c_i, a_i) prem $robust$. This is weak prematurity since $robust$ will entail the asserted condition action pair (c_i, a_i).

The second case of low premature commitment is a negative example — it is not the case that the user has to assert, say, (c_j, a_j) in order to achieve the goal of having the operation defined. Since the derived operation $drvd$ is the primary goal, its lack of robustness is not a concern. Thus, assuming the derived operation $drvd$ includes (c_j, a_j), then: $\neg(c_i, a_i)$ prem $drvd$.

3.1.2 Visual Programming

In many visual programming environments programs are constructed out of icons representing data and operations and arcs (or wires) linking them. As a result the programmer 'draws' a program and often has to guess as to appropriateness of physical locations for the icons used without a full awareness of their best location when the program is complete. Hence, the user's primary goal may be to declare a data source, without having to commit themselves to a physical location for the data source icon (Green and Petre, 1996)

Assuming that for a required data source, the source can be identified as well as its location, we have: $locationIDed$ prem $dataSourceIDed$. The premature commitment is weak since within the domain of visual programming the identification of the data source cannot be achieved without providing a location.

3.1.3 Prototype Objects

In some event based programming environments, a prototype object sort can only be built from an object instance. Hence, ideally the user has to create an instance object with the characteristics that will suit the prototype. However, the mechanism can prematurely commit the inexperienced programmer to prototype objects with the instance specific characteristics of the object from which it was built (Gilmore, 1997).

A prototype object with generic attributes cannot be created without creating an instance object with specific attributes. Since the prototype object does not necessitate specific attributes, we have:

$$specificAttributes \text{ PREM } prototypeObject$$

4. EFFECTS OF PREMATURE COMMITMENT

Here we examine the interpretations developed and consider how their formal properties inform our understanding of the informal dimensions, and how an analysis of the interpretations can motivate their refinement and their scope of applicability.

4.1 Prematurity under composition

It is valuable to be able to assess the influence of module composition upon premature commitment, since it can help inform system development involving the extension and the combination of sub-systems. As with viscosity, the formal interpretation of premature commitment enables the effect of composition upon the dimension to be easily assessed. We consider combining two alternative interfaces (A and B) which access the same underlying functionality. The combined interface ($A \oplus B$) allows users to freely move between and use A and B independently. The interpretation of premature commitment under this type of composition shows that both types of prematurity can be reduced:

If p prem q for A, **and not** p prem q for B, **then not** p prem q for $A \oplus B$,

Hence, the degree of prematurity for $A \oplus B$ is less than (or equal to) that of A or B.

This concurs with our intuitions, consider a system A involving a case of premature commitment, making another system B equally available to the user has the potential to allow the user to still satisfy their goal while avoiding the prematurity embodied in A. Hence cases of premature commitment can be avoided by the provision of additional tool support. Thus for the visual programming example, a tool offering an alternative view, such as text, would enable a data source to be identified and used (*dataSourceIDed*) without having to commit to its specific visual location (*locationIDed*).

4.2 Relations with Viscosity

4.2.1 Knock-on Viscosity

Knock-on viscosity characterises a change which affects the overall integrity of the object being altered. As a result knock-on viscosity is not so much concerned with resistance to change but with the impact that alterations can have upon a system, or object, as a whole. The notion has been interpreted formally with the concept of 'disruption' which relates two goals and an input, such that: if the input results in the first goal being satisfied, then the second goal is negated.

In principle, formal association between the characterisation of knock-on viscosity and that of premature commitment can be sought. It is possible to employ formal methods to determine in what cases disruption may entail premature commitment and vice-versa. Several potential dependencies between the two have been examined yielding highly specific conditions qualifying the dependency relation. On reflection, these qualifying conditions are sufficiently specific that we conclude there to be minimal inherent dependencies linking the two dimensions.

4.2.2 Repetitive Viscosity

Repetitive viscosity has been characterised by the language of user inputs capable of achieving a specified change, and the subsequent assessment of the complexity of that language. Relating this to premature commitment, it can be shown that instances of prematurity imply an inequality between two comparable languages. This suggests that premature commitment contributes to the viscosity of satisfying the primary goal.

Assuming an instance of premature commitment q prem p, the repetitive viscosity of achieving p from the initial conditions is $(\neg p \wedge \neg q)\mathsf{REP}p$, and the repetitive viscosity of achieving q is $(\neg p \wedge \neg q)\mathsf{REP}q$. The definition of q prem p entails the satisfaction of q prior to p, hence for the above two languages: *there is an input sequence achieving the secondary goal q which is a prefix of an input sequence achieving the primary goal p.* This links the languages, showing that the two are not independent, the complexity of one can influence the other. Taking the minimal language as a measure of repetitive viscosity, the above observation shows that achieving the secondary goal may be less viscous than achieving the primary.

The linkage of the concepts of premature commitment and repetitive viscosity is weakened by the fact that premature commitment is specific to the initial conditions of an interactive use, where as repetitive viscosity is not specific to any temporal context.

The weak dependency between premature commitment and both types of viscosity can be of benefit — it informs us that the dimensions may be addressed independently. Such an observation supports the feasibility of 'design guidelines' which propose that the impact one dimension can be compensated for by another. For example, Gilmore (Gilmore, 1997) proposes that impact of high premature commitment can be combated with low viscosity in order to allow premature decisions to be easily revised.

5. CASE STUDY

Having introduced a formal interpretation for the notion of premature commitment we illustrate its application in more detail by examining an interactive tool. The particular tool to be examined is called "WiZe", it is a WYSIWYG-style editor for writing specifications in the formal language 'Z'. We use an example of WiZe's behaviour to illustrate the manner in which our account of premature commitment relates to properties of the tool which would be informally judged as imposing unwarranted ordering and load upon users.

WiZe has been developed as part of an on going research project which is now nearing completion (Morrey et al., 1996). The tool is used by both staff and students in the preparation of papers and teaching related material.

WiZe is designed to help its users author and prepare system specifications in the Z notation. The Z notation has been developed to enable the specification of systems in terms of discrete mathematics (Spivey, 1988). One distinctive feature of Z is that is provides a structuring mechanism for specifications which enables a collection of related elements, termed schemas, to be introduced and then used in various combinations to define more complex elements and systems.

WiZe provides a basic word processor interface with the addition of menus and dialogues providing access to the mathematical symbols of Z and schema constructs. Schemas are created using a dialogue in which the user identifies the type of the new schema and a new schema name. (Note that for purposes of this examination we only consider labelled schemas within the Z notation.) The new schema is then created without any content and the user is free to enter details when they wish to. WiZe provides a number of schema specific operations, such as schema-cut and schema-copy, and automatically maintains the uniqueness of each schema name.

In order to characterise premature commitment within WiZe, we consider the following possible user goals orientated to schema creation:
- sc = a schema exists with a specific content
- sn = a schema exists with a specific name

Different styles of use of WiZe can be characterised within the context of these goals by considering alternative combinations of them as primary user goals. For example:
- The primary goal of just sc corresponds to use focused upon the expression of specific schema content without consideration for the type of schema required or its name.
- An alternative type of use which maybe viewed as more strategic and promoting the structure and readability of a specification is for the primary goal to be sn. In this case the user is focusing upon naming specification elements, and not detailing their content or formal meaning.
- The final example is where the primary goal is $sc \wedge sn$. Here, both aspects of the specification being prepared are of equal importance. One can think of this case as being close to the use of WiZe purely as a type-setting tool where a previously prepared specification is being transcribed using the tool.

When creating a schema WiZe's dialogue requires the name of the schema before any schema construct appears in the document and before any content can be provided. This behaviour can be characterised as prematurely committing the user to the schema name.

The initial condition is a WiZe document in which a required schema is not given in terms of its content, its type, or its label: $\neg sc \wedge \neg sn$.

Satisfying the goal of having a new schema with the required content is only possible following the dialogue in which the user has to assert the schema name. This behaviour conforms with: $A (\neg sc) \ U \ [\text{assert}_{sn}]sn$.

Finally, WiZe maintains a degree of specification integrity which prevents the author from creating some specifications which are ambiguous in various respects. Within WiZe although a schema can be created without content, a schema without a name cannot be created. Thus we have: $AG \ (sc \Rightarrow sn)$.

Combining these formal properties together yields a weak premature commitment to a schema name: $sn \ \text{prem} \ sc$.

The biases that instances of premature commitment reflect have been described in terms of primary and secondary goals. More generally such biases reflect often implicit assumptions about the way in which a tool is intended to be used, and thus they can be seen as claims about what are users' primary goals. For example, the examination of WiZe suggests premature commitment to sn, however this can be viewed as claim about WiZe users — *Claim: WiZe users primary goal within the context of schema creation is the schema name.*

In fact since users frequently adapt to the nuances of the tools they employ, we can look towards user experiences of WiZe for evidence of adopting sn as a primary goal, in preference to sc. A survey examined this hypothesis, novice and experienced WiZe users were encouraged to reflect on the best ways in which to use the tool by asking them to select instructional statements suitable for new WiZe users. The outcome of the survey showed that more experienced WiZe users favoured instructions which encouraged the choice of schema name prior to its creation. Out of 23 users a total of nine expressed an opinion on the choice of schema name prior to creating a schema. Of the nine, four of the more experienced users, and one inexperienced user, recommended the choice of schema names, and the other four inexperienced users rejected the same advice. In summary:

experience	recommended	no opinion	rejected
≥ 6 hours	4 (17%)	19 (83%)	0 (0%)
< 6 hours	1 (4%)	18 (79%)	4 (17%)

Although this survey did not form part of a planned experiment, the outcome does provide some supportive evidence for sn being adopted as a primary goal. In addition, this suggests that the behaviour classed as premature commitment is relevant in assessing how tools such as WiZe get used.

6.   SUMMARY AND CONCLUSION

This paper contributes to an investigation into the formal characterisation of psychologically motivated measures of notations and tools. This work is novel in adapting a primarily cognitive perspective to a system based framework. Positioning the dimensions within a well defined framework has enabled their precise exposition, this not only enables trade-offs and comparisons between dimensions to be investigated but it also encourages the re-examination, and informal exposition, of the dimensions currently used. In addition we have also addressed a major weakness of cognitive dimensions by employing an interpretative framework relating directly to the characteristics of interactive systems. This not only allows the dimensions to provided with a system-based meaning, but is serves as basis for employing them constructively in development.

In summary, generalising from the formal examination:

• at least two formally distinct classes of premature commitment can be distinguished

• cases of premature commitment can be reduced by the introduction of complementary sub-systems.

• cases of both knock-on viscosity and repetitive viscosity are not strongly related to instances of premature commitment.

There have been a variety of approaches to capturing interface usability issues within formal frameworks. The formal frameworks developed have been motivated by concerns, ranging from cognitive modelling and requirements engineering through to enabling rigorous software development and appropriate software architectures. In many cases these approaches have been driven by a rich set of examples, or scenarios, and have demonstrated a 'craft' approach to modelling which is largely conducted and employed by experts but not widely exploited.

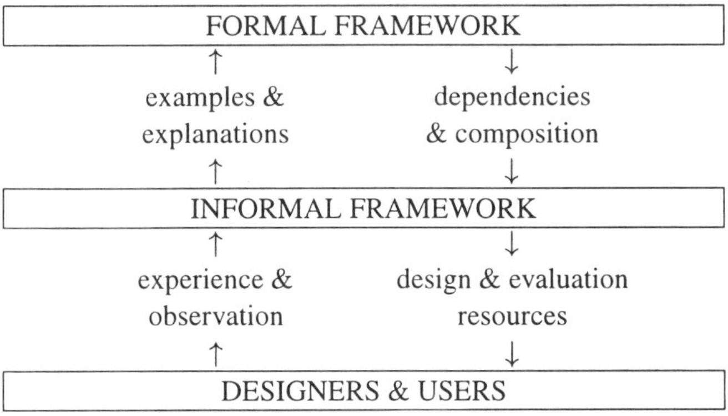

Figure 1: A role for generic formal modelling in HCI

By contrast, the modelling conducted in this paper is orientated towards developing the underlying framework upon which the informal and compelling notion of cognitive dimensions may depend. Hence, the specifics of the formal framework inform and elaborate the foundations for conceptual tools which have been developed for widespread adoption and exploitation (figure 1). This approach places modelling in context where its utility lies in contributing to the understanding, and subsequent effective use of, what would otherwise be informal tools for design and evaluation.

ACKNOWLEDGEMENTS

The author is indebted to staff within the Requirements Engineering interest group at Sheffield Hallam University for comments and reflections upon the WiZe tool. In addition, the author is grateful for the constructive advice provided by anonymous reviewers of an earlier version of this paper.

REFERENCES

Barnard, P. J. and Harrison, M. D. (1992). Towards a framework for modelling human computer interactions. In Gornostaev, J., editor, *Proceedings International Conference on HCI, EWHCI'92*, pages 189–196. Moscow:ICSTI.

Blandford, A. and Green, T. (1997). OSM an ontology-based approach to usability engineering. In *Representations in Interactive Software Development*. Workshop at Queen Mary and Westfield College, Department of Computer Science.

Dearden, A. M. and Harrison, M. D. (1997). Abstract models for hci. *The International Journal of Human-Computer Studies*, (46):151–177.

Dix, A. J. (1991). *Formal Methods for Interactive Systems*. Academic Press.

Duke, D. J., Barnard, P. J., May, J., and Duce, D. A. (1995). Systematic development of the human interface. In *Proceedings of APSEC'95: Second Asia-Pacific Software Engineering Conference*. IEEE Computer Society Press.

Gilmore, D. J. (1997). Cognitive dimensions as a tool for comparative evaluation. Technical report, Psychology Department, University of Nottingham.

Green, T. and Petre, M. (1996). Usability analysis of visual programming environments: a 'cognitive dimensions' framework. *The Journal of Visual Languages and Computing*, 7(2):131–174.

Green, T. R. G. (1989). Cognitive dimensions of notations. In Sutcliffe, A. and Macaulay, editors, *People and Computers V*, pages 443–460. Cambridge University Press.

Harrison, M. D., Blandford, A. E., and Barnard, P. J. (1993). The software engineering of user freedom. Technical Report Amodeus 2 Document, University of York.

Jackson, M. (1997). The meaning of requirements. *Annals of Software Engineering*, 3.

Lavery, D., Cockton, G., and Atkinson, M. (1996). Cognitive dimensions: Usability evaluation materials. Technical report, Deparment of Computing Science, Uiversity of Glasgow.

Markopoulos, P., Rowson, J., and Johnson, P. (1997). Composition and synthesis with a formal interactor model. *Interacting with Computers*, 9(2):197–223.

Modugno, F., Green, T. R. G., and Myers, B. A. (1994). Visual programming in a visual domain: A case study of cognitive dimensions. In Cockton, G., Draper, S. W., and Weir, G. R. S., editors, *People and Computers IX*, pages 91–108.

Morrey, I., Siddiqi, J., Buckberry, G., and Hibberd, R. (1996). A toolset to support the constrcution and animation of formal specifications. *Journal of Systems and Software*.

Nicola, R. D., Fantechi, A., Gnesi, S., and Ristori, G. (1991). An action based framework for verifying logical and behavioural properties of concurrent systems. In *Proceedings of 3rd Workshop on Computer Aided Verification*.

Palanque, P. A. and Bastide, R. (1997). Synergistic modelling of tasks, users, and systems using formal specification techniques. *Interacting with Computers*, 9(2):129–154.

Paterno, F. (1997). Formal reasoning about dialgoue properties with automatic support. *Interacting with Computers*, 9(2):173–196.

Roast, C. R. (1997). Formally comparing and informing design notations. In Thimbleby, H., O'Conaill, B., and Thomas, P., editors, *People and Computers XII*, pages 315–336.

Roast, C. R. (1998). Designing for delay in interactive information retrieval. *Interacting with Computers*, 10:87–104.

Roast, C. R. and Siddiqi, J. I. (1996). Relating knock-on viscosity to software modifiability. *Proceedings of OZCHI 96, Hamilton, New Zealand*, pages 222–227.

Roast, C. R. and Siddiqi, J. I. (1997b). Usability requirements as specification constraints — an example of WYSIWYG. *IEE Proceedings Software Engineering*, 144(2):101–110.

Siddiqi, J. I. and Roast, C. R. (1997). Viscosity as a metaphor for measuring modifiability. *IEE Proceedings — Software Engineering*, 144(4):215–223.

Spivey, J. M. (1988). *The Z Notation: A Reference Manual*. Prentice Hall International.

Yang, S., Burnett, M., DeKoven, E., and Zloof, M. (1995). Representation dfesign benchmarks: a design-time aid for VPL navigable static representations. Technical Report TR 95-60-3, Oregon State University.

Discussion

Gilbert Cockton: What would a developer lose by using UAN rather than modal logic to specify and analyse premature commitment?

Chris Roast: IT is not for developers, it is for theory developers, to improve cognitive dimensions.

Gilbert Cockton: Okay, so what would I lose from using UAN for theory development?

Chris Roast: What you lose and gain depends on the inferential mechanisms that come with UAN and logic.

Gilbert Cockton: UAN has no inferential mechanisms, but I can still spot premature commitment.

Chris Roast: That is okay, but you may not be able to prove it with UAN alone.

Ken Fishkin: What is the difference between formal statements and textual statements

Chris Roast: The property is more precisely represented in the formal statements and the inferences associated with them are more reliable.

Nick Graham: Have you attempted to use model checking techniques to examine the properties expressed by your ACTL specifications?

Chris Roast: Just started using model checking techniques.

Fabio Paterno: To apply model checking techniques you need to provide also some specification of the system that you want to analyse, what notation do you use for this purpose?

Chris Roast: We have started first exercises using Augmented State Machines encoded in Prolog.

John Grundy: I have been using cognitive dimensions in the analysis of high level design tools. In the case of premature commitment I've found that some users see premature commitment within such tools as a 'good' reflection of the methodology the tool supports, where as other users see the premature commitment as restrictive and under-desirable.

Chris Roast: The traditional view of cognitive dimensions is that there is no value judgement with a dimension hence one could not say whether a case of premature commitment is 'good' or 'bad' out of context. In the context you describe one account would be say that the same tool is being used in significantly different ways: one use is for those who prefer the premature behaviour and adherence to a methodology; and, the other use is one which is not so closely allied to a prescribed method of use.

Joelle Coutaz: What about using the length of interaction trajectory to reason about premature commitment?

Chris Roast: I have related only viscosity with respect to interaction trajectory length. Hence trajectory length may give an measure of severity, however in the paper we only look at the concept and not its severity.

Henrik Christensen: How to relate premature commitment with technical description?

Chris Roast: Clearly the technical description looses characteristics of the informal concept. The work has progressed with aim of interpreting cognitive dimensions in terms that are relevant to interface engineers while remaining meaningful for usability engineers. Reflecting this, the interpretations examined so far are not "written in stone" but are best viewed as potentially valuable interpretations of cognitive dimensions, we are keen to entertain other interpretations and their refinement.

Using the B formal approach for incremental specification design of interactive systems

Yamine Aït-Ameur, Patrick Girard & Francis Jambon
LISI / ENSMA, BP 109, Téléport 2, F-86960 Futuroscope cedex, France
Tel.: (+33/0) 5 49 49 80 63, Fax: (+33/0) 5 49 49 80 64
E-mail: {yamine, girard, jambon}@ensma.fr, Web: http://www.lisi.ensma.fr/cao.html

Abstract: This paper introduces a new technique for the verification of interactive systems. It first presents the use of a model oriented formal method for specifying interactive systems, i.e. the B method. Then, it suggests formally based solutions which allow solving difficulties that are inherent to interactive systems specification, like reachability, observability or reliability. Our claim is that this model-oriented technique that uses proof obligations can be used together with model checking techniques, where automatic proofs of properties can be performed.

Keywords: Model oriented notation, B method, specification refinement, interaction properties verification, specification of interactive system.

1.   INTRODUCTION

Formal specification techniques become more and more used in the area of computer science and particularly for the development of secure systems namely "critical systems". These systems require a high level of correctness and consistency, which encourages formal development. Several approaches in formal methods have been proposed in the last decade. They are divided in different categories depending on the kind of semantics they are based on (Brun and Beaudouin-Lafon, 1995, Feather, 1987, Sannella, 1988). Conversely, formal specification of interactive systems can be split into different ways. Historically, the first way concerns the dialogue description (Dix et al., 1993). Related to the natural language decomposition, human-computer interactions have been broken down into three hierarchical levels, the *lexical* level, the *syntactic* level and the *semantic* level. The dialogue description mainly concerns the syntactic level. It involved several formalisms, grammars, state-based diagrams or event models (Green, 1986). More recently, the development of GUI-Builders (Graphical User Interface Builders) has considerably increased the graphical power of user interfaces. GUI-Builders allowed rapid prototyping of interactive systems, and authorised incremental development. Nevertheless, lack of precise specifications is becoming a more and more critical issue.

On the one hand, user-centred design leads to semi-formal but easy to understand notations, such as UAN (Hix and Hartson, 1993) and MAD (Scapin and Pierret-Golbreich, 1990) for interactive design, or GOMS (Card et al., 1983) for evaluation. On the other hand, adaptation of well-defined approaches, combined with interactive models, brings partial but positive results. These are for example the interactors and related approaches (Duke and Harrison, 1993b, Paternó, 1994, Palanque, 1992), using model oriented approaches (Duke and Harrison, 1993a), algebraic notations (Paternó and Faconti, 1992), Petri nets (Palanque, 1992) or Temporal Logic (Brun, 1997, Abowd et al., 1995)

In this paper we deal with model oriented formal methods. State transition networks use finite automata to describe the transition systems, Petri nets and temporal logic gave interesting results from the automatic verification point of view by providing automatic algorithms allowing to check critical properties of interactive systems like liveness, reachability, safety and so on. However, building these transition models incrementally is a heavy task. These approaches are based on the building, by composition, of a whole model (transition system) which represent the system to be described. Then, properties can be checked and the transition system is interpreted to generate a program implementing the behaviour it describes. The difficulty in such techniques is to build the whole (Dix et al., 1993). Other model-oriented approaches have been suggested. They are neither based on transition systems nor they provide an automatic procedure for the verification of the properties of the system. These systems are based on the generation of proof obligations that are checked by the user (with the help of a theorem prover). Among these techniques, VDM is based on preconditions and postconditions (Bjorner, 1987) and on the theory of partial functions, Z is based on set theory (Spivey, 1988), and B is based on the weakest precondition calculus (Abrial, 1996). They allow the description, in high abstraction level language, of the different components of a given system. However, these approaches require an important work to describe the different functions of the system.

Our claim is that neither the first approaches nor the second ones solve the whole problems, but the merging of both techniques seems to be a promising approach. Indeed, the first one allows the control of properties by model checking and neglects the development aspects. In opposite, the second approach allows a complete development of a system and controls all the properties by the verification of all the proof obligations (automatically or by the user). So, several interaction properties can be proved. The more important advantage of this second technique is that it avoids the state explosion problem that becomes crucial when systems grow and it allows the development of the whole system by refinement. As we stated above, our paper deals with the last category of formal methods. We focus on the B method (Abrial, 1996, Lano, 1996). Compared to VDM and Z, it allows the definition of a constructive process to build whole applications, with the respect of all the rules by the use of a semi-automatic tool (Steria méditerranée, 1997). Finally, notice that we did not address the other approaches mainly the ones based on algebraic techniques, rewriting, or concurrent languages.

This paper is organised as follows. In the next section, we briefly present a case study, which stems from the French group on formal specification for highly interactive systems FLASHI (Palanque and Girard, 1996), and we outline the major properties we want to ensure. Section 3 explains the B-method and presents a short overview of proving methods for interactive properties. Section 4 outlines some aspects of the B language over a well-known example, the mouse. Last, section 5 gives examples of B analysis in the context of our example, and details the usage of the B-tool, that allows proving properties.

2. CASE STUDY

Our case study is a co-operative version of a Post-It®[1] Note software. It appears on the screen as a *block* that can be iconified, but cannot be moved. Clickable areas allow direct manipulation of the block, for iconification, and close (quit). It is possible to enter text into the Post-It® Note on the block, which always exists. Last, it is possible to detach the upper Post-It® Note from the block, and then to drag it anyway. Post-It® Notes have a similar behaviour, that differs in four ways: (1) the detach area is restricted to a drag command area, (2) the close area becomes a kill area, (3) a resize area is defined in the lower-right corner, corresponding to a standard resize behaviour, and (4) a send behaviour is defined. This behaviour consists in emitting the Post-It® Note to a receiver that is visualised as a special icon. The interactive trigger is a drop (mouse up event) onto the icon.

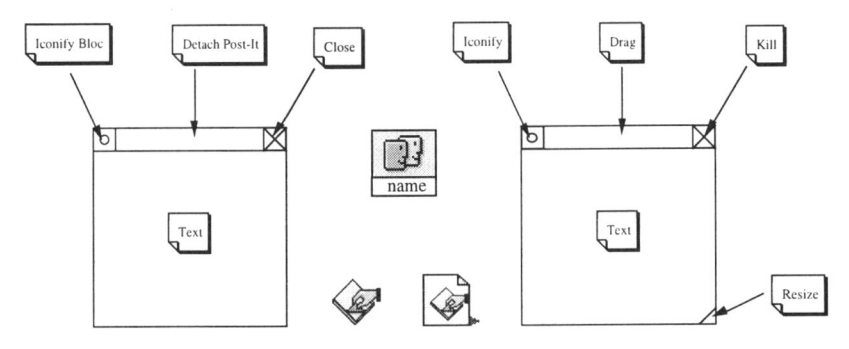

Figure 1. From the left to the right, The Post-It® block, the three icons (Post-It® block, User, and Post-It®), and the Post-It® Note itself, together with his active areas.

Defining good properties of Interactive Systems is an open problem. Several approaches have proposed classifications of properties. For example, (Dix et al.,

[1]   "Post-it" is a registered trademark of 3M

1993) define three main categories of principles to support usability, which are then refined into about fifteen more specific principles. In their article, J. Campos and M. Harrison (Campos and Harrison, 1997) give a good framework for classifying user interface properties, separating them among three classes that address the user (*visibility*), the user interface (*reachability*), and the underlying system (*reliability*):

- **Visibility** relates to feedback and information perception by the user. In our case study, can we ensure that the user can perceive internal state of the system? Does every Post-It® Note move rely to hidden/exposed status of all the perceivable Post-It® Notes?
- **Reachability** deals with what can be done at the user interface and how can it be done. In our application, it concerns for example the way we can move the Post-It® Notes. How can the mouse be taken into account? Is it always possible to move a Post-It® Note? Can it move away from the screen?
- **Reliability** concerns the way the interface works with the underlying system. Does some predicate on the state of the system always hold? Is it possible to ensure that an empty Post-It® Note cannot be sent?

3. THE B METHOD AND INTERACTION PROPERTIES

The B method allows the description of different modules, i.e., abstract machines that are combined by programming in the large operators. This combination allows building complex systems incrementally and correctly when all the proof obligations are proved. Moreover, the interest of this method in our case is the tool it provides.

3.1 The abstract machine notation

The abstract machine notation is the basic mechanism of the B method. J. R. Abrial defined three kinds of machines identified by the keywords MACHINE, REFINEMENT and IMPLEMENTATION. The first one represents the high level of specification. It expresses formal specification in a high abstract level language. The second one defines the different intermediate steps of refinement and finally the third one reaches the implementation level. Note that the development is considered to be correct only when every refinement is proved to be correct with respect to the semantics of the B language. Gluing invariants between the different MACHINES of a development are defined and sets of proof obligations are generated. They are used to prove the development correctness. A theorem prover including set theory, predicate logic and the possibility to define other theories by the user, achieves the proof of these proof obligations. The proving phase is achieved either automatically, by the theorem prover, or by the user with the interactive theorem prover.

3.2 Description of abstract machines

J. R. Abrial has described several important clauses for the definition of abstract machines. Depending on the clauses and on their abstraction level, these clauses can be used at different levels of the program development. In this paper, a subset of these clauses has been used for the design of our specifications. We will only review these clauses. A whole description can be found in the B-Book (Abrial, 1996). The typical B machine starts with the keyword MACHINE and ends with the other keyword END. A set of clauses can be defined in between. In our case, these clauses appear in the following order:

- EXTENDS is a programming in the large clause that allows to import instances of other machines. Every component of the imported machine becomes usable in the current machine. This clause allows modularity capabilities.
- SETS defines the sets that are manipulated by the specification. These sets can be built by extension, comprehension or with any set operator applied to basic sets.
- CONSTANTS defines all the constants that are used in the machine. Notice that the constants described can have any type (naturals, elements of sets, constant functions, and so on).
- PROPERTIES are logical expressions that are satisfied by the constants described in the previous clause.
- VARIABLES is the clause where all the attributes of the described model are represented. In the methodology of B, we find in this clause all the selector functions which allow accessing the different properties represented by the described attributes.
- DEFINITIONS is a set of definitions introduced by the user. They are rewritten everywhere they are used in a machine. It allows simplification of machine notation.
- INVARIANT clause describes the properties of the attributes defined in the clause VARIABLES. The logical expressions described in this clause remain true in the whole machine and they represent assertions that are always valid.
- INITIALISATION clause allows giving initial values to the variables of the corresponding clause. Note that the initial values must satisfy the invariant.
- OPERATIONS clause is the last clause of a machine. It defines all the operations (functions and procedures) that constitute the abstract data type represented by the machine. Depending on the nature of the machine, the OPERATIONS clause authorises particular generalised substitutions to specify each operation. The substitutions used in our specifications and their semantics is described below.

Other syntax possibilities are offered in B, and we do not intend to review them in this paper, in order to keep its length short enough.

3.3 Semantics of generalised substitutions.

The calculus of explicit substitutions is the semantics of the abstract machine notation and is based on the weakest precondition approach of Dijkstra (Dijkstra, 1976). Formally, several substitutions are defined in B. If we consider a substitution S and a predicate P representing a postcondition, then [S]P represents the weakest precondition that establishes P after the execution of S. The substitutions of the abstract machine notation are inductively defined by the following equations. Notice that we restricted ourselves to the substitutions used for our development. The reader can refer to the literature (Abrial, 1996, Lano, 1996) for a more complete description:

```
[SKIP]P                      <==>  P
[S1 || S2]P                  <==>  [S1]P and [S2]P
[PRE  E  THEN  S  END ]P     <==>  E and [S]P
[ANY v WHERE E THEN S END]P  <==>  ∀ v (P =>[S]P)
[x:=E]P                      <==>  P(x/E)
```

The last one represents the predicate P where all the free occurrences of x are replaced by the expression E. Notice that when a given substitution is used, the B checker generates the corresponding proof obligation, i.e., the logical expression on the right hand side of the operator "<==>". This calculus propagates a precondition that must be implied by the precondition set by the user. If not, then the user proves the precondition or modifies it.

3.4 Interaction properties

Proving interaction properties can be achieved by the way of *model checking* or *theorem proving* (Campos and Harrison, 1997). Theorem proving is a deductive approach to the verification of interactive properties. Unless powerful theorem provers are available, proofs must be made "by hand". Consequently, they are hard to find, and their reliability depends on the mathematical skills of the designer. On the opposite, model checking is based on the complete verification of a finite state machine, and may be fully automated. However, one of the main drawbacks of model checking is that the solution may not be computed due to the high number of states (Campos and Harrison, 1997). The last sessions of EHCI'95 and DSV-IS'97 show a wide range of examples of these two methods of verification.

As an example, *model checking* is used by Palanque et al. who model user and system by the way of object-oriented Petri nets –ICO– (Palanque et al., 1995). They argue that automated proofs can be done to ensure that there is no cycle in the task model; a specific task must precede another specific task (enter_pin_code and get_cash in the ATM example); and that the final functional core state is the final user task (get_cash and get_card). These proofs are relatives to reachability. Lauridsen uses the RAISE formalism to show that an interactive application – functional core, dialogue control and logical interaction– can be built using translations from the functional core adapter specification (Lauridsen, 1995). Then, Lauridsen shows that this refinement method can prove interaction properties relatives to predictability, observability, honesty, and substitutivity.

In the meantime, Paternó and Mezzanotte check that unexpected interaction trajectories expressed in a temporal logic –ACTL– cannot be performed by the user. The system –a subset of an air traffic control application– is modelled by interactors specified with LOTOS (Paternó and Mezzanotte, 1995). Brun et al. uses the translation from a semi-formal task-oriented notation –MAD– (Scapin and Pierret-Golbreich, 1990) to a temporal logic –XTL– (Brun, 1997) and prove reachability (Brun and Jambon, 1997).

Our approach –using the B method– deals with the first method, i.e., *theorem proving*. Yet, the method does not suffer from the main drawbacks of theorem proving methods, i.e., proving all the system "by hand". Most of the proofs, regarding *visibility* or *reachability*, which are compulsory in the building process are checked by the B-Tool "Atelier B". Notice that in our case study, about 95% of the proofs obligations are automatically proved. Moreover, since the specification is incrementally built, the proofs are also incrementally built. Indeed, compositionality in B ensures that the proofs of the whole system are built using the ones of the subsystems. This technique considerably simplifies the interaction properties verification. And then, this incremental conception of applications asserts that the proofs needed at the low levels B-machines of the application, i.e. the functional core, are true at the higher levels, i.e. presentation. So, the *reliability* is checked by construction. The following sections give examples of verification of *visibility* and *reachability* properties in our case study using the B technique.

4. FORMALISATION OF THE MOUSE INTERACTION

This section presents a simple example of the use of the B notation for the specification and for the verification of the operations related to the mouse. It is derived from the case study described in the section 3. The complete formalisation of this case study in B can be found in (Aït-Ameur et al., 1998a, Aït-Ameur et al., 1998b). This specification has been designed using reverse engineering techniques starting from an already existing toolkit implementing mouse manipulation. This reverse engineering task to re-design the mouse specification is a crucial phase in our work. It allows using the B language in a uniform manner even for already designed programs. However, this step of development needs to be achieved for other parts of an interactive application (e.g. keyboard). Below, we specify the only operations we are interested in.

4.1 Specification

The machine we define is named POSTIT_MOUSE. It defines two sets: the POST_MOUSE representing all the possible values for a mouse (it behaves as a type) and a finite enumerated set MOUSE_STATE for the states of the mouse.

```
MACHINE POSTIT_MOUSE

SETS
    POST_MOUSE;
    MOUSE_STATE ={up, down, clicked}
```

For convenience, we have considered three states only. Without loss of generality, we have voluntarily omitted the other states because they are not used in our application. Notice that they could have been included.

```
CONSTANTS
    max_post_mouse,
    x_mouse_position_default,
    y_mouse_position_default,
    max_mouse_position_wide,
    max_mouse_position_high
PROPERTIES
    max_post_mouse = card(POST_MOUSE) &
    x_mouse_position_default = 20 &
    y_mouse_position_default = 20 &
    max_mouse_position_wide = 300 &
    max_mouse_position_high = 250
```

The previous part defines a set of constants. The *max_post_mouse* constant is the maximum of mouse positions we can have. The *x_mouse_position_default* and *y_mouse_position_default* are the default coordinates of the mouse. The *max_mouse_position_high* and *max_mouse_position_wide* are the maximum values of the mouse coordinates. They correspond to the dimensions of the screen.

```
VARIABLES
the_post_it_mouse,
x_post_it_mouse_position, y_post_it_mouse_position,
post_it_mouse_state, post_it_mouse_creation
INVARIANT
the_post_it_mouse<:POST_MOUSE &
x_post_it_mouse_position :the_post_it_mouse --> NAT  &
y_post_it_mouse_position :the_post_it_mouse --> NAT &
post_it_mouse_state:the_post_it_mouse --> MOUSE_STATE &
post_it_mouse_creation:the_post_it_mouse --> BOOL &
!xx (xx:the_post_mouse ==>
(x_post_it_mouse_position(xx):
          1..max_mouse_position_wide) &            (1)
(y_post_it_mouse_position(xx):
          1..max_mouse_position_high) )
```

For a given mouse in the set *the_post_it_mouse*, the previous selectors define a set of functions that allow retrieving the coordinates of a mouse, its state and its creation. The last predicate expresses that every mouse position remains in the screen. Several operations on the mouse (creating, moving, clicking...) are defined below. We only give the details for creating and for moving the mouse (! xx stands for $\forall$ xx).

98

```
OPERATIONS
   pp <--create_mouse_position=
         . . .
   Move_mouse_with_drag(pp, aa,bb)=
PRE
   pp : the_post_it_mouse &
   aa : NAT &
   aa : 1..max_mouse_position_wide &
   bb : NAT &
   bb:1..max_mouse_position_high &
   post_it_mouse_state(pp)=down &
   post_it_mouse_creation(pp)=TRUE
THEN
   x_post_it_mouse_position(pp):=aa ||
   y_post_it_mouse_position(pp):=bb
END;
   move_mouse(pp, aa, bb)=
         . . .
   mouse_up(pp)=
         . . .
   mouse_down(pp)=
         . . .
   mouse_clicked (pp)=
         . . .
END
```

The *create_mouse_position* creates a mouse and gives it the status up, and default position as coordinates. The *move_mouse_with_drag* allows the moving of the mouse with its state to down and it moves it to the coordinates (*aa,bb*), where a precondition requires *aa* and *bb* to be in the screen. This precondition is **mandatory** to prove that the mouse never goes out of the screen. In other words this precondition is an example of a *visibility* property.

4.2 Proofs

The previous machine generates a set of 33 proof obligations. All of them were **automatically** proven by the "Atelier B" tool. Among these proof obligations, let us consider the ones of the *move_mouse_with_drag*. There are 6 proof obligations, and among them, the ones that says that the invariant assertion (1) is preserved. There, the precondition:

(aa : 1..max_mouse_position_wide & bb : 1..max_mouse_position_high)

is used to prove the invariant assertion (1) in the clause INVARIANT.

Let us now, try to write the following for the *move_mouse_with_drag* operation. We obtain:

99

```
Move_mouse_with_drag(pp,aa,bb) =
PRE
    pp : the_post_it_mouse &
    aa : NAT &
    bb : NAT &
    post_it_mouse_state(pp)=down &
    post_it_mouse_creation(pp)=TRUE
THEN
    x_post_it_mouse_position(pp):=aa ||
    y_post_it_mouse_position(pp):=bb
END;
```

If we violate the precondition in the *move_mouse_with_drag* operation by omitting that:

(aa : 1..max_mouse_position_wide & bb : 1..max_mouse_position_high)

Then the system is not capable to prove the correctness of the operation. It generates a proof obligation saying that there is a need to prove the invariant assertion (1) of the INVARIANT clause which is violated.

5. INTEGRATION OF THE MOUSE INTERACTION

Linking two abstract machines is possible thanks to programming in the large operators offered by the B method. These operators allowed us to incrementally build complex and sound formal specifications. In this section we present an abstract machine which specifies a simple window manager, and we mainly focus on the moving operation of a window. Then, this abstract machine and the one corresponding to the mouse are used to build another complete and sound abstract machine, which specifies the window manager with an interaction by the mouse. We do not give the complete specification and we focus on the proof aspects. The whole-annotated abstract machine is defined in (Aït-Ameur et al., 1998b).

5.1 The window manager without mouse interaction

The POSTIT_VISU_WITHOUT_INT is the abstract machine that defines a simple window manager related to our case study.

5.1.1 Specification

The following abstract machine defines a set of windows (to support a post it). It represents the module of all the allowed window manipulations.

```
MACHINE POSTIT_VISU_WITHOUT_INT
EXTENDS POSTIT_VISUALIZATION

CONSTANTS
   . . .
PROPERTIES
   max_post_visu=card(POST_VISU)                &
   max_post_it_wide=300                         &
   max_post_it_high=250                         &
VARIABLES
. . .
```

The previous properties define the values of the dimensions of the screen. The variables of the INVARIANT describe the accessors to the different components of a window. *the_post_it_visu* is the set of all the windows effectively created, and *get_new_post*, *block_state* and *post_it_window_status* are the functions which respectively imports a window from the POSTIT_VISUALIZATION machine, gives the state of the block and computes the status of the window from the one on the imported window.

```
INVARIANT
   the_post_it_visu <:POST_VISU &
   get_new_post :the_post_it_visu --> post_new &
   block_state :block_VISU &
   post_it_window_status:the_post_it_visu-->SCREEN_STATE &
   (!xx. (xx : the_post_it_visu =>
      (x_post_it_position(xx) : 1..max_post_it_wide &      (2)
       y_post_it_position(xx) : 1..max_post_it_high ) ) )
```

The previous logical expression (2) is an important invariant. It states that all (!) the windows of the set *the_post_it_visu* have their upper-left corner in the screen. This invariant is conserved and proved for all the operations. We will now describe the *move_window_position* action, and every element it uses. In this machine, *move_window_position* is not strictly constrained. For example, it is possible to partially quit the visualisation window while moving a Post-It® Note. This constraint will be put later on. We only take into account the constants, variables and invariants that are needed by *move_window_position*.

```
OPERATIONS
move_window_position(pp, aa, bb)=
   PRE
      aa : 1..max_post_it_wide &
      bb : 1..max_post_it_high &
      pp : the_post_it_visu   &
      block_state = block_open   &
      (  post_it_window_status(pp)= displayed   or
         post_it_window_status(pp)= hidden )
```

The previous preconditions say that the new coordinates of the upper-left corner of a window (aa,bb) must belong to the screen, that the window *pp* is effectively created (belongs to the_post_it_visu set), that the block of Post-It® Notes is effectively open and that the window can be displayed or hidden.

```
THEN
      x_post_it_position(pp):= aa
      y_post_it_position(pp):= bb                    ||
      update_hidden(get_new_post(pp))
END
```

Here, a parallel substitution is used. It says that after executing this operation the new coordinates of the upper-left corner become (*aa,bb*) and that the operation *update_hidden* (of another non described machine) is called. This last operation is called in order to update the status of the windows that become hidden or displayed after the current window has been moved. We take into account here a visibility property we have expressed in section 2.

5.1.2 Proofs

From these previous preconditions, we can infer the following properties:
- Windows never can be moved when they are iconified,
- Windows never can be moved when the block is not opened,
- Windows never have their upper-left corner outside of the screen. This is very important for windows manipulation. It is directly derived from the invariant assertion (2).

All these proofs show that *reachability* properties can be checked in the top-level B-machine.

5.2 Specification of the window manager with mouse interaction

Now, we get two abstract machines: one for the mouse and another for the window managing. The goal of the third abstract machine is to merge these two abstract machines in order to build a new one that integrates the manipulation of the windows using a mouse.

5.2.1 Specification

The following abstract machine, named POSTIT_VISU_WITH_INT_MOUSE extends (by a programming in the large operator) the abstract machines for mouse and for windows.

```
MACHINE POSTIT_VISU_WITH_INT_MOUSE

EXTENDS
   POSTIT_MOUSE , POSTIT_VISU_WITHOUT_INT
PROPERTIES
   . . .
   screen_wide = max_mouse_position_wide            &
   screen_high = max_mouse_position_high            &
   max_post_it_wide=max_mouse_position_wide         &
   max_post_it_high=max_mouse_position_high
```

102

The previous properties are named gluing properties. They make connections between the constants of all the imported machines. Indeed, it specifies that the dimensions of a screen for a window are the same as the ones for a mouse.

```
INVARIANT
    the_post_it_visu_with_mouse <:
        POSTIT_VISU_WITH_MOUSE &
    post_it_visu_with_mouse_creation :
        the_post_it_visu_with_mouse --> BOOL &
    get_the_mouse :
        the_post_it_visu_with_mouse --> the_post_it_mouse &
    get_the_post_it_visu :
        the_post_it_visu_with_mouse --> the_post_it_visu
```

The set *the_post_it_visu_with_mouse* records all the windows manipulated by a mouse. The selectors define a set of functions that allow extracting a window by *get_the_post_it_visu* and the mouse by *get_the_mouse*. Let us give the details of the action *move_window_with_mouse* that allows moving a window combining the interaction of the mouse. This action has a set of preconditions, which needs to be valid before the action is performed. They are commented below.

```
OPERATIONS
move_window_with_mouse(pp, aa, bb) =
PRE
    aa : NAT &
    bb : NAT &
    aa : 1..max_post_it_wide &
    bb : 1..max_post_it_high &
    pp : the_post_it_visu_with_mouse &
```

The new coordinates of the upper-left corner of the window must define a point in the limits of the screen. Notice that these preconditions imply:

- The ones of the *move_window* without the use of the mouse. It remains to assert that the window is displayed,
- and the ones of *move_mouse*. It remains to assert that the mouse is down to ensure that the drag is possible.

```
    post_it_window_status(get_the_post_it_visu(pp))
        = displayed &
    post_it_mouse_state(get_the_mouse(pp)) = down &
    block_state = block_open &
```

The block of Post-It® must be open, otherwise the window of a Post-It® Note cannot be moved.

```
    post_it_visu_with_mouse_creation(pp) = TRUE &
    post_it_visu_creation(get_the_post_it_visu(pp)) = TRUE &
    post_it_mouse_creation(get_the_mouse(pp)) = TRUE &
```

The different elements manipulated by the operation (mouse, a window, a window with mouse interaction) must be already created.

```
x_post_it_position(get_the_post_it_visu(pp))+5 :
       1..max_mouse_position_wide &
y_post_it_position(get_the_post_it_visu(pp))+5 :
       1..max_mouse_position_high &
x_post_it_window(get_the_post_it_visu(pp))-5 :
       1..max_mouse_position_wide &
```

The coordinates delimiting the moving zone of the window must belong to the screen, i.e., must appear in the screen.

```
x_post_it_mouse_position(get_the_mouse(pp)):
     x_post_it_position(get_the_post_it_visu(pp))+5..
     x_post_it_window(get_the_post_it_visu(pp))-5  &
y_post_it_mouse_position(get_the_mouse(pp)):
     y_post_it_position(get_the_post_it_visu(pp))..
     y_post_it_position(get_the_post_it_visu(pp))+5
```

The mouse position must be in the moving zone delimited previously. This is an additional precondition which is strictly related to the fact that there is a mouse interaction and that the mouse must be in the moving zone. This precondition could not be expressed in one of the imported machines.

```
THEN
   move_window_position(get_the_post_it_visu(pp),aa,bb) ||
   Move_mouse_with_drag(get_the_mouse(pp),aa,bb)
END
```

Calling the *move_window_position* action of the POSTIT_VISU_WITHOUT_INT moves the window and the mouse is also moved by the action *move_mouse_with_drag* of the machine POSTIT_MOUSE. Notice that this action is one of the actions that combine the mouse toolkit and the window manager toolkit.

5.2.2 Proofs

From the PROPERTIES assertions, we derive that the coordinates of the upper-left corner of a window and the ones of the mouse take their values in the same domain. Therefore, we can prove that a mouse can manipulate every window. This is an important *reachability* property. The previous abstract machine gives supplementary preconditions on the objects. These preconditions imply the ones of the corresponding operations in the machines imported by extension. Therefore, the prover is capable to complete the proof of correctness. This is an important issue of the B method that shows that B is not only capable to structure the development of specifications, but it allows the structuration and the modularization of the proofs. Moreover, this approach shows that it is possible to structure the specifications hierarchically with respect to the implication of the preconditions. Here, the implication plays the role of an ordering relation from weak to strong. Indeed, the preconditions of the last machine are stronger than the ones of the imported machines. Finally, this mechanism of weakest precondition conserves the coherence of the whole specification. This previous machine has shown that it is not possible to:

- move a window with a mouse whose position is not in the moving zone,
- move a window if there is no mouse,
- move a window if it is eliminated: this property is inherited form the imported machine.

We can prove the previous properties by removing the corresponding assertions from the preconditions and then the prover will complain because we are not capable to prove some proof obligations.

6. CONCLUSION AND FUTURE WORK

This paper has shown the use of the B method on a non-trivial case study. It has illustrated the capability of B to handle different aspects of the software life cycle in the area of interactive systems. The described approach showed that:
- The approach is completely formalised and most of the proof obligations are proved automatically. The other ones needed only few steps of proof. They allow controlling the development of the whole program.
- It is possible to check properties of the specifications, thanks to the weakening of the preconditions (Aït-Ameur et al., 1998a).
- Reverse engineering aspects can be handled with this approach and the specifications of already existing programs can be used to develop new ones. Therefore, reusability issues appear.
- The specifications are incrementally built, in contrast with state based approaches. Indeed, programming in the large operator allows to compose abstract machines and therefore to build more complex specifications. Yet, this process needs to follow a given methodology issued from the area of interactive system design.

However, several open issues raised from this work:
- There is a need to merge both state models and B models in heterogeneous approach. We will get the benefits of both the developments aspects and the model checking ones.
- The validation aspects need to be tackled in the context of B. There seems to be a possibility to generate tests from such B specifications.
- The B specifications must be developed, in an ascending manner for linking the task analysis to the derivation of specifications and in a descending manner to show the refinement the specifications to implementation.

Finally, we plan to adapt the B approach to the different architectures proposed in the area of interactive systems for handling the formal specification design process. We suggest to define generic abstract machines that implement a given architecture model in order to avoid the user to be a B-expert.

7. REFERENCES

Abowd, G. D., Wang, H.-M. and Monk, A. F. (1995) A Formal Technique for Automated Dialogue Development, in DIS'95 (Eds, Olson, G. M. and Schuon, S.) ACM, Ann Arbor, Michigan, pp. 219-226.

Abrial, J.-R. (1996) The B Book: Assigning Programs to Meanings. Cambridge University Press.

Aït-Ameur, Y., Girard, P. and Jambon, F. (1998a) A Uniform approach for the Specification and Design of Interactive Systems: the B method, in 5th International Eurographics Workshop on Design, Specification, and Verification of Interactive Systems (DSV-IS'98) (Eds, Johnson, P. and Markopoulos, P.) , Cosener's House, Abingdon, UK, pp. 333-352.

Aït-Ameur, Y., Girard, P. and Jambon, F. (1998b) Using the B formal approach for incremental specification design of interactive systems. Laboratoire d'Informatique Scientifique et Industrielle (LISI/ENSMA). Research report. 98-001.

Bjorner, D. (1987) VDM a Formal Method at Work, in VDM Europe Symposium'87 Springer-Verlag. LNCS.

Brun, P. (1997) XTL: a temporal logic for the formal development of interactive systems, in Formal Methods for Human-Computer Interaction (Eds, Paterno, F. and Palanque, P.) Springer-Verlag, pp. 121-139.

Brun, P. and Beaudouin-Lafon, M. (1995) A taxonomy and evaluation of formalisms for the specification of interactive systems, in 10th annual conference of the British Human-Computer Interaction Group (HCI'95) , University of Huddersfeild, UK.

Brun, P. and Jambon, F. (1997) Utilisation des spécifications formelles dans le processus de conception des Interfaces Homme-Machine, in Neuvièmes journées francophones sur l'Interaction Homme-Machine (IHM'97) Cépaduès-Éditions, Poitiers-Futuroscope, France, pp. 23-24-27-25-26-28-29.

Campos, J. C. and Harrison, M. D. (1997) Formally Verifying Interactive Systems: A Review, in Eurographics Workshop on Design, Specification, Verification of Interactive Systems (Eds, Harrison, M. D. and Torres, J. C.) Eurographics, Springer-Verlag, Granada, Spain, pp. 109-124.

Card, S., Moran, T. and Newell, A. (1983) The psychology of Human-Computer Interaction. Lawrence Erlbaum Associates.

Dijkstra, E. (1976) A Discipline of Programming. Prentice Hall, Englewood Cliff (NJ), USA.

Dix, A. J., Finlay, J., Abowd, G. and Beale, R. (1993) Human-Computer Interaction. Prentice Hall.

Duke, D. J. and Harrison, M. D. (1993a) Abstract Interaction Objects. Computer Graphics Forum, 12, 25-36.

Duke, D. J. and Harrison, M. D. (1993b) Towards a Theory of Interactors. Amodeus Esprit Basic Research Project 7040. System Modelling/WP6.

Feather, M. S. (1987) A Survey and Classification of some program Transformation Approaches and Techniques, in IFIP world congress (Ed, Meertens, L. G. L. T.) Elsevier Science Publishers B.V. (North-Holland), pp. 165-195.

Green, M. W. (1986) A Survey of three Dialogue Models. ACM Transactions on Graphics, 5, 244-275.

Hix, D. and Hartson, H. R. (1993) Developping user interfaces: Ensuring usability through product & process. John Wiley & Sons, inc., Newyork, USA.

Lano, K. (1996) The B Language Method: A guide to practical Formal Development. Springer.

Lauridsen, O. (1995) Systematic methods for user interface design, in IFIP TC2/WG2.7 working conference on engineering for human-computer interaction (EHCI'95) (Eds, Bass, L. J. and Unger, C.) Chapman & Hall, Grand Targhee Resort (Yellowstone Park), USA, pp. 169-188.

Palanque, P. (1992) Modélisation par Objets Coopératifs Interactifs d'interfaces homme-machine dirigées par l'utilisateur. PhD of Univ. Toulouse I, Toulouse.

Palanque, P., Bastide, R. and Sengès, V. (1995) Validating interactive system design through the verification of formal task and system models, in IFIP TC2/WG2.7 working conference on engineering for human-computer interaction (EHCI'95) (Eds, Bass, L. J. and Unger, C.) Chapman & Hall, Grand Targhee Resort (Yellowstone Park), USA, pp. 189-212.

Palanque, P. and Girard, P. (1996) Groupe de travail GP3-FLASHI (Formalismes et Langages Appliqués aux Systèmes Hautement Interactifs). GDR-PRC Communication Homme-Machine. Rapport d'activité.

Paternó, F. (1994) A Theory of User-Interaction Objects. Journal of Visual Languages and Computing, 5, 227-249.

Paternó, F. and Faconti, G. P. (1992) On the LOTOS use to describe graphical interaction, Cambridge University Press, pp. 155-173.

Paternó, F. and Mezzanotte, M. (1995) Formal verification of undesired behaviours in the CERD case study, in IFIP TC2/WG2.7 working conference on engineering for human-computer interaction (EHCI'95) (Eds, Bass, L. J. and Unger, C.) Chapman & Hall, Grand Targhee Resort (Yellowstone Park), USA, pp. 213-226.

Sannella, D. (1988) A Survey of Formal Software Developement Methods. Laboratory of Fundamental Computer Science. LFCS Report series. ECS-LFCS-88-56.

Scapin, D. L. and Pierret-Golbreich, C. (1990) Towards a method for task description : MAD, in Work with display units 89 (Eds, Berliguet, L. and Berthelette, D.) Elsevier Science Publishers, North-Holland.

Spivey, J. M. (1988) The Z notation: A Reference Manual. Prentice Hall Int.

Steria méditerranée (1997) Atelier B version 3.0.

8.   BIOGRAPHY

Yamine AIT-AMEUR, obtained his Ph.D in 1992 and is currently senior lecturer at École Nationale Supérieure de Mécanique et d'Aérotechnique (ENSMA) at Futuroscope, France. He performs his research at the Laboratory of Industrial and Scientific Computer Science at ENSMA. His main interests are formal verification of programs and of data models. He is leading the research group on formal verification.

Patrick GIRARD is senior lecturer at the University of Poitiers, and belongs to the Laboratory of Industrial and Scientific Computer Science at ENSMA. He received his Ph.D in 1992. His main research interest concerns Programming by Demonstration and Formal approaches in HCI.

Francis JAMBON is assistant professor at the University of Poitiers. He received is Ph.D from the University Joseph Fourier (Grenoble, France) in 1996. Currently working in the LISI/ENSMA laboratory, his research interest covers human error handling and formal modeling of HCI.

Discussion

Gilbert Cockton: You said that 95% of the proofs were automatically generated. Was it that 95% of the proof obligations were completely proved automatically, or 95% of each proof was typically automatic?

Patrick Girard: The former - only 5% of the proof obligations required manual intervention with machine assistance.

John Grundy: What do we gain with B rather than a constraint language?

Patrick Girard: B can solve many other problems and provides a uniform approach. More, instead of being a constraint language with eventually a constraint solver, B is a constructive approach allowing building a program satisfying some specification.

Fabio Paterno: Even in the formal area many notations have been applied in the HCI field. What aspect can be better expressed in B or in which phase can it provide more support?

Patrick Girard: It can give good support to refine code. Moreover, it allows us to modularize developments, prove the refinements and to reuse several existing specifications.

Fabio Paterno: You have not spoken about code refinement.

Patrick Girard: It will be described in a next work.

Chris Roast: What is you opinion about how to relate B with other notations?

Patrick Girard: B could be integrated with dialogue specifications done by Petri Nets.

Shijian Lu: How can B help with incremental specification?

Patrick Girard: You can first develop a specification with mouse interaction and then add to it.

John Grundy: Can B be used to specify collaborative applications?

Patrick Girard: I have not done it but I think it could be possible as it has been used for real-time applications.

Engineering Component-based, User-configurable Collaborative Editing Systems

John Grundy

Department of Computer Science, University of Waikato, Private Bag, Hamilton, New Zealand
jgrundy@cs.waikato.ac.nz

Abstract: The ability to collaboratively edit work artefacts is important in many kinds of editing tools, including Computer-Aided Design (CAD) tools, Computer-Aided Software Engineering (CASE) tools, drawing packages, and document editors. However, most existing such tools either do not support collaborative editing or provide limited collaborative editing facilities. We describe our recent work in adding collaborative editing support onto a previously single-user CASE tool, using a component-based approach. Our collaborative editing components allow users to move from asynchronous to synchronous editing as desired, and even allow a user to support different levels of collaborative editing with different other users simultaneously. Major advantages of our approach include no changes to the implementation of the component-based CASE tool, nor the collaboration-supporting components, were necessary. Additionally, our components that facilitate collaborative editing are readily reusable in other tools adopting a similar component-based software architecture.

Keywords: groupware, component-based software, CASE tools, reusability, CSCW

1. INTRODUCTION

As cooperating workers have become increasingly distributed in geography and time, support for collaborative editing has become increasingly important in many editing tools. For example, users of software development tools generally require facilities to support asynchronous work, e.g. version and configuration management tools and merging capabilities. They also often desire synchronous editing capabilities, which allow for example designers to closely collaborate on evolving systems, debugging to be done co-operatively, or documentation and reverse-engineered designs to be discussed. Users may also want editing capabilities in between these extremes. For example, being kept aware when other users modify a shared design but not having their own design modified.

Unfortunately most existing editing tools do not support this range of collaborative editing facilities for the same kind of work artefact, or only support one particular approach for different kinds of artefacts. It is also often difficult to seamlessly move between different "levels" of collaborative editing as desired. An additional problem from a tool engineering perspective is that almost all editing tools have to be specifically engineered to support even one type of collaborative editing. It is usually a large effort to retrofit such capabilities onto existing tools, and such modifications are often infeasible from an organisational or engineering perspective.

We describe our recent work in adding user-configurable collaborative editing facilities onto an object-oriented CASE tool. We have done this using a software component-based approach i.e. we have developed software components which support collaborative editing facilities and "plugged" these components into our CASE tool without modifying the CASE tool implementation or architecture in any way. These collaborative editing components can also be plugged into other editing tools using a component-based software architecture, without necessitating any change to the components nor the tool.

2.   COLLABORATIVE EDITING REQUIREMENTS

The screen dump in Figure 1 is from the JComposer object-oriented CASE and meta-CASE tool (Grundy et al., 1997; Grundy et al., 1998). JComposer provides editable graphical and textual views of object-oriented and component-based software systems, supporting their specification, design, implementation, documentation and reverse-engineering. It also supports generation of CASE tools based on a component-based software architecture and framework. The diagram ("view") in Figure 1 shows a process support tool repository being specified. JComposer will subsequently generate a component-based implementation of this graphical specification. Other views can be developed which specify e.g. multiple views of a process model as graphical and/or textual editors (Grundy et al., 1997).

Users of JComposer often wish to collaborate to develop specifications and designs, as well as to implement, debug and reverse-engineer systems. For example, collaborating developers may want to synchronously edit a view to closely collaborate in building a specification or design. When one user makes changes to the view at this close "level" of collaboration, the exact same change is made to the other user's view. Sometimes users will want to have a description of changes made shown to collaborators, rather than automatically actioned. They can then decide whether to have the change made immediately to their version of the view, whether to discuss the change further, or whether to reject it. At other times developers will work asynchronously, not having changes broadcast to others' working on different versions of the same view. Subsequently developers will exchange modifications and merge some or all of them with their own changes to a view. Users may simply request they be informed when some change or sequence of changes are made to a view they are interested in, with some automatic processing to take place (e.g. to record the change(s), to inform them of the change(s), etc.).

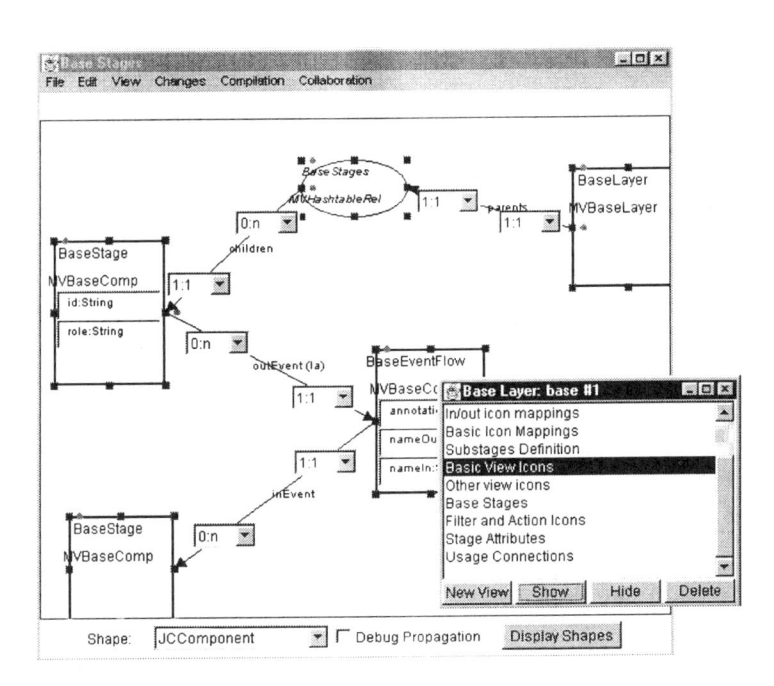

Figure 1. Example of an editable view from the JComposer environment

It has been our experience with developing tools such as JComposer that all of these levels of collaborative editing are required for all kinds of views of software development, at one time or other during the software development lifecycle. Thus tools like JComposer should allow any view to be edited in any of the above levels of collaborative editing, but moreover users should be able to easily move between any of these levels as desired.

JComposer was originally developed with no specific multi-user editing capabilities, but does use a component-based software architecture, allowing new software components to be "plugged into" the environment without modifying existing components. We could have substantially modified the tool to support the kinds of collaborative editing facilities outlined above, but instead chose to take a longer-term view, as we wanted to be able to leverage these kinds of facilities in other editing tools. Thus we required an engineering approach which would, ideally, involve no modifications to JComposer or its software architecture, but instead utilise a component-based approach with reusable collaborative editing components plugged into a tool if required. Advantages of this approach include: ability to reuse collaborative editing components without modification; ability to add collaborative editing to tools without modification; and upgradeable components, i.e. unplugging components to add improved ones.

113

3.   A COMPONENT-BASED SOFTWARE ARCHITECTURE

3.1   3.1. JViews Software Architecture

JComposer is built using a component-based software architecture called JViews (Grundy et al., 1997). Component-based systems are comprised of units of data and functionality, which are composed to build a complete software product. The difference between component-based systems and more conventional software systems (e.g. using function libraries and class frameworks) is that component-based systems allow components to be "plugged" in at run-time, or unplugged and interchanged with other components with comparable interfaces and functionality. This supports user-configuration of systems, reusbility of components, and a more versatile and potentially robust "building block" approach to system architectures.

JViews is built on top of the Java Beans componentware API of Java 1.1 (Javasoft, 1997). The basic structure of a JViews component-based system is illustrated in Figure 2. Components (rectangles) are linked by relationship components (ovals) or simple reference links (solid lines). When a component undergoes a state change, it sends a "change description" object describing this change to "interested" linked components and relationship components. Interested components choose to listen before and/or after the state change occurs, or can even listen when other components receive change description objects. Change descriptions can be stored and used to implement a wide range of system functionality, including undo/redo for diagrams, attribute recalculation and constraint enforcement, versioning and collaborative editing (Grundy et al., 1996).

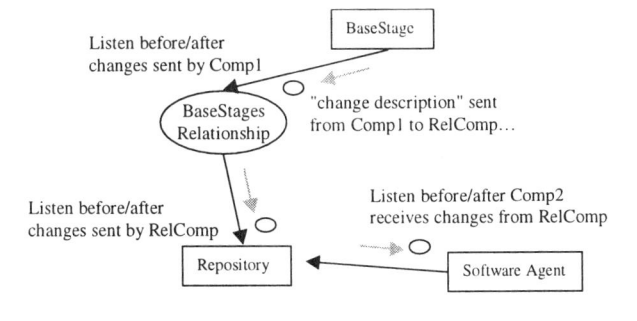

Figure 2. The JViews component-based software architecture

JViews-based environments support multiple views of work artefacts via "view relationships" between repository components and view components. View components are rendered in graphical or textual forms, and provide appropriate editing functionality. Ideally all JViews-based environments should provide the collaborative editing capabilities described in the previous section. However, we did not build such capabilities directly into JViews. In order to support such capabilities, each view in a JViews-based system, such as JComposer, needs additional components "plugged" into the view i.e. components supporting distributed, multi-user editing are connected to JComposer view components. These collaborative

114

editing components "listen" to change descriptions (i.e. editing events) generated by components in the view, and these changes propagated to collaborating user's environments. When an environment receives such changes, the changes must be forwarded to the appropriate view and actioned as appropriate to support the level of collaborative editing required.

3.2   Collaborative Editing Components

Figure 3 shows some existing JComposer view and repository components and links, for the process model repository in Figure 1, coloured grey. The JViews-based collaborative editing components we have developed are shown in black. The main collaborative editing component is the "collaboration menu", which provides the user interface to configuring the level of collaborative editing on a view, and handles change propagation to/from other users' environments. Each JComposer view has an instance of this component connected to it, and this collaboration menu component "listens" before and after any changes are made to the view. Listening for all view component changes both before and after they are made allows the collaboration menu component to implement locking protocols for synchronous editing, and to lock out changes produced by other users when at a synchronous level of collaborative editing on this or other views. This is necessary as our Java implementation of these collaborative editing components uses multithreading, with separate execution threads handling receiving and actioning of other users' edits.

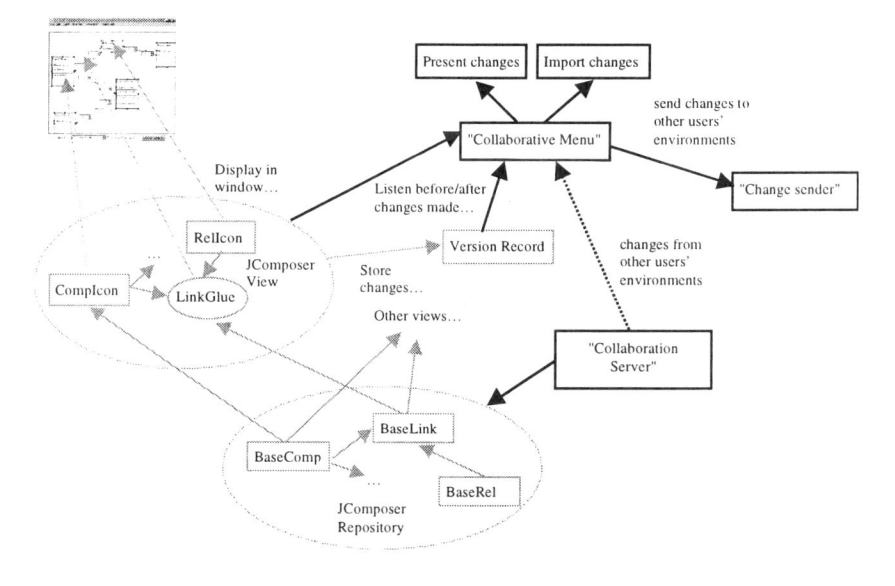

Figure 3. Example of adding groupware components to JComposer

Each JViews view component has a "version record", storing changes made to the view to provide a modification history and to support undo/redo of all view changes. The collaboration menu component listens to this version record, and

115

before a change description is stored in the version record, the collaboration menu annotates it with the name of the user from whom the change originated. After the change has been stored in the view's version record, it is propagated to other collaborating users who are collaboratively editing the view. We propagate the changes stored by the view in its version record, not all change descriptions generated by the view's components. This is because some view component state changes are caused by the actioning user editing, which we want to propagate and record, but others are caused by these edits (e.g. resizing a line if one of its connected icons is moved). Thus only the *initiating* changes need be stored and propagated, as these "follow-on" changes will be made by the other user environments' editor semantics.

3.3   Change Sending

Changes are sent to collaborating users' environments via a "change sender" component, which runs in a separate execution thread to the collaboration menu and JViews view components. This multi-threading ensures that no editing performance loss occurs for the user of the environment while changes are propagated to collaborators i.e. no blocking of user I/O occurs. The change sender queues change descriptions to be broadcast to other users' environments, and uses point-to-point communication with the other user environment's "collaboration server" components to send the change descriptions. We used the JViews change description serialisation mechanism to serialise change description objects into byte streams and to send them via socket connections to other users.

A "collaboration server" component is attached to each JViews environment's repository component, and allows multiple client socket connections from other collaborators' "change senders". The collaboration server, on receiving change descriptions, forwards them to the appropriate view's collaboration menu component, which deserialises the broadcast change description and actions it appropriately. The collaboration menu has a version record to present changes in (if at "presentation" level), and a version record to import changes into (when at an asynchronous editing level). Figure 4 illustrates the propagation of change descriptions between users' environments. We used this multi-point broadcasting model, rather than relying on a single-server model to provide efficient, robust collaborative editing capabilities. However, a major advantage of our component-based approach is that we could replace the change sender and collaboration server components with ones that implement e.g. an Remote Method Invocation (RMI)-based approach to propagating changes, rather than use sockets, or use a shared single-server architecture.

An additional lightweight "registration" server is provided for registering user names and the user's host and port numbers (to establish socket connections between change senders and collaboration servers). This also allocates unique component ID numbers for each user as they are required. The collaboration menu uses sets of unique ID numbers generated by this server to uniquely tag every JViews view component with an ID number. Each user then has a their own version of view data, with copied view components uniquely numbered, rather than have users distributively share the same component data. This replicated data approach once again provides a very robust implementation, but more importantly allows us to seamlessly move between asynchronous editing approaches (which require copied view versions) and synchronous editing, which assumes the "same" data is being edited. In our approach, users who are synchronously editing a view actually still have their own version of the view data, but these replicated versions are kept synchronised by automatically applying all changes made by other users to them.

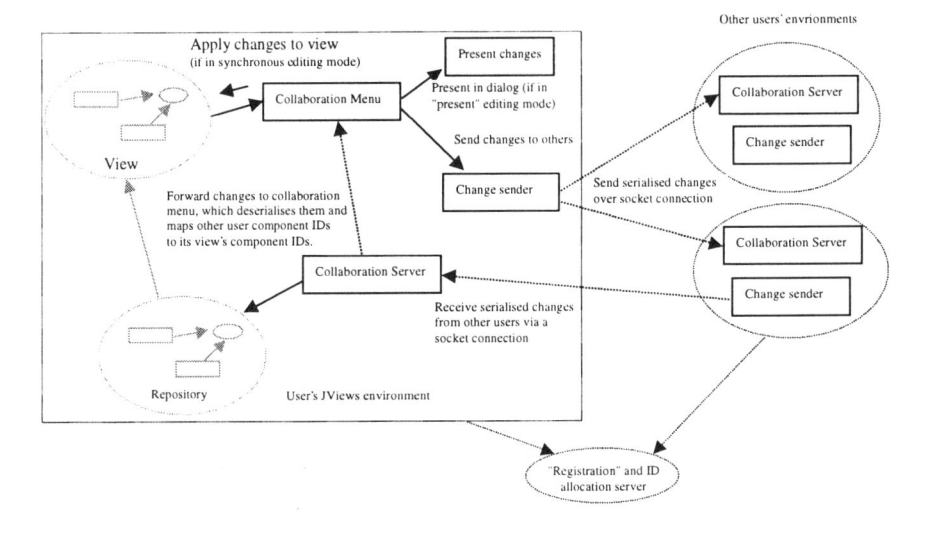

Figure 4. Communication of events between user environments

4. USER INTERFACE COMPONENTS FOR COLLABORATION

This section illustrates the human-interface aspects of our collaborative editing components, using JComposer as an example environment. We also relate the user interface characteristics to the various collaboration components described in the previous section.

4.1 Configuring Collaboration

When a JViews-based environment is first started, a saved JViews component must be opened by the user. When opened this automatically instructs the environment to add a collaboration menu to every new view, and initialises a single collaboration server for the environment. It also registers the user's name and host/port with the collaboration registrar server.

Whenever a JComposer view is created, a collaboration menu component is created and attached to this view. This component adds a "Collaboration" menu item to the view's pull-down menu bar, as illustrated in Figure 5. This menu allows the user of the JComposer environment to add collaborators, change the level of collaboration with specific collaborators, and to exchange the view components or

117

change descriptions with other users (for asynchronous work). We chose this simple, menu-based interface for simplicity and to allow users to configure collaborative editing from one place.

When the user selects the "Add Collaborator" item, the collaboration menu component queries the collaboration registrar server for all other users names and host/port numbers. A selected collaborator is added and the collaborative editing mode with this collaborator set to "asynchronous" (level 1). Multiple collaborating users can be specified in this manner for the same view, and collaborative editing can be undertaken at different levels for each collaborator. The user changes the collaboration level using the Current Collaborators item and the collaborator's name subitems, as shown in Figure 5. We have found this approach allows for quick, seamless transition between levels of collaboration.

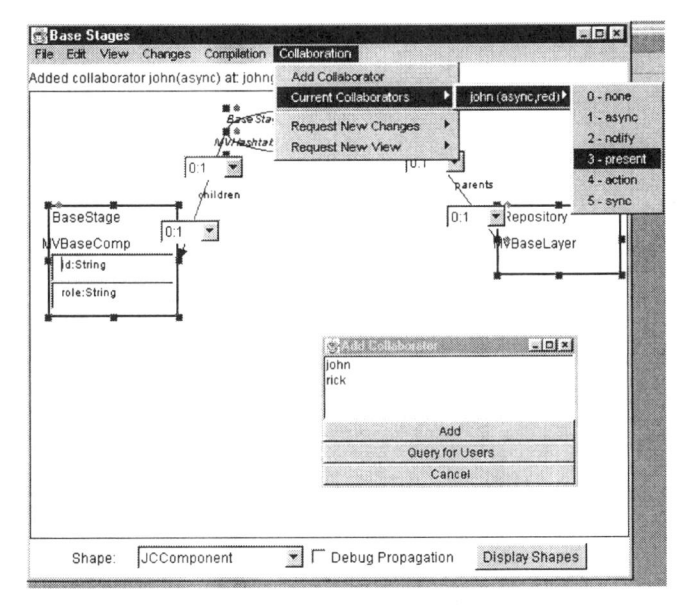

Figure 5. Specifying the collaboration "level" with other users for a view

When the collaboration level with another user is changed, a message is sent to the other user's collaboration server which changes their collaboration level with this user to match the one specified. We inform the user with whom the collaboration level has changed of the new level with a short text message displayed below the pull-down menus.

When a user first initiates collaborative editing of a view with another user, the collaboration menu component checks to see if the other user in fact has a copy of the view. If not, the view components are serialised and sent to the other user's environment. The components are then deserialised, given new unique ID numbers and the copy of the view displayed. The original ID numbers of the copied components are stored and used to map component ID numbers between different users' environments. Users always have a copy (i.e. alternate version) of a view they are collaboratively editing, resulting in fast editing response (no database or server-

118

based data needs updating). This also allows users to move from asynchronous to synchronous editing seamlessly.

4.2 Asynchronous Editing

When users are editing a view with asynchronous collaboration ("level 1"), no changes to the view made by either users are propagated to the other user's environment. Instead, changes are only exchanged using the "Send Changes" menu item. Users can also choose to send a whole view definition to a collaborator, if preferred. When "Send changes" is used, as shown in Figure 7, all changes made to the view by the user since the last sending of changes are sent to the specified other user. These changes are then presented in a version record dialogue box, and the other user can selective merge them into their version of the view by selecting changes and clicking the "redo" button. At present we do not allow users to request changes from other users via a menu option, but rather leave the sending of changes under the control of the person who made them. This could be easily modified, if desired, but we feel users should communicate e.g. using audio or messaging, to ensure changes sent as required.

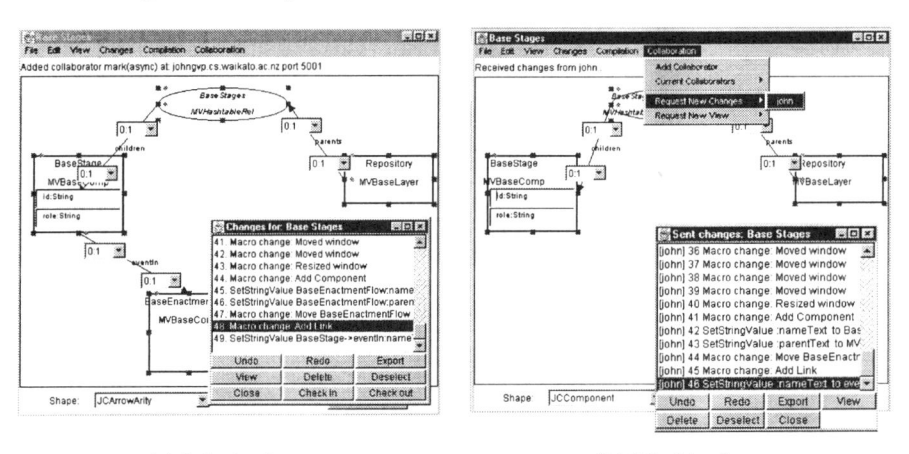

(a) John's view.   (b) Mark's view.

Figure 6. Asynchronous editing of a JComposer view

Components and change descriptions are sent to other users by the collaboration menu component by serialising them, sending them to the specified user's collaboration server, and then having the receiving user's view deserialise them and map the originating view's component IDs to the receiving view's component IDs. Changes that can not be applied by the receiver e.g. they have deleted a view component the other user has edited, are marked as "invalid".

4.3 Presentation

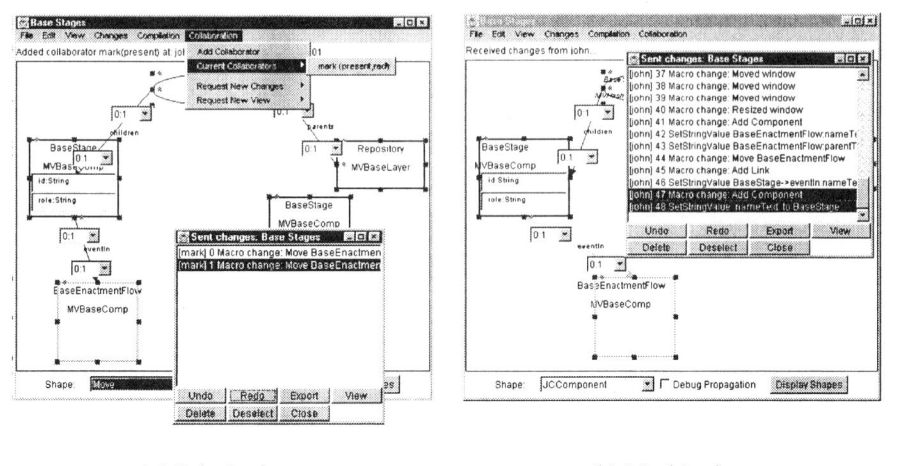

(a) John's view.   (b) Mark's view.

Figure 7. Presenting changes as they are made by other users

In the presentation level of collaborative editing ("level 3"), changes are broadcast as they are made to collaborating users, but then are presented in a dialogue box, as illustrated in Figure 8. Users then select the changes they desire to be made to their version of the view, and clicking on the "redo" button applies these changes to their view. Changes are tagged with the name of the user who originally made the change and are actioned by a receiving user. We have found this mode of collaborative editing very useful when users wish to keep informed of changes being made by other users to a shared view, but don't want these changes automatically performed on their version of the view.

4.4 Synchronous Editing

We provide two levels of "synchronous" - actioning ("level 4") and fully synchronous ("level 5"). Actioning changes simply involves the collaborative menu component applying received changes immediately to the view, rather than presenting them in a dialogue like level 3 presentation of changes. No locking or total ordering of changes protocols are used so users can potentially simultaneously edit view items, resulting in one change being immediately superseded by another when they are propagated to collaborators' environments.

Level 5 (fully synchronous) editing is the same as actioning changes but a locking protocol is employed, ensuring simultaneous edits do not occur. When a user begins to make an editing change, the collaboration menu component detects this (it is listening before and after state changes in the view occur, so gets a "before change" event from the view), and tries to "lock" the view component being changed. This is done by broadcasting a lock message to all other collaborators in level 5 collaboration mode on this view and waiting for a reply from each. Simultaneous attempts to edit the same view component result in neither user being

120

able to obtain a lock, and we colour the view item red to indicate this. The users then must wait and try and make their change again. Figure 9 illustrates synchronous editing in use, with the history of changes made by John and Mark shown in dialogues.

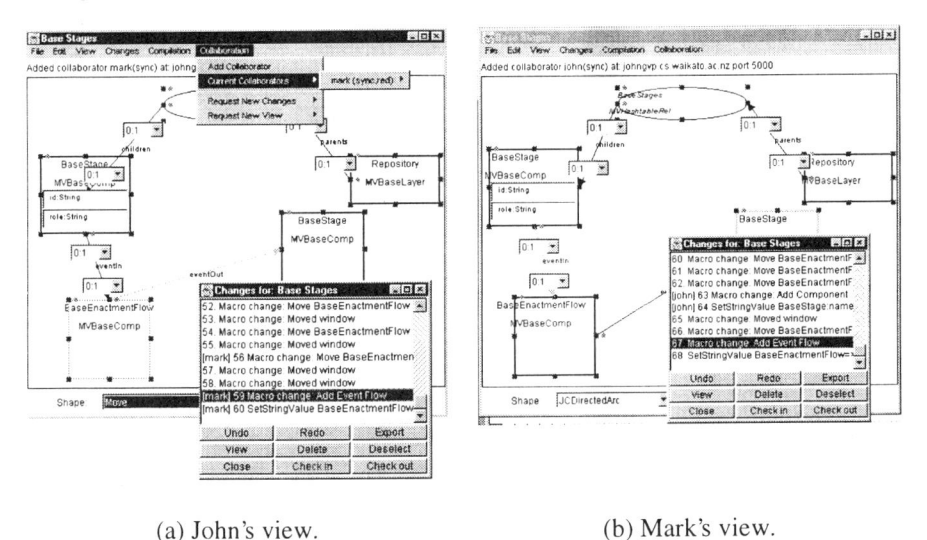

(a) John's view.   (b) Mark's view.

Figure 8. Example of synchronously editing JComposer views

4.5   Mixed-Levels of Collaborative Editing

A user, "John", can simultaneously be at e.g. presentation level of collaborative editing with another user, "Mark", and at e.g. the synchronous level with a third user, "Steve". When synchronous changes between John and Steve are processed, Mark has the change presented to him. When Mark edits the view, John has the change presented to him, and when he asks for these changes to be actioned, Steve sees the changes made synchronously. At any time the collaboration levels between these three users can be changed, a user can end collaboratively editing their version of the view, or a fourth user can begin collaboration at any level.

JViews view inconsistency management techniques are used to ensure views are kept consistent or that users are aware of inconsistencies (Grundy et al., 1996). JViews allows users to incrementally merge asynchronous and presented changes with their views, and can detect if a change can not be actioned e.g. the user deleted the view item the change refers to, the user has not yet actioned a create view item change when trying to action a subsequent change etc. This allows users to very flexibly choose when changes made by others are actioned for their views, and tolerates view inconsistency for a period of time, which we have found very useful. Our environments can be configured to highlight and/or query for those view items which have unactioned changes associated with them, allowing users to monitor such inconsistencies and to later resolve them.

121

5.   DISCUSSION

Many tools support asynchronous editing, such as Mjølner software development editors (Magnusson et al., 1993), the BSCW document management tool (Bently et al, 1995), Lotus Notes (Lotus, 1993), and editors like emacs. Other tools support synchronous collaborative work, such as GroupKit (Roseman and Greenberg, 1996), CoolTalk (Netscape Communications, 1995), and NetMeeting (Microsoft, 1997a). Some of these systems, such as NetMeeting and Mjølner, support aspects of both synchronous and asynchronous editing, but do not allow users to readily move between these modes of collaboration for the same view.

Other examples of combining different modes of collaborative work include SPADE/ImagineDesk (Di Nitto and Fuggetta, 1995), wOrlds (Bogia and Kaplan, 1995), Oz (Ben Shaul and Kaiser, 1997), TeamRooms (Roseman and Greenberg, 1997), and W4 (Gianoutsos and Grundy, 1996). These approaches generally separate the synchronous editors from the asynchronous ones, with little ability to seamlessly move between modes of operation. Additionally all of these systems have had these facilities built in from scratch. To add such capabilities to single-user tools usually requires major tool rearchitecturing and reimplementation.

Some component-based approaches to supporting collaborative editing include Orbit (Kaplan et al, 1997), CoCoDoc (ter Hofte et al, 1997; ter Hofte, 1998) and Emmerich (Emmerich, 1996), all which use CORBA-based object management and change propagation mechanisms. CoCoDoc supports collaborative compound document editing with multiple coupling levels, that can be changed independently for each component in a compound document. However, it does not allow users to have different levels for different pairs of users and does not support one user to have multiple views of a compound document open simultaneously. Other systems generally do not allow users to change collaboration levels on the same views, nor can these collaboration facilities be plugged into single-user environments in the manner we have provided.

Suite supports flexible coupling of user interface components (Dewan and Choudhary, 1991), allowing users to move between tightly coupled (synchronous) and loosely coupled (asynchronous) editing, with a variety of intermediate strategies. While the Suite approach to specifying coupling levels is similar to ours, and levels of coupling have some correspondance, we have found from our experiences with JComposer that setting coupling levels for whole views is sufficient. We have also found the use of change objects to be more flexible and provide a viewable, interactable history of work, in contrast to the Suite approach of less-flexible database-style querying to synchronise values. Our plug-in approach to adding collaborative editing is quite different to the attribute-based scheme of Suite, and we believe more reusable in general as tools continue to move to component-based software architectures. COAST (Schuckmann et al, 1996) provides a component-based approach to building primarily synchronous collaborative editing systems. This utilises an MVC-style architecture, similar to that of JViews, but has much more limited view consistency management strategies and asynchronous support. Our use of the JViews, and hence Java Beans, event mechanism to support collaboration is different to COAST which provides its own message passing infrastructure. The JavaBeans composition tool of (Banavar et al., 1998) allows end users to compose their own collaborative editing applications using direct manipulation. However, these composed editors do not provide the degree of flexible coupling of our JComposer tool, nor does this architecture allow users to add collaborative editing facilities directly to any JavaBean.

In order to use our approach, however, does require tools to utilise a component-based architecture, and an architecture with the flexible nature like JViews. Listening both before and after changes have been carried out, and even before changes sent to a listened component have been handled by it, is necessary to support both fully synchronous editing and to be able to multithread sending changes, receiving changes and user edits without interference. Unfortunately conventional component-based architectures like COM/DCOM (Microsoft, 1997b), JavaBeans (Javasoft, 1997), and that of TeamRooms (Roseman and Greenberg, 1997b), do not directly support such flexible component interconnection and event subscription. This makes reuse of our components with tools built with such architectures difficult, without substantial change of the tools to ensure appropriate event generation and propagation.

Collaborative editing components have aspects which involve human computer interaction e.g. the collaboration menu for configuring collaboration, the dialogue box to present changes in, and the highlighting of icons to indicate changes made by other users. There are limitations to what degree of seamless awareness and interaction can be provided using a component-based approach without modifying existing tool implementations or making collaboration components overly-dependant on particular tools. For example, generally the way icons are drawn can not be changed, and only certain kinds of highlighting of view items can be achieved. This limited the degree of interaction and awareness capabilities we provided when building our collaboration components for JViews-based environments. Aspects that involve the management of distributed objects, the propagation of change notifications between environments, and the handling of received changes are also important. We found it relatively straightforward to build these capabilities using JViews, although our use of unique IDs to tag JViews components is simplistic. We did not encounter any performance problems when using a component-based approach, compared to building similar collaborative editing facilities for a predecessor of JViews using conventional programming techniques (Grundy et al., 1995).

A final observation is the need for additional communication techniques to complement collaborative editing facilities. We found email-like messaging useful in conjunction with asynchronous editing, and an audio link useful with synchronous editing. An audio link and/or textual synchronous chat is useful with presentation level of collaborative editing, allowing users to discuss changes.

6.   SUMMARY

We have described a component-based approach to adding user-configurable collaborative editing facilities to existing component-based design tools. This approach has numerous advantages over conventional approaches of building in collaboration facilities into editing tools. Users can move between different levels of collaborative editing for any diagram; components supporting collaborative editing can be plugged into any component-based tool implemented with our JViews architecture with no changes to the tool or collaborative editing components needed, and these components can be easily replaced with new versions which provide better performance or facilities.

We are currently building additional collaborative work supporting capabilities into our collaboration components, including semantic telepointers for use in synchronous editing mode which show other users' mouse movements and menu interactions. We are investigating the use of CORBA or DCOM object persistency mechanisms to replace the simple object serialisation and persistency of JViews, and to provide an improved approach to object identification. We are also developing formal specifications of our collaborative editing components using Object-Z, to more formally specify their interfaces, behaviour and the kinds of tools into which they can be plugged.

ACKNOWLEDGEMENTS

The many helpful comments of the anonymous reviewers are gratefully acknowledged, as are the efforts of Henri ter Hofte, who's freely offered advice, comments and editing of earlier versions of this work go well above and beyond the call of duty. This work was supported in part by a grant from the Public Good Science Fund.

REFERENCES

Banavar, G., Miller, Doddapaneni, S., Miller, K., and Mukherjee, B. 1998. Rapidly Building Synchronous Collaborative Applications By Direct Manipulation, *Proceedings of the 1998 ACM Conference on Computer-Supported Cooperative Work*, ACM Press.

Ben-Shaul, I.Z., Heineman, G.T., Popovich, S.S., Skopp, P.D. amd Tong, A.Z., and Valetto, G. 1994. Integrating Groupware and Process Technologies in the Oz Environment, *Proceedings of the 9th International Software Process Workshop,* IEEE CS Press, Airlie, VA, October, pp. 114-116.

Bentley, R., Horstmann, T., Sikkel, K., and Trevor, J. 1995. Supporting collaborative information sharing with the World-Wide Web: The BSCW Shared Workspace system, *Proceedings of the 4th International WWW Conference,* Boston, MA, December.

Bogia, D.P. and Kaplan, S.M. 1995. Flexibility and Control for Dynamic Workflows in the wOrlds Environment, *Proceedings of the Conference on Organisational Computing Systems,* ACM Press, Milpitas, CA, November.

Dewan, P. and Choudhary, R. 1991. Flexible user interface coupling in collaborative systems, *Proceedings of ACM CHI'91,* ACM Press, April 1991, pp. 41-49.

Di Nitto, Di and Fuggetta, A. 1996. Integrating process technology and CSCW, *Proceedings of IV European Workshop on Software Process Technology,* Lecture Notes in Computer Science, Springer-Verlag, Leiden, The Netherlands, April.

Emmerich, W. 1996. An Architecture for Viewpoint Environments Based on OMG/CORBA, *Proceedings of 1996 International Workshop on Multiple Perspectives in Software Development,* ACM Press, San Francisco.

Gianoutsos, S. and Grundy, J. 1996. Collaborative work with the World Wide Web: adding CSCW support to a Web browser, *Proceedings of Oz-CSCW'96,* University of Queensland, Brisbane, Australia, August, pp. 14-21.

Grundy, J.C., Hosking, J.G., Mugridge, W.B., Amor, R.W. 199.5 Support for Collaborative, Integrated Software Development, *Proceedings of the 7th Conference on Software Engineering Environments*, IEEE CS Press, Noordwijkerhout, the Netherlands, April.

Grundy, J.C., Hosking, J.G., Mugridge, W.B. 1996. Supporting flexible consistency management via discrete change description propagation, *Software - Practice & Experience*, **20** (9), September, 1053-1083.

Grundy, J.C., Mugridge, W.B., and Hosking, J.G. 1997. A Java-based toolkit for the construction of multi-view editing systems, *Proceedings of the Second Component Users Conference,* SIGS Books/CUP, Munich, Germany, July 14-18.

Grundy, J.C. and Hosking, J.G. 1998. Serendipity: integrated environment support for process modelling, enactment and work coordination, *Automated Software Engineering*, **5** (1), January, 26-60.

Grundy, J.C., Hosking, J.G., Mugridge, W.B. 1998. Experiences in using Java on a software tool integration project, *Proceedings of 1998 Software Engineering: Education and Practice Conference*, IEEE CS Press, Dunedin, New Zealand, January 22-26 (in press).

Javasoft, 1997. *The Java Beans 1.0 API Specification*, Sun Microsystems Inc., See: http://www.javasoft.com/beans.

Kaplan, S., Mansfield, T., Phelps, T, Fitzpatrick, M., Qui, W., Taylor, R., Fitzpatrick, G., Berry, A. 1997. Orbit - supporting social worlds, *Proceedings of INTERACT97*, Chapman-Hall, Sydney, Australia, 114-116.

Lotus Corporation, 1993. *Lotus Notes Release 3*, See: http://www.lotus.com/.

Magnusson, B., Asklund, U., and Minör, S. 1993. Fine-grained Revision Control for Collaborative Software Development , *Proceedings of the 1993 ACM SIGSOFT Conference on Foundations of Software Engineering,* Los Angeles, December, pp. 7-10.

Microsoft, 1998a. *Microsoft NetMeeting 2.1*, Microsoft Corporation, See: http://www.microsoft.com/netmeeting/.

Microsoft, 1998b. *Component Object Model*, Microsoft Corporation See: http://www.microsoft.com/com/.

Netscape, 1996. *CoolTalk for NETSCAPE NAVIGATOR 3.0 BETA*, Netscape Communications, See: http://home.netscape.com/.

Roseman, M. and Greenberg, S. 1996. Building Real Time Groupware with GroupKit, A Groupware Toolkit, *ACM Transactions on Computer-Human Interaction*, **3** 1, 1-37.

Roseman, M. and Greenberg, S. 1997a. A Tour of Teamrooms, *Video Proceedings of ACM SIGCHI'97,* ACM Press, Atlanta, Georgia, March.

Roseman, M. and Greenberg, S. 1997b. Simplifying Component Development in an Integrated Groupware Environment, *Proceedings of the ACM UIST'97 Conference*.

Shuckman, C., Kirchner, L., Schummer, J. and Haake, J.M. 1996. Designing object-oriented synchronous groupware with COAST, *Proceedings of the ACM Conference on Computer Supported Cooperative Work*, ACM Press, November 1996, pp. 21-29.

ter Hofte, G.H. and H.J. van der Lugt, CoCoDoc : A framework for collaborative compound document editing based on OpenDoc and CORBA. In J. Rolia, J. Slonim and J. Botsford eds, *Open distributed processing and distributed platforms : Proceedings of the IFIP/IEEE international conference on open distributed processing and distributed platforms*, Toronto, Canada, May 26-30, 1997. Chapman & Hall, 1997, pp. 15-33.

ter Hofte, G.H., *Working apart together : Foundations for component groupware. Telematica Instituut Fundamental Research Series, vol. 001*. Telematica Instituut, Enschede, the Netherlands, 1998, See: http://www.telin.nl/publicaties/1998/wat/wat.htm.

BIOGRAPHY

John Grundy is a Senior Lecturer in Computer Science at the University of Waikato, New Zealand. He holds the BSc(Hons), MSc and PhD degrees, all in Computer Science from the University of Auckland. His research interests include software engineering environments, software architectures and component-based software development, groupware systems, human-computer interaction and user interface technology, and object-oriented systems.

Discussion

Helmut Stiegler: Why is flexibility of collaboration useful, and who decides on which level (e.g. per object, session or system)?

John Grundy: There are many examples for different synchronization levels. When you design a new object oriented system, for instance, you design first an architecture and progressively add things. For that you need the same workspace. But later, you want to be able to diverge because you are interested in different parts of the system, or you want to try different architectures. For coordination, we use other social protocols: telephone or email.

Henrik Christiansen: Is it decided on a session level?

John Grundy: Yes

Len Bass: Can you change dynamically?

John Grundy: Yes

Christian Gram: Can I press changes on another user even though he has gone to asynchronous mode?

John Grundy: Usually, we use the other channels of communication for that (email, etc.)

Prasun Dewan: Yes, you should be able to force information on a receiver. In Suite, transmission and listening are independent dimensions.

Gilbert Cockton: Are users aware of the other users' levels?

John Grundy: Yes, a user's current level is indicated in the 'Users' menu, but you must click on the menu to see this. There is no notification. We probably need to develop this further, but the basic mechanisms are there.

Ken Fishkin: What about dependencies between changes? You present a list of changes to the user, of which the user can accept only those they want. But some changes may only make sense if earlier changes are accepted. How does your system deal with this?

John Grundy: We don't handle it explicitly. The system generates an error if you try to perform an action that has no meaning without a previous action you did not commit.

Prasun Dewan: How do you handle merging?

John Grundy: Syntactical conflicts are handled through errors as I just said. Semantic conflicts are presented in a separate dialogue box.

Generic and Composable Latecomer Accommodation Service for Centralized Shared Systems

Goopeel Chung, Prasun Dewan and Sadagopan Rajaram
Department of Computer Science, University of North Carolina at Chapel Hill, Chapel Hill, NC 27599-3175, {chungg,dewan,rajaram}@cs.unc.edu

Key words: multi-user interface, collaboration system, logging, groupware, latecomer, newcomer, window system, genericity, composability

Abstract: It is important that a shared application allow a latecomer to join other users who are already working together with the application. We have developed a latecomer accommodation service framework for centralized shared systems (applications and infrastructures). It employs an independent latecomer accommodation server that is dynamically composable with its clients. The server, also called the logger, logs a shared application's user interface (UI) changes in response to calls made by the client, also called the loggable. Later, when the time comes to accommodate a latecomer, the logger replays the logged changes to the loggable, which, in turn, creates the latecomer's user interface. To deal with UI protocols at different levels of abstraction, we have defined the API in terms of a generic UI model. This reduces the burden on a loggable from a complete service implementation to a translation between its specific UI protocol and our generic UI model. To reduce the space and time overhead, the logger performs complex log compression. The extent of compression depends on the amount of semantic knowledge that the loggable provides to the logger. In this paper, we motivate, describe and illustrate the approach, and outline how it is implemented.

1. INTRODUCTION

The composition of users participating in a collaboration session with a shared application can change dynamically. A collaboration session can begin with some number of users, and later, some additional users may late-join the collaboration session, and some users may leave early. Moreover, users may not be able to finish the collaboration within one session - they may have to stop the session temporarily, and resume later at another session using the previous session state. Latecomer accommodation service allows latecomers/resumers to join/resume a collaboration session that has already made some progress. We will use the term, latecomer, to also mean resumer.

The essential part of the latecomer accommodation service is to create a new user interface for the latecomer that shows some part of the shared application state. How this is accomplished can vary. The exact part of the state shown may depend on the latecomer's role in the collaboration. Moreover, before displaying the state, the latecomer accommodation service may also show a quick animation of how the user interface reached its current state.

In general, implementing a latecomer accommodation service is difficult, and hence, should ideally be done by a collaboration infrastructure. This is the approach taken in many systems such as Suite (Dewan, Choudhary, 1992), XTV (Chung, Jeffay, Abdel-Wahab, 1994), a system by (Manohar, Prakash, 1995), and Habanero (NCSA). However, each of these systems provides its own latecomer accommodation service. Thus, there is no code sharing among these systems. Moreover, the latecomer accommodation service is tightly integrated with other aspects of the system. It is not possible for applications to use the latecomer service without using other protocols offered by the system such as those for user interface, concurrency control, and access control. It is often the case that these protocols are too rigid for an application.

Therefore, it would be useful to provide an independent latecomer accommodation service that can be used by a variety of systems and applications. In this paper, we present our first step towards such a service. It has the following distinguishing features.

– Composability: We provide a separate server module that is dynamically composable with a latecomer client (a system or an application). The latecomer server can share the same address space with the client, or be in a different address space of the same host, or on a different host. It exports an API that separates the latecomer accommodation service from other collaboration functions. Through the API, the latecomer client sends the UI state change information as often as necessary, and the latecomer server logs this information. When the time comes to accommodate a latecomer, the latecomer server replays the log back to the latecomer client. The latecomer client, in turn, can use the replayed log to create the latecomer's user interface. Our log and replay approach implies "You Get What You Log" - the latecomer client determines what actions are logged and replayed. Since we are using a log and replay approach, we will refer to the latecomer server as the logger, and the latecomer client as the loggable.

– Genericity: Different loggables can provide UI change information based on different UI protocols, which can be at different levels of abstraction. In order to support various protocols, the logger's API is based on a generic UI model that makes few assumptions about how a shared application makes changes to its user interface.

– Log Compression: Our log and replay approach allows animation of how the user interface reached its current state before the latecomer joins the session. However, it may be the case that the latecomer does not want such animation, but simply wants to see the current UI state as quickly as possible. We provide special support for such a situation by compressing the log so that not all of the UI changes sent by the loggable are actually logged. The extent of the compression performed by the logger is proportional to the amount of semantic information given to it by the loggable.

– Ease of Programming: The service should not require a significant burden on the loggable. Instead of implementing the latecomer service, the loggable takes on a translation role, simply converting between its specific UI protocol and our generic model. Such a translation module can be built for a whole class of systems and applications, and we believe that the effort required to build such a module is small.

The rest of the paper is organized as follows. We first describe the related work on which our research is based. Next, we describe our approach. Finally, we give conclusions and directions for future work.

2.   RELATED WORK

Many collaboration systems such as Suite (Dewan, Choudhary, 1992), XTV (Chung, Jeffay, Abdel-Wahab, 1994), GroupKit (Roseman, Greenberg, 1996), a system by (Manohar, Prakash, 1995), and Habanero (NCSA) support latecomer accommodation using different approaches.

Suite is a collaboration infrastructure that provides to its application programmers the high-level abstraction of a shared active variable. Suite determines how an active variable is displayed based on its type. The Suite architecture is based on the model-view framework - where a central model implements the shared application state, and multiple views implement interfaces of different users. Suite allows different users' views to be different, thereby supporting non-WYSIWIS interaction. It also supports transactions, where not every change made to a view is immediately committed in the model. When a latecomer joins a collaboration session, Suite calls a load method on the model, which sends to the latecomer's view data structures that have been committed by pre-existing views. Thus, the new user cannot see any uncommitted values.

XTV is an extension of a single-user window system called X that allows users to share existing single-user X applications. The X window system provides to its application programmers the abstraction of a window, which is much lower level than Suite's active variable. An X application sends to an X server a series of requests to create and update windows, and the X server sends to the X application user input in the form of low-level mouse and keyboard events. XTV enables sharing of a single-user X application by intercepting and distributing the X requests to multiple X servers, and by relaying the user input events from the multiple servers to the shared application. The latecomer accommodation service in XTV works by logging the low-level window requests from the shared application, and replaying them to the latecomer's X server. XTV has to use the logging approach since it is not possible to look inside existing X applications for internal data structures. This is different from Suite, which has its application export the data structures. XTV also performs log compression by maintaining only the current UI state. However, the log compression algorithm is closely tied to the X protocol.

These two systems assume a single centralized component that represents the shared application state, and multiple UI components for different users. Some collaboration systems replicate the shared application component as well as creating multiple UI components. A replicated system provides good response times to its users, because all of their input is locally processed. However, it must perform an additional step of replicating the shared application component for the latecomer. The replicated approach is taken by many systems such as GroupKit, a system by (Manohar, Prakash, 1995), and Habanero, and we will look at those systems now.

GroupKit is a toolkit that lets developers build groupware applications. In GroupKit, when a latecomer joins a collaboration session, the run-time infrastructure sends an event called updateEntrant to an existing application replica, which, in turn, communicates with the latecomer's replica to update the latecomer's user interface. What specific actions are taken during this time totally depends on the shared application. For example, a group drawing program could send the entire drawing to the latecomer, and a text chatting program could send the text contents of all the existing chat windows. Therefore, the latecomer accommodation service is flexible in that it can be whatever the application needs. However, it has to be implemented manually by the application programmer.

A system by (Manohar, Prakash, 1995) allows flexible support for resuming a collaboration session by using a data artifact called a session object. A session object captures a user's interaction with an application, and records window events such as mouse and keyboard actions. When a latecomer resumes the collaboration session, the system replays the session object's window events to a fresh copy of the application, and, in this process, the application creates the user interface for the latecomer. During replay, the system shows the previous user's actual interaction as faithfully as possible by controlling the rate of replay. The system also provides a VCR-like user interface, so that the latecomer can pause, skip, and fasten the replay. In order to support skipping to an uncoming portion of replay, the session object also has intermittent state checkpoints where the previous application wrote its entire current state information. The new application can use one of these checkpoints to load the entire application state without replaying prior window events. The system reduces the burden on the application programmer since history replay is managed by it. This is unlike GroupKit, where an application has to be totally responsible for latecomer accommodation. This is more like the XTV approach, which also logs and replays window system level protocols. But it is different from XTV in the

132

following respects. First, it works for a replicated system as mentioned before. Second, it allows UI change animation, and allows users to control its replay, while XTV simply creates the current UI state. Third, unlike XTV, it does not compress events.

Habanero is a collaboration system that allows users to interact with a shared application called a hablet. A hablet is a Java applet program extended for multi-user collaboration. When a latecomer arrives, Habanero calls a marshallSelf method that is to be implemented by the hablet. In response to this call, the hablet marshalls itself (i.e. saves its state information) to a marshall object. Habanero, then, migrates this marshall object along with the hablet code to the latecomer's workstation, where the migrated hablet code unmarshalls the previous hablet state from the marshall object. In addition to updating its state, the migrated hablet has to update the latecomer's user interface. Habanero also supports session record and replay feature, but this is a separate mechanism that is automatically supported by the system. Therefore, a hablet programmer is to be concerned only about marshalling and unmarshalling the hablet state when it comes to latecomer accommodation.

As we can see, none of these systems (both centralized and replicated) has a separate module for latecomer accommodation service; the latecomer accommodation service is closely integrated with the system or individually implemented by each application. Moreover, an application that wants to use the latecomer accommodation service from one of these systems must follow all the protocols offered by the system, including those not relevant to latecomer accommodation such as the active variable abstraction of Suite, the low level X protocol of XTV, the groupware programming abstractions of GroupKit, the window events protocol of the system by (Manohar, Prakash, 1995), and the Java applet "habanerization" of Habanero. In the next section, we will describe how these limitations can be overcome for a centralized system. We leave handling latecomers in a replicated system as future work.

3.   APPROACH

3.1   Architecture

The architecture that should be formed for our latecomer accommodation service to work is illustrated in *Figure 1*. This architecture assumes that a shared system consists of an application client and multiple UI servers, one for each user. Each server manages the interface of a user for the client. The client sends requests to change the user interface in terms of some UI abstraction the server defines, such as a window or an active variable. The client can also ask the server to notify the client

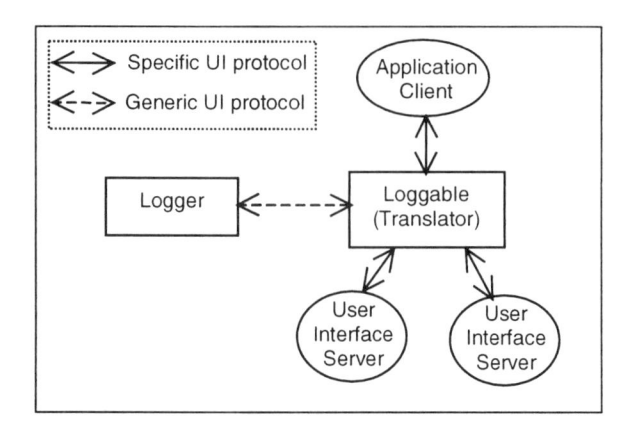

Figure 1. Latecomer Accommodation Service Architecture.

through events when certain aspects of the user interface are changed by the user (for example, mouse movements or active variable changes). Therefore, in a shared system, a client and multiple servers send messages (requests and events) back and forth following a specific UI protocol based on the UI abstraction.

A logger and a loggable work together to provide latecomer accommodation service for the shared system. The logger is a separate, log and replay module. The loggable is positioned between the client and the servers, and listens to messages exchanged between them. The logger and the loggable talk to each other using a generic UI protocol to which a specific UI protocol can be translated.

The loggable translates requests from the client into abstract primitives defined by our generic model, and sends them to the logger, which, in turn, logs them. The loggable has the discretion to decide which request it translates and sends to the logger. When a latecomer needs to be accommodated, the loggable asks the logger to replay the abstract primitives that are needed to create the latecomer's user interface. The logger, in response, sends these primitives. When the loggable receives a primitive, it reverse-translates the abstract primitive to a request of the specific UI protocol. Once the translation is done, the loggable sends the request to the latecomer's UI server.

The major factor in determining the efficiency of our latecomer accommodation service module is the compression ratio of the actual log size to the total size of all the primitives sent by the loggable. The compression ratio is greatly affected by how much semantic information the loggable can provide about the client requests. We roughly classify the extent of information into three cases, and provide an approach for each case. We will describe the three approaches in the sections that follow. Each approach assumes a different model of how the client makes changes to the user interface depending on the amount of semantic information that it can get from the loggable. Each approach will be a generalization of the previous approach, and assumes more semantic knowledge. We could have described the third approach directly, but we are doing it incrementally for motivation and explanation purposes. Since our implementation is in Java, we use Java syntax for describing operations defined by our approaches.

3.2   Brute Force Approach

This approach is to accommodate loggables that cannot provide any semantic information about a client request. The basic idea here is to record all the client requests in the log, and replay without modification to a new server. The main complication in this approach is the synchronization, which is described using *Figure 2*.

Initially, the logger and loggable start in the log and play modes, respectively. While in the play mode, the loggable treats each client request as just an encoded message that it knows nothing about, and simply relays the message as is to the logger. The loggable calls logMessage(Object message) to send the message to the logger. The logger logs each of these messages in chronological order. When the time comes to accommodate a latecomer, the loggable sends a REPLAY signal asking the logger to start replaying the logged messages. On sending/receiving the

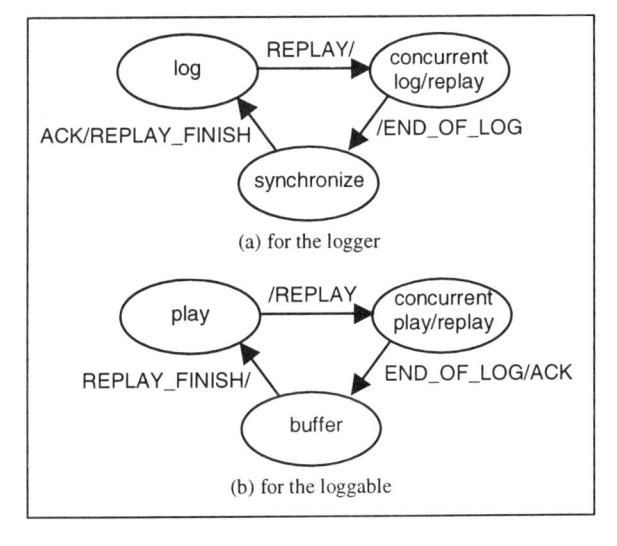

Figure 2. Mode Transition Diagram.

REPLAY signal, the loggable and logger go into the concurrent play/replay and concurrent log/replay modes respectively.

While in the concurrent log/replay mode, the logger simply replays the logged messages one by one to the loggable in exactly the same order in which they were logged. The loggable can, in turn, send these replayed messages directly to the latecomer's UI server.

While replay is going on, the client can send new messages to the loggable, which, in turn, sends them to the logger as well as to the pre-existing UI servers. The logger simply appends the new messages to the message log. When the logger has consumed the entire message log, it sends an END_OF_LOG signal to the loggable, and goes into the synchronize mode. The loggable responds to the END_OF_LOG

135

signal with an ACK signal, and goes into the buffer mode. The ACK signal defines a synchronization point, and it indicates to the logger that the loggable will send no new message until the logger replays all the messages sent so far and goes back into the log mode.

While in the synchronize mode, the logger waits for the ACK signal to arrive. While waiting, the logger can receive additional new client messages that the loggable may have sent before the ACK signal. The logger simply records these messages in the log, and replays them at the same time. When it finally receives the ACK signal, the logger sends a REPLAY_FINISH signal to the loggable, and goes back into the log mode. The buffer mode for the loggable is the same as the concurrent play/replay mode except that the loggable now buffers any new messages in its own temporary log. As soon as the loggable receives the REPLAY_FINISH signal from the logger, it sends the buffered new messages directly to the latecomer's UI server and to the logger, and then goes back into the play mode.

This brute force approach is inefficient because every client message has to be logged and replayed. This can consume a large amount of memory as the collaboration can last a long time. Additionally, the time needed to create the latecomer's user interface is strictly proportional to the entire collaboration time. If we have some semantic information about each of the client messages, we may be able to use less log space, and drastically reduce the time needed to create a latecomer's user interface. The following section describes a better approach assuming that the loggable can provide some semantic information about the client messages.

3.3 Independent Objects Approach

When we want to create the latecomer's user interface as quickly as possible, it is not necessary to show how the interface changed since the collaboration started. It is sufficient to show only the current state of the interface. For example, if the users changed the background color of a window many times, we do not have to save the history of all the background color changes, but only the latest background color.

Our approach here is based on observations such as this one, and its entire basic model of how the client makes changes to the UI server assumes that each of the client requests can be translated into one of the following abstract primitives.

- instantiate: The client instantiates some objects (e.g. windows, or active variables) on the UI server for interaction with the user.
- modify attributes: The client asks the server to change some attributes of an interaction object by specifying their new values. For example, the client can change the background color attribute of a window by specifying its new color value. An attribute value may not just be data, it may be a high level command that changes the attribute value. For example, it may be a command to draw a circle on a window foreground (which we assume to be modelled as an attribute of the window). The logger does not need to interpret the attribute values. It simply passes them to the loggable in the form it received them.
- destroy: When one of the interaction objects is no longer necessary, the client can send a request to destroy it.

136

For our approach to work, we require that the loggable translate the client's requests into the abstract primitives given above, and send them to the logger in order to report how the client is making changes to the user interface.

The logger maintains a record for each object instantiated by the client, and represents each attribute as a field of the record. Whenever the client modifies one of the attribute values, the logger replaces the old value with the new one for the corresponding field. The client can also modify attribute values of objects it did not instantiate when the objects are shared with other clients. For example, in the X window system, multiple clients can make changes to the shared default colormap. In this case, the logger depends on the loggable to report the objects as pre-existing before any modify primitives are applied to them. Since most of the client requests will involve changing certain attributes of interaction objects, this approach can accomplish drastic saving of the memory space needed to log the UI changes. Furthermore, we can accomplish more saving of log space by freeing memory allocated for objects that have been destroyed.

Now, when creating a latecomer's user interface, all the logger needs to do is just replay to the loggable the primitives to instantiate the objects (modify in case the objects are pre-existing) with the current attribute values, and the loggable can, in turn, translate the primitives into corresponding client requests and send them to the latecomer's UI server.

However, the model we assume in this approach so far may be too simple for some cases, since the client can make cumulative changes to an object attribute. For example, let us say that a logger and a loggable are working to provide latecomer service for a text editor application. The loggable has modelled the text window as a single object on the logger, and the foreground of the text window as a single attribute of the object. The loggable's intention is to translate a client request that displays characters on the window into a modify attribute - the loggable uses the request itself (without modification) as the value parameter of a modify primitive that changes the foreground attribute. When the "value" is replayed later, the loggable can simply send the "value" to the latecomer's UI server. The text editor client can display characters one after another through different text drawing requests as the users enter them using the keyboard. Instead of refreshing the whole window foreground each time a new character needs to be displayed, each request can change a part of the screen where the new character needs to be displayed. We refer to such a value change as cumulative since it cannot replace the previous value of the associated attribute. We extend our model to allow the loggable to specify the cumulative nature of some attribute value changes.

With this change in our model, the logger now looks at the cumulative nature of the value change, and if it is cumulative, it simply appends the new value to the previous value of the associated attribute. When a non-cumulative (replacing) value change needs to be applied to an attribute, the whole list of values attached to the attribute is replaced by the new value. During replay, the logger replays the value changes in the list one by one in chronological order.

Another good use of this extension arises when the loggable wants the logger to log the history of value changes even when they are not actually cumulative in nature. For example, as mentioned before, a latecomer may want to view the history of all the changes in a certain window.

Hence, the log space we need to use is more or less proportional to the number of objects that the client is maintaining on the UI server, but not exactly proportional due to some cumulative value changes. Moreover, the time needed to create the latecomer's user interface is not necessarily subject to the length of the total collaboration time.

The mode changes that the logger and the loggable take are basically the same as in the brute force approach. However, the logger in the concurrent log/replay mode works a little differently in how it deals with new primitives coming from the loggable.

If the new primitive involves an object that has already been set up on the latecomer's UI server, the new primitive is simply applied to the object record for a future latecomer accommodation service, and also sent to the loggable as a replay primitive. If the new primitive is about an object that is yet to be set up on the latecomer's UI server, it is simply applied to the object record, but is not sent to the loggable as a replay primitive. This is because the new primitive's effect will be replayed later when the logger gets to the associated object. Finally, if the primitive is about an object which the logger is in the middle of setting up on the latecomer's UI server, the application of the primitive to the record is temporarily delayed until the object is completely set up, and when the set up is complete for the object, the delayed primitives are applied to the object record for a future latecomer accommodation service, and sent to the loggable one by one in the order that they were received by the logger.

Our independent objects approach subsumes the previous brute force approach. If the loggable is sending client messages using the model assumed in the brute force approach, we simply instantiate one log object with one attribute, and we treat each client message as a cumulative value change to the attribute of the log object, thereby simulating the brute force logging of the previous approach.

3.4 Dependency Handling Approach

We saw in our previous approach that cumulativeness of attribute value changes enforces an order during replay. A cumulative value change for an object attribute cannot be replayed unless its previous value change is first replayed. Put another way, cumulativeness of an attribute value change forms a replay dependency of the attribute value change on its predecessor. Since this particular form of dependency is made within the same object, we call it an intra-object dependency (or cumulative dependency). In this subsection, we extend our model to include clients issuing primitives that create other kinds of dependencies (i.e. inter-object dependencies), and describe how it affects our log and replay approach. We first motivate the need to make such dependencies.

Windows for some applications often have repetitive tiles of an arbitrary pattern as the background. If the application client were to draw the repetitive pattern on the entire window, it would be very cumbersome and error-prone. To make programming easier in such a case, window systems such as X provide the programmers with a scratch-pad-like abstraction, called a pixmap, which itself is not directly displayable, but can be used in combination with other abstractions such as windows. To create a window with a tiled background in X, the X client would first draw the unit pattern on a pixmap, and modify the window's background attribute to refer to the pixmap. In response to the request, the X server can copy the pixmap content and repeatedly draw the pattern on the window. Later, the client can modify the pixmap to use it for some other purposes, or delete it when it is no longer needed without affecting the background pattern of the window.

In this example, the tiled window (depender) object is said to depend on the pixmap (dependee) object. Such dependency relationships between different objects (inter-object dependencies) affect how we log and replay the client request primitives in the following ways.

First, dependencies affect the order in which we instantiate and modify objects on the latecomer's UI server during replay. In our example, primitives that create the pixmap, and update it with the attribute values should be replayed before the primitive that forms the window's dependency on the pixmap.

Second, a destroy primitive from the loggable does not mean an immediate removal of the associated object record from the logger, because some other object may have formed a dependency on it. If we do remove the record, we would not be able to build the dependee object on the latecomer's UI server at all, which, in turn, means that the depender object cannot have one of its attributes set correctly.

We represent each of the dependencies as a directed edge that has its tail on the depender object node and its head on the dependee object node. The graph thus created can be used to replay client request primitives in the correct order: i.e. replay the dependee object first, and then the depender object. Also, when we delete a node in response to a destroy primitive, we check whether an edge has its head on the associated node: i.e. whether any other object depends on it. If there is indeed a depender object, we do not delete the object node, but we just mark it as destroyed. If there is no depender object, we delete the object node along with all the edges that originate from the deleted node. Then, we recursively follow the deleted edges to find and delete any node that could not be deleted because its depender node still existed.

There is another, related, problem to be resolved, however. This problem occurs when the client tries to modify a dependee object. We cannot apply the attribute value changes implied in the modify primitive to the object because we assume that its depender object depends on all the current attribute values of the object. We resolve this problem by object versioning. We consider the instantiation of an object as creating the first version of the object, which becomes its current version. Later, the loggable may send a primitive that modifies the object. In response to this primitive, the logger first finds out whether any other object depends on the current object to be modified. If there is no such object, the logger applies the change to the current version of the object. Otherwise, the logger creates a new version copy of the current version. The new version is a copy of the previous version except that all its attribute values are initialized to null. The logger then applies the change to the new version, which becomes its current version. To indicate the replay order of the two versions, we create a dependency of the new version on the previous version. We refer to this dependency as version dependency. Any subsequent modification made to the object is about the most current version of the object. With the introduction of versioning, the dependency graph is now made up of different versions of objects, some of which are connected by version and inter-object dependencies. Version dependency imposes another restriction on how we replay primitives: an object version cannot be replayed unless its previous version and all other object versions that depend on the previous version have been replayed. This is because we lose the previous version's context by replaying its next version.

Versioning not only preserves the dependee object context for the depender object, but also removes cycles in the dependency diagram. Without versioning, cycles can occur. For example, when creating a pixmap in X, the X request should specify a hierarchy of windows for which the pixmap can be used, by including, as an attribute of the pixmap, a window that belongs to the window hierarchy. We refer to this window as the reference window of the pixmap. So let us say that when creating a pixmap A, the client specified a window B, thereby creating a dependency of pixmap A on window B. Now, after the client draws some basic pattern on pixmap A, it designates pixmap A as the background pattern of window B. Assuming there is no versioning, this modification creates a dependency of window B on pixmap A. Thus, we have a cycle formed with the two object nodes and the

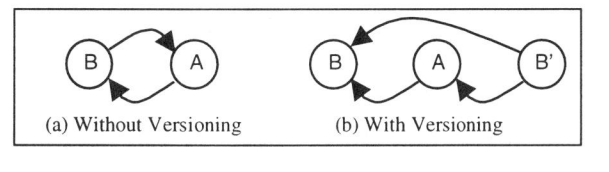

(a) Without Versioning   (b) With Versioning

Figure 3. Cycle Removal through Versioning.

two dependency edges between them. Such a cycle creates a problem when we replay primitives to create objects on a latecomer's UI server: we cannot create window B without creating pixmap A, or vice versa, because they depend on each other. Deleting nodes creates a similar problem. Let us say that a primitive to destroy the window arrives. It cannot be deleted because pixmap A depends on it. Now, if a primitive to destroy pixmap A arrives, it too cannot be honored, since the undeleted window B depends on it.

Let us illustrate how versioning works to prevent such a cycle. When making the background pattern attribute change in window B, we find that pixmap A depends on it. Instead of applying the new value in the current version of window B, we create a new version B' of window B and apply the value change to B'. Since we are effectively adding a new node (which does not have any incoming edge) and making the dependencies from there, we never have a cycle in the dependency diagram. The versioning process is illustrated in *Figure 3*.

With the guarantee that there is no cycle in the entire object dependency diagram, we can use the same procedures described above for logging and replaying.

Our dependency handling approach follows basically the same mode changes as described before. However, the logger in the concurrent log/replay mode works a little differently in how it deals with each of the new primitives coming from the loggable. Unlike the previous approach, which applies the new primitive's value

140

changes to the logger data structures and optionally sends the primitive on the fly depending on whether the associated object has been replayed, we take a rather simple solution for now. We log any new primitive coming from the loggable in a temporary log. When we finish replaying all the versions in the dependency diagram, we take each primitive in the temporary log, and send it back to the loggable. Before sending the primitive, we also apply the primitive's value changes to the dependency diagram in order to prepare for a future latecomer accommodation service. We take this simple approach because the new primitive's effect during replay is not necessarily confined to a single object version due to inter-object and version dependencies, and it is probably not worth the effort to try to determine the new primitive's effect during replay when we can simply apply it to the data structures and send it back to the loggable when the replay is over.

Our new dependency handling approach subsumes our previous independent objects approach in a straightforward manner, since the previous approach is just a special case of our new approach, where there is no dependency among different objects.

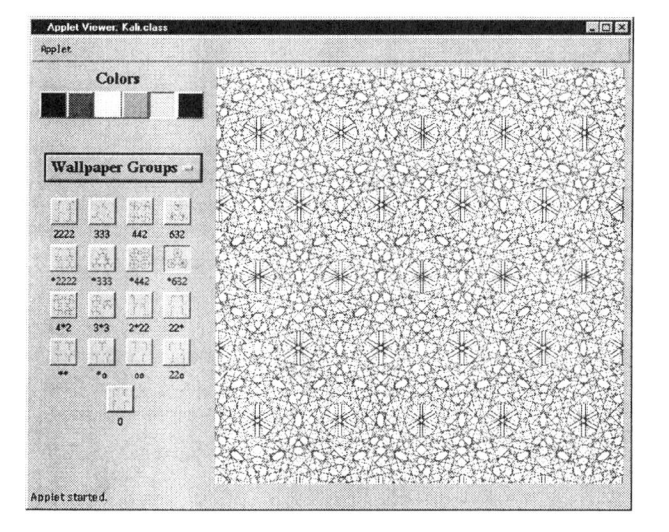

3.5   Evaluation and Implementation

Figure 4. A User Interface Snapshot of an Application Program Kali

Let us evaluate our latecomer accommodation service framework based on the requirements described in the introduction. It is composable by design as shown in its architecture (*Figure 1*), and it imposes no policies or protocols that are unrelated to latecomer accommodation support. It compresses the log by design, though the extent of the compression depends on the amount of semantic knowledge provided

141

by the loggable. It is easy to program since the loggable takes on a translation role instead of implementing the entire service. However, there is a trade-off between log compression and ease of programming - the more compression the service provides, the more work the loggable has to do in order to provide more semantic information. But, we still believe that even with the dependency handling approach, the effort required to build a loggable will be less than what is required to implement the log compression. For example, it is easier to describe the dependencies than to interpret them. Indeed, compression comes at a cost, but the loggable only has to specify the parameters of the compression algorithm. The framework is generic because it does not make any assumptions about the UI abstraction. For instance, the abstraction could be a Suite active variable, or an X window system window.

We have implemented the logger in Java. So far in our paper, only X examples were used to motivate the description of our work. To verify that our logger implementation is useful for higher-level abstraction systems beyond X, we added latecomer accommodation service to a Java application called Kali.

Figure 4 shows a snapshot of the user interface created by the application program Kali. The left portion of the interface is the control panel, while the right portion is the canvas on which a user can draw the pattern that he desires. The control panel is divided into the color panel and the group panel. The color panel controls what color is used to draw on the canvas while the group panel is used to

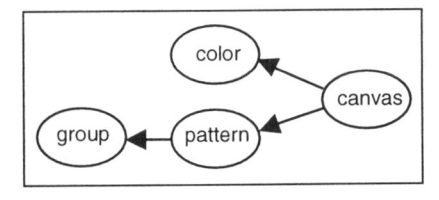

Figure 5. Dependency Relationship among Kali State Objects.

set a pattern to lay on the canvas. There are three alternative groups of patterns a user can choose from a drop-down group menu, and for each different group selection, the application displays a different set of patterns that the user can choose as buttons below the group menu. Selection of a color or a pattern affects only subsequent drawing the user lays on the canvas, but does not influence previous work. No effect is seen when the group is changed, but the canvas is cleared when a particular pattern is chosen for the first time after the group change.

As illustrated in *Figure 5*, there are basically four states maintained within the application program: i.e. those of color, group, pattern, and canvas. The loggable models these states as four state objects, each of which has a single attribute used to log events that change the associated state object. Each selection in the color buttons, the group menu, and the pattern buttons is modeled as a single event, and it is non-cumulative since its effect on the associated state object replaces that of a previous selection event. Each event associated with the canvas state object is cumulative since its effect adds to the current drawing of the canvas, except that the first canvas event after each new group selection followed by a pattern selection is

142

non-cumulative. *Figure 5* also illustrates the inter-object dependencies the loggable specifies to enforce a correct replay order.

As can be seen from the nature of the application, logging is a more attractive alternative since state capture is rather complex. The state is not only dispersed in the canvas but also in the control panel since the effect of the next event in the canvas depends on the state in the control panel. The importance of this method is that by clearly defining the dependencies which are natural to the application, and the properties of the attributes being logged, the entire compression is automated. Moreover, the change to the application program was minimal – only a small portion of event handling code within the program had to be changed to both send events to the logger and to receive replayed events.

We ran the application using the logger for latecomer accommodation and obtained the following statistics. *Table 1* covers the entire spectrum where we use all the events that are logged while in other cases, only necessary events are replayed.

In the first case, the control panel was used to change only the color. In the second case, the group of patterns in the control panel was changed. In the last case, the entire canvas was cleared and a design recreated. We had two Color events before the group was changed to redraw a new design. In the replay, all the events that occurred before the pattern change, which include the two color events, are purged and we can see effective log compression. The number of replayed events are exactly equal to the events that occur after the last clear occurred and hence offer an advantage of a compact log.

Table 1. Logger Performance on Log Size Reduction

Logged Events					Replayed Events		
Canvas	Button	Group	Color	Total	Canvas	Control Panel	Total
387	0	0	3	390	387	3	390
229	0	1	3	233	229	4	233
463	1	1	4	469	215	4	219

4.   FUTURE WORK

In both of our latter two approaches, the loggable can have the logger replay the whole history of a certain window's state changes by specifying all the drawing requests to the window as having the cumulative characteristic. However, just replaying the value changes of an object's attributes (e.g. just showing what went on within only the main window of a drawing application) may not be sufficient for some latecomers. A latecomer who is also a novice user of the shared client may want to learn how to work with the client's interface while watching the request replay, such as which menus are used. But simply replaying primitives according to the dependency relationships cannot satisfy such needs, because some of the windows used for menus may be temporarily created, used by the user, and destroyed immediately, and hence immediately removed from the data structure. We plan to define a playback dependency, which basically defines a playback sequence of window drawing requests.

We also plan to use our system to provide a composable latecomer service for a variety of systems. Since our implementation is coded in Java, it is easiest to compose it with systems implemented in Java. We plan to compose it with the Java applications we plan to build as part of the Collaboration Bus project going on in our department.

ACKNOWLEDGMENTS

This research was supported in part by National Science Foundation Grants IRI-9408708, IRI-9508514, IRI-9627619, and CDA-9624662, and by DARPA/ONR grant N 66001-96-C-8507.

REFERENCES

Abdel-Wahab, H. M. and Feit, M. A., XTV: A Framework for Sharing X Window Clients in Remote Synchronous Collaboration, *Proceedings, IEEE Conference on Communications Software: Communications for Distributed Applications & Systems*, Chapel Hill, NC, pp. 159-167, April 1991.

Chung, G., Jeffay, K., and Abdel-Wahab, H., Dynamic Participation in Computer-based Conferencing System, *Journal of Computer Communications*, 17(1): 7-16, January 1994.

Dewan, P. and Choudhary, R., A high-level flexible framework for implementing multi-user user interfaces, *ACM Transactions on Information Systems 10*, 4, 345-380, October 1992.

Manohar, N. R. and Prakash, A., The Session Capture and Replay Paradigm for Asynchronous Collaboration, *Proceedings of the Fourth European Conference on Computer-Supported Cooperative Work*, September 10-14, Stockholm, Sweden, 149-164, 1995.

NCSA, Habanero, http://www.ncsa.uiuc.edu/SDG/Software/Habanero/.

Roseman, M. and Greenberg, S., Building Real Time Groupware with GroupKit, A Groupware Toolkit, *ACM Transactions on Computer Human Interaction*, 1996.

BIOGRAPHY

Goopeal Chung is a Ph.D. student in the Department of Computer Science at the University of North Carolina at Chapel Hill. He received a B.S. degree in Computer Engineering from Seoul National University, and a M.S. degree in Computer Science from University of North Carolina at Chapel Hill. His research interests are flexible shared window systems and process migration.

Prasun Dewan is a professor in the Department of Computer Science at the University of North Carolina at Chapel Hill. Before joining UNC-Chapel Hill, he was on the faculty of Purdue University. He received a B.Tech. degree in Electrical Engineering from the Indian Institute of Technology of New Delhi and a Ph.D. in

Computer Science from University of Wisconsin at Madison. His research interests are in frameworks for implementing single-user and multi-user applications, collaborative software engineering, object-oriented databases, operating systems, process migration, mobile computing, and interoperability.

Sadagopan Rajaram received the B.Tech degree in Computer Science and Engineering from the Indian Institute of Technology, Madras (Chennai), in 1997. He is currently working towards his Masters degree in Computer Science from the University of North Carolina at Chapel Hill. His interests include CSCW, particularly in the area of access control and security.

Discussion

Ken Fishkin: I have a question about your loggable filtering. If one views an event as a command to a virtual machine, then the event log is like a sequence of commands in assembly language. So, the filtering you describe is similar to classic code optimisation. For instance, some of the techniques you describe in the paper are similar to peephole optimisation, dead code removal, and code hoisting. Would it be useful to strengthen this similarity and investigate the use of available code optimisation packages?

Prasun Dewan: Our system is flexible, and whoever implements the loggable filter certainly can do any optimisation. I need to think about this similarity, however.

Christian Gram: Can you log "Undo" and manage it without losing information?

Prasun Dewan: Yes, I think it should work.

John Grundy: Is Kali a single-user application?

Prasun Dewan: Yes. We is turned it into a multi-user application, then added latecomer management.

Nick Graham: You seem to be biased towards applications that are WYSIWIS, and artifact-based, where artifacts can be represented by a set of graphical calls.

Prasun Dewan: As to WYSIWIS, yes. As to artifacts, I do not quite agree. It is up to you to describe how your application is to be rendered.

Len Bass: How would you handle users with different levels of synchronisation? Would you have one logger for each?

Prasun Dewan: Yes, we would have one logger per user in that case.

Stephane Chatty: Can you do fast-forward and rewind through your event logs?

Prasun Dewan: We can log enough events to support these operations, but have not implemented them so far.

Franck Tarpin-Bernard: After a long session , what is the size of a log file? Isn't it very large?

Prasun Dewan: If you want fast-forward and rewind, then yes it would be very large, since you would have to log all events. Otherwise, you can have checkpoints and shorten your file.

Help generation for task based applications with HATS

García, F.[*], Contreras, J.[*], Rodríguez, P.[*] and Moriyón, R.[*,†]
Escuela Técnica Superior de Informática. Universidad Autónoma de Madrid

†*Instituto de Ingeniería del Conocimiento. ADIC.*

Abstract: This paper describes HATS, a system for the generation of context sensitive help for interactive applications. HATS delivers help based on a hierarchy of tasks the user can perform. As the user interacts with the application and accomplishes the tasks, the help messages are updated automatically, and give him context sensitive information about the actions needed to accomplish the desired task, including graphical references to the places in the application window where the tasks can be performed. HATS includes a reduced environment that simplifies the design of the help system.

Keywords: Help generation, Task models, Formal notations, Intelligent interfaces

1.   INTRODUCTION

During the last years, interactive applications have become increasingly harder to use. This process, that has taken place in despite of a great improvement in the design and evaluation methodologies in the life cycle of these systems, has brought special attention to the key role played by the help components, integrated in those applications.

However, these help components have not followed the rapid development pace of the applications they serve. The most extended paradigm employed at the present moment consists in using hypertext, or hypermedia, to inform the user about the steps that must be undertaken to accomplish the tasks furnished in the application. This could be seen as recipes, the hyperlinks being used to change from one recipe to another.

The main drawbacks of this approach have been analyzed in detail in (Contreras, 1998). The two most important ones are, in the first place, the fact that all the explanations are given to the user at a very low level, related uniquely with atomic interactions s/he must perform. Secondly, the absence of feedback and interaction between the application and the help system.

These deficiencies observed in current help systems may have important consequences. Bhavnani points the type of help provided to users of such complex systems as CAD applications, as one of the reasons that could explain the small productivity increases in firms using those systems (Bhavnani, 1996).

In the present work, we describe a system that generates high level help, with a minimum development cost for designers. This system, called HATS (Help for ATOMS Task System) is able to automatically generate help for those interactive applications for which the user tasks have been defined according to ATOMS.

ATOMS (Rodriguez, 1997), is a system that permits the specification of hierarchical user tasks for interactive applications. These tasks may include context information, so as to describe under which circumstances the tasks are carried out; they are defined by means of a declarative language. This system is also comprised of a tasks manager, in charge of following the user activity in the application with respect to the tasks defined. It is important to note that the task model is general enough so as to be used by other tools who can reason about, providing services such as help, tutoring, macro and undo facilities, etc. A detailed discussion of the advantages of hierarchical task models can be found in (Zeiliger, 1997).

Using the benefits provided by ATOMS, HATS gives help to the user of an application that is substantially different to the one offered by current help systems as described above, and is mainly characterized by:

- It is task oriented. Explanations are generated by analyzing the task model. Thus, they are more expressive and have greater semantic content.
- Help is provided *just in time*, i.e., at every moment only the pertinent explanations are given according to the state of execution of the task being performed. This is possible thanks to the capabilities found in ATOMS. Since the system is able to detect the state of the application, HATS uses this knowledge to provide the user with relevant information, such as feedback about finished tasks or what steps should be performed next.
- The help system makes direct references to the widgets of the application where the user is supposed to act next, in a graphical manner. By means of highlighting in the application window, HATS indicates in a very clear way where interactions described in the help window should take place.

Finally, the cost for the designer when using HATS to generate help for her/his application is reduced: s/he just has to specify the tasks for the application, along with the corresponding help information for those tasks.

This paper is organized as follows. We first describe previous related work, followed by an example originating from a CAD application, that we will be using to illustrate the main characteristics of our help system. We continue with a brief description of ATOMS, just to introduce HATS in detail. We finish discussing some conclusions and research lines for future work.

2. RELATED WORK

In the last years there has been an important amount of research work in the field of generating help for interactive applications, using different paradigms. In this section we describe previous work that overcomes some of the drawbacks of traditional help systems pointed out in the introduction.

Humanoid Hyper Help, H3 (Moriyón, 1994), is a system that generates hypertext based help about the data presented in application displays, the commands to manipulate the data, and the interaction techniques to invoke the commands, for applications that have been developed according to the Humanoid model based paradigm (Szekely, 1992). It can derive the help automatically from the model used to implement the interface. Although it simplifies in a great deal the work of the designer generating a first version of a help system that can be refined a posteriori, it is not able to produce task oriented help about high level questions like *How do I merge these two files?* or *How can I add an arrow head at the end of this line?*. Moreover, help design in systems like H3 is more complex than it is in HATS, since a set of production rules is needed. This is due to the fact that HATS is task oriented, while H3 is widget oriented.

Cartoonist (Sukaviriya, 1990) is another interesting system that has in common with H3 the fact of generating help automatically from the models used to construct the interface. The originality of this system, though, lies in that it uses animation to convey the information to the user. Cartoonist uses backchaining reasoning in order to show how to satisfy preconditions.

The work by Pangoli and Paternó (Pangoli, 1995) has in common with our system the fact of being specialized in giving task oriented help; hence, the help given is more expressive that the one found in traditional help systems. However, this system does not use the tasks descriptions to follow the user actions, and thus it cannot synchronize help messages and user actions, as it happens with HATS.

Finally, Teach me While I Work, TWIW (Contreras, 1998), is another system centered around a model that describes the tasks that can be performed by the user. Although it can be used as a help system, it goes one step further and it is aimed at being used mainly as a tutoring tool. In this sense, it can not only inform the user about the actions to be performed, but also filter these actions in case they are not the appropriate ones. The absence of parameters in the task model used by TWIW makes it less context sensitive than the system we propose in this paper; the task model is less rich than the one used in HATS, specially in sequencing issues.

3. AN EXAMPLE

A very graphical way of introducing the problem we are interested in, is by making use of a real world based example. In order to do that, we have chosen one of the excellent examples presented in (Bhavnani, 1996). That paper focuses on the unrealized potential of Computer-Aided Drafting, even in the case of experienced users, that still employ suboptimal strategies to perform complex CAD tasks. The examples presented in that paper are quite convenient for our own purposes; that is, to introduce HATS, our ATOMS based help system on user tasks. Concretely, the example we will use is the one there referenced as Example 1, consisting of Adding Fire Protection to a Column:

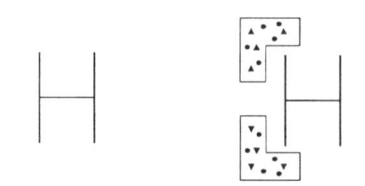

Figure 1. Drawing L-shaped fire protection enclosures for a column.

As described by the authors, the fire protection task consists of drawing 'fire protection enclosures around columns in a floor plan'. The fire protections are L-shaped polygons patterned with dots and triangles symbolizing concrete. So, the picture that represents a column must end up with two identical poched (patterned) L-shapes once the task is finished. This can be seen in Figure 1.

There are two main possibilities of drawing the protections that surround the column. The first one consists of drawing both L-shaped protections, patterning them afterwards. The second one consists of drawing one of the shapes, patterning it and then mirror copying the shape with respect the column axis. Of course, there are some other mixed possibilities. After completing the task in a CAD system, it becomes evident that the second possibility corresponds to the optimal task scheduling, while all the others can be considered as suboptimal.

One of the objectives of the help system we propose, is to provide the users with a global perspective of the task, guiding him/her through the appropriate sequencing of subtasks. This possibility is suggested in Bhavnani's paper as one way of providing users with strategic information that is not part of the application itself; that is, by including knowledge that is not in help manuals.

The inclusion of strategic knowledge in complex systems, secondary or non existent few years ago, is growing in interest within the CAD community, given that commercial CAD products are continuously resulting in more featured systems, often with more than a thousand commands. Of course, all these commands are detailed in manuals or consult books, where several pages are often devoted to the characteristics and parameters of most of them. However, higher level strategies are not usually included, at least as substantial chapters.

Next, we briefly describe ATOMS, the task oriented system HATS is based on.

4. ADVANCED TASK ORIENTED MANAGEMENT SYSTEM

ATOMS, *Advanced Task Oriented Management System*, is a system aimed to deal with complex user tasks. ATOMS tasks include context information that is updated dynamically as the user performs different activities. The task hierarchy is defined by rules. The definition of tasks and rules is declarative, being similar to the definition of grammar rules in natural language processing systems. ATOMS uses a parser, able to identify the global tasks being accomplished, as well as the context determined from partial information taken from the user actions. More details about the system can be found in (Rodríguez, 1997).

ATOMS based applications incorporate a set of task patterns and rules that constitute its task model. Part of it is common for all the applications, and another part is application dependent. Some tasks are tagged as *application tasks*, in the sense that they are completely meaningful from the user point of view.

On the other hand, task patterns can be *atomic*, supporting the definition of direct user interactions, or *composed*, defining high level actions in terms of simpler ones. Both types of patterns admit the inclusion of parameters, that serve as context information for the tasks. Selecting a graphical object of a window could be an instance of an atomic task pattern, whose parameter is the selected object. Similarly, drawing a polygon could be an example of a composed application task pattern in which the polygon itself becomes the task parameter.

Apart from task patterns, the application task model includes rules. Those rules include information about (a) subtasks that constitute a composed task, (b) constraints over the values of parameters from related tasks, including not only immediate propagation of values, but also methods for assigning new values, (c) task preconditions that indicate the conditions under which the rule holds and (d) task sequencing, that can be sequential, parallel or alternative. Sequential order holds for the consecutive execution of the subtasks, while parallel assimilates to 'any order' and alternative to 'exclusive or'.

Tasks can also be qualified according to the number of times they can be executed. So, for instance, a task can be labeled as *optional*, meaning that its execution is not necessary for the global objectives, and also as *multiple*, meaning that it can be executed several times. In this last case, the number of repetitions can be specified.

Not all the information associated to tasks can be specified declaratively: task preconditions are predicates that must be satisfied whenever the task is accomplished. ATOMS allows the definition of preconditions by means of task patterns, that can be defined in a declarative way, but general preconditions are also possible, and they have to be programmed. The same happens with the methods used for parameter passing.

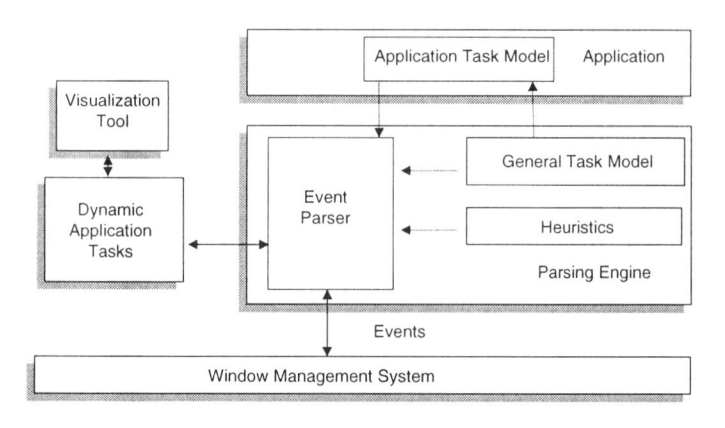

Figure 2. ATOMS architecture

The implementation of ATOMS is based on the AMULET framework (Myers, 1997). AMULET allows the designer to deal with high level events, based on interactors, which represent the basic actions a user performs. This feature, together with the fact that it supports a complete prototype/instance object system, is extensively used in ATOMS. The ATOMS architecture is shown in Figure 2.

At runtime, a set of *dynamic application tasks* reflects which actions the user is performing, including contextual information. The *event parser* analyzes the interactions of the user with the application, on the basis of user events, the task model, and the dynamic application task set. This parsing process allows the event

parser to maintain the state of the application tasks in the dynamic application tasks area.

In next section, where we explain how HATS is used to provide help to the user on the task of adding fire protection to a column, most of the above mentioned ATOMS features will reveal.

5. HATS

HATS generates task based help for applications that incorporate an ATOMS task model. HATS provides two kinds of information: on one hand, like in the work of Pangoli and Paternó, (Pangoli, 1995), it explains complex tasks in terms of simpler ones, something that is much easier to comprehend than just a list of elementary interactions like mouse clicks, as it happens in most conventional help systems. On the other hand, somehow as in H3, (Moriyón, 1994), HATS gives context sensitive graphical information about the locations in the window where the user can interact in order to achieve the goals described in the different tasks, and how this interaction should take place. The context sensitivity of HATS is due to the fact that ATOMS is able to distinguish actions that simpler task management systems would consider as being similar.

The user can ask for help in two ways: either by selecting a task from a hierarchically organized list of application tasks, or by selecting a part of the window and asking for actions that can be performed there.

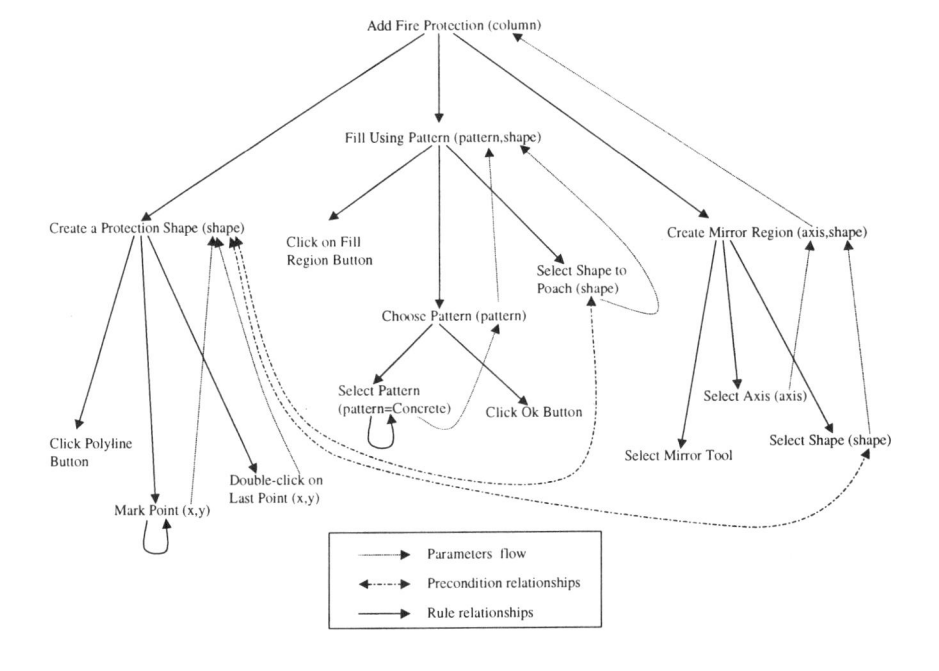

Figure 3. An optimal decomposition of the task: *Add Fire Protection to a Column.*

Once an application task is selected, there are two types of help the user can obtain: on one hand, s/he can navigate through the subtasks of the application task s/he has asked help for, getting descriptive information about them; hence, at each moment there is a *current help task.* On the other hand, the user can get help about the actions that have to be performed, and the relevant information is updated as the user accomplishes the task s/he is getting help for; hence, at each moment there is also a set of *next pending tasks.*

When the current help task is not one of the next pending tasks, HATS is in *descriptive mode.* Then, the messages it generates tell the user about how the current help task can be accomplished. Otherwise, the system is in *active mode,* and the corresponding help messages tell the user about the actions to be done.

By default, when giving help about a subtask, HATS does not give information about the higher level tasks in whose context it is accomplished. This policy is enforced in order to avoid the proliferation of long messages and large windows that make the use of HATS uncomfortable. The user can ask for additional task context information that shows him/her the super-tasks of the current help task.

In the rest of this section we will give first an overview of the kind of help provided by HATS, centered around the help the user can get for the adding fire protection task previously described. The task decomposition we will use is presented in Figure 3. This example has been implemented on a prototype of a CAD system for which a task model has been specified. Afterwards, more general aspects, like the architecture of the HATS system, and issues about the design of help for applications are treated.

5.1   HATS message window

When the user requests help for a task like *Add Fire Protection to a Column,* the HATS message window appears, as can be seen in Figure 4, showing basic information for the task. In our example, the following *task description message* is shown (both underscored and bold text are emphasized only for explanation purposes later on in the paper):

*You have requested help about how to **Add Fire Protection to a Column***.
*This task **adds L-shape concrete blocks around the outer corners of the column to be protected.***
You can do this task on <u>any of the highlighted objects</u>.

Simultaneously, all the columns that appear in the drawing area of the application window will be highlighted. The HATS message window includes just simple messages, like the one above, and a button, *NextToDo,* that focuses HATS on one of the next pending tasks, hence switching the system to active mode.

The user can also enforce focus based modifications to the help message through the items in the *Focus* menu *(Go To Next Task, In Context,* and *DeContext),* and explore alternative ways to accomplish the current help task through the items in the *Alternatives* menu *(All Alternatives, Next Alternative,* and *Previous Alternative).* The *Show Task Hierarchy* item in the *View* menu opens a window that displays the state of the tree of the subtasks that are being explained. Besides the buttons, the user can also interact with the HATS message window by clicking on the lines of the message being shown, as we will explain later.

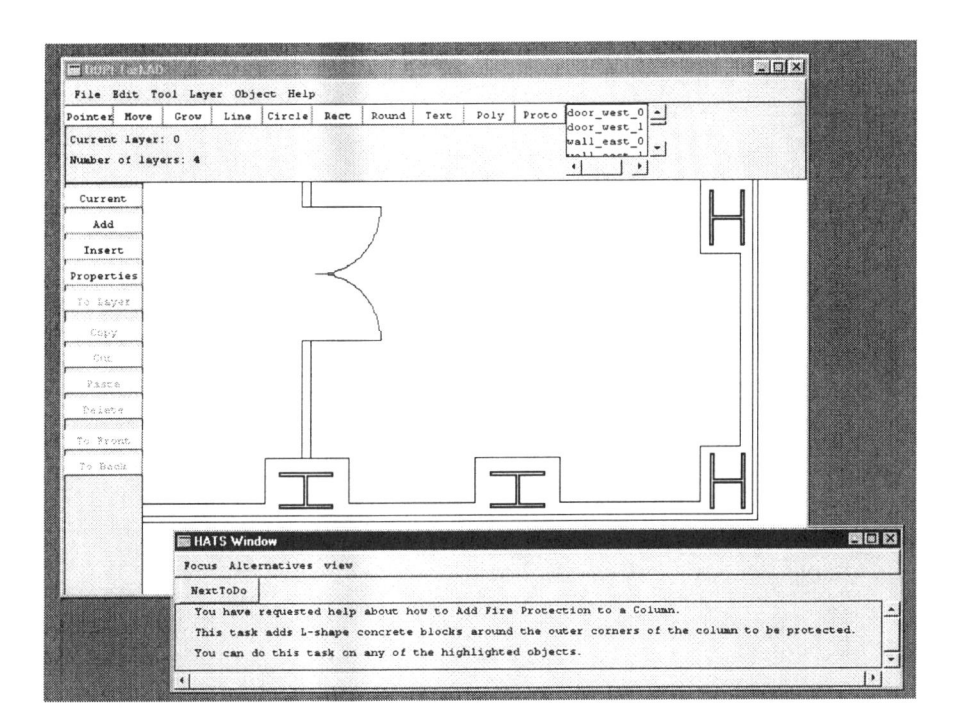

Figure 4. Requesting help for the adding fire protection task.

All the events generated on the HATS message window will be called *HATS* events, while those generated on the application window will be called application events. Application events that match with one of the next pending tasks, as well as the NextToDo button in the HATS message window, turn HATS mode into active, while, in general, HATS events turn the mode into descriptive. Context and alternative commands do not have any effect on the systems mode.

5.2   Descriptive Mode Navigation

When the initial message appears, the current help task is the application task *Add Fire Protection to a Column,* and its first atomic subtask, *Click on the Create Polyline Button* becomes the next pending task. Hence, HATS is in descriptive mode. We shall see now how the user can navigate from here and get information about the different subtasks of the application task.

Double clicking on the initial message will substitute it by a corresponding *task action message* (still a message shown in descriptive mode) obtained by substituting the second part of the previous one by an explanation of the subtasks that correspond to fire protection for columns, as follows:

*You have requested help about how to **Add Fire Protection to a Column**.*
In order to do this task you have to fulfill the following subtasks:
***Create a Single Protection Shape**.*

157

Fill the Region Using a Concrete Pattern.
Create a Mirror Region with respect to the Axis of the Column.

The user can now double click on any of the lines that explain one of the subtasks, and a corresponding *task description message* will appear. For example, if the user double clicks on the first subtask, the message will be:

You have requested help about how to **Create a Single Protection Shape.**
You can do this task on <u>the part of the window that is highlighted.</u>

At any moment the user can also ask for contextualization by using the *In Context* item in the *Focus* menu, and a higher level of the task hierarchy is shown. The message below shows a contextualized action message for the previous task.

You have requested help about how to **Add Fire Protection to a Column.**
In order to do this task you have to **Create a Single Protection Shape.**
In order to do this task you have to fulfill the following tasks:
Click on the Create PolyLine button.
Mark a point <u>*(This has to be done 5 times)*</u>.
Double click on the last point.

The *In Context* item of the *Focus* menu, together with the double clicking action, allows the user complete navigation through the task tree corresponding to the initial application task. Navigation is supplemented through the possibility to *Go To Next Task*. The default behavior of HATS allows the user to see description and action help messages for any subtask, together with a context that consists of a variable amount of its supertasks. The user can also choose the *verbose* behavior, that includes in the HATS message window the messages that correspond to all the subtasks s/he has explored at each moment.

5.3   Automatic Update in Active Mode

If the user starts the execution of the application task s/he is requesting information for, HATS switches from descriptive to active mode. Active messages are similar to task action ones, except for the fact that they speak about the actions that are being done, and the next action or actions to be performed. When switching to active mode, HATS shows the task context formed by the supertasks of the current help task that were not present in the previous context. In our example, once the user has finished the first subtask (creation of a single protection shape) the HATS window will show the following active message, that includes a precondition:

You have finished the task **Create a Single Protection Shape.**
You have done this task on <u>the highlighted object.</u>
Next you have to **Poach the Shape Using a Concrete Pattern.**
The following condition must hold: you must poach the shape you just created.
In order to do this task first you have to **Click on the Fill Region Button.**

*In order to do this task you have to click with the **left** button of the mouse on the highlighted object.*

As the user follows the instructions on the HATS window, HATS updates them, showing her/him constantly the successive actions s/he has to perform. After the user has clicked on the Fill Region button, the help message will be:

*Next you have to **Choose a Pattern for the Protection.***
*In order to do this task first you have to **Select a Filling Pattern**. This can be done one or more times.*
*You can do this task on any of the objects highlighted in green by clicking with the **left** button of the mouse.*
*After this, you have to **Click on the OK Button**.*
*You can do this task on the object highlighted in yellow by clicking with the **left** button of the mouse.*

This message differs from previous ones in that the task being explained can be repeated an undetermined number of times. We have already seen a repetition task with a fixed number of repetitions. Repetition tasks are updated in a different way depending on whether the number of repetitions is fixed a priori or it can be determined by the user. In the first case the number of times the task still has to be performed is updated automatically in the messages generated by HATS; in the second case, the help message doesn't change until the user performs the atomic task that follows the one that can be repeated.

Finally, once the user has chosen the filling pattern, the help window will show:

*You have finished the task **Choose a Pattern for the Protection**.*
*Next you have to **Select the Shape to be Poached**.*
The following condition must hold: the selected shape must be the one you just created.
*You can do this task on the highlighted object by clicking with the **left** button of the mouse.*

In the previous message, the precondition on the next pending task is used to determine automatically that only one of the shapes can be selected, and that shape is the only one that is highlighted. The underlined part of the message is generated according to this situation.

5.4   Sequencing

The example we have studied is representative of a typical situation. The main situations that can arise besides those shown here correspond to different types of sequencing. As previously mentioned, ATOMS admits the specification of sequential, parallel, and alternative sequencing among subtasks of a given task. The previous subsections have been devoted to an example where only sequential subtasks have appeared. Next we shall outline the main features that characterize the help given by HATS in case of other types of sequencing.

159

In case of alternative sequencing HATS includes a message stating this, followed by a list of the alternative tasks, and, if in active mode, an explanation of how to start them. Double clicking on one of these tasks shows a corresponding description message for it. When in active mode, as soon as the user starts one of the alternative subtasks, HATS treats the situation as if that was the only alternative. The items in the Alternatives menu apply when the current help task is any of the mentioned ones, allowing the user to navigate through the different alternatives.

In case of parallel sequencing, HATS shows the list of subtasks, as in the previous case. Later on, in active mode it shows the task message corresponding to the task that follows the last atomic task that has been accomplished. When asked for context, HATS shows the list of those subtasks that are not finished, together with their corresponding next pending subtasks. HATS never shows information about nested alternative or parallel subtasks, unless it is in verbose behavior.

5.5   Design issues

The design of HATS help for a given application involves two parts: first, the task model has to be defined; after that, the designer must add help information to it. This information is formed by textual descriptions of tasks and preconditions, and the tasks that, when accomplished, will make preconditions to be satisfied.

Naming tasks, although simple, is an essential part of help design. Most parts of the messages previously shown that are highlighted with bold face are task names; they are inserted automatically by HATS in the corresponding help messages.

The descriptions of tasks and preconditions are just character strings that are included automatically by HATS in help messages when the corresponding tasks are being described. Previously we have seen messages that include these descriptions.

Parameter patterns are used to determine the parts of the window to be highlighted as complementary information to the help messages. They are specified in a way similar to task patterns (actually, both of them are instances of *Object Patterns,* a general object prototype that can be matched against other objects in the underlying object system). Moreover, preconditions are used as filters to the list of parts to be highlighted.

The reduced HATS design environment just allows task names and descriptions that appear in the HATS messages window to be edited. This is an essential feature, since usually, when visualizing help messages in context for the first time, the help designer finds out that the names and descriptions of many tasks, as well as those of preconditions, are not appropriate. All the remaining information included in help messages is automatically generated.

Tasks hierarchies and their associated help information can be reused in different applications. Tasks and their components are objects in the AMULET object system. Hence, each task is a potential prototype for instances of it, that inherit its properties, including help information. For example, multiple tasks are instances of a *multiple task* prototype that includes additional information like the number of repetitions.

A higher degree of reusability can be obtained by associating tasks to widgets. HATS based buttons include an instance of the *Click on the $Label button* task prototype. Their name is automatically generated using the label of the corresponding button. Dialog boxes are among the widgets for which defining corresponding tasks that include help information can be useful. For example, the dialog box for the selection of filling patterns in the example described at the beginning of this section is an instance of a generic widget for pattern selection, that includes a corresponding selection task.

5.6   HATS Architecture

The HATS system works in conjunction with the application it provides help for, and with ATOMS. Figure 5 shows the overall architecture. The system is driven by user events. Application events and the flow of information they generate are represented by solid arrows, while dashed arrows correspond to HATS events.

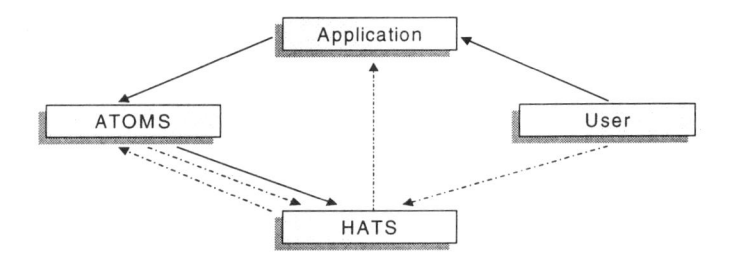

Figure 5. HATS framework.

As the diagram shows, both types of events are sent to HATS after passing through the ATOMS manager. HATS then displays help messages in its own window, and sends highlighting requests to the application window.

The generation of help messages is done as follows: according to what has just been said, HATS receives its input from ATOMS, that indicates the kind of event that has taken place (HATS or application), together with the relevant information at the task level, including any possible changes that affect one of the next pending tasks. HATS uses the information given by ATOMS in order to set a new state, and then a grammar is used for the generation of the messages.

TaskMsg = TaskDescrMsg | TaskActionMsg | TaskActiveMsg
TaskDescrMsg   = [Context] [TaskContentsMsg] TaskLocMsg
TaskActionMsg = [DescrContext] ActionMsg
DescrContext   = (IntroMsg | TaskContentsMsg | TaskLocMsg) (TaskContentsMsg
            | TaskLocMsg)*
IntroMsg = You have requested help about how to **TaskName**
TaskContentsMsg   = TaskRef **TaskDescr**
TaskRef = The task **TaskName** | IndTaskRef
IndTaskRef   = this task | its [first | last] subtask [,] **TaskName** [,]
TaskLocMsg = You can TaskAction on TaskLocDescr
TaskAction   = **TaskName** | do IndTaskRef
ActionMsg   = In order to TaskAction you have to ActionDescr
ActionDescr = fulfill the following tasks: **TaskName*** | EventDescr on TaskLocDescr
EventDescr   = [Double] Click with the **ButtonPosition** button of the mouse on
        TaskLocDescr

```
TaskActiveMsg  = [ ActiveContext ] ActiveMsg
ActiveContext  = [ FinishedMsg ] ActiveDescrMsg⁺
FinishedMsg = You have finished the task TaskName. You have done it on
     TaskLocDescr
ActiveDescrMsg = [ OptPendingDescr ] You are accomplishing the task TaskName
     I [ OptPendingDescr ] PendingDescr TaskName.
OptPendingDescr    = In order to do this task
PendingDescr    = ( First I Next I Finally ) you [ still ] have to
ActiveMsg    = PendingDescr EventDescr on TaskLocDescr
```

Figure 6. Grammar for help message generation (non verbose version).

Figure 6 shows a portion of the grammar, that is relevant for the example described in this section. The parts of the grammar that deal with keyboard events, sequencing, graphical references, and repetitions are omitted. The nonterminal elements of the grammar, encircled in a rectangle, represent single or composite messages; task names and other information accessible from each individual task are typed with bold letters, as it happens in the messages we have seen, and nonterminal elements that correspond to graphical references are underlined.

HATS includes a planner that chooses among the alternatives that appear explicitly in the grammar, and those that are implicit in references to graphical objects. For example, a task can be referred by its name or by an indirect reference like *this task*, depending on whether its name has appeared recently in the message. In the same way, the help message can refer to graphical objects or to a region where they are supposed to be, depending on the information HATS has at generation time. In case there is more than one graphical reference in the message, different colors are used, and corresponding references are included in the text.

6.   CONCLUSIONS AND FUTURE WORK

We have presented a system for the generation of task oriented help for interactive applications, that allows the design of the help component in a simple way once a task model for the application has been specified. The type of help provided by the system has many advantages, including the fact that help messages and instructions are updated automatically as the user accomplishes the corresponding tasks, and that they include references to parts of the window where actions can be performed. The system provides support for context sensitive complex tasks; this is achieved by means of a task model that includes task parameters.

Future work is aimed in three main directions: allowing the interactive specification of the task model for the application and the corresponding help information, developing a more sophisticated tool that allows the generation of tutorials about interactive applications that keep track of the student's work and interact with him, and extending our ideas to a distributed environment. The development of these plans also presents challenges about the integration with techniques developed in other user support systems, like Brad Myers' Topaz macro system (Myers, 1998), and Romain Zeiliger and David Kosbie's ACCEL distributed task system (Zeiliger, 1997).

7. ACKNOWLEDGMENT

This work has been partially supported by the Spanish *Plan Nacional de Investigación*, project number TIC96-0723-C02-01/02.

8. REFERENCES

Bhavnani, S.K. and John, B.E. (1996), Exploring the Unrealized Potential of Computer-Aided Drafting, in *Proceedings of CHI 96*, Vancouver, BC Canada, ACM Press.

Contreras, J. (1998) A Framework for the Automatic Generation of Software Tutoring. Phd. Thesis, Université René-Descartes, Paris.

Moriyón, R., Szekely, P. and Neches, R. (1994) Automatic Generation of Help from Interface Design Models, in *Proceedings of CHI'94*, ACM Press.

Myers, B.A., McDaniel, R.G., Miller, R.C., Ferrency, A., Faulring, A., Kyle, B.D., Mickish, A., Klimovitski, A. and Doane, P. (1997) The Amulet Environment: New Models for Effective User Interface Software Development. *IEEE Transactions on Software Engineering*, **23-6**, pp. 347-65.

Myers, B.A. (1998) Scripting Graphical Applications by Demonstration, to appear in *Proceedings CHI'98*, ACM Press.

Pangoli, S. and Paternó, F. (1995) Automatic Generation of Task-oriented Help, in *Proceedings UIST'95*, Pittsburgh, ACM Press.

Rodríguez, P., García, F., Contreras, J. and Moriyón, R. (1997) Parsing Technologies for User-Task Recognition, in *Proceedings of 5th International Workshop on Advances in Functional Modeling of Complex Technical Systems* (ed. M. Modarres), forthcoming.

Sukaviriya, P. and Foley, J.D. (1990) Coupling a UI Framework with Automatic Generation of Context-Sensitive Animated Help, in *Proceedings UIST'90*, ACM Press.

Szekely, P., Luo, P. and Neches, R. (1992) Facilitating de Exploration of Interface Design Alternatives: The HUMANOID Model of Interface Design, in *Proceedings SIGCHI'92*, ACM Press.

Zeiliger, R. and Kosbie, D. (1997) Automating Tasks for Groups of Users: A System-Wide "Epiphyte" Approach, in *INTERACT'97* (ed. S. Howard, J. Hammond and G. Lyndgaard), Chapman & Hall Press, IFIP, Sydney.

9. BIOGRAPHY

Federico García is a Ph.D. student at the Department of Computer Science of the U. Autónoma de Madrid since 1996. He is interested in tools for task model management.

Javier Contreras teaches at the Department of Computer Science of the U. Autónoma de Madrid since 1995. He is a former researcher at the Madrid IBM SC. He obtained his Ph.D. in U. Paris V, developing a tutoring system.

Pilar Rodríguez teaches at the Department of Computer Science of the U. Autónoma de Madrid since 1996. She is a former researcher at the Instituto de Ingeniería del Conocimiento and at the Madrid IBM SC. She holds a PhD in Physics.

Roberto Moriyón is Professor of the Department of Computer Science of the Universidad Autónoma de Madrid since 1980, and a researcher at the Instituto de Ingeniería del Conocimiento since 1989. He holds a PhD in Mathematics from Princeton University.

Discussion

Claus Unger: In your example, the task to be performed by the user is defined in a very precise way: why can't the user simply
- select the columns to be protected
- select the shape of the fire protection
- select the fill pattern

Federico Garcia: Because what the users usually want is to learn how to use a computer program. They usually have advanced domain knowledge from paper drawings, and they want to perform the same tasks with a computer. What we propose is not a tool for automating some common tasks, but a way to help users to perform common tasks in terms of simpler ones within the standard working context, so that later they are able to perform other similar tasks by themselves. If we just automated the execution of specific tasks, they wouldn't be able to learn how to perform similar ones.

Claus Unger: To my understanding, there is a fundamental difference between a tutorial system and an active help system. Your example more or less emphasizes the tutorial aspect of your approach.

Federico Garcia: Yes, there are similarities between our system and tutorial systems. Actually, our work is the basis for a more advanced tool whose focus is to provide designers with an environment for the creation of software courses. So, HATS is the first approach to address the problem of easily generating software courses, and it incorporates a guidance quite similar to tutoring guidance.

Fabio Paterno: I would prefer a task system that when the user performs a disabled action provides task-oriented explanation of why that action is disabled, and how to enable it, rather than a task system that explains which tasks cannot be done

Federico Garcia: The problem with our system is that it cannot detect such input events, only events that the underlying AMULET system sends to the application, so we can not receive that kind of input about disabled widgets.

Philipe Palanque: Couldn't you even get mouse positions?

Federico Garcia: Yes, that's possible, but then we wouldn't get one of AMULET's main benefits, which is portability over different platforms.

Prasun Dewan: Doesn't your task generation facility provide what Claus wanted?

Federico Garcia: I would reformulate the question as follows: Doesn't your HATS system provide automation for a task once the system has realised which task the user is currently performing?

Yes, but our objective is not to auto-execute but to instruct. Moreover, in many cases we cannot realise which task the user is performing until the final steps. For example, you cannot know which column the user wants to apply fire protection to until he chooses it. So, once the system knows the next concrete action, it can offer to perform it. Actually, in the current implementation, HATS provides a facility for automatic execution of tasks when all their needed parameters are bound.

Jean Scholtz: Do you have any plans to do user studies on your help system

Federico Garcia: Not yet. The system has been tested by some partners, but we agree that is not enough of a representative population.

Jean Scholtz: Oh, well please clarify the difference between descriptive help mode and active help mode.

Federico Garcia: In Descriptive help mode, the system provides meaning and hierarchical task decomposition, while in Active help mode more concrete and widget-oriented explanations are given, explaining only the next action to be performed in order to achieve the task that is currently being explained.

Joelle Coutaz: Do you plan to provide help within the application workspace (as in the MAC OS finder) rather than in a separate window (as in your current system)?

Federico Garcia: We've not considered that. The problem is that it is easier to provide that kind of integrated messages for a widget-oriented help system, while for a task-oriented help system the given explanations are usually more sophisticated and, as a consequence, longer and more difficult to integrate with the application interface. Of course, a separate window wouldn't be needed and an integrated pane could be added to application window.

Joelle Coutaz: Do you plan to work on helping the user to ask for help? The problem is that it is hard to formulate questions to the help system

Federico Garcia: Our aim is not to focus on how a user can ask for help on some topic. Currently, the user selects a task from a hierarchically sorted list of modelled tasks, or by hitting the help-key after beginning to perform a specific task.

Joelle Coutaz: That would constrain the vocabulary

Federico Garcia: Of course, ideally a user would request help by writing a question using natural language, and the system should have to extract the semantic information from that question to provide explanations. But this is out of our scope at this moment.

Laurence Nigay: You spoke of exploring groupware help - how would you specify tasks for groups?

Federico Garcia: The task modelling language we have developed to specify task models should be augmented to incorporate the notion of users and groups. From this notion, things such as constraints about what users (or groups) are allowed to perform some steps, or who has to perform some activities and under which circumstances, should be allowed to be expressed with our task-modelling language. Our current model includes parallelism among tasks, so extending our event parser to a distributed environment would not be a big problem.

Claus Unger: The same task can be performed in many different ways. Have you considered more flexible representations such as precedence graphs?

Federico Garcia: There is the need to reach a trade off between a representation flexible enough to express many different alternatives and a representation easy to provide help from. Task models may have powerful capabilities by using both pre and post conditions and different sequencing in a correct way. Moreover, the hierarchical decomposition of this representation provides a semantic content not present in precedence graphs. An additional advantage of task models is its growing use from the design point of view, being present in many current model-based development environments.

Toward the Automatic Construction of Task Models from Object-Oriented Diagrams

Shijian Lu[†], Cécile Paris[†] & Keith Vander Linden[‡]

[†] *CSIRO/MIS, Locked Bag 17, North Ryde, NSW 1670, Australia,*
{shijian.lu, cecile.paris}@cmis.csiro.au

[‡] *Department of Computer Science, Calvin College, Grand Rapids, MI 49546, USA,*
kvlinden@calvin.edu

Abstract: Task models bridge the gap between HCI and Software Engineering. They are useful both for interface design and for generating user interface code and user documentation. These benefits, however, are difficult to achieve because building task models from scratch is difficult. In this paper, we describe an approach for automatically constructing task models from object-oriented diagrams in a CASE tool. The approach exploits the common semantic ground between task models and system-behaviour models, namely use cases, use case diagrams and sequence diagrams. We identify the useful information contained in these diagrams and how it can be augmented to support task model construction. A prototype system is then described, together with a working example.

Key words: Formal models of user interfaces, Task models, information reuse, methodology, tools, Object-Oriented analysis and design

1.   INTRODUCTION

Task models are becoming popular in software development. They are employed in the early stages of the software development life-cycle, e.g., in requirements analysis (Sebillotte, 1995) and in design (Hix and Hartson, 1993). They are also used for implementation (Smith and O'Neill, 1996) and evaluation (Card *et al.*, 1983). They can drive prototyping of user interfaces (Johnson *et al.*, 1995) or act as communication tools between all participants in the software design process, i.e., between software engineers, HCI specialists, end users and even technical writers (O'Neill, 1996, Balbo and Lindley, 1997). Properly formalised, task models can be used to generate user interface code (Szekely *et al.*, 1993, Wilson and Johnson, 1996, Puerta, 1997) and to produce user documentation (Paris and Vander Linden, 1996b).

Given that task models are so useful in software development, the question of how they can be produced becomes important, as building them by hand from scratch can be difficult and time consuming (Paris and Vander Linden, 1996a). It is thus desirable to acquire automatically as much of them as possible from existing information sources.

One possible source of information for task models is Object Oriented (OO) models as used in Computer Aided Software Engineering (CASE) tools. While CASE tools have traditionally been used to assist in software design, implementation and validation, the system behaviour models they contain can also be reused to build the task models required for other purposes, such as the generation of user interface code and user documentation. We have built a task model acquisition module (TMAM) to automate this process. A typical usage scenario for this type of software development environment is as follows:

1. Designers build OO diagrams during system analysis and design. They could also build them as part of reverse engineering or system re-engineering;
2. Designers use the TMAM to automatically construct task models from the OO diagrams;
3. Interface designers and writers then load the task models into a task model editor, modify them as appropriate, and use them to generate prototypes of the user interface and drafts of the user documentation.

In addition to speeding up the software development process, the automatic acquisition of task models has other benefits. First, if the user documentation and on-line help are generated automatically from the acquired task models, they are guaranteed to be consistent with the underlying application they document, even if the functionality of the application changes during the development process. The task of producing the documentation in a timely fashion and yet ensuring its consistency with the application's functionality is otherwise a difficult task. Second, the user interface designed from the task models will be easier to integrate with the rest of the application modules because the task models were constructed with reference to the actual elements of the application design.

This paper presents a practical approach for augmenting information contained in OO diagrams in order to construct coherent task models. Although this approach is generally useful for interface design, it is directly motivated by reducing design information for the generation of user or task-oriented documentation. Throughout the paper, we illustrate our points with a sample application, STE (Simple Text Editor). STE is a simple freeware text editor that we reverse-engineered.

The paper is structured as follows. Section 2 gives a brief account of Diane+, the formal representation of task models we have chosen in our work. It is followed, in section 3, by an analysis of the different diagrams offered by the Unified Modeling language (UML) as supported by Rational Rose™ version 4.0, the tool we employ.[1] Use cases, use case diagrams and sequence diagrams are identified as primary information sources for constructing task models. Sections 4 and 5 give a detailed comparison of task models with use cases and with scenario diagrams respectively. The prototype system is described in section 6 together with a working example.

Table 1. Some of Diane+ task attributes and their graphical representation

Task Attribute	Graphical form	Explanation
Interactive		Task in which user interacts with system
Manual		Task performed solely by user
Automatic		Task performed solely by system
Elementary		Task without a decomposition (no shading)
Composite		Task with a decomposition (shaded box)
Decomposition		Task refinement
Feed back		Feedback provided to the user by the application (e.g., message printed)
Mandatory		Task must be performed (box in solid lines)
Optional		Task is optional (box in dotted lines)
Parallelism		Tasks can be performed in parallel
Task sequence		Order of task to be performed
Sequence precondition.	If a>0	Condition under which the link is to be followed
Comment	(text area)	Task Comment
Task precondition		Condition that must be true for the task to be applicable
Terminal node		Normal end of the task

---

[1] Note that the diagrams offered by this software are fairly typical of the diagrams used in Object-Oriented CASE tools.

171

2. DIANE+ NOTATION

We chose Diane+ (Tarby and Barthet, 1996) as our task model formalism. It is a typical task model formalism in that it allows for the representation of hierarchically structured tasks and provides a variety of procedural annotations for these tasks. We chose Diane+ over other task models because of its coverage of the information required to produce documentation. (The interested reader is referred to (Paris *et al.*, 1997) for a more detailed account of the motivation for this choice.) Diane+ employs a graphical notation to represent task decomposition as well as temporal and logical relationships amongst the tasks. In a Diane+ diagram, tasks are represented by boxes which contain the name of the task and, when appropriate, the constraints on the number of times the task can be executed. The shape of the box represents the actor of the task, i.e., whether it is the end user, the system, or combination of both. Table 1 lists the attributes provided by Diane+ that we use in our work.[2]

3. WHICH UML DIAGRAM?

Task models as defined in HCI provide a user-oriented view of a system. Object-oriented modelling languages, on the other hand, tend to offer two system-oriented views, one describing the application's structure and the other the application's behaviour. UML (UML, 1997), the OO modelling language we have used in this project, is no exception. It models the application's structure with class diagrams and the application's behaviour with use cases, use case diagrams, state transition and interaction diagrams.[3] Task models and OO models of the application's behaviour can be seen as semantically equivalent; with the former representing an overt, user-oriented view of application's behaviour, and the latter representing an internal, system-oriented view of that behaviour. In essence, thus, they are *both* concerned with dynamic behaviour of the application. Therefore, in our attempt to automatically generate task models, we focus our investigation on the models of the application's behaviour provided by a CASE tool, i.e., use cases and use case diagrams, interaction diagrams, and state transition diagrams. This section briefly describes each in turn. The next two sections then discuss how they can be exploited to construct task models automatically.

---

[2] We added the notion of *feedback* to the original Diane+ formalism, as this concept is an important one for documentation

[3] As in any rapidly evolving field, people often use different terms to refer to the same thing, or use the same term to refer to different concepts. For example, Booch's (1993) object diagrams and interaction diagrams are equivalent to collaboration diagrams and sequence diagrams respectively in UML (1997). However, in UML, object diagrams comprise static and dynamic forms, while interaction diagrams or scenario diagrams include both collaboration diagrams and sequence diagrams. In this paper, we use UML's terminology.

3.1   Use cases and use case diagrams

Use cases are created during object-oriented requirements analysis. Each identifies a thread of potential use for the system to be constructed (Pressman, 1997). Use case diagrams show the relationship between users and the use cases within an application. Together, use cases and use case diagrams identify the agents that will use the application and the high-level goals that these agents have with respect to the application. They are thus useful to describe the tasks a user will perform with the application.

3.2   Interaction diagrams

Interaction diagrams describe how objects collaborate to carry out the activities of a use case. They specify the sequence of messages that are passed between the application objects, some of which are user perceivable objects (e.g., interface widgets) and others are non-perceivable objects (e.g., internal application objects). Interaction diagrams are useful for constructing task models in that they indicate what actions the user performs, and what the system does in response to those actions.

Interaction diagrams come in two forms based on the same underlying information, but each emphasising on a particular aspect of it. *Sequence diagrams* show interactions arranged in time sequence, i.e., the messages that objects exchange are arranged in time sequence. *Collaboration diagrams* show interactions organised around the objects, and relationships amongst objects. Since these two forms of interaction diagrams can be automatically generated from each other, either can be used. We have arbitrarily used sequence diagrams in this study.

3.3   State (transition) diagrams

In UML, state diagrams can be used to show the sequence of states that either a single object, or perhaps the entire system, goes through during its life in response to received stimuli, together with its responses and actions. State diagrams for single objects are of limited use because an end user task is normally achieved through interactions between multiple objects. State diagrams for the entire system, on the other hand, would be a good source of information for task models. When fully developed, a state diagram for a system would contain exhaustive information about the application's behaviour in response to the user's actions. However, this comprehensive state diagram tends to be too complicated to build, and is, therefore, seldom used in practice. For these reasons, we have excluded state diagrams from further investigation, until such time as they are used more fully in practice.

4.   USE CASES AND USE CASE DIAGRAMS *VS* TASK MODELS

As mentioned earlier, use cases capture the user requirements for an application by describing how and to what ends an application will be used (Jacobson *et al.*, 1995). Semantically, they also define abstract or composite tasks. Consider the example shown in Figure 1. It provides a simplified use case for the composite task of saving a file in STE, the application we employed for our test-bed. This use case gives a clear description of how the user interacts with the system to accomplish the task of saving a file. Task models expect these composite tasks to have explicitly defined attributes and to be hierarchically decomposable. This section discusses UML's support for these two things.

4.1   Composite task attributes

Although use cases and composite tasks are equivalent semantically, they are not equal. For instance, composite tasks in a task model, such as a Diane+ model, have task attributes explicitly defined (refer to Table 1). This is not the case for use cases. While some task attributes may be explicitly defined, others are defined implicitly and some may be of no concern at all:

- *Explicitly defined attributes* – In UML, the name and textual description are explicitly represented for a use case;
- *Implicitly defined attributes* – Although not explicitly defined, one can determine whether the task is manual, automatic, or interactive (see table 1) based on the actor specified for the task;
- *Unrepresented attributes* - Some information required to construct task models is difficult if not impossible to extract automatically from a UML use case. Examples include task preconditions and feedback. For example, the last statement in the Figure 1 is an expression of task feedback. Because UML has no explicit representation for task feedback, such information is usually included in the use case description. Extracting this information from free text would require sophisticated language processing.[4] The same is true of preconditions in UML.

---

[4] While it would not be possible to process free text, we are investigating the use of a *controlled language* for these descriptions, from which it is then possible to obtain information, because of the regularity it imposes on the text.

174

1)	The user chooses the save option from file menu.
2)	The system checks the document status.
3)	If it is an existing file, the system saves the file.
4)	If it is a new file, the Save File dialog appears.
5)	The user chooses a folder.
6)	The user enters a file name.
7)	The user clicks the Save button.
8)	The system saves the file.
9)	When saving, the saving progress bar can be observed by the user.

Figure 1. A simplified use case: Save file.

4.2   Hierarchical decomposition

In task modelling languages, composite tasks can be hierarchically decomposed. This is also true in UML. In Rose's implementation of UML, a use case is elaborated by attaching either a subordinate use case diagram (if it is relatively complex) or a sequence diagram (if it is relatively simple). In UML version 1.0, apart from communicate relationships between an actor and a use case, there are two types of elaboration relationships between use cases: *extend* and *use*. The extend relationship is used to express conditional behaviour while the use relationship is used to describe common behaviour between two or more use cases. For example, a possible use case diagram for Figure 1 would be something like Figure 2. There are 3 use cases in this diagram, Start saving, Execute saving, and Specify file information. Start saving will typically cover the behaviour described by (1) and (2) in Figure 1 while Execute saving from (8) to (9) and Specify file information from (4) to (7). The relationships between Start saving and Execute saving, Specify file information are extend relationships. That is, an instance of Start saving may include the behaviour specified by use case Execute saving or Specify file information depending on whether the file being saved is an existing or a new file. Specify file information is related to Execute saving by a use relationship. In other words, the behaviour described in Execute saving is mandatory to Specify file information.

175

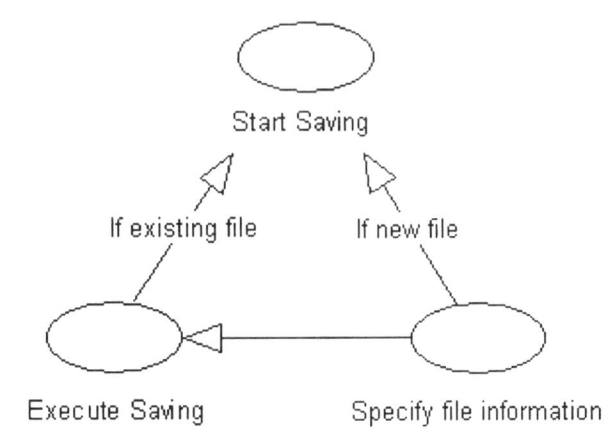

Figure 2. A use case diagram that elaborates Save file use case.

Based on the discussion above, we conclude that the nesting between use cases and use case diagrams is equivalent to task hierarchical decomposition. In particular, we see the following:

- All use cases inside a use case diagram can be seen as sub-tasks of the composite task corresponding to the use case diagram;
- Extend relationships (with associated preconditions) between use cases can be seen as conditional task sequence relationships, from the extended task to the extending task;
- Use relationships between use cases can be seen as task sequence relationships, from the using task to the used task;
- Unrelated use cases can be seen as tasks parallel to each other.

Given these similarities, we can automatically convert use cases and use case diagrams into hierarchically decomposed task models. The task attributes that cannot be determined automatically have to be added manually as appropriate.

5.   INTERACTION DIAGRAMS VERSUS TASK MODELS

A use case is semantically equivalent to a composite task, and sequence diagrams are used to elaborate use cases. What is the relationship between sequence diagrams and task models? To answer this question, we need to explore how much information contained in sequence diagrams could be reused to generate task models. To help focus our comparison between these two formalisms, we have specified the behaviour of STE, our simple text editor, using both a sequence diagram, Figure 3, and a Diane+ task model, Figure 4.

The sequence diagram in Figure 3 was obtained by reverse engineering the STE application, by experimenting with it, and by referring to the system code. The diagram in Figure 3 describes a scenario in which the application contains a newly created document, and the user saves the document before quitting. As we can see, the selection of the "Quit" option leads to a series of messages being passed to a number of objects, including:

- When the user selects the "Quit" option, the menu object sends the "quit()" message to the application's main object, "instance STE".
- The "instance STE" object sends a "close()" message to "myDoc", the main document object.
- The object "myDoc" checks whether it has been saved. (event 4)
- If "myDoc" has not been saved, it sends a message to open the "toSave" dialog box. This "if" condition is specified textually in the comment column on the left.
- The user presses the "OK" button. (event 11)
- The system determines that this is a new document, so it calls the "Save File Dialog".
- The user selects a folder, enters a file name, and clicks the "OK" button.
- The system saves the document and exits the application.

We also built the corresponding Diane+ task model for the exit task, based on our experience using the application. This task model is presented in Figure 4. As shown there, "Quit STE" is an interactive composite task that is decomposed in a sequence of elementary tasks. The interactive task "select quit option" is followed by an automatic task "show toSave dialog", and so on. By comparing Figures 3 and 4, it becomes clear that sequence diagrams contain much more system-internal information than do their corresponding task models, and that sequence diagrams do not allow for the specification of all task attributes present in task models.

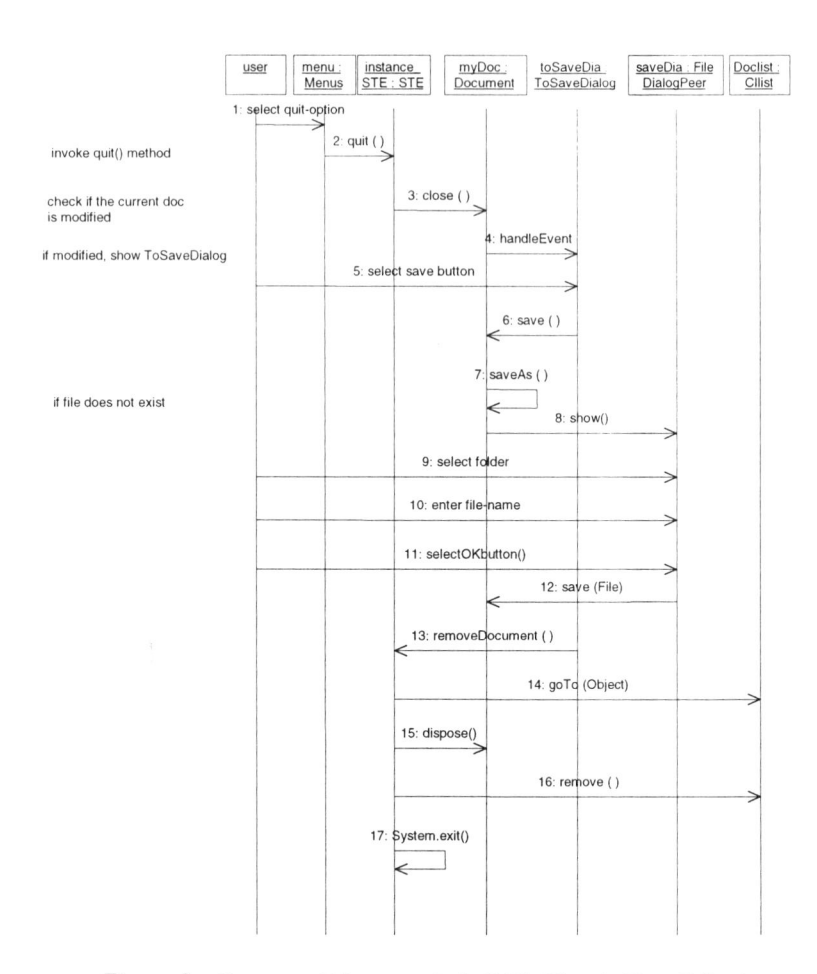

Figure 3.   Sequence Diagram: Quit STE (Simple Text Editor).

5.1   Overt and Internal Behaviour

Sequence diagrams focus on system-internal, inter-object message activity.   In Figure 3, for example, we can see that, when the user selects the quit button, the menu item instance sends a "quit()" message to the "instance STE" object. That object in turn sends a "close()" message to the document instance. These system details are largely invisible to the end user. This focus on internal activities is not surprising.   Sequence diagrams are intended to facilitate system design, and therefore focus on how objects, whether visible or invisible, collaborate with each other to deliver the required functionality. Task models, on the other hand, are intended to describe how users interact with a system in performing certain tasks. They must, therefore, focus more on overt behaviour.

We should note that task models do capture some system actions. For example, message 4 in the sequence diagram roughly corresponds to the sub-task "[system]show toSave dialog box" in the task model. Similarly, message 8 corresponds to the action "[system] show Save-as dialog box", and, finally, message 12 to the action "[system] save file". A closer look at messages 4 and 8 reveals that they both display interface elements to the user. Message 12 saves the file, which is also discernable by the user.

Based on the above analysis and other examples, we conclude that sequence diagrams are a superset of task models in that task models mainly describe the overt behaviour of the users and the system, while sequence diagrams additionally represent the system's internal behaviour.

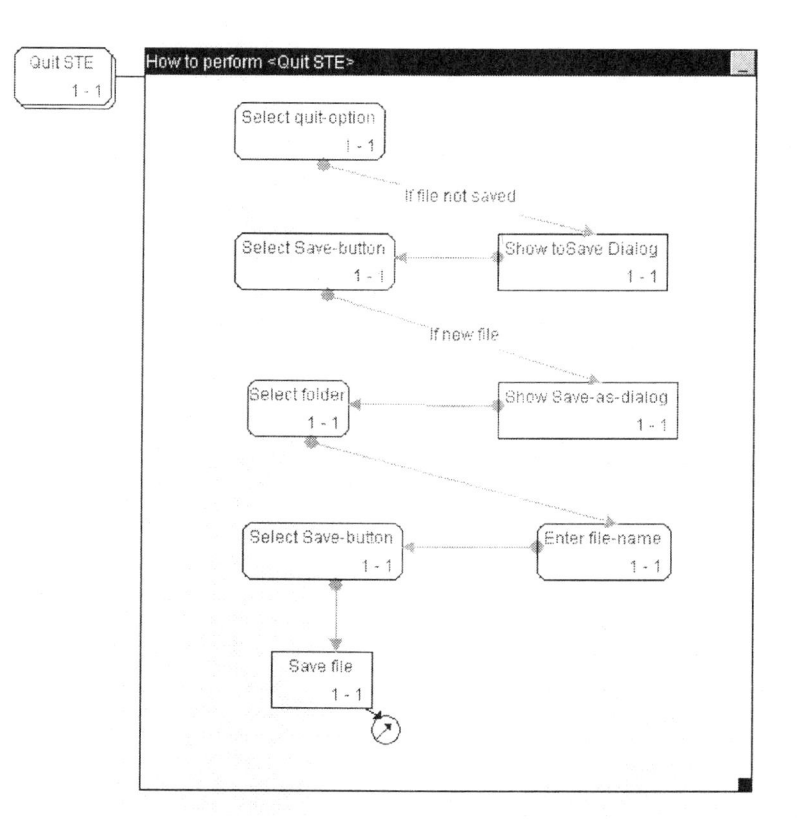

Figure 4. Diane+ model for quitting STE.

179

5.2   Non-Composite Task Attributes

A second difference between sequence diagrams and task models is that messages in sequence diagrams do not explicitly specify all the task attributes present in task models. We made a similar observation concerning use cases in section 4.1:

- *Explicitly defined attributes* – Many task attributes are explicitly specified in the sequence diagram. For example, the temporal relationships amongst tasks;
- *Inferred attributes* – Some task attributes can be inferred from sequence diagrams. For example, whether a task is interactive or automatic can be inferred from whether the sender of the message is the user or not;
- *Unrepresented attributes* – Some task attributes are not captured in sequence diagrams. For example, sequence diagrams do not specify multiple paths of execution, task repetition, or whether the action is optional or required. Textual notes may be placed in the left column to indicate these attributes, but these texts, at least in general, are too unstructured to be converted easily into task attributes.

5.3   Summary

In summary, then, we have the following relationships between sequence diagrams and task models:

- sequence diagrams are roughly equivalent to composite tasks in a task model;
- messages between objects in a sequence diagram are roughly equivalent to elementary tasks;
- all messages inside a sequence diagram are roughly equivalent to sub-tasks of the composite task corresponding to the sequence diagram.

Given these similarities, we can design an algorithm to construct automatically a task model from a sequence diagram. Generally, the sequence diagram messages can be converted to task model tasks of the appropriate types. However, it is clear that the sequence diagram contains a considerable amount of system-internal information that is not needed in the task model. To address this problem, we use a number of heuristics that filter out irrelevant messages:

- keep all user-initiated messages;
- if the first message is not a user-initiated message, then keep the message immediately before the first user-initiated message;
- keep the message immediately following the last user-initiated message, if there is one;
- if the message immediately following the last user message is not the last the message in the sequence diagrams, then keep the last message as well.

6.   THE SYSTEM AND A WORKING EXAMPLE

We have developed a task model acquisition module (TMAM) which automatically

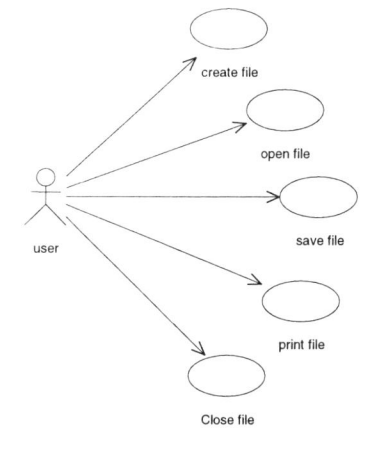

Figure 5. Use case diagram: use stePro.

constructs Diane+ task models from UML use cases, use case diagrams, and
sequence diagrams. The algorithms employed by this tool are based on the analysis
given in the previous sections and are implemented within the Rational Rose CASE
tool using Rose script.

The TMAM starts from the top-level use case diagram in an UML system
behaviour model. After transforming all use cases and their relationships into partial

Figure 6. Use case diagram: save file.

task models, it will iterate through each use case and transform its subordinate use
case diagram(s) or sequence diagram(s).

For STE, the TMAM first creates a use case diagram called "use stePro". It is
shown in Figure 5. This diagram models the fact that a user could perform 5 basic
tasks with STE: "create file", "save file", "open file", "print file", and "close

181

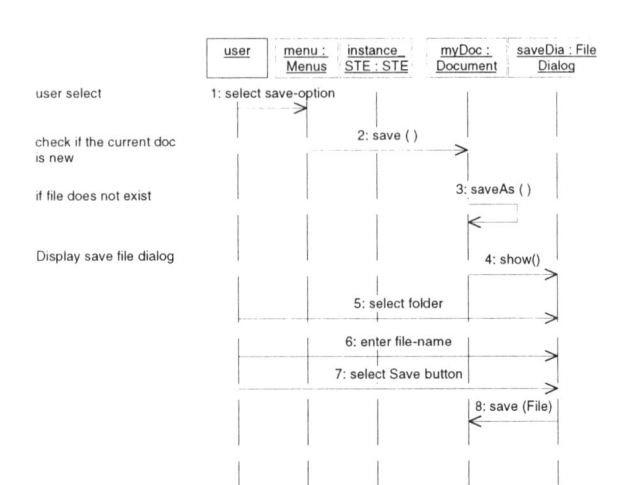

Figure 7. Sequence diagram: save new file.

file". All of these tasks are internally complex, but for the sake of simplicity, only the "save file" use case is further elaborated here. Its elaboration, the "save file" use case, is shown in Figure 6. This use case diagram models the fact that the user may save either a new file ("save new file") or an existing file ("save existing file"). At this point, the designer decides that this is a sufficient level of detail for the use case analysis. He or she then defines the "save new file" sequence diagram, shown in Figure 7. This diagram specifies exactly how the objects in the application will collaborate to deliver the functionality required by the "save new file" use case. Briefly, the sequence diagram shows that, when the user chooses save option from file menu, a series of internal system actions will eventually bring up a "save file" dialog box. At this point, the user must select the desired folder, enter a file name, and click on the "save" button. This results in the application actually performing the action of saving the file. A similar sequence diagram would be created for the "save existing file" use case.

Given the UML behavioural model just created, the TMAM automatically constructs the corresponding task model, as shown in Figure 8.[5] This model is displayed using a task model editor (TAMOT), which we built in JAVA. In Figure

---

[5] The layout has been modified. The TMAM does not yet produce a totally acceptable layout for the task model derived automatically. This is due to the fact that coordinates have to be added to the task model on the fly. We are currently working on obtaining a reasonable layout automatically.

8, composite task "use stePro" is decomposed into 5 parallel composite sub-tasks, one of which, "save file", is further decomposed into "save new file" and "save existing file". The "save new file" task is decomposed into a sequence of elementary tasks which correspond to the "save new file" sequence diagram. Note that messages 2 and 3, modeled in the "save new file" sequence diagram, have been filtered out using the heuristics presented in the previous section.

Although the task model shown in Figure 8 is accurate and useful, it is seldom the case that automatically constructed task models can be used without modification. This is the motivation for building the dedicated editor, the TAMOT. It allows one to modify various aspects of the task model. Typically, changes will include:

- *The names of elementary tasks* - The displayed name of an elementary task depends on whether its corresponding message is the user or not. If it is the user, the name of the message is taken as the task name (e.g., "select save-option" and "enter file name"). Otherwise, the name of the message together with the name of the receiving object's class name is used (e.g., "show File Dialog" and "save Document"). While the names are acceptable in this example, it is possible that inaccurate names may be constructed. TAMOT allows the user to modify them manually.
- *The number of elementary tasks* - The number of elementary tasks that get created in the task model is determined by the filter heuristics described in Section 5. The filtering rules worked nicely for this example, but their effectiveness in a large example is yet to be tested. It is likely that in some cases the user will have to add or remove elementary tasks.
- *Task preconditions and feedback* - As discussed earlier, it is difficult to automatically derive task preconditions and feedback from the textual comments in the UML model. The user, therefore, will need to add them manually by referring to the ancestral use case description.

183

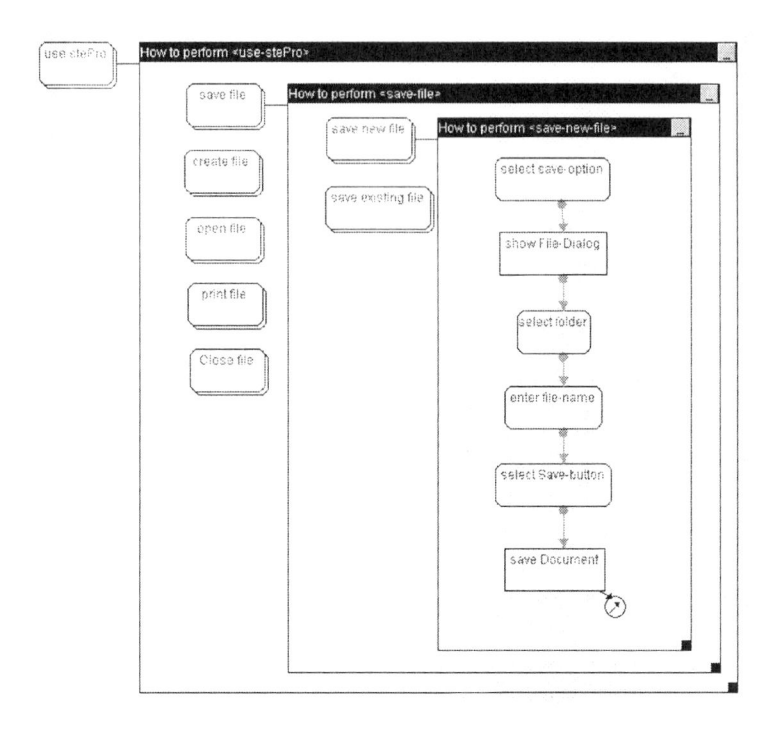

Figure 8. Resulting task model (displayed by TAMOT).

7.   SUMMARY AND CONCLUSIONS

Task models are increasingly used for a variety of purposes, but constructing them remains a difficult task. In this paper, we presented a practical way of automatically acquiring task models from system behaviour models defined by object-oriented diagrams. In particular, we focussed on UML use cases, use case diagrams, and sequence diagrams.   By successfully exploiting the common semantic ground covered by system behaviour models and task models, we showed how information contained in these diagrams could be augmented and filtered to construct task models. We then presented a working prototype, demonstrating that substantial portions of a task model can be obtained automatically.

Of course, it is not clear that building UML behavioural models is any easier than building Diane+ task models. However, it is clear that OO CASE tools are gaining widespread acceptance. This means that we will be able to take advantage of pre-existing knowledge sources by reusing the information they contain in order to cut the effort required to build task models.

In addition, our approach brings the software engineering and interface design communities a step closer together. This is important as the two communities need to work together to produce software systems that are correct and useful. Furthermore, the approach may also allow for the documentation production to be better integrated into the software development life cycle, as task models serve as a basis to produce documentation.

In our work, we have successfully used our derived task models to generate on-line user documentation (Paris *et al.*, 1998). In future work, we intend to apply our technique in a "real world" setting. This will generate the empirical data that we need to improve our system to the point where it is truly practical and deployable. We also intend to investigate the use of the task models for generating user interface code. Finally, we are exploring the possibility of building a unified model that integrates task models and OO diagrams (Lu *et al.*, 1998). This unified model would further tighten the relationship between human computer interaction and software engineering.

ACKNOWLEDGMENTS

This work is partially supported by the Office of Naval Research (ONR) – Grant N00014096-1-0465 – in the program for User Centred Direct Interaction Systems. We gratefully acknowledge the participation of Sandrine Balbo and Nadine Ozkan, and are thankful to Valery Anciaux and Christophe Plier for their contribution to the implementation of the task model editor.

REFERENCES

(Balbo and Lindley, 1997) Balbo, S. and Lindley, C. Adaptation of a task analysis methodology to the design of a decision support system. In *Proceedings of Interact'97*, Sydney, Australia, 1997.

(Booch, 1993) Booch, G. *Object-oriented Analysis and design with applications.* Benjamin Cummings, Redwood City, 2nd edition, 1993.

(Card *et al.*, 1983) Card, S.K., Moran, T.P. and Newell, A. *The psychology of human computer interaction.* Lawrence Erlbaum Associations, 1993.

(Hix and Hartson, 1993) Hix, D. and Hartson, R. *Developing user interfaces, ensuring usability through product and process.* Wiley, 1993.

(Jacobson *et al.*, 1995) Jacobson, I, Christerson, M, Jonsson, P. and Overgard, G. *Object oriented software engineering: a use case driven approach.* Menlo Park, California, Addison-Wesley, 1995.

(Johnson *et al.,* 1995) Johnson, P. Johnson, H. and Wilson, S. Rapid prototyping of user interfaces driven by task models. In *Scenario based design: envisioning work and technology in system development* (ed. J.M Carroll), John Wiley, New York, 1995.

(Lu *et al.*, 1998) Lu, S., Paris C. and Vander Linden K. Integrating task modelling into the object oriented design process: a pragmatic approach. Position paper at CHI'98 workshop on Incorporating Work, Processes and Task Analysis into Industrial Object-Oriented Systems Design. April, 1998.

(O'Neill, 1996) O'Neill, E.J. Task model support for cooperative analysis. In *Proceedings of CHI'96*, 1996.

(Paris and Vander Linden, 1996a) Paris, C. and Vander Linden K. An overview of on-line documentation and CASE tool: Isolde, Report on task 1 and 3. Technical report ITRI-95-16, ITRI, University of Brighton, UK, 1996.

(Paris and Vander Linden, 1996b) Paris, C. and Vander Linden K "DRAFTER: An interactive support tool for writing multilingual instructions", *IEEE Computer*, 29(7):49-56, 1996.

(Paris *et al.*, 1997) Paris, C., Balbo, S. and Ozkan, N. Novel uses of task models: two case studies. Presented at the *NATO/ONR workshop on cognitive tasks*, CSIRO Technical Report, 1997.

(Paris *et al.*, 1998) Paris, C., Vander Linden, K. and Lu, S.: Automatic Document Creation from Software Specifications. In the *Proceedings of the 3rd Australian Document Computing Symposium (ADCS'98)*, J. Kay and M. Milosavljevic (eds), Sydney, August 1998.

(Pressman, 1997) Pressman, R.S. (1997) *Software Engineering: A Practitioner's Approach*. International Edition, McGraw-Hill.

(Puerta, 1997). Puerta, A.R A model-based interface development environment. *IEEE Software*, July/August, 1997.

(Sebillotte, 1995) Sebillotte, S. Methodology guide to task analysis with the goal of extracting relevant characteristics for interfaces. Technical report for Esprit project P6593, INRIA, Rocquencourt, France, 1995.

(Smith and O'Neill, 1996) Smith, M.J and O'Neill, J.E. Beyond task analysis: Exploiting task models in application implementation. In *Proceedings of CHI'96.* (1996)

(Szekely *et al.*, 1993) Szekely, P. Luo, P. and Neches, R. Beyond Interface builders: Model-based interface tools. In *Proceedings of InterCHI'93*, ACM, 1993.

(Tarby and Barthet, 1996) Tarby, J-C and Barthet, M-F (1996) the Diane+ method. In *Proceedings of the second international workshop on computer-aided design of user interfaces*. Namur, Belgium, June, 1996.

(UML, 1997) UML Notation Guide: unified modelling language version 1.0, Rational Software corporation, 1997.

(Wilson and Johnson, 1996) Wilson, S. and Johnson, P. Bridging the generation gap: from work tasks to user interface design. In *Proceedings of CADUI'96* 1996

BIOGRAPHY

Dr Shijian Lu is currently a senior research scientist in CSIRO Mathematical and Information Sciences, Australia. Before joining CSIRO in 1995, he was a research fellow in the Center for Cognitive Science, Denmark. He holds a BS degree from Shandong Institute of Mining and Technology, China and PhD degree from Leeds University, UK. His research interests include many aspects of HCI such as information and knowledge representation, multimedia multimodal interface design, and incorporating HCI into object oriented software development process.

Dr Cécile Paris is the research leader of the Intelligent Interactive Technology Project (IIT) at CSIRO, the Australian National Research Center. This research group is part of the Mathematical and Information Sciences Division, and is concerned with a variety of issues dealing with human-computer interaction (HCI). Dr Paris' research is primarily in language research engineering, but also involves multimedia presentation, user modeling, user interface design and evaluation, authoring tools, integration of HCI into software engineering, and software internationalization and localization. Dr Paris received a BA in computer science from the University of California in Berkeley, and an MS and a PhD in computer science from Columbia University (New York).

Dr Keith Vander Linden is a faculty member in the department of Computer Science at Calvin College, Grand Rapids, MI, USA. He received an MS in Computer Science from the University of Iowa and a PhD in Computer Science and Cognitive Science from the University of Colorado. His research interests include Artificial Intelligence, Cognitive Science, Software Engineering and User Interface Design.

Discussion

Gilbert Cockton: Do you really think use cases represent the user context?

Shijian Lu: Yes, I do. Use cases do capture SOME aspects of user context. This is one of the main reasons why use cases are popular in the OO community. Having said that, however, I, by no means claim that use cases capture ALL aspects of user context.

Fabio Paterno: So why do you use cases rather than task specifications?

Shijian Lu: Because they are mainstream within OO software engineering

Fabio Paterno: But they do not address good design, they do not start with a good set of task descriptions

Shijian Lu: Yes/no, but I think there are two different issues here. The first issue is that given that use cases are widely used in OO community, is there anyway in which use cases as defined in the design specification can be put into uses other than motivating system design? And that is the concern of this paper. The second issue is that use cases as a mechanism for capturing requirements have aforementioned short-comings, how can we do better in the future? The latter was addressed at the CHI'98 workshop on incorporating work, process and task analysis into commercial and industrial Object-Oriented systems development, where suitable extensions to UML were proposed.

Fabio Paterno: So would you try to base use cases on task modelling?

Shijian Lu: Ideally, in my view, it would be better to use task analysis and modelling to replace use cases altogether. But, the pragmatic may lead to different courses.

Remi Bastide: Wouldn't that put ergonomists out of a job? They currently begin the software lifecycle with task modelling. Their results are then used by engineers. Your implicit lifecycle is different

Shijian Lu: No, typically, what gets constructed would be a draft task model. Therefore, ergonomists are still needed for fleshing out the model. You are right in that, the lifecycle here is different. We are concerned with re-using information contained in an existing design specification.

Joelle Cockton: One things to remember in system design is that the initial task model will not match the final task model for the user once the system has been developed.

Len Bass: The question of whether use cases or task models should be done first is a marketing question, not a technical question. The fact is that use case modelling is the only modelling technique that is used by software developers, and levering off this fact may increase the usage of task models

Morton Borup Harning: Given that task models that your system generate are not sufficient when seen from a user's point of view, could you edit the generated task models and then feed these changes back into the original use cases, improving or at least pointing out its short comings

Shijian Lu: That's a good idea, that we need to explore.

Methods for Identifying Usability Problems with Web Sites

Jean Scholtz
National Institute of Standards and Technology, Gaithersburg, MD USA, jean.scholtz@nist.gov

Laura Downey
Vignette Corporation,Austin, TX USA,laura@vignette.com

Abstract: The dynamic nature of the Web poses problems for usability evaluations. Development times are rapid and changes to Web sites occur frequently, often without a chance to re-evaluate the usability of the entire site. New advances in Web developments change user expectations. In order to incorporate usability evaluations into such an environment, we must produce methods that are compatible with the development constraints. We believe that rapid, remote, and automated evaluation techniques are key to ensuring usable Web sites. In this paper, we describe three studies we carried out to explore the feasibility of using modified usability testing methods or non-traditional methods of obtaining information about usability to satisfy our criteria of rapid, remote, and automated evaluation. Based on lessons learned in these case studies, we are developing tools for rapid, remote, and automated usability evaluations. Our future work includes using these tools on a variety of Web sites to determine 1) their effectiveness compared to traditional evaluation methods, 2) the optimal types of sites and stages of development for each tool, and 3) tool enhancements.

Key words: Usability testing, Web development, Web site design, Remote usability testing, Web site evaluation

1. WEB DEVELOPMENT CONSTRAINTS ON USABILITY EVALUATION

Web development places severe time constraints on developers and evaluators because of the rapid development and release cycle. The tight coupling of content, navigation, and appearance of Web sites means that separate evaluation of any one component is not meaningful. Web sites also change frequently. We feel it is safe to assume that in the majority of cases, there is no testing of the entire site to see how the new portion fits in, even if the new portion has been evaluated. Web sites must evolve as users' expectations change and as new software and hardware developments are implemented in the Web sites of others and content becomes outdated. This implies that usability evaluations for Web sites should be a continuous effort. But the traditional usability tests, and even Nielsen's (1989) "discount usability testing," take time, especially if one has to test an entire Web site.

Web sites reach a diverse audience. Getting representative users to come to a usability laboratory to participate in an evaluation is often not feasible. More importantly, users view Web sites with different types of browsers, preferences, and internet connections. Testing under all these different conditions adds to the time and complexity of setting up and conducting laboratory tests. Therefore, tools to monitor existing sites for potential usability problems should be very useful to Web site developers.

While traditional software has the same constraints, we maintain that these constraints are more severe when developing Web sites and Web-based applications. However, the Web facilitates quick and widespread delivery of information. Moreover, Web server logs record much information about user interactions with Web sites. We wanted to see if we could take advantage of these two properties in developing some methods for obtaining usability information for Web-based software.

2. TRADITIONAL USABILITY EVALUATION METHODS

Jeffries et al. (1991) compared usability evaluation methods and identified advantages and disadvantages of several techniques, including usability testing. John and Marks (1997) compared the effectiveness of several usability evaluation methods to laboratory usability tests and found that less then half of the problems predicted were observed in usability tests. Nielsen (1993) found laboratory testing of users to be the most effective source of information for identifying usability data. In-house user testing is expensive and places limits on the type and number of users geographically available. Moreover, in-house testing does not allow evaluators to view use in the context of other work activities and the users' hardware and software configurations.

Remote testing has been getting increased attention in the evaluation community. Remote testing can be done synchronously by using software tools that allow the evaluator to view the remote user's screen. Audio connections may be provided by the software or by using additional phone lines. Asynchronous tests can be done by electronically distributing the software and the test procedures and providing a way for the results to be captured and returned to the evaluator.

Hartson et al. (1997) discussed advantages and disadvantages of several types of remote evaluations and presented two case studies: one using teleconferencing and the second using a semi-instrumented method of evaluation. The focus in these two cases was to obtain qualitative information to be used in formative evaluations.

Our work focuses on using remote testing to obtain quantitative information to supplement work done in the laboratory or to identify potential usability problems in existing software. While we believe that qualitative data is needed in order to produce better designs, we are focusing on what quantitative data can be collected in a remote, automated, and rapid fashion to identify usability problems.

3. OBJECTIVES AND METHODOLOGY

3.1 Objectives

Our objective is to develop tools and techniques to facilitate evaluation of Web sites and Web site designs. Our long-term plan is to:

- Carry out case studies to determine what useful quantitative data can be collected in a remote, automated, and rapid fashion;
- Develop tools based on what we learn from the case studies;
- Use these tools on a wide variety of sites, comparing the effectiveness of individual tools as well as combinations of tools and remote testing;
- Redesign tools as needed and develop new tools suggested by the effectiveness comparisons; and
- Generate guidelines about which tools should be used under which conditions.

This paper reports on the first set of case studies and the lessons learned from them. Our first three tools have just been released and two more are in the design stage.

3.2 Methodology for Case Studies

In order to design effective tools, we carried out three initial case studies to investigate the usefulness of quantitative information that can be collected remotely. In these case studies, we looked at the effectiveness of evaluations based on:

- User satisfaction ratings on usability questions
- The time and success users have in carrying out tasks on Web sites
- Usage patterns

3.3   Web Sites Selected

We selected three different services in the NIST Web site representing three different types of sites. The sites selected were a form fill-in application, a general-purpose library site, and a special purpose technical site. The owners of these sites were enthusiastic about our experiments and were grateful for any recommendations that we could provide them in the course of our research. In the next paragraphs, we briefly explain each site and its use.

3.3.1   The NIST Technicalendar Wizard

A printed calendar is published every week at NIST. It contains notices about meetings and talks to be held at NIST or given by NIST employees at other locations, as well as meetings elsewhere that might be of interest to NIST scientists. The calendar is distributed to NIST personnel in hardcopy. It is also viewable on the Web and e-mailed to others outside of the agency. The URL for the calendar is at http://nvl.nist.gov/pub/nistpubs/calendars/techcal/techcal.htm.

Previously, articles for inclusion in the technicalendar were faxed, phoned in, or e-mailed to a staff person who spent at least one day per week collecting any missing information for items submitted and formatting them correctly. To streamline this activity, an on-line wizard was developed so that submissions could be made via the Web. It was hoped that this would considerably reduce the time spent in publishing the technicalendar and make the submission process easier for NIST staff.

3.3.2   The NIST Virtual Library

The NIST Virtual Library (NVL) is a service available to both NIST staff and the public from the NIST home page. The NVL gives users access to an online catalog, assorted electronic journals, various databases (some of which are limited to NIST personnel), and NIST publications. Access is also provided to several other resources, including NIST maps and phonebooks, yellow pages, other government agency information, and weather forecasts.

This site supports both NIST personnel conducting scientific research as well as outside visitors who range from school children writing reports to researchers in business and universities. The NVL site designers are considering various possibilities for redesign and are interested in any recommendations we can provide. The current version of this site can be viewed at http://www.nist.gov/.

3.3.3   The Matrix Market

The Matrix Market is a specialized service provided by NIST staff in the form of test data for comparing algorithms for numerical linear algebra. The mathematics group has compiled a set of sparse matrices and matrix generators that can be downloaded from their Web site. The users are mathematicians from all over the world. Viewers of these pages can get information about the individual matrices and can download any matrix test data. This data can take considerable time to download so the group is especially interested in ensuring that visitors can quickly and accurately locate the test set they need. The Web site used in the case study was similar to the current page at http://math.nist.gov/MatrixMarket/.

4.   STUDY ONE: THE TECHNICALENDAR WIZARD

4.1   Methodology

We used this case study to determine the usefulness of collecting subjective satisfaction ratings. As the wizard had not yet been released, we incorporated this data collection into a beta test. While the beta test method is often used to collect bug information, it is usually not used specifically to collect data about usability problems. We had questions about how useful beta testing would be as a substitute for usability testing. In particular, would users be willing to participate in the beta test and what types of usability problems would be identified this way?

We hoped to address the first question by advertising the availability of the online wizard in the paper bulletin. NIST personnel were told that after the trial period the online submission procedure would be the sole submission method. They were informed about the usability study and were given the opportunity to "test" the wizard if they did not have actual calendar items to submit.

One problem with using beta testing to uncover usability problems is the difficulty of correlating user reports of problems with the task the user was doing when the problem occurred. As this Web application is quite simple, containing only a few high-level tasks, we hypothesized that, by collecting the submitted calendar item, we could identify the user task that was being done when the usability problem was encountered.

We were interested to see what types of usability problems could be identified using this approach. The authors conducted independent heuristic evaluations of the Technicalendar Wizard first. We listed the issues that at least one of us had identified as a problem. We used this list of problems as a comparison for the actual problems identified during the beta test. While we realize the limitations of heuristic reviews, we were faced with some real-world constraints. First, we needed some input for constructing our rating questionnaire. Secondly, we wanted a baseline to compare the usability problems identified during the beta test. A comparison based on an actual user test would have been more desirable but there are issues about charging administrative staff time for usability tests in government institutions which raise the cost of in-house user testing.

We constructed an evaluation form for users to fill out and e-mail to us after they had used the Technicalendar Wizard. The evaluation form included six questions for rating usability and an open-ended comment field.

After a month of use, we compiled the data collected from the user test and looked to see what, if any, overlap we had with the problems identified in the heuristic evaluation. We reviewed the user data along with the problems identified in the heuristic review and fixed a number of problems. We continued collecting user data for the next six weeks to see if our redesigns were construed as better.

4.2   Results

During the first month of testing, there were 24 electronic submissions. Of these, 16 were real submissions and 8 were test submissions. Any given Technicalendar contains between 25 and 40 items. Some of the items are published in more than one Technicalendar, so a very rough guess is that the 16 real submissions constituted between 15% -25% of the total submissions for the month. Of the 24 electronic submissions, 13 filled out evaluation sheets. Eight questionnaires were from real submissions and five were from test submissions.

The second phase of testing lasted six weeks. During this time there were 59 electronic submissions. Of these, 43 were real submissions and 16 were test submissions. We received 15 evaluation questionnaires, 10 from the real submissions and 5 from the test submissions.

Twenty usability problems were identified in the heuristic evaluation. Of these 20, 4 were fixed prior to the beta test. We wanted to see if and how the remaining problems were identified during beta testing and what problems were discovered in beta testing that were not identified during the heuristic evaluation. Usability problems discovered during beta testing could be identified in one of three ways: a low rating in the rating section of the questionnaire, a calendar submission with missing or incorrectly formatted data, or user comments. As shown in Table 1, the most problems (including two we thought we had fixed prior to beta) were identified through user comments. However, the calendar submissions and the ratings yielded three more problems. In addition, all these methods helped us identify usability issues.

What problems were noted in the heuristic review that were not identified as problems during the beta test? Of the eight problems identified by the heuristic review that were not identified during beta testing, two had to do with alignment of fields and grouping of fields. Two others were terminology and inconsistent labeling problems. No keyboard navigation was provided to move between steps and no numbers were provided on the wizard steps. No field was provided for a title for a speaker. And finally, directions for selecting an item in a drop-down list appeared as the first item in the list.

What problems were identified by users that were not identified in the heuristic review? Users described difficulties in submitting some unusual items. For example, a user had difficulty using the wizard to fill in the proper information for a panel with six speakers. There was no way to specify that this was a panel and it was difficult to list the names of all six speakers nicely formatted. This individual usually wrote nicely formatted descriptions for the calendar items and then submitted them. The wizard did not support her formatting preferences. The open-ended comments were especially useful for identifying unusual problems.

Table 1. Ways in which Problems were Identified during Beta Testing

Identification Method	Number	Type of problem
Calendar submission	2	Text field formatting
Low ratings	1	Determining optional fields
User comments	5	Access to help
		Relationship between fields
		Terminology
		Layout
		Missing defaults

4.3   Discussion

The response rate from the users was good. We collected more input than we would have been able to during a typical laboratory usability test. We worked with the Web master to correct the problems identified and a second version was installed on the Web site. The second round of beta testing uncovered no new problems and allowed us to verify our redesign by comparing the usability ratings.

The case study suggested that a useful tool would include functionality to automatically generate satisfaction questionnaires along with an analysis capability. In the case of transaction-based Web applications, it may be feasible to generate rating questions in response to the completion of a checklist of the components of the site.

5.   STUDY TWO: THE NIST VIRTUAL LIBRARY

5.1   Methodology

The NIST Virtual Library (NVL) is a scientific library accessible to the public from the NIST Web site. While some of the databases are restricted to NIST personnel, most of the library resources are open to the general public. The NVL staff was considering a redesign of the web interface and was very interested in obtaining data that would help them focus on specific areas to target.

197

The usability test consisted of three parts: a matching exercise to test existing categorization, ten representative tasks, and a short demographic and satisfaction questionnaire. We recruited five subjects from different scientific disciplines who worked at the NIST site in Gaithersburg, MD. It is important to note that we did NOT conduct this test remotely. We designed the test so that, given the appropriate software, it could be conducted remotely. In simulating remote testing, we kept the experimenter interaction with the users during the test to a minimum.

In the matching task, users were asked to match 29 items to one of ten choices, nine categories from the NVL home page plus a "none" category. We collected the results of this variation of a card-sorting task (Nielsen, 1993). In the performance task we collected the time it took users to complete each of ten tasks and their answers for each task. We also collected users' perceived difficulty ratings for each task. After the test was over, the experimenter conducted a retrospective interview with the users to identify qualitative information in order to determine what kinds of information we would miss in a purely automated asynchronous remote test.

We needed a benchmark to compare the results of our subjects. We had two experts complete the matching exercise, the ten tasks, and the satisfaction questionnaire. One expert was a reference librarian at NIST who was very familiar with the NVL site. The second expert was the designer of the NVL Web site.

5.2   Results

5.2.1   The Matching Task

Our baseline users misidentified two items out of the 29 total. Our non-expert subjects misidentified 13 items. Out of the nine categories, two of them, Databases and Hints & Help, were misidentified the most times. Figure 1 shows some of the categories and items in the matching task.

Category	Items
Subject Guides	Weather forecasts
Visiting NIST	CD-ROM databases
Hints and Help	Street map of NIST
Web Resources	Online Commerce Business Daily
E-Journals	Britannica Online
NIST Publications	List of Federal Library Web sites
Databases	NIST Tour Information
	NIST index to technical activities

Figure 1. A Sample of Categories and Items in the Matching Exercise

5.2.2　　The Performance Test

> **Tasks**
> Find 6 computer science journals.
> Find a list of the periodic tables.
> Find at least one NIST person to contact on the subject of visualization.
> Find a link in the NVL site that lets you look up U.S. area code information.
> Find the link to physics dissertation abstracts.

Figure 2. A Sample of the Tasks used in the Performance Test

Figure 2 shows a sample of the tasks users were asked to do. Our expert users were able to do nine of the ten tasks. However, each expert user missed a different task. Our five non-expert users were able to successfully complete between six and seven of the ten tasks.

The expert users took just over eight minutes to complete the ten tasks. The non-expert users needed over 31 minutes to complete the same tasks. Looking at individual tasks, we find an interesting issue. All the non-expert users missed one task. However, the users did not rate this task as the most difficult. This is probably because many of them thought they had located the answer.

5.2.3　　The Satisfaction Questionnaire

Users rated the difficulty for the tasks quite high given their success and the time they needed to complete these tasks. A seven-point scale was used, with one being an unacceptable rating and seven being an excellent rating. Experts gave an average difficulty rating of 5.7 compared to an average of 4.8 for the non-experts.

Originally, we had intended to use only success or failure in completing the task. However, we found instances where users thought they had located information but had not. Therefore, recording the users' answers was necessary.

5.3　　Discussion

Because we were not actually conducting this test remotely, we were able to observe users and interview them after the test. We did this to get an idea of the data we would not be able to collect remotely. Our observations of users' strategies and retrospective interviews gave us some insights into user search strategies. We found that users tended to use a search engine if they didn't know where to start a search, i.e., under which category to begin searching. If they did know the category, they preferred to use that.

We also noted that users preferred the category icons in the menu frame to jump to those pages, rather than the links within the home page. Alphabetical listings of links were more helpful than other groupings when the material was unfamiliar.

This qualitative information could not have been easily obtained using asynchronous remote testing, although a comparison of the paths users take to optimal paths could be used to identify critical decision points. Was the quantitative information we collected useful? The results of the matching tasks pointed to two category names that were difficult for users to understand. The performance test identified four tasks that were difficult for users. Looking at the paths these users took compared to the paths of users who obtained the correct answers could have helped isolate where the confusion occurred.

What lessons did we learn in order to design successful, remote testing tools? We need to collect users' answer to specific tasks to ensure the task really was successfully completed. Additionally, collecting the paths that the users take in information seeking tasks allows us to determine how well our Web site organization matches users' mental models. An automatic way to compare these paths to ideal paths would also be useful. Quantitative measures of time, success, and perceived difficulty can be obtained remotely and automatically. The matching task can be easily automated and used for remote testing.

6. STUDY THREE: THE MATRIX MARKET

6.1 Methodology

As we noted earlier, the Matrix Market is a very specialized site used primarily by mathematicians in testing numerical linear algebra algorithms. The developers of this site told us that visitors to the site would primarily be interested in 1) finding information about a particular test set or 2) downloading a particular test set. While the information contained in the site made it quite large, the use of the site was limited to two primary uses. We used this case study to determine if usage patterns derived from server log data would be effective in identifying usability problems. We recognize the numerous problems with using server log data as the sole source of information (Stout, 1997). However, server log data can still be used to determine overall patterns of traffic, changes in traffic patterns and dead areas in a site. Sullivan (1997) describes the use of server logs to provide inferential statistics about Web site usability.

6.2 Heuristic Review

We first did a heuristic review of the site to use as an indicator of potential problems. We used this data to get an indication of the type of information to look for in the server log data. In the review, we identified 17 problems that we grouped into eight basic kinds of problems. In Table 2, we list the eight categories of problems identified in the review and our hypotheses about what information from the server log might be used to confirm or deny these potential problems. We also included a result column to show our conclusions based on examination of one month of server log data.. We plan to extend this study to use more data in the

future.   Please   note   that   the   web   page   of   the   Matrix   Market
(http://math.nist.gov/MatrixMarket) has changed somewhat since the time of our
case study and some problems discussed here are no longer present.

6.3   Results

Our analysis was done mostly by "brute force"; that is, we used scripts to filter
and sort the data. Our long-term goal is to develop queries and visualizations that
usability professionals can use to analyze traffic on Web sites, with an emphasis on
uncovering usability problems.

For each of the potential problems identified by our heuristic, we hypothesized
what data in the server log might be used to determine if the problem actually
existed in real use. We simplified the access log file by removing all references to
graphics and to scripts. We built paths of user visits each day, recognizing that
caching prevents us from seeing the complete picture. We placed a time limit on
visits and discarded visits lasting longer than 30 minutes.

6.3.1   Overall Results

In one month, we counted 1199 visits and 1010 unique IP addresses. To see
whether users were having any major problems with the site, we looked at the
percent of visits where help was accessed at least once. Just over 5% of the visits
used help.

The home page provided six ways for users to browse through the matrices. We
found that for this month, the percentage of visits using each access method ranged
from 4% to 19%. This gave us an indicator of the top two or three access methods.
We also found that 40% of the visits started from the home page, while 24% of the
visits started from a page explaining one of the matrices. However, almost 70% of
the visits requested the home page at some time.

The site developers told us that they expected two types of users. Users might
come to the site, having read a research publication about an algorithm for numerical
linear algebra, to read a description of the matrix that was referenced. Users would
also come to the site to determine if the supplied matrices would be useful in testing
their algorithms and if so, download the appropriate file. We found that 52% of the
visits looked at the matrix descriptions. However, only 6% of the visits downloaded
a file.

6.3.2   Comparing Server Log Data with Heuristic Results

Of the eight potential problems we investigated using server log data, we verified
that one (the scrolling problem) was a significant problem. Two remain to be
verified (the long search form and the download problem) and five others were not
verified as significant problems. Table 2 shows the results of looking at usage
patterns to see if the potential usability problems affected users doing their work.

The next step is to do actual user testing on this site to determine how accurately
the server log data reflects these usability problems. We must also determine other

usability problems not identified in the heuristic and look for indications of these in the server log data.

Table 2. Usage Pattern Results

Problem	Usage Data Examined	Results
Behavior inconsistency	% of users using inconsistent behavior	< 8% of users used inconsistent behavior
Terminology inconsistency	% of users using help	Only 5% of users used help
Need to scroll long lists	% of users viewing page	20% - potential problem
Discriminating between link names for data files	Average number of links followed from this page to data files would be greater than from other pages to access data files	29% of users accessed more than one data file but only 7% accessed more than one data file from this page
Scrolling was most likely needed to view several groups of links on home page	Most frequently accessed pages by visits	Most frequently accessed pages were in easily visible area
Extra step needed to access some information	% of users viewing this data	Only 5% of visits went to this data
Need to scroll to view entire search form	Search followed immediately by another search	Unable to validate at this time
Estimates for download times are not given	% of users stopping transfer of data downloads	Unable to validate at this time

6.4   Discussion

We believe that for specialized Web sites with limited uses, the following usage questions can be answered through server log data:
- From the home page, which links are most frequently used?
- Do users have a difficult time discriminating between names of links from a given page?

- Do users have difficulty locating information via searching and need to make multiple attempts?
- Do visitors use help frequently?
- What pages are used most frequently as entry points by users?

Server log analysis allows us to estimate the percentage of users that a potential usability problem affects. We concluded from this case study that a useful tool would construct user paths from server log data and display the appropriate visualizations in response to usability questions such as those listed above.

7.   CONCLUSIONS

We believe that usability evaluation techniques that will prove effective for the Web must be rapid, remote, and automated. We have investigated the data that could be collected in such a fashion and shown the usefulness of that data in identifying usability problems through three case studies of different types of web sites. We have also gathered some requirements for tools that could provide much of this information.

7.1   Gamma Testing

We suggest the term "gamma testing" for a variation of beta testing focusing on identifying usability problems. We showed that this type of testing is useful for Web applications consisting of forms. A tool to support this type of data collection would generate rating questions based on information supplied by the developer about the components of the form. While we have not yet developed this tool, we have written a document about using this methodology.

7.2   Automated Testing

We conducted a usability test to see if specific information-seeking tasks could be automated. We found that a category-matching exercise was quite useful and could easily be automated. Our abbreviated usability test, collecting whether or not users were successful in carrying out a task and the time they needed to complete the task, can also be automated. We have released the first version of the NIST WebMetrics tool suite (http://zing.ncsl.nist.gov/~webmet/)which contains a category matching tool (WebCAT) and an automated path collection tool (WebVIP). We are currently working on visualizations to facilitate the analysis of the user paths obtained through WebVIP.

7.3   Server Log Analysis

For specialized Web sites, using server logs to obtain more information about the use and usability of the site is an excellent starting point. We found server log data useful in giving indications of the relative amount of use of various portions of the site and in judging the possible effect of potential usability problems. We are currently designing a tool to construct approximate paths and provide appropriate visualizations for investigating potential usability problems.

8.   FUTURE WORK

We based our designs for the tools on a few case studies with specific types of Web sites. As our first set of tools is now available, we are requesting feedback from the hundreds of developers who have downloaded the tools. We plan to document their experiences using the tools on various types of Web sites. Based on this feedback, as well as our continuing case studies, we plan to revise the existing tools and to design new tools to facilitate rapid, remote, and automated usability evaluations of Web sites.

9.   REFERENCES

Hartson, H., Castillo, J., Kelso, J., and Neale, W. (1996) Remote Evaluation: The Network as an Extension of the Usability Laboratory. *Proceedings ACM CHI'96 Conference,* (Denver, CO, April 13-18), 228-235.

Jeffries, R., Miller, J., Wharton, C. and Uyeda, K. (1991) User Interface Evaluation in the real world: A comparison of four techniques. *Proceedings ACM CHI'91 Conference,* (New Orleans, LA, April 28-May 2), 119-124.

John, B.E. and Marks, S.J. (1997) Tracking the effectiveness of usability evaluation methods. *Behaviour and Information Technology,* Vol. 16, no. 4/5, 188-203.

Nielsen, J. (1993) Usability Engineering, Academic Press, Boston.

Nielsen, J. (1989) Usability engineering at a discount. In *Designing and Using Human-Computer Interfaces and Knowledge Based Systems,* (ed. G. Salvendy and M.J. Smith) Elsevier Science Publishers, Amsterdam, 394-401.

Stout, R. (1997) Web Site Stats: Tracking Hits and Analyzing Traffic. Mc-Graw-Hill, Berkeley, CA.

Sullivan, T. (1997). *Reading Reader Reaction: A Proposal for Inferential Analysis of Web Server Log Files.* 3rd Annual Conference on Human Factors and the Web, (Denver, CO. June 12). For proceedings see:
http://www.research.att.com/conf/hfweb/conferences/prev_conferences.en.html

10.   BIOGRAPHY

Dr. Jean Scholtz is currently a researcher in the Visualization and Virtual Reality Group at NIST. Her interests are in tools for evaluating software from the user perspective, primarily CSCW systems and Web applications. Dr. Scholtz has a PhD in computer science.

As a researcher at NIST in the Natural Language Processing and Information Retrieval Group, Laura Downey focused on evaluation and analysis techniques. She is the designer of several of the tools in the NIST WebMetrics tool suite.

Discussion

Kenneth Fishkin: The usability of a Web site can be affected drastically by the browser people are using. Can WebSAT accommodate this?

Jean Scholtz: Yes. Firstly, some of the guidelines are browser-specific, warning the user about features which may work on some browsers and not others. Secondly, the trace log contains browser information. So you can tell what browser was used if you use Webvip to log links.

Morten Harning: Do your tools support dynamically generated HTML pages?

Jean Scholtz: No, but they are next on the list.

Prasun Dewan: If you allow applets in your pages, then Web applications would not be a special case of interactive applications, since Java lets you write arbitrary applications.

Jean Scholtz: Yes! However, we would still need to modify our work as we currently apply only guidelines about informational-type sites.

Fabio Paterno: How do you plan to use information on usage of a Web site to improve its design?

Jean Scholtz: We plan to develop some models of web usage and compare the actual usage to what the designers intended to support.

Christian Gram: A pessimistic comment to user testing of Web sites based on an experiment where many students made "thinking aloud" tests on commercial Web sites: They agreed on a few (serious) errors, but all in all there was only little overlap. That means, each Web site contains a lot of errors, and it is impossible to find all - or just the major ones.

Michael Freed: Responding to Christians comment, I just want to point out that tools for detecting usability problems in a design have not to detect all such problems in order to be useful. Such tools can be very useful if, e.g., they sometimes draw attention to problems that would be obvious from hindsight, but are unlikely to be considered from advance. Also, such tools can complement designers' intuition by considering usability problems that cannot be predicted on the basis of common sense.

Employing simulation to evaluate designs: The APEX approach

Michael A. Freed, Michael G. Shafto, Roger W. Remington

NASA Ames Research Center, Mail Stop 262-4, Moffett Field, CA 94035-1000
{mfreed,mshafto,rremington}@mail.arc.nasa.gov

Key words: human performance modeling, human error, simulation, usability, design

Abstract: Computer simulation could be used to reduce the cost of designing human-machine systems, just as it is currently used in the design process for inanimate systems such as electronic circuits. However, past efforts have met with limited success due to difficulties modeling the human components of these systems. We have constructed a software framework and methodology for modeling human performance, APEX, that addresses several of these difficulties. This paper describes a methodology for using APEX to evaluate designs in complex, dynamic task environments; we then illustrate this process using an example from the domain of air traffic control.

1.   ITERATIVE DESIGN

The enormous cost of fielding a complex human-machine system can be attributed in part to the cost of discovering and eliminating usability problems in its design. In general, evaluation costs increase as the design process progresses. By the time a system has come into use, fixing a design problem involves not only redesigning and re-testing, but also modifying fielded devices and possibly retraining users. To manage engineering design costs, large new systems are usually developed by a process of *iterative design* (Gould, 1988). As a design progresses from idea to fully fielded system, decisions are evaluated at each stage. If problems are discovered during evaluation, the system is partially redesigned and further evaluation takes place on the new version. This process is repeated until a satisfactory version results.   Of course, the ability to determine whether the current version is satisfactory is limited by the effectiveness of the evaluation methods employed.

Evaluation methods applicable at a late design stage are generally more expensive but also more effective than methods that can be used at earlier stages. In particular, once a working prototype of the new system has been constructed, evaluation by user testing becomes possible. Observing users employing the system in a wide range of scenarios and operating conditions can tell a designer a great deal about how well it will function once in the field.   This process is widely recommended in discussions of human factors and routinely practiced in the design of safety-critical and high-distribution systems.

However, user testing suffers from a number of drawbacks and limitations. For instance, subjects are often more highly motivated than true end-users and, in some cases, become too knowledgeable about the developing system to be useful in discovering certain problems. Another drawback is cost. When designing new air traffic control systems, for example, such tests typically require hiring highly paid expert controllers as subjects, often for extended periods (Shafto, 1990; Remington, 1990b).   The limited amount of testing that results from high cost can stifle innovation, slow development, and even compromise safety.

Designers can reduce the amount of user testing required by discovering problems early in the design process, and thus reducing the number of design iterations. To discover problems with usability, the primary early-phase evaluation method involves checking the design against human factors guidelines contained in numerous handbooks developed for that purpose (Smith, 1986). Guidelines have proven useful for some design tasks, but have a number of fairly well-known problems (Mosier, 1986). In particular, guidelines focus on static, relatively superficial factors affecting human-machine performance such as text legibility and color discrimination.   But when addressing topics relating to the dynamic behavior of a system or to the mental activities of the user, guidelines are often lacking or are too general to be of much use. Thus, "for the foreseeable future, guidelines should be considered as a collection of suggestions, rather than distilled science or formal requirements. Understanding users, testing, and iterative design are indispensable, costly necessities" (Gould, 1988).

Scenario-based approaches, such as Cognitive Walkthrough (Polson et al., 1992), "thinking aloud," and human simulation modeling, offer alternative methods for early-stage design evaluation. These techniques trade off some of the guideline-based method's generality for greater sensitivity to human cognitive factors and for an increased ability to predict performance in complex, dynamic task domains. The idea of a scenario-based approach is to achieve some of the benefits of user testing at an early design stage when no usable prototype has been constructed. Designers follow the behavior of a real or hypothetical user employing imaginary or simulated equipment to achieve specified task goals in specified operating conditions.

Focusing on specific scenarios allows designers to consider situation-dependent aspects of performance such as the varying relevance of different performance variables, the effects of changing workload, and the likelihood and consequences of interactions between a user's tasks. However, complexity and dynamic elements in a task domain pose difficulties for any scenario-based approach. While an improvement over guidelines in this respect, all of these approaches become more difficult to use in more demanding task domains as task duration, situation complexity, number of actors, number of activities that each actor must perform, and the number of scenarios that need to be considered all increase.

By exploiting the computer's speed and memory, human simulation modeling overcomes obstacles inherent in other scenario-based methods and thus has the greatest potential for predicting performance in more demanding task environments. A large, accurate memory overcomes the problem of tracking innumerable scenario events. Processing speed helps compensate for the need to examine more scenarios by, in principle, allowing each scenario to be carried out more quickly than in real-time. The computer's ability to function continuously adds further to the number of scenarios that may be explored.

However, despite its potential, human simulation has been used to inform design almost exclusively in simple design domains – i.e. domains where tasks are brief, situational complexity is low, few actors and forces determine events, and so on.

Predicting performance in more challenging task domains requires an operator model that can function effectively in demanding task environments. Existing human models have typically lacked several very important capabilities including those needed to cope with varied forms of uncertainty inherent in many task environments; manage limited cognitive, perceptual, and motor resources; and, manage multiple, periodic tasks. These capabilities have been incorporated into a human operator model called APEX (Freed, 1997a; Freed, 1997b) by adapting techniques from the field of artificial intelligence.

APEX has been applied to simulate air traffic controller behavior (ATC), a task domain that presents a variety of challenges for human modeling. Expert performance in this domain requires coping with uncertainty, managing limited resources, and managing multiple tasks – challenges one would expect in many other design domains of practical interest. This paper uses the air traffic control domain to illustrate a five-step process for employing APEX to aid design in a new

Method	when	Redesign cost	method cost	demanding task environments	method effectiveness
User testing	late	high	high	yes	high
Guidelines	early	low	low	no	low
Walkthrough	early	low	low	no	medium
Simulation	early	low	medium	yes	medium

Table 1 Comparison of usability evaluation methods

209

domain.

1. Constructing a simulated world
2. Task analysis
3. Scenario development
4. Running the Simulation
5. Analyzing simulation results

The paper is organized as follows. Section 2 describes a scenario that sometimes occurs in an APEX ATC simulation; the scenario illustrates how APEX simulation fits into the overall design process and exemplifies its use in predicting operator error. Subsequent sections discuss each of the five steps listed above for preparing and using an APEX model to aid in design.

2.   EXAMPLE SCENARIO

At a TRACON air traffic control facility, one controller will often be assigned to the task of guiding planes through a region of airspace called an arrivals sector. This task involves taking planes from various sector entry points and getting them lined up at a safe distance from one another on landing approach to a particular airport. Some airports have two parallel runways. In such cases, the controller will form planes up into two lines.

Occasionally, a controller will be told that one of the two runways is closed and that all planes on approach to land must be directed to the remaining open runway. A controller's ability to direct planes exclusively to the open runway depends on remembering that the other runway is closed. How does the controller remember this important fact? Normally, the diversion of all inbound planes to the open runway produces an easily perceived reminder. In particular, the controller will detect only a single line of planes on approach to the airport, even though two lines (one to each runway) would normally be expected.

However, problems may arise in conditions of low workload. With few planes around, there is no visually distinct line of planes to either runway. Thus, the usual situation in which both runways are available is perceptually indistinguishable from the case of a single closed runway. The lack of perceptual support would then force the controller to rely on memory alone, thus increasing the chance that the controller will accidentally direct a plane to the closed runway.

Designing to prevent such problems is not especially difficult – it is only necessary to depict the runway closure condition prominently on the controller's information display. The difficulty lies in anticipating the problem. By generating plausible scenarios, some containing operator error, APEX can direct an interface

210

designer's attention to potential usability problems. Though perhaps obvious from hindsight, such errors could easily be overlooked until a late stage of design.

The ability to explicate events (including cognitive events) leading to the error can help indicate alternative ways to refine an interface. For example, one of the difficulties in designing a radar display is balancing the need to present a large volume of information against the need to keep the display uncluttered. In this case, by showing how the error results from low traffic conditions, the model suggests a clever fix for the problem: prominently depict runway closures only in low workload conditions when the need for a reminder is greatest and doing so produces the least clutter.

3.   CONSTRUCTING A SIMULATED WORLD

The first step in simulating a human-machine system involves implementing software components specific to the task domain. Because the domain model used for simulation will almost inevitably require simplifying from the real domain, the exact nature of the tasks the simulated operators will have to carry out cannot be known until this step is accomplished. Constructing software to model the domain thus precedes representing task knowledge for the operator model. This software, the **simulated world**, should include several components:

- a model of the **immediate task environment** including **equipment models** specifying the behavior of devices employed by the simulated operator. In ATC, these include a radar scope, two-way radio, and flightstrip board.
- a model of the **external environment** specifying objects and agents outside the operator's immediate environment. In ATC, the external environment comprises a region of airspace over which the controller has responsibility, airspace outside that region's boundaries, a set of airplanes, and the aircrews controlling those airplanes.
- a **scenario control** component that allows a user to define scenario events (e.g. airliner emergencies, runway closures) and scenario parameters (e.g. plane arrival rate) and then insures that these specifications are met in simulation. See section 5.

In addition, a **simulation engine** controls the passage of simulated time and mediates interactions within and among all simulated world and simulated operator components. A simulation engine provided by the CSS simulation environment, discussed in section 6, is currently used to run the APEX human operator model as well as the air traffic control simulated world described below.

4.   TASK ANALYSIS

APEX, like other human simulation models, consists of general-purpose
components such as eyes, hands, and working memory; it requires the addition of
domain-specific knowledge structures to function in any particular task domain.
Task analysis is the process of identifying and encoding the necessary knowledge
(Mentemerlo, 1978; Kirwan, 1992). For highly routinized task domains such as air
traffic control, much of the task analysis can be accomplished easily and fairly
uncontroversially by reference to published procedures.

For instance, to clear an airplane for descent to a given altitude, a controller
uses a specific verbal procedure prescribed in the controller phraseology handbook
(see Mills, 1992) – e.g. "United two one niner, descend and maintain flight level
nine thousand." Other behaviors such as maintaining an awareness of current
airspace conditions do not correspond to any written procedures. These aspects of
task analysis require inferring task representation from domain attributes and general
assumptions about adaptive human learning processes. This section introduces the
notational formalism (PDL) used in APEX to represent task analyses and discusses
the role of adaptive learning in determining how agents come to perform tasks.

4.1   An expressive language for task analyses

In APEX, tasks analyses are represented using the APEX Procedure Definition
Language (PDL), the primary element of which is the **procedure**. A procedure in
PDL represents an operator's knowledge about how to perform routine tasks. For
instance, a procedure for clearing a plane to descend has the following form:

```
(procedure
    (index  (clear-to-descend ?plane ?altitude))
    (step s1 (determine-callsign-for-plane ?plane
        => ?callsign))
    (step s2 (say ?callsign) (waitfor ?s1)
    (step s3 (say "descend and maintain flight
        level") (waitfor ?s2))
    (step s4 (say ?altitude) (waitfor ?s3))
    (step s5 (terminate) (waitfor ?s4)))
```

The **index clause** in the procedure above indicates that the procedure
should be retrieved from memory whenever a goal to clear a given plane for descent
to a particular altitude becomes active. **Step clauses** prescribe activities that need to
be performed to accomplish this. The first step activates a new goal: to determine
the identifying callsign for the specified airplane and to make this information

available to other steps in the procedure by associating it with the variable *?callsign*. Achieving this step entails finding a procedure whose index clause matches the form

(determine-callsign-for-plane ?plane)

and then executing its steps. After this, *say* actions prescribed in steps s2, s3, and s4 are carried out in order. This completes the phrase needed to clear a descent. Finally, step s5 is executed, terminating the procedure.

The activities defined by steps of a PDL procedure are assumed to be concurrently executable. When a particular order is desired, this must be specified explicitly using the **waitfor clause**. In this case, all steps but the first are defined to wait until some other task has terminated. Second, although this task is complete when all of its steps are complete, it is sometimes desirable to allow procedures to specify more complex, variable completion conditions. For example, it may be useful to allow race conditions in which the procedure completes when any of several steps are complete. Thus, rather than handle termination uniformly for all procedures, termination conditions must be notated explicitly in each procedure.

The ability to specify how concurrent execution should be managed and to specialize termination conditions for each procedure exemplify an attempt with PDL to provide a uniquely flexible and expressive language for task analysis. In particular, PDL can be considered an extension to the GOMS approach (Card, 1983) in which tasks are analyzed in terms of four constructs: goals, operators, methods, and selection rules. Procedure structures in PDL combine and extend the functionality provided by GOMS methods and selection rules. GOMS operators represent basic skills such as pressing a button, saying a phrase, or retrieving information from working memory; executing an operator produces action directly. PDL does not produce action directly, but instead sends action requests (signals) to cognitive, perceptual, and motor resources in the APEX resource architecture. What action, if any, should be executed is determined by the relevant resource model.

It is important to distinguish PDL procedures from externally represented procedures such as those that appear in manuals. PDL procedures are internal (cognitive) representations of how to accomplish a task (Anderson, 1995). In some cases, as above, there is a one to one correspondence between the external prescription for accomplishing a task and how it is represented internally. But written procedures might also correspond to multiple PDL procedures, especially when written procedures cover conditional activities (i.e. carried out sometimes but not always) or activities that take place over a long period of time. Similarly, PDL procedures may describe behaviors such as how to scan the radar display that result from adaptive learning processes and are never explicitly taught.

4.2 Approximating adaptive learning

Task analysis is often used to help designers better understand how human operators function in *existing* human-machine systems (Hutchins, 1995). In such cases, task analysis can be usefully (though not altogether accurately) viewed as a linear process in which a task analyst observes operators performing their job, infers underlying cognitive activities based on regularities in overt behavior, and then represents these activities in the context of some general cognitive model.

A different process is required to predict how tasks will be carried out with newly designed equipment and procedures. In particular, analysis can no longer start with observations of overt behavior since no real operators have been trained with the new procedures and no physical realization of the new equipment exists. Instead, cognitive structures underlying behavior must be inferred based on task requirements and an understanding of the forces that shape task-specific cognition: human limitations, adaptive learning processes, and regularities in the task domain.

For example, to model how a controller might visually scan the radar display to maintain awareness of current airspace conditions, an analyst should consider a number of factors. First, human visual processing can only attend to, and thus get information about, a limited portion of the visual field at any one time. By attending to one region of the display, a controller obtains an approximate count of the number of planes in that region. He or she identifies significant plane clusters or other Gestalt groups and can detect planes that differ from all others in the region on some simple visual property such as color or orientation.

But to ascertain other important information requires a narrower focus of attention. For example, to determine that two planes are converging requires attending exclusively to those planes. Similarly, to determine that a plane is nearing a position from which it should be rerouted requires attending to the plane or to the position. These visual processing constraints have important implications for how visual scanning should be modeled. For example, to maintain adequate situation awareness, the model should shift attention not only to display regions but also to individual planes within those regions.

An assumption that the human operator adapts to regularities in the task environment has further implications. For instance, if a certain region contains no routing points and all planes in the region normally travel in a single direction, there would usually be no reason to attend to any particular plane unless it strayed from the standard course. Adaptive mechanisms could modify routine scanning procedures to take advantage of this by eliminating unnecessary attention shifts to planes in that region. This saves the visual attention resource for uses more likely to yield important information.

A fully mature approach to human modeling will require techniques for identifying or predicting regularities in the domain and detailed guidelines for predicting how adaptive learning processes will shape behavior in accordance with these regularities. A few such guidelines have been considered in discussions of particular knowledge representation problems (Freed, 1997a), and somewhat more general principles were discussed as part of APEX's overall modeling methodology (Freed, 1997b). However, the present work has only begun to address this important issue.

5.   SCENARIO DEVELOPMENT

The third step in preparing an APEX simulation run is to develop scenarios. A scenario specification includes any parameters and conditions required by the simulated world. In general, these can include initial state, domain-specific rate and probability parameters, and specific events to occur over the course of a simulation (see list below). In the current implementation of the simulation, initial conditions do not vary. In particular, the simulated controller always begins the task with an empty airspace (rather than having to take over an active airspace) and with the same set of goals. The goals are to maintain safe separation between all planes, get planes to their destination in a timely fashion, stay aware of current airspace conditions, and so on.

- initial agent goals
- initial operating conditions
- specialized parameters such as the rate and likelihood of certain events
- specific events to occur during the simulation run

At minimum, a scenario must include a duration D and an aircraft count C. The scenario control component will randomly generate C plane arrival events over the interval D, with aircraft attributes such as destination, aircraft type, and point of arrival determines according to default probabilities. For instance, the default specifies that a plane's destination will be LAX with p(.7) and Santa Monica airport with p(.3). The default includes conditional probabilities – e.g. the destination airport affects the determination of airplane type – e.g. a small aircraft such as a Cherokee is much more likely to have Santa Monica as its destination.

Scenario definitions can alter these default probabilities, and thereby affect the timing and attributes of events generated by the scenario control component. Users can also specify particular events to occur at particular times. For example, one might want to specify a number of small aircraft arrivals all around the same time in order to check how performance is affected by a sudden increase in workload. Currently, arrivals are the only kind of event that the scenario control component generates randomly. Special events such as runway closures and aircraft equipment failures must be specified individually.

6.   RUNNING THE SIMULATION

To employ the operator model, world model, and scenario control elements in simulation requires a simulation engine. APEX currently uses the simulation engine provided by CSS (Remington, et al., 1990a), a simulation package developed at NASA Ames that also includes a model development environment, a graphical interface for observing an ongoing simulation, and mechanisms for analyzing and graphing temporal data from a simulation run.

CSS simulation models consist of a network of **process** and **store** modules, each depicted as a "box" on the graphical interface. Stores are simply repositories for information, though they may be used to represent complex systems such as human working memory. Process modules, as the name implies, cause inputs to be processed and outputs to be produced. A process has five attributes: (1) a name; (2) a body of LISP code that defines how inputs are mapped to outputs; (3) a set of stores from which it takes input; (4) a set of stores to which it provides output; and (5) a stochastic function that determines its finishing time – how much simulated time is required for new inputs to be processed and the result returned as output. A process is idle until a state change occurs in any of its input stores. This activates the process, causing it to produce output in accordance with its embedded code after an interval determined by its characteristic finishing time function.

The CSS simulation engine is an event-driven simulator. Unlike time-slice simulators, which advance simulated time by a fixed increment, an event-driven simulator advances until the next active process is scheduled to produce an output. This more efficient method makes it practical to model systems whose components need to be simulated at vastly different levels of temporal granularity. In particular, the APEX human operator model contains perceptual processes that occur over tens of milliseconds, motor and cognitive processes that take hundreds of milliseconds and (links to) external simulated world processes modeled at the relatively coarse temporal granularity of seconds. CSS provides further flexibility by allowing processes to run concurrently unless constrained to run in sequence.

The process of incorporating a model into a CSS framework is fairly straightforward, but a user must decide how much detail to include regarding the model's temporal characteristics. In the simplest case, one could model the world and the operator each as single processes. Because processes can have only a single finishing time distribution, such a model would assume a uniform duration for all operator activities. For instance, a speech act, a gaze shift, a grasp action, and a retrieval from memory would all require the same interval. The process-store network used to simulate and visualize APEX behavior models each component of the APEX architecture as a separate process.

Once the process-store network has been constructed, and simulated world and APEX elements incorporated into the code underlying processes, the simulation can be run. CSS provides a "control panel" window with several buttons. SHOW toggles the visualization function, causing information in processes and stores to be displayed and dynamically updated. START and STOP initiate and freeze a simulation run. STEP causes time to advance to the next scheduled process finish event, runs the scheduled process, and then freezes the simulation.

7.   SIMULATION ANALYSIS

The final step in using APEX is to analyze the results of simulation. CSS provides tools for analyzing and graphing temporal aspects of behavior. For example, if interested in predicting how much time the controller took to respond when a new airplane appeared on the radar display, the modeler could specify that interest when constructing the process-store network (see Remington et al., 1990a for how this is accomplished). CSS automatically stores specified timing values from multiple simulation runs and graphs the data on demand.

7.1   Design-facilitated errors

APEX is intended to help predict **design-facilitated errors** – i.e. operator errors that could be prevented or minimized by modifying equipment or procedure design. The current approach assumes that people develop predictable strategies for circumventing their innate limitations and that these strategies make people prone to error in certain predictable circumstances. For instance, to compensate for limited memory, people sometimes learn to rely on features of their task environment to act as a kind of externalized memory. If, for whatever reason, the relied on feature is absent when it should be present (or vice-versa), error may result.

In the *wrong runway scenario* described in section 2, the controller's error stemmed from reliance on a visually observable feature – an imbalance in the number of planes approaching to each runway to signal – to act as a reminder of runway closure. When workload dropped too low for this feature to remain observable, the controller reverted to a behavior consistent with its absence. In particular, the controller selected a runway based on factors that had nothing to do with runway availability such as airplane type and relative proximity to each runway approach path.

When this error occurs in simulation, the sequence of events that led up to it can be extracted from the **simulation trace**, a record of all the events that occurred during the simulation run. However, this "raw" event data is not very useful to a designer. To inform the design process, the events must be interpreted in light of general knowledge about human performance. For instance, most errors can be partially attributed to the non-occurrence of normal events. The raw simulation data will not contain any reference to these events, so normative knowledge must be used to complete the causal story that explains the error.

As an additional constraint on what constitutes a useful analysis, the explanation for an error assign blame to something that the designer has control (Owens, 1991, makes a similar point). For instance, citing human memory limitations as a cause of the above described error is correct, but not very useful. In contrast, blaming the failure on the absence of expected perceptual support for memory implies ways of fixing the problem. The designer could enforce the perceptual support (in this instance, by insuring that planeload never drops too low), provide alternative perceptual support (a runway closure indicator on the display), or train the operator not to expect perceptual support and to take other measures to support memory.

7.2   Error patterns

We would like to facilitate the generation of analyses in which non-occurring normal events are made explicit and causal explanations trace back to elements of the task environment that the designer might be able to control. One way to do this is to represent general knowledge about the cause of error in **error patterns**. An error pattern is a specific type of explanation pattern (Schank, 1986) – i.e. a stereotypical sequence of events that end in some kind of anomaly that needs to be explained (an error in this case). When an error occurs in simulation, error patterns whose characteristic anomaly type matches the "observed" error are compared against events in the simulation trace. If the pattern matches events in the simulation trace, the pattern is considered an explanation of the error.

Because an APEX human operator model can only be a coarse approximation of a real human operator, error predictions emerging from simulation will not necessarily be problems in reality. The designer must evaluate the plausibility and seriousness of any error predictions on the basis of domain knowledge and a common sense understanding of human behavior. Current scientific knowledge about human error-making is inadequate for prediction. The APEX approach only attempts to make designers more effective at applying their common sense knowledge about when and why people make errors. Thus, the need for the user to evaluate model predictions should be considered compatible with the APEX approach.

One other aspect of simulation analysis presents more of a problem. Currently, the modeler must interpret simulation event data "by hand" on the basis of informally specified error pattern knowledge. This approach is far from ideal and, given the massive mount of simulation data that must be examined, probably unacceptable for practical use. To automate analysis, simulation mechanisms must be augmented to check observed (i.e. simulated) behavior against expected behavior and to signal errors when specified deviations occur. Error patterns indexed by the anomaly and successfully matched against the simulation trace would then be output to the user as error predictions.

218

8.   CONCLUSION

In safety-critical domains, such as nuclear power, aerospace, military, medical, and industrial control systems, the cost and risk of implementing new technology are major barriers to progress. The fear of innovation is not based on superstition, but on the common experience of failure in complex system development projects (Curtis et al., 1988). Retaining the status quo, however, becomes less and less tenable as existing systems become obsolete and the cost and risk of maintaining them escalate.

Replacement or significant upgrading of such safety-critical systems eventually becomes inevitable. Therefore, it is necessary to attack the core problem, namely, the lack of a systematic design method for complex human-computer systems. It is the absence of such a methodology that lies at the root of valid concerns about the safety (Leveson, 1995) and economic benefit (Landauer, 1995) of new human-computer systems.

APEX is intended to be a contribution toward improving the design of safety-critical human-computer systems, for example, the next-generation air traffic control system. APEX incorporates and extends many of the functional elements of the MIDAS system (Corker and Smith, 1993), particularly computational models of the physical and informational environment: equipment, geography, regulatory constraints, documents, and displays.

The key innovations of APEX are its integrated approaches to task analysis, procedure definition, and intelligent, resource-constrained multi-tasking. This paper has presented a step-by-step description of how APEX is used, from scenario development through trace analysis.

The development of APEX is itself an exercise in iterative design. Current work is aimed at extending the modeling framework, developing new applications, and validating partial models (see Homer, 1997). The goal remains to reduce the cost and risk of the implementation of complex human-computer systems, by addressing key human-interaction issues as early as possible in the design process.

REFERENCES

Anderson, J.R. (1995) *Cognitive psychology and its implications* (fourth edition), San Francisco: W.H. Freeman.

Card, S.K., Moran, T.P., & Newell, A. (1983). *The psychology of human-computer interaction.* Hillsdale, NJ: Lawrence Erlbaum Associates.

Corker, K.M., & Smith, B. (1993). *An architecture and model for cognitive engineering simulation analysis: Application to advanced aviation analysis.* AIAA Conference on Computing in Aerospace. San Diego, CA.

Corker, K.M. & Pisanich, G.M. (1995). Analysis and modeling of flight crew performance in automated air traffic management systems. *Proceedings of the 6th IFAC/IFIP/IFORS/IEA Symposium: Analysis, Design, and Evaluation of Man-Machine Systems.* Boston, MA.

Curtis, B., Krasner, H., & Iscoe, N. (1988). A field study of the software design process for large systems. *Communications of the ACM,* **31,** 1268-1287.

Freed, M.A. & Remington, R.W. (1997). Managing decision resources in plan execution. In *Proceedings of the Fifteenth Joint Conference on Artificial Intelligence.* Nagoya, Japan.

Freed, M. & Shafto, M. (1997). Human-system modeling: some principles and a pragmatic approach. *Proceedings of the Fourth International Workshop on the Design, Specification, and Verification of Interactive System.* Granada, Spain.

Gould, J.D. (1988). How to design usable systems. In M. Helander (Ed.), *Handbook of Human-Computer Interaction.* New York: North-Holland.

Homer, J.B. (1997). Structure, data and compelling conclusions: Notes from the field. *System Dynamics Review,* **13,** 293-309.

Hutchins, E. (1995). *Cognition in the wild.* Cambridge, MA: MIT Press.

Kirwan, B. and Ainsworth, L. (1992). *A guide to task analysis.* London: Taylor and Francis.

Landauer, T.K. (1995). *The trouble with computers.* Cambridge, MA: MIT Press (Bradford).

Leveson, N.G. (1995). *Safeware: System safety and computers.* Reading, MA: Addison-Wesley.

Mentemerlo, M.D. and Eddowes, E. (1978). The judgmental nature of task analysis. In *Proceedings of the Human Factors Society,* pp. 247-250. Santa Monica, CA.

Mills, T.S. & Archibald, J.S. (1992). *The pilot's reference to ATC procedures and terminology.* Van Nuys, CA: Reavco Publishing.

Mosier, J.N. & Smith, S.L. (1986). Applications of guidelines for designing user interface software. *Behavior and Information Technology,* **5,** 39-46.

Owens, C. (1991). A functional taxonomy of abstract plan failures. In *Proceedings of the Annual Conference of the Cognitive Science Society.* Chicago, IL.

Polson, P., Lewis, C., Rieman, J., Wharton, C., and Wilde, N. (1992). Cognitive Walkthroughs: A method for theory-based evaluation of user interfaces. *International Journal of Man-Machine Studies,* **36,** 741-773.

Remington, R.W., Johnston, J.C., Bunzo, M.S., & Benjamin, K.A. (1990). The Cognition Simulation System: An interactive graphical tool for modeling human cognitive processing. In *Object-Oriented Simulation.* San Diego: Society for Computer Simulation, pp. 155-166.

Remington, R.W., & Shafto, M.G. (1990). *Building human interfaces to fault diagnostic expert systems I: Designing the human interface to support cooperative fault diagnosis,* Seattle, WA. CHI'90 Workshop on Computer Human Interaction In Aerospace Systems.

Schank, R.C. (1986). *Explanation patterns.* Lawrence Erlbaum Associates, Hillsdale, NJ.

Shafto, M.G., & Remington, R.W. (1990). *Building human interfaces to fault diagnostic expert systems II: Interface development for a complex, real-time system.* Seattle, WA: CHI'90 Workshop on Computer-Human Interaction in Aerospace Systems.

Smith, S.L., & Mosier, J.N. (1986). *Guidelines for designing operator interface software.* Tech. Rept. No. MTR-10090. McClean, VA: MITRE Corporation.

220

BIOGRAPHY

Michael Freed received his B.S. degree in 1988 from the University of Massachusetts, and his Ph.D. in Artificial Intelligence in 1998 from Northwestern University. He has worked and published in several areas of artificial intelligence including plan execution, case-based reasoning, machine learning, and expert systems. Since 1994, Dr. Freed has been a research scientist at NASA Ames Research Center. His main area of research uses diverse methods from the field of artificial intelligence to help simulate complex human behavior. His current research interests also include intelligent interfaces, computer-aided interface design and automated support for human decision-making.

Roger Remington received his B.S. degree from the University of California at Los Angeles in 1974. He received his M.S. and Ph.D. degrees in Human Experimental Psychology in 1978 from the University of Oregon where he worked with Profs. Michael Posner and Steven Keele on issues of visual selective attention and human performance. Dr. Remington served as a Research Psychologist at the Naval Aerospace Medical Research Laboratory in Pensacola, Florida, working on programs to optimize attentional demands in fighter aircraft. From 1980 to the present, Dr. Remington has been a Research Psychologist in the Aerospace Human Factors Research Division at NASA-ARC. From 1993-1994 Dr. Remington was a visiting scientist at the School of Computer Science at Carnegie Mellon University. He has published numerous papers on visual attention and its affects on display design. Dr. Remington has served as the lead human factors designer on NASA projects responsible for developing human interfaces for intelligent systems. His current interests include visual attention, task switching, and integrative models of human cognition.

Michael G. Shafto received his Ph.D. from Princeton University in 1974. He has published in the areas of experimental and quantitative methods, systems engineering, human-computer interaction, developmental and educational psychology, applied social psychology, and psycholinguistics. In 1987 he transferred from the Office of Naval Research (Cognitive Science Division) to NASA-Ames Research Center, where he has served in several technical and management roles. He is currently the Branch Chief for Human-Automation Integration Research in the Human Factors Research and Technology Division (Information Systems Directorate), and Program Manager for Human-Automation Integration Research in NASA's Aeronautics research program. His current research interests are in the area of formal modeling and simulation-based analysis of complex human-machine systems.

Discussion

Len Bass: How do you validate models, i.e. how does one know the sufficient set of primitives in a system, and how does one know that a task is modelled correctly?

Michael Freed: Validity of a modelled task is basically done by the engineer who utilizes a model. If predictions are reasonable, then the engineer will consider the predictions in the design. If the predictions are not reasonable, then the engineer will ignore them. Validity of primitives comes from psychological literature.

Gilbert Cockton: Only a comment: There are better ways to establish an intial task or activity model, and they reveal problems with existing ATCs, e.g., the wind down cost is too high for scenarios where the user must abandon the interaction (e.g. threat of attacks, see someone you must speak to, catch a bus).

Fabio Paterno: How do you represent in your approach the cooperation among multiple users as it happens in ATC applications?

Michael Freed: We consider such interactions as all other interactions.

Stéphane Chatty: I am not quite clear about how you use your model of the user. What do you simulate against what, at what level does it occur (mouse clicks or tasks?) and what does that produce?

Michael Freed: We take the model of the user and of the environment. We run that against one another and get event traces.

Remi Bastide: How do you exploit the event traces of a simulation?

Michael Freed: The event traces are large amount of output. There are some problems in exploiting the amount of data.

Joelle Coutaz: How do you specify the perceptual appearance of the system to be tested?

Michael Freed: You specify a data structure which represents the content of the screen, such as icons, their movement, and their colour.

Robert Spence: In the introduction to your talk you mentioned electronic circuit design and similar activities. I have been involved in the design of computer-aided design tools for people such as chip designers, and I am very much aware of the fact that (for example) circuit designers often find it difficult to identify the tasks, sub-tasks, sub-sub-tasks, etc. they have to address in the course of (say) a few weeks. Equally, it is extremely difficult to elicit, from those designers, any measure of urgency, importance and the like. How does your research relate to such users who, I think, are undertaking a very different task to that of the Air Traffic Controller?

Michael Freed: Eliciting and representing a human operator's underlying task knowledge can certainly be difficult and time consuming. Techniques from the expert-systems subfield of "knowledge acquisition" can be used to assist in this process and keep its costs under control. In addition, several aspects of APEX have been developed to ease this process. For example, the PDL notation for task knowledge balances the need for a powerful, expressive language against the need to keep is simple, intuitive, and suggestive. Another example is the inclusion of libraries of generic task knowledge for activities such as using a mouse, typing on a keyboard, and finding information on a graph or table. Because these activities recur in many domains, including representations of them simplifies the task analysis problem.

Philippe Palanque: You have only talked about what is called mistakes. Do you have ideas on how to extend your work to slips?

Michael Freed: In fact, what I presented is precisely slips made in knowledge due for example to high workload.

Philippe Palanque: Ok, so what about more low level slips, such as selecting the wrong icon on the screen?

Michael Freed: We are not dealing at the moment with this level of detail.

Christian Gram: Could you handle it by introducing slips stochastically?

Michael Freed: Yes, but that is not the focus of our work.

Frameworks and patterns for synchronous groupware : AMF-C approach

F. Tarpin-Bernard, B.T. David, P. Primet
GRACIMP - ICTT, Ecole Centrale de Lyon, France
{Franck.Tarpin-Bernard, Bertrand.David, Pascale.Primet}@ec-lyon.fr

Abstract: Frameworks and design patterns are emerging technologies in software engineering. They increase software quality in terms of reusability, modularity and extensibility. Synchronous groupware can benefit of these new technologies. This article describes AMF-C, a multiagent model which structures each agent with a various number of facets, and two associated frameworks. Indeed, a cooperative application can use either a fragmented framework (facets are dispatched into the network) or a replicated one (each agent is totally replicated). Design patterns are identified for the definition and the interconnection of facets. In this last case, an expressive graphical formalism is used to wire control components. The design and implementation tasks are largely reduced and mainly rely on a good choice and combination of patterns. Finally, we introduce the associated tools and methodology that holds great promise in addressing the design issues.

Key words: Framework, design pattern, synchronous groupware, CSCW, AMF-C

1. INTRODUCTION

"Object-oriented application frameworks are a promising technology for reifying proven software designs and implementations in order to reduce the cost and improve the quality of software" (Fayad, 1997). Indeed, they enhance modularity by encapsulating volatile implementation details behind stable interfaces which reduce the effort required to understand and maintain existing software. Related to the framework technology, the design patterns have recently emerged in software engineering (Gamma, 1995). These patterns are supposed to describe recurring solutions that have stood the test of time. A single framework usually contains many patterns, so these patterns are smaller than frameworks. Therefore, they are also more abstract. They are the micro-architectural elements of frameworks (Johnson, 1997). But for many authors, since some frameworks have been implemented several times, they represent a kind of pattern, too. For instance, Model/View/Controller is a user-interface framework that is described as a pattern in Bushmann & al. (1996), whereas Johnson considers that it can be decomposed into three major design patterns and several less important ones, referring to Gamma's work. Actually, both notions are complementary and their importance in software engineering is increasing regularly.

Computer supported cooperative work is also a recent field of investigation. Many models, tools and interaction patterns have been developed for experimental groupware. Few of them are becoming specialised frameworks. For instance, the National Center for Supercomputing Applications built *Habanero* (NCSA, 1996), a framework for sharing Java objects with colleagues distributed around the Internet. *TCL-TK DP* (see Smith, 1996) can also be considered as a cooperative framework. It is used by Roseman's team to implement the new version of *Groupkit* (Roseman, 1993).

As the number of CSCW experiments and observational studies is increasing, new sociological and psychological consequences of this new way of working are identified. One of the most important conclusions about these systems is that, most of the time, they are well adapted for one kind of cooperative work but can not be applied in all situations (meetings, collaborative design, teletraining, etc.). For all these reasons, we consider that groupware, and especially synchronous groupware, should provide a very wide range of patterns of interaction. But more importantly, they should provide services which allow the user (or the leader of a group) to switch at run-time from one pattern to another.

Considering these different issues, our purpose is to help design and development of flexible groupware, building cooperative frameworks and associated design patterns. This paper describes AMF-C, an architectural model which defines two cooperative frameworks, and some of the main patterns which have been identified. It concludes with the related design methodology and tools.

2. FRAMEWORKS FOR GROUPWARE

Referencing to well known works such as (Rodden, 1991) or (Ellis, 91), we have identified different forms of control (Tarpin-Bernard, 1998), among these, the most relevant are:
- **Interaction control** : management of the relations between user actions and internal data changes.
- **Notification control** : management of the notifications of actions from or to the group.
- **Access control** on data and processings : management of rights and duties of users in relation to their roles in the group.

– **Concurrency control** : coordination activity of concurrent access to shared resources in multi-user systems.

As groupware engineering can not be done from scratch, it is necessary to identify different levels of development. These four controls can be dispatched into three functional layers (see figure 1), corresponding to the three main actors involved in groupware : users, groups and computers.

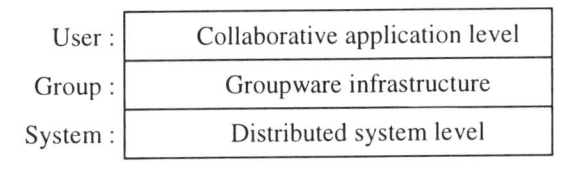

User :	Collaborative application level
Group :	Groupware infrastructure
System :	Distributed system level

Figure 1. The three functional layers of a groupware environment

The first layer corresponds to the **collaborative applications** level. It contains all the cooperative software used by the users. This level is definitely user-centred, which means that it manages interaction control and proposes interfaces for notification and access controls. It uses multiusers services provided by a second layer called the **groupware infrastructure**. This layer contains all the common elements of group activities and acts as an operating system dedicated to groups. It supports collaborative work managing sessions, users and groups ; provides generic cooperative tools (e.g.: telepointer) and is responsible for concurrency control. It also implements notification protocols and provides access control mechanisms. In many groupware, these tasks are assumed by toolkits. It is a generic layer between applications and **distributed system** which constitutes the third level of our model. This last layer is essentially in charge of message multicast and consistency control. Usually, it is a computer-centred layer that provides transparent mechanisms for communication and synchronisation of distributed components which misfit with CSCW aims but which are very useful.

In the next sections, we will only develop the collaborative application level and especially our AMF-C model (Tarpin-Bernard, 1997b).

2.1   AMF : a framework for single-user software

Architectural models for groupware have to combine the knowledge of models developed for single-user applications and the constraints introduced by cooperative work. For many years, HCI community has been very interested in designing models for interactive software. One of the most important class of such models is the multiagent one. These models organise an interactive system as a set of agents that collaborate to support the dialogue between men and computers. Most of these agents are based on three components (facets) mapped on the HCI paradigm (presentation to the user, functional kernel, and interaction control). But, these models present two main disadvantages :
1. They define very large facets which mix different thematic functions.
2. They do not provide powerful mechanism to express interaction control.

To bring some solutions to these shortages, we chose to develop a multiagent model called AMF (Ouadou, 1994).

Indeed, to solve the first problem, AMF organises each agent in an appropriated number of facets. These facets can be similar to the classical components of PAC model (Coutaz, 1990) or MVC (Krasner, 1988). They can also either come from a finer split of *control* components, or from the identification of new characteristics of agents (e.g.: management of the user model), or from the duplication of classical facets (several *presentation* facets corresponding to different views). For instance, we can identify the following facets: *presentation* (I/O relations with the user), *abstraction* (logical data - functional kernel), *evaluation* (capture of the user's actions), *help* (contextual and on-line helps linked to a user model) or *user model* (information for adaptive interface). In the multiuser version of AMF we will present other facets related to the cooperative work requirements.

Finally, to solve the second problem, AMF expresses interaction control with two kinds of components:

1. Each facet presents several *communication ports* (allowing input, output or both). These ports avoid to having a permanent binding between an abstraction (a port) and its implementation (a function). Moreover, it is possible to implement the body of the functions in various languages.

2. The *Control* "facet" is an abstract facet mainly defined by *control administrators*. A control administrator has three roles:
   - To *connect,* managing logical relations between the communication ports (sources and targets) that are connected to it;
   - To *translate,* transforming the messages which come from the source ports in understandable messages for target ports;
   - To express *behaviour,* and so control strategies, using different rules of activation between a source port (A) and a target port (B). We have identified several administrators, such as : simple (if A then B), sequence (if A1, next A2, next ... An then B), conjunctive (if A1 and A2 and ... An then B)...

An example of interaction control in a single-user application.

Using the AMF concepts, it is possible to model an interaction control in a single-user application. In the simplest case, when only one agent is implicated, two simple administrators (A_1 & A_2) generally manage the relations between an action starting from the *Presentation* facet and the associated command defined in the *Abstraction* facet (see figure 2).

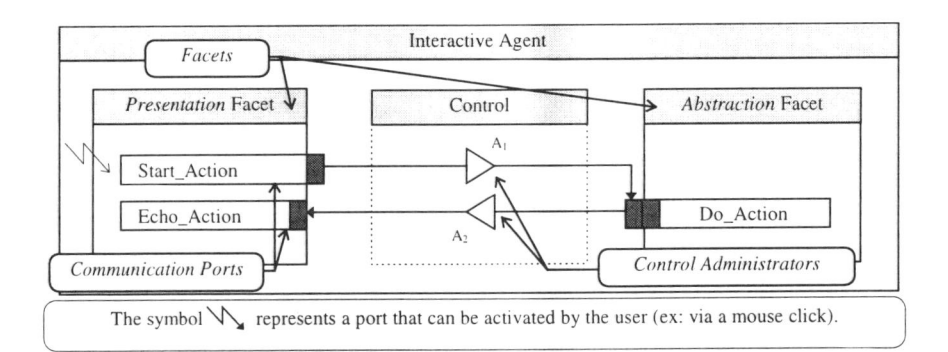

Figure 2. An interaction on a single-user agent modelled with AMF

In a multi-user context, an application must be able to notify each action of one user to the other members of his group, and each agent must be able to reproduce the actions of remote users. To solve this problem, we created AMF-C a cooperative extension of AMF (Tarpin-Bernard, 1997a). This model can adopt a fragmented form when shared agents are split and their facets distributed, and a replicated form when each agent has a representative on each workstation.

2.2   A fragmented framework for groupware

Analysing distributed systems studies, we have found the original concept of fragmented object (Gourhant, 1994). The methods and data of a fragmented object are distributed on the network and "transparent" mechanisms let it look like a classical object in a single computer. Applying fragmentation to AMF model offers an interesting approach for modelling CSCW applications. Indeed, their facets define a natural boundary for fragmentation. Thus, we can study the distribution of the facets into the network. According to the desired architecture, we can distribute *presentation*, *control* or *abstraction* facets.

The figure 3 presents a centralised architecture with three shared agents manipulated by two users. Each agent is defined by four facets : the *abstraction* and *control* facets, and two *presentation* facets corresponding to specific views of each user. In this context, each *presentation* facet can be adapted to the role of each user ($P_{Ai} \neq P_{Bi}$). It is the *control* facet which is in charge of the propagation of input/output events from or to the different facets, and especially between multiple *presentation* facets.

229

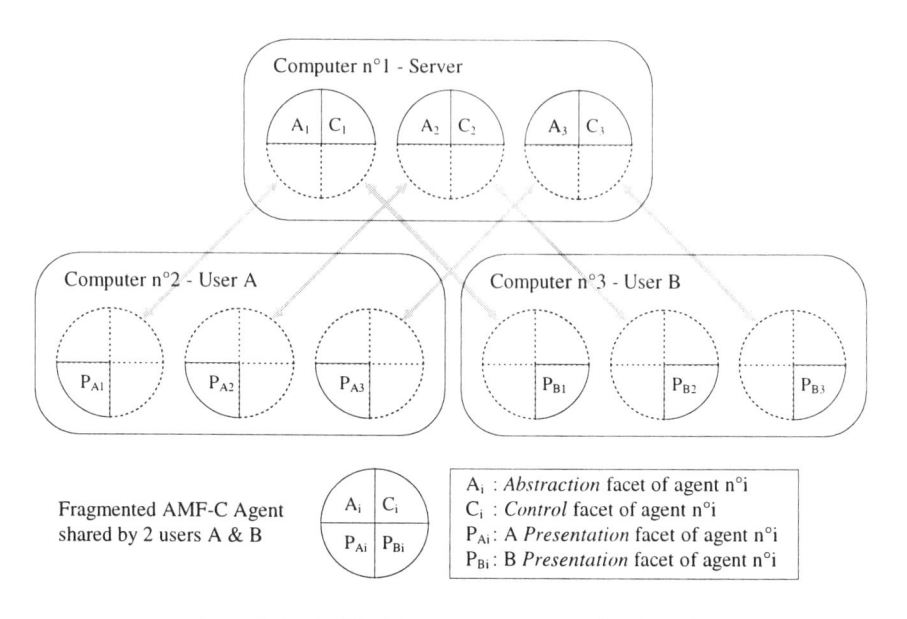

A_i : *Abstraction* facet of agent n°i
C_i : *Control* facet of agent n°i
P_{Ai}: A *Presentation* facet of agent n°i
P_{Bi}: B *Presentation* facet of agent n°i

Fragmented AMF-C Agent
shared by 2 users A & B

Figure 3. An AMF-C fragmentation - centralised version

If we try to model an elementary interaction (e.g.: a button triggers an action on an agent), we can consider a situation in which a first user is responsible of the agent, whereas a second user can just interact with its presentation. In this case, we can imagine that the agent is mainly located on the first user's workstation (Figure 4). To assume concurrency control and maintain the consistency of the shared agent, it is necessary to define new types of administrators. In the example given on the figure 4, we have built a lock administrator which filters the access to the agent.

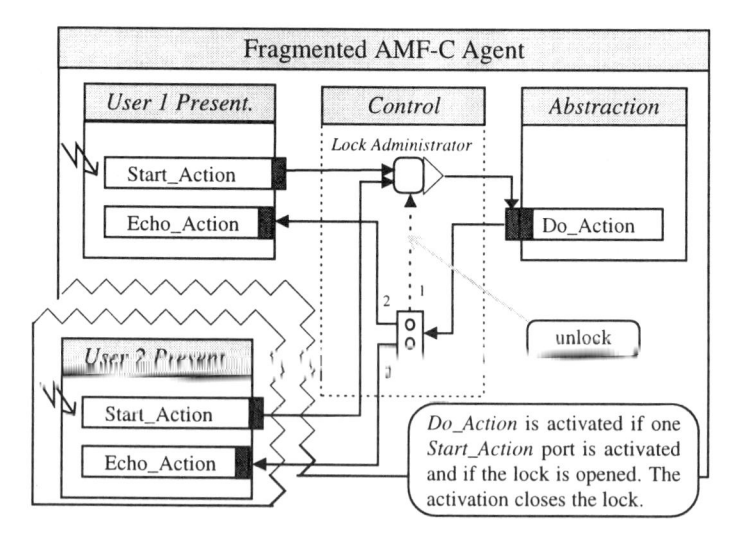

Figure 4. An example of elementary interaction on a fragmented AMF-C agent

230

The dynamicity property of AMF-C agents allows to formalise the adaptation of each agent to the current user's role. Indeed, the number and the form of facets is not static, any change of role can lead to substitute a facet, and especially a *presentation* one.

The fragmented AMF-C framework is well adapted to represent hybrid architecture in which some facets are centralised whereas others are replicated. Moreover, the use of a distributed object-oriented language can really ease the implementation of such a model. Indeed, in our first implementation of AMF, with C++, each facet is an object. The activation of a communication port leads to the invocation of a method of these objects. In a distributed context, this corresponds to a remote method invocation as defined in CORBA (Siegel, 1996) or Java-RMI.

However, we can notice that, to introduce more flexibility in notification control and so propose WYSIWIS relaxations, we need to multiply the number of *control* and *abstraction* facets. Indeed, if we want to process remote actions differently than local ones, we need some new *control* facets. On the other hand, several *abstraction* facets are necessary if we want to authorise users to work on their own data and let do some versioning. If we insist in this way of facet personalisation, agents fragmentation becomes an unadapted paradigm. As a consequence, looking for a maximum flexibility implies to replicate each agent and so to choose the replicated AMF-C framework.

2.3   A replicated framework for groupware

Replication is based on both notions of **reference agent** and **local agent**. When a reference agent is shared by *n* participants, *n* local representatives are distributed on the local workstations. The local agents of a same reference agent are called **brother agents**. These local agents support the manipulations of the users. The form and the content of each local agent depend on its owner's characteristics expressed in terms of roles and viewpoints. To define work contexts, which means memorise agents states, the reference agent notion is particularly interesting. Actually, reference agents can be real or virtual (figure 5).

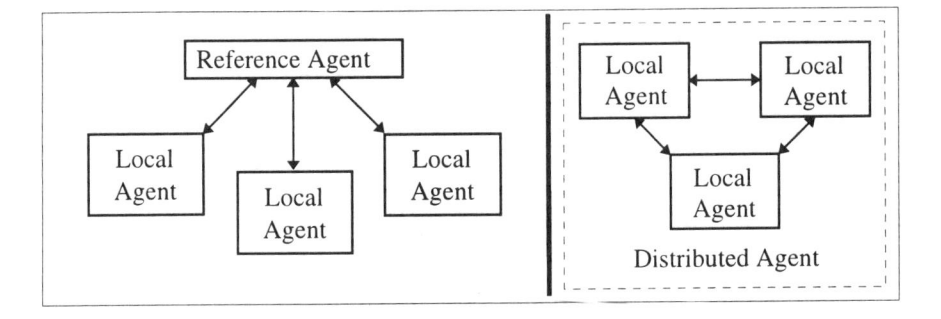

Figure 5. Two visions of reference agents : centralised or distributed

In the first case, reference agents can be localised on a server, with all the advantages (simplicity, regularity, etc.) and disadvantages (rigidity, bottleneck, etc.)

231

of such a situation. In the second case, each reference agent is virtual, which means that it is defined by the whole set of local agents. This approach presents other advantages (more interactivity, best fault tolerance) and disadvantages (complexity, etc.). As an intermediate solution, the reference agent can be one of the local agent and its localisation can be static or dynamic. In the static case, it is always in the same place, whereas in the dynamic case, it can be situated on the workstation of the group leader or on the workstation of its creator. In all these cases, each action (creation, modification and deletion) performed on the local agent should be notified to the other brother agents.

2.3.1   An example of replicated AMF-C framework

In our laboratory, we have experimented this framework using the ECooP groupware infrastructure (Primet, 1996a). In order to introduce a maximum flexibility in the four control presented in the beginning of section 2, we consider that four steps are relevant in a "group interaction": selection (OS : Object Selection), validation (AV : Action Validation), execution (AE : Action Ending) and unselection (OF : Object Freeing). Several sequences of actions can happen between the selection - unselection phase (figure 6a).

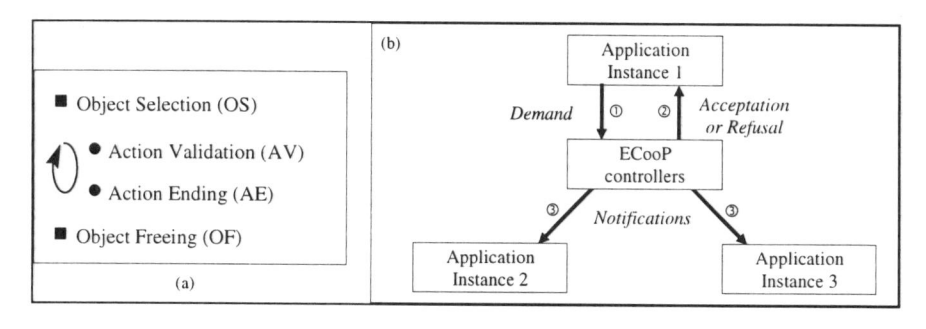

Figure 6. The four steps of the control dialogue (a) and the NCP protocol (b)

A specific **control and notification protocol** and a set of associated generic functions have been defined in order to ease the dialogue between a cooperative application and the groupware infrastructure (Primet, 1996b) and to provide flexible concurrency control mechanisms. It relies on four types of messages - D: Demand, A: Acceptation, R: Refusal and N: Notification - (figure 6a).

2.3.2   Concurrency control flexibility

At each phase of a "group interaction", a demand is systematically sent to the ECooP local controller so that it is always informed of the application state. Depending on the chosen concurrency policy and the initial control parameters, the controller answers immediately without any control or submits the request to the ECooP decision component before answering to the application. For instance, in a pessimistic policy with an earliest control (since object selection), the control is

232

performed with the reception of an "Object Selection Demand". The decision component accepts or refuses and the local controller transmits this "collective" decision to the application. Then, the other messages are systematically accepted and notified as the lock assumes that there will be no problems with these operations. On the other hand, in an optimistic policy with a latest control (at the end of processing), the "Object Selection" and "Action Validation" demands are always accepted. The real control is only done at the end of the action execution. If a conflict occurs, its solving is related to a collective decision and the application must undo the action. A notification of this undo action is also sent to the remote applications.

In this context, whatever the decision component is (the community of local controllers or a central controller), the application interface does not have to change. Only behaviour of controller agents depends on the policy.

The replicated version of the AMF-C model fits very well with ECooP. Indeed, to implement flexible concurrency control, we first need to define specific administrators able to dialogue with local controller using functions of the ECooP API and second to build a new facet, called *Distant*, which receives the notifications of remote actions. Figure 7 presents the schematic representation the four administrators which realise the four phases of the dialogue (a) and two additional administrators (b) which can be used to implement direct manipulations (Object Selection and Action Validation can be simultaneous).

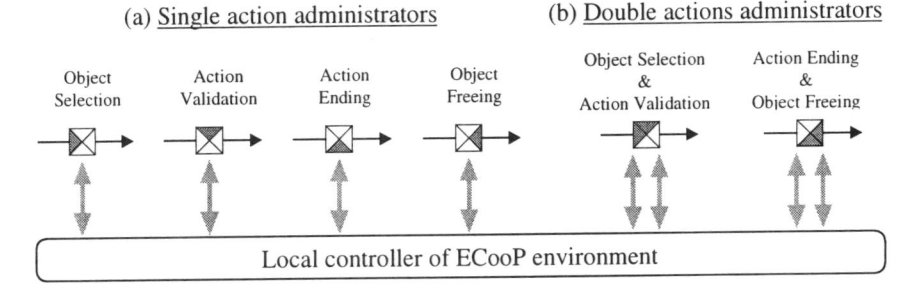

(a) <u>Single action administrators</u>   (b) <u>Double actions administrators</u>

| Object Selection | Action Validation | Action Ending | Object Freeing | Object Selection & Action Validation | Action Ending & Object Freeing |

Local controller of ECooP environment

Figure 7. The cooperative administrators of AMF-C

3.   DESIGN PATTERNS

Considering both AMF-C frameworks, we can imagine various design patterns related to the choice of thematic facets or to the choice of control mechanisms. In this section, we develop the patterns associated to the replicated framework.

The identification of specialised CSCW facets can lead to various solutions. For instance the PAC* model (Calgary, 1997) maps the three common functional spaces of groupware (production, communication and coordination) on the structure of PAC agents. As a consequence, the authors propose several patterns dealing with various combinations of dispatching. For instance, each component (Presentation, Abstraction and Control) can be sliced into three parts corresponding to the three spaces. Another pattern dedicates PAC agents to treat the production, communication and coordination functions independently. A first adaptation can leads us to define communication and coordination facets whereas production facets can be assimilated to abstraction facets. A large presentation facet or three smaller ones then will also be defined. In practice, we met some difficulties to split agents this way because considering fine grain agents we found that they are often dedicated to one main space so that the model lost its interest.

So, in addition to the *Distant* facet which receives all the remote notifications, we introduce a second one, called *Access,* which is in charge of the adaptation of presentations according to the users' roles. It activates and deactivates the interactive control objects of the user interface according to his rights. At least we define a *Private* facet which deals with the choice of group retroaction and notification control (see next section). The AMF-C model is definitely dynamic and allows, at each instant, to modify, create or delete some agents, facets or administrators. The *Private* facet lets users change structurally the agent via an adapted interface.

Using the six administrators that we have presented in §2.3 and referring to the standard interaction pattern presented figure 1, we can define a first pattern of cooperative interaction (Figure 8). When the message sent by *Start_Action* crosses the A_1 administrator, all the remote agents receive from ECooP a message which activates the *Replay_*Action port of the *Distant* facet, so that the action is replayed on each replica of the agent.

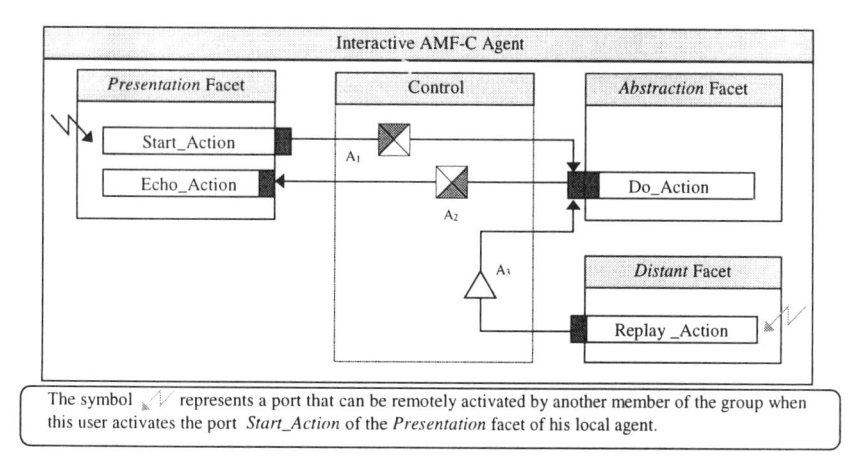

The symbol ⩘ represents a port that can be remotely activated by another member of the group when this user activates the port *Start_Action* of the *Presentation* facet of his local agent.

Figure 8. A first interaction pattern on a shared agent modelled with AMF-C

It is also possible to define a second pattern of interaction in which selection and unselection phases are clearly distinct from the action phases (see figure 9). This pattern allows users to see the objects which are locked (locally or remotely).

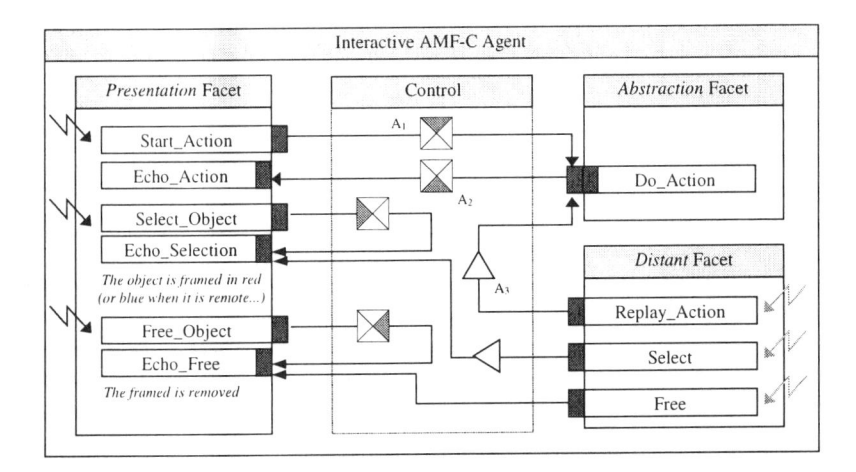

Figure 9. A second interaction pattern on a shared agent modelled with AMF-C

Considering all the specific facets presented before, we can propose a generic interactive and cooperative AMF-C agent (figure 10). This pattern only shows one direct interaction (once it is finished, the object is freed). Of course, for each action, a real agent contains one of the previous patterns.

This last figure also details the structure of the *Private* facet. As we introduced it in the previous section, relaxation of WYSIWIS can be done with AMF-C according to **several strategies**.

The first one consists in modifying the administrators linked to the *Distant* facet in order to change its connection with the *Presentation* facet or even with the *Abstraction* facet. In the second one, we can modify the implementation of the input port *Echo_Action* of the *Presentation* facet for it to have a different behaviour depending on the source of the activation message. Finally, in some cases, we can completely disconnect some communication ports (e.g.: do not propagate some scrolling actions of other participants). For instance, to disconnect a user from the others, one solution is to not notify his actions of the other members. To make such a change, it is necessary to modify the administrators which are linked to *Presentation* facets. These three strategies are represented by the three generic ports of the *Private* facet which are presented on the figure : *Change_Propagation*, *Change_Echo* and *Change_Updating*. As a consequence, the *Private* facet has a structural knowledge of the agent.

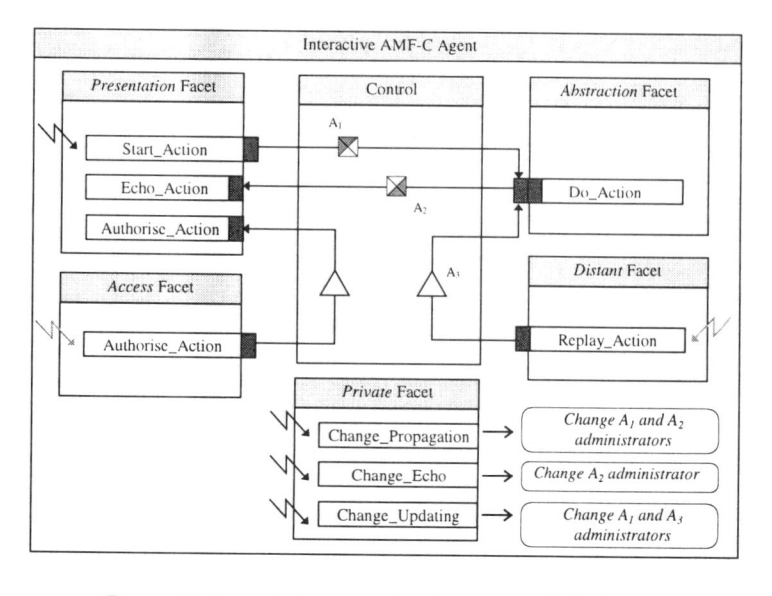

Figure 10. General structure of an interactive AMF-C agent

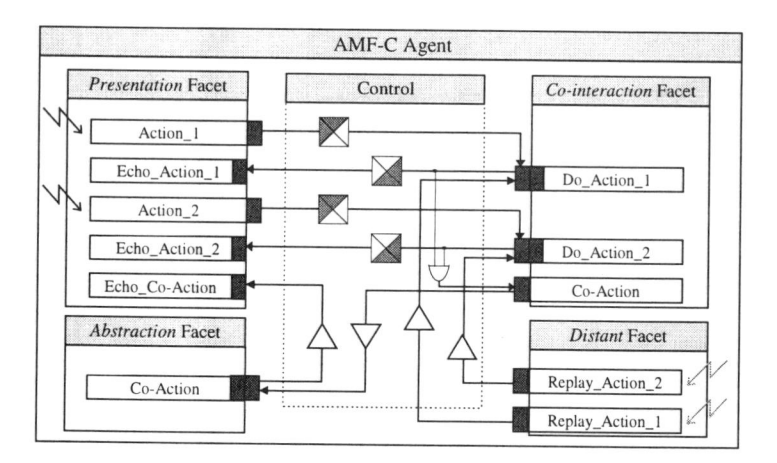

Figure 11. A design pattern of co-interaction on an AMF-C agent

Combining the definition of new facets and the use of new control mechanisms, designers can imagine now kinds of interaction. As a short example, we propose in figure 11, a pattern which models a co-interaction. We call co-interaction, a complex interaction between two or more users where each of them execute a part of the action (e.g. : two users should turn 2 different keys to open a secure door). To implement a co-interaction, we define a new facet which monitors the elementary interactions and triggers the co-interaction when all requirements are achieved (completion, timing, etc.).

4.   METHODOLOGY AND TOOLS

In this paper, we have focused our attention on the presentation of AMF-C frameworks for groupware, and some of their associated design patterns. However, we did not forget, that such a work is really useful only if a methodology is also proposed and if design tools are provided.

Currently, thanks to our first design and development experiments we have started to define some rules that should be used by a comprehensive methodology. The first one deals with the choice of the AMF-C framework. According to us, the main criteria of selection is the degree of autonomy and personalisation that is looked for. Indeed, if the wanted application respects simple rules of coordination (e.g. only one kind of WYSIWIS is needed) and if the groups are homogeneous, the fragmented framework which is the simplest one is a good choice. In other cases, the replicated framework is the only one that lets you introduce a maximum of flexibility in the group processes.

Once the designer have chosen his framework, his task is now divided into two main phases :
1. Identify the agents and their services
2. Choose design patterns associated to each service

Indeed, as in other multiagent models it is often difficult to identify the agents of the application. On this particular point, AMF-C does not introduce specifities, so that all the common methods can be used. However, the situation changes concerning the choice of structural patterns for agents. It is necessary to choose what facets should be defined and how to dispatch the services into these facets. At least, designers have to choose a pattern of interaction for each service. Each time that it is meaningful to define new facet in terms of reusability and modularity we advise to do it.

Of course, because of our flexibility principle, the choice of these patterns is not static. Initially, the designer chooses what pattern is the most relevant according to his point of view. But, whether the end-user wants to change some controls, the dynamicity of AMF-C lets him choose his own pattern.

Finally, as we mentioned it in the beginning of this section, the design pattern approach fits very well with the definition of associated tools. The builder tool which is under construction will propose a catalogue of design patterns to ease groupware design. The design and implementation tasks are largely reduced by the direct building of AMF-C diagrams. In the future, this tool will also be used for the definition of new patterns and for the dynamic evolution of cooperative applications.

5.   CONCLUSION

Frameworks and design patterns are both notions that have recently emerged in object-oriented software engineering. They have been proposed to ease design of large and complex software thanks to their good properties in terms of reusability, modularity, extensibility are more generally quality improvement. Groupware are among the most complex software that should be designed. Because they involve groups of users in work processes, they must combine all the advanced technologies studied in single-user situations but also take in account dynamics of work sessions and sociological rules.

Our proposal tries to cover a wide range of problems from groupware design to dynamic adaptation of cooperative applications. Our key model is the multifaceted multiagent AMF model. Its cooperative extension AMF-C leads us to propose two frameworks for groupware based on both paradigms : fragmentation and replication. The graphical formalism of AMF-C eases the building of various design patterns corresponding to several kind of problems.

Designers' tasks then consist of choosing these patterns in respect with these frameworks. The methodology and its associated tools are the keys elements for the success of this approach. Currently, we focus our efforts on the development of both elements continuing to implement and evaluate our own synchronous groupware. Today, we have already developed a kinematic diagram editor and a 3D scene builder that validates the concepts presented in this paper.

Finally, the AMF-C graphical notation mainly describes the organisation of multiagent applications in terms of structures and relationships. Referring to Kruchten's work (1995), we consider that it can be used to express logical views on a system. However, this notation only shows static views. It needs to be completed by scenarios in order to fully use the dynamic property of AMF-C.

6. REFERENCES

Coutaz J., Nigay L. (1997), From Single-User Architectural Design to PAC*: A Generic Software Architecture Model for CSCW, CHI'97, Atlanta, ACM Publ., 242-249.

Coutaz J. (1990) Architecture Models for interactive software: Failures and Trends, in G. Cockton (eds.): *Engineering for Human-Computer Interaction*, Elsevier Sc. Publ., 137-153.

Ellis C.A., Gibbs S.J. & Rein G.L., (1991), Groupware : some issues and experiences, Communication of ACM, Vol 34. n°1, 39-58.

Fayad M.E., Schmidt D.C. (1997), Object-Oriented Application Frameworks, *Communications of the ACM*, Oct., Vol 40. n°10, 32-38.

Gamma E., Helm R., Johnson R., Vlissides J. (1995), Design Patterns : Elements of Reusable Object-Oriented Software, Addison Wesley, Reading, MA.

Gourhant Y., Makpangou M., Le Narzul JP., Shapiro M. (1994), Fragmented objects for Distributed Abstractions, in Readings in Distributed Computing Systems, Eds Casavant & Singhal, IEEE Computer Society Press, 170-186.

Johnson R.E. (1997), Frameworks = Components + Patterns, *Communications of the ACM*, Oct., Vol 40. n°10, 39-42.

Krasner G.E., Pope S.T., (1988), A cookbook for using the model view controller user interface paradigm in Smalltalk 80, *Journal of Object-Oriented Programming*, 1(3), 26-49.

Kruchten P. (1995), The 4+1 View Model of Architecture, *IEEE Software*, November, 12 (6), 42-50.

NCSA (1996), Habanero Home Page : http://www.ncsa.uiuc.edu/SDG/Software/Habanero/

Ouadou K. (1994), AMF : Un modèle d'architecture multi-agents multi-facettes pour Interfaces Homme-Machine et les outils associés, Ph D, Ecole Centrale de Lyon, France.

Primet P. (1996a), ECooP a flexible CSCW Environment, Technical Report, Ecole Centrale de Lyon, France

Primet P. (1996b), Contrôle de concurrence dans les collecticiels: mise en oeuvre de la flexibilité, Proceedings of CRAC'96, Paris, France

Rodden T. (1991), CSCW and Distributed Systems: the problem of Control, *Proceedings of the ECSCW '91*, Amsterdam, Kluwer Academic Press.

Roseman M. (1993), Tcl/Tk as a Basis for Groupware, *Proceedings of Tcl 93 Workshop*, University of Calgary, Alberta Canada,

Siegel J. (1996), CORBA - Fundamentals and Programming, John Wiley.

Smith B., Rowe L. A. (1996), An Introduction to Tcl-DP, Cornell University, http://www.cs.cornell.edu/Info/Projects/zeno/Tcl-DP/Tutorial/tutorial.html

Tarpin-Bernard F. (1997a), "Travail Coopératif Synchrone Assisté par Ordinateur : Approche AMF-C", Ph D, Ecole Centrale de Lyon, France.

Tarpin-Bernard F., David B.T. (1997b), AMF a new design pattern for complex interactive software ?, *Proceedings of International HCI'97*, San Francisco, in Design of Computing Systems, 21 B, Eds Elsevier, 351-354.

Tarpin-Bernard F., Primet P. (1998), *Flexibility in synchronous groupware*, paper submitted to the Journal of Computer Supported Collaborative Work, Kluwer Academic Publishers

7. BIOGRAPHY

Franck Tarpin-Bernard is an associate professor graduated in 1997 (PhD). He is also engineer of the Ecole Centrale de Lyon and has been working on CSCW and software engineering for four years. Bertrand David is professor and co-director of the GRACIMP laboratory. He works on HCI, CSCW, Concurrent Engineering and cooperative learning. Pascale Primet is an associate professor in computer science. She mainly studies groupware, distributed computing and high speed networks.

Discussion

Len Bass: How do you handle time constraints between distributed events?

Franck Tarpin-Bernard: Co-Action will manage the time constraints between two distributed events that must be combined to obtain a complete command.

Prasun Dewan: What is the difference between an administrator and a facet?

Franck Tarpin-Bernard: A facet is a set of communication ports. Administrators are sub-components. They can be considered as a special kind of facet. The control facet includes all the administrators.

Prasun Dewan: You showed us how the collaborative behaviour can be changed by changing the patterns. At what time is the pattern bound , at application creation time or at runtime? If it is at runtime, then users could change dynamically from, say synchronous to asynchronous coupling.

Franck Tarpin-Bernard: Currently the set of patterns must be defined at application creation time by the designer but users can change dynamically from one pattern to another at run-time.

Prasun Dewan: But users do not think in terms of facets.

Franck Tarpin-Bernard: Yes, but the Presentation facets are in charge of presenting the interaction patterns to the user and triggering the structural adaptations of agents. So the application could adapt its structure automatically to the user's needs.

Helmut Stiegler: Your focus is on synchronous co-operation. Groupware in general has a broad scope, including workflow systems, which are asynchronous. Do you know already how to include asynchronous collaboration?

Franck Tarpin-Bernard: We thought about it. Maybe we only need a new facet. For each specific problem, a new kind of facet is created. We need new facets and maybe new administrators to handle this problem.

Nick Graham: How many controller styles (i.e., concurrency, control policies) have you implemented?

Franck Tarpin-Bernard: We developed various pessimistic approaches. About optimistic approaches, we only tried one. Undo conflicting actions.

Nick Graham: The dialogue protocol seems to restrict us to relatively simple object-function dialogues. Is this correct?

240

Franck Tarpin-Bernard: Not at all. If the designer needs to manage complex objects such as sets of objects he will consider them as a new class of agent. Moreover, like in Object Oriented languages, we have defined the notion of inheritance for agents. So you can build a large hierarchy of agents.

Prasun Dewan: Do you provide a general undo function?

Franck Tarpin-Bernard: We tried to create a new facet Undo similar to the coordinator. We are not sure that we can reuse undoing functions in different CSCW systems.

Joelle Coutaz: Can the model cope with a mixture of fragmented and replicated agents?

Franck Tarpin-Bernard: Conceptually it is quite feasible but in practice the implementation tools and the infrastructure you use may lead to only one of the policies.

Joelle Coutaz: How does AMF-C cope with heterogeneity of styles?

Franck Tarpin-Bernard: Just like in PAC-Amodeus. The Dialogue Controller is expressed as AMF-C agents whose facets call external functions.

MAMP: A Design Model for Object-Oriented Visualization Systems

Ricardo Orosco* & Marcelo Campo**

Univ. Autonoma de Madrid – UAM – Dep. Ing. Informatica. Ciudad Univ. Cantoblanco, 28049, Madrid, Spain. Email: orosco@acm.org . Also UNCPBA – ISISTAN –Argentina
***Univ. Nac. Centro Bs. As. – UNCPBA - Fac. Cs. Exactas - ISISTAN. 7000, Tandil, Argentina. Email: mcampo@exa.unicen.edu.ar.*

Abstract: The difficulty to build interactive visualizations that allow complex data explorations is a well-known fact. Some reasons for this difficulty are the dynamic nature of data exploration process and the diversity of goals and requirements in visualization applications, among others. The usage of design models for implementing information visualization systems (IVS) appears as a convenient approach to reduce this complexity. However, current HCI design models are insufficient from the point of view of the needs of IVSs. In a similar way, tools or environments specially developed to build IVSs have limitations for the implementation of highly dynamic exploration process. In this work, MAMP, a design model for the construction of object oriented visualization applications is presented. This model combines the advantages of current HCI design models (in particular, MVC) with the requirements of data visualization process. A software architecture and an object-oriented application framework, Telescope, based on MAMP are also described, along with several ways for implementing the characteristic features of any visualization, using these tools. Finally, two visualization applications developed according to the MAMP design model are briefly described: *CityVis*, a system for visualizing city data, and *WarVis*, a system for visualizing information about military conflicts.

Keywords User interface architectures, visualization, object-oriented frameworks

1.   INTRODUCTION

This paper is devoted to the description of a design model for visualization systems construction, *MAMP*, and an associated software architecture that can be used to simplify the development of Information Visualization Systems, IVS. A corresponding Object-Oriented framework, *Telescope*, has been built and tested through the development of visualization systems with a sophisticated functionality in different domains.

The difficulty to build interactive visualizations that allow complex data explorations is a well-known fact (Chuah 96)(Kazman 96)(Roth 94). There are some reasons for this intrinsic difficulty: on one hand, advanced visualization systems require highly dynamic data exploration processes, in which data are subject to successive transformations using composition, decomposition and filtering mechanisms, as well as different degrees of abstraction and detail are needed. The decision about the use of one of these operations is taken by the user on the basis of the result of the exploration process itself, in an unpredictable way. The exploration of the same data with different goals, at different moments or by different users, can rise the need for different exploration techniques, so a framework for the development of IVSs must simplify the adaptation of the system to the users needs. On the other hand, data also shows a dynamic behavior, and very often the information conveyed by it can not be predicted when the IVS is developed. Finally, IVSs are usually conceived to be used in a number of applications related to a specific field, but there are always differences between the requirements of different applications, so the exploration techniques being used have to be adapted frequently. The development of an IVS is generally a process based on successive approximations, where the reuse of techniques from previous systems is essential, and the availability of a clear model can make a big difference.

One of the consequences of the above facts is that the development of IVSs is in general very different from the development of generic interactive applications for which significant portions of their interactive functionality can be built using modern interactive graphical tools like interface builders. In fact, the development of IVSs requires in general a big amount of programming, and a lot of redesign and adaptation of critical parts. In this context, the most powerful support that can be given to the design and development of IVSs is through a simple conceptual design model that simplifies the designer the decomposition of the system into different components, and their integration, reuse, and adaptation.

Finally, one of the main facts that differentiate IVSs is what we can refer to as their *visualization functionality,* that is, the different ways they allow the user to manipulate data visualization. As a matter of fact, the appearance of data flow based visualization systems, like AVS (Upson 89), can be considered as a major step in the simplification of the design and use of IVSs. The work presented here puts together ideas coming from this recent trend with others from HCI modeling, allowing the use of techniques that can already be seen as classical within the HCI context, but that are highly insufficient from the point of view of the needs of IVSs, and at the same time giving more flexibility to the techniques of data flow based visualization.

The model proposed in this paper consists of an extension to the *Model View Controller* software architecture (MVC) (Krasner 88), adding an Abstraction component and a Mapping component. These new components receive requests from visualization component, and return elaborate data representations after consulting the real data component. On the other hand, abstraction components can be organized in several ways, allowing the implementation of highly dynamic visualization systems, with a visualization functionality that depends very heavily on the application state.

The rest of this paper is organized as follows: in §2 current paradigms for HCI modeling and their limitations for implementing IVS are described. Section 3 describes MAMP design model, its derivation from MVC and the advantages of its usage. In §4 and §5 a possible implementation for this model is described, through the Telescope framework. Section 6 describes the construction of some of main visualization features, using Telescope. Section 7 describes (briefly) two visualization applications developed with this model. Finally, §8 cites some conclusions of this work.

2. MODELS, ARCHITECTURES AND TOOLS FOR VISUALIZATION DEVELOPMENT

Current HCI design models provide essentially the same functional capabilities: presentation, application and dialogue control. These models addressed the same quality goals, but differences in how these goals were applied led to two main architectural styles: the object-oriented style, as exemplified by MVC and PAC (Coutaz 87), and the layered style, first exemplified by the Seeheim model (Green 85) and then followed by the Arch/Slinky meta-model (UIMS 91).

Within object-oriented style, MVC is the most common and used model. In particular, in object-oriented visualization systems with direct-manipulation capabilities, MVC is the predominant approach. This model promotes the independence between the data representation (Model) and its visual presentation (View), assigning to the View component the responsibility of producing the visual presentation of data contained in its Model.

From the point of view of a reusable architecture for IVS, MVC fails in providing an adequate architectural guide that allows the independent incorporation of additional functionality. Indeed, to provide an adequate support for tasks such as exploration process control and semantic processing of data, the identification of additional components should be considered. Particularly, some of the major limitations that can be identified are:

- *Semantic Analysis.* From a design perspective, MVC does not promote the implementation of mechanisms of semantic analysis of the information independently of classes representing information or views. That is, data analysis algorithms must be located in classes implementing either the information representation or visualizations. When new algorithms need to be added, this solution forces the modification of existent classes with behavior related to specific applications. In this way, MVC can induce designs hard to extend and adapt.
- *Abstraction levels filtering.* In general, complex information defines several levels of abstraction that can be visualized or hidden according to the detail level desired by the user. Using a pure MVC architecture, the filtering of different detail levels of the data to be visualized has to be implemented for any particular visualization.

This complicates the programming of alternative visualizations, reducing also its reusability.

- *Data enhancement / enrichment processes.* The usage of some visualization techniques can require a process of data enrichment or enhancement over the data to be visualized, such as an interpolation process. However, the process to be applied depends both on the selected visualization technique and the visualized domain, in order to avoid undesirable phenomena such as misrepresentation (Duce 93). The implementation of these processes by means of the distribution of their functionality among the views and model classes, reduces the possibilities of reuse of these components, and limits the usage of different processes.

The layered style has similar goals, although its emphasis is in the portability of application components across different domains and visualization toolkits. It presents similar drawbacks to the ones cited for the MVC approach. For example, in Arch/Slinky, the features previously described are generally distributed among the dialogue component, the functional core adapter and the presentation component.

The usage of specific tools or environments for visualization construction also presents some limitations for implementing visualizations with a high functionality. Some of these tools attempt to alleviate the construction task by means of techniques and methods for automatic generation of visualizations (BOZ (Casner 91), APT (Mackinlay 86)). This approach facilitates the construction of presentations by non-programmers. These tools, however, are focused on the determination and construction of adequate presentations for particular data types and tasks, without considering aspects such as the adaptation of visualization techniques to specific application needs, or the inclusion of visualization functionality. Another approach is to use special-purpose toolkits and libraries, specially designed for visualization construction (OpenGL (Neider 93), Visualization Toolkit (Schroeder 96)). These tools attempt to provide a high performance, but the degree of abstraction provided by them is far away from the needs of designers of complex visualization.

One successful approach, in particular in commercial visualization communities, is to use dataflow-based systems or environments (such as AVS). These environments have a modular approach for visualization design. The designer must compose a particular visualization through the construction of a network consisting of predefined modules (which include different visualization techniques, filters and operators), generally contained in libraries. This approach has a wide acceptance, although its applicability is mainly oriented to scientific visualization applications. However, it also presents some limitations for implementing visualizations with complex functionality. In most cases, designed networks have a static nature that makes the implementation of highly dynamic visualizations difficult. Additionally, providing an adequate support for the implementation of dynamic data exploration processes, such as the incorporation of domain-specific tasks or user-assistance techniques, is a complex task.

The usage of a software architecture for visualization construction is an approach that has not been sufficiently explored. VANISH (Kazman 96) is one of the few examples in this area. This architecture adapts the Arch/Slinky metamodel for building visualization applications of hierarchically structured information. In this work, a similar approach is pursued, using an object-oriented approach instead of a pure layered approach, incorporating the specific features of visualization processes.

246

3.   PROPOSED MODEL

In order to provide a design model for the structuring of object-oriented visualization applications, MVC was selected as the base architecture model, mainly because its wide acceptance in developing interactive object oriented applications. To solve the previously described limitations of this model, the specific features of visualization processes were considered from the perspective of a conceptual model of visualization process, *Visualization Idioms* (Habber 90). This model focuses on the description of a data visualization process, but it does not considerate very important aspects such as user interaction. Its integration with MVC allows to obtain a domain specific software architecture for implementing object oriented visualization applications with highly dynamic capabilities, as it is required to perform successful data exploration processes.

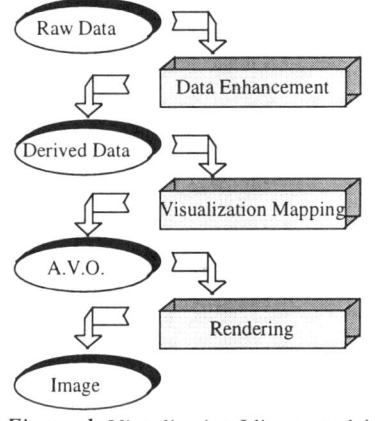

Figure 1. Visualization Idioms model

The *Visualization Idioms* model identifies the three main transformations occurring in most visualization processes (fig. 1), that convert raw data (source data to be visualized) into a displayable image:
– *Data enhancement or enrichment:* it operates on raw data, which is modified into derived data for subsequent visualization operations.
– *Visualization Mapping*: it constructs an imaginary object (abstract visualization object – AVO) from the derived data produced by data enhancement transformations. This imaginary object has extensions in space and time, and contains attributes such as geometry, color, transparency, luminosity, etc.
– *Rendering:* it operates on the AVO to produce at least a displayable image, generally using familiar operations from computer graphics and image processing.

All of these transformations can be implemented using standard MVC. For example, in most object-oriented applications based on MVC, the rendering transformation is included in the views, while other transformations and raw data administration are included within the model. Taking into account the limitations described in §2, this fact produces designs hard to understand and with little reusability.

To obtain a better design, the MVC's model component was divided into three new components, considering those transformations described by *Visualization Idioms*:

– *Data Representation or Application Model*: it manages the raw data to be visualized, that is, the analyzed information. Generally, these data can be available in several forms: data contained in a database or gathered from another application.

– *Visualized Data Determination or Data Abstraction*: it determines which data will be effectively visualized at run-time. To do this, it uses the data provided by the application model, and determines the information that will be presented to the user taking into account aspects such as: visualization state (selected items, current zoom level, user actions, etc.), user preferences, user directives, detail levels, etc.
This component implements the specific functionality of particular visualization applications; and it is described with more detail in §4 and §5.

– *Data Objects – Graphical Objects Association or Mapping*: it performs the association between visualized data objects and their correspondent graphic representation. This association consists of a tuple detailing the type of graphical object used to represent each item. It also contains associations with the form <visual channel, data attribute> indicating the visual channels used to show some properties of data provided by abstraction level.

According to this subdivision of MVC's model component in three new components, a new design model, specially oriented to the construction of object-oriented visualization applications can be derived: ***MAMP (Model-Abstraction-Mapping-Presentation)*** (fig.2). The first three components correspond to the ones above described, while the Presentation component includes the functions of MVC views and controllers. However, this last component can be further subdivided into two components: representation and interaction, according to the application needs.

The addition of these new components facilitates the construction of visualization in several ways. First, it is possible to build different visualization applications of the same dataset, using the same visualization techniques, but with different functionality. With this design, the view and application components are fully reused; the designer only needs to specify the tasks to be performed, the abstraction levels to be used for visualizing the data, the selection criteria, the analytical algorithms to be applied over the data, and so on. In this way, the designer may build systems that perform different exploration processes of the same data.

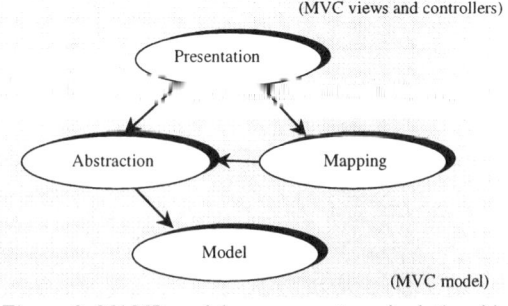

Figure 2. MAMP model: components and relationships

248

Also, it is possible to reuse different data enhancement or analysis algorithms in visualizations of distinct domains. The visualizer may explore the data through different analysis, using algorithms with different characteristics. These algorithms can be stored in a library, from which the designer can select them for other visualizations. Obviously, it is also possible to build visualizations of the same domain with different visualization techniques, or to use the same visualization techniques in different domains.

The separation of the mapping component from the application model allows encapsulating the knowledge about the presentations used for each data item. Thus, the representation of each data item is determined according to the mapping specification, independently from the model, the visualization functionality and the visualization techniques. This means that the same mapping specification could be used with different visualizations.

Application-specific tasks and/or user-assistance techniques can be easily included in the design of the application. This feature allows the adaptability of the application to the domain or applications needs, and to the user preferences or expertise degree. Abstraction and Mapping components can include user or interaction models that tailor information presented to the user.

An additional feature of this approach is the possibility to dynamically change the application functionality. The algorithms and techniques can be replaced by similar ones at run-time, according to the user directives. The possibility to dynamically change the visualization functionality is a powerful feature for IVS. In this way, it is possible to build a visualization application that can be dynamically adapted at run-time to the visualization process performed by the user. This means that the behavior of the application can be modified, according to the user or application requirements. Also, it allows to the user perform fully dynamic exploration processes, doing different analysis of the data during his interaction, without rebuild the application.

It can be argued that some of these features can also be implemented using standard MVC, without explicitly including the abstraction component. But, the reusability of such designs would be very poor, because of the inclusion of application-specific knowledge in only two components. The inclusion of this knowledge as separated components facilitates its reusability, as well as enables designs with a higher flexibility and generality.

4.   ABSTRACTORS

The described model admits different alternative implementations. In this work, the concept of *abstractor objects* to implement the abstraction component is introduced, emphasizing dynamic object composition to increase the reusability of the solutions. These objects are entities that can access the data representation (contained within the application model), and determine which objects (and properties) will be effectively visualized. To perform this determination, abstractors encapsulate the specific functionality of visualization applications, such as analysis algorithms, selection criteria, data enhancement/enrichment techniques, user assistance techniques, user or interaction models, etc.

Essentially, abstractors behave as *proxies* of the data models, controlling the access to these objects from visualization classes. In this way, abstractors can be composed to provide independent control over each object contained in the model. Also, they can be dynamically composed to combine different functionality, as for example, filtering on a specific selection of the visualized information.

Following the conventional communication mechanism among views and models in MVC, MAMP views request their models the information to be visualized through direct messages. In MAMP, an abstractor plays the role of a MVC model and decides whether to ask the original MAMP model for the requested information. The key idea behind the design of the abstractor support is the definition of a standard protocol, through which visualizations can ask their models for data to be visualized. Each view must ask this information through standard messages, such as *getItems*, *getNodes*, *getLinks* and so on.

Also, making the existence of abstractions explicit, abstractor allows to implement a mechanism to control the abstraction or detail level of the visualization, through the concept of *abstraction scales*, as explained in section 6.

The implementation and usage of abstractors using an object-oriented application framework is described with more detail in next sections.

5.   TELESCOPE FRAMEWORK

MAMP is currently implemented by an object oriented framework, named *Telescope* (Orosco 97a), that materializes a software architecture for *MAMP*. *Telescope* was implemented in *Visual Works – Smalltalk*, using OpenGl as 3D graphics platform. Its main components are:

• *Data Representation:* storage and access to the data items to be visualized.
• *Data Abstraction:* this level determines which elements will be visualized, and classifies them into sets of related items.
• *Data Objects - Graphical Objects Mapping:* this component performs the association between the data objects (and their properties) and the correspondent graphical objects.
• *Visualization:* it comprises graphical data presentation and user interaction. It is sub-divided into two components:
    • *Presentation:* it consists of presentation building, according to the graphical objects specified in the mapping.
    • *Interaction:* it consists of all aspects related to the user interaction: item selections and manipulations, user navigation, etc.
• *Visualization State:* it contains the current visualization state, which can include the current selected items, current visualization focus, previous user actions, etc.

Each *Telescope*'s component is implemented by means of classes (generally abstract classes) providing its generic behavior. Each visualization application developed using *Telescope* must implement the particular behavior for each component. Fig. 3 shows relationships among the main classes of each component.

The visualization component consists of a set of *Views*, hierarchically organized. Each view contains a graphical presentation (an instance of a *GraphicalObject*

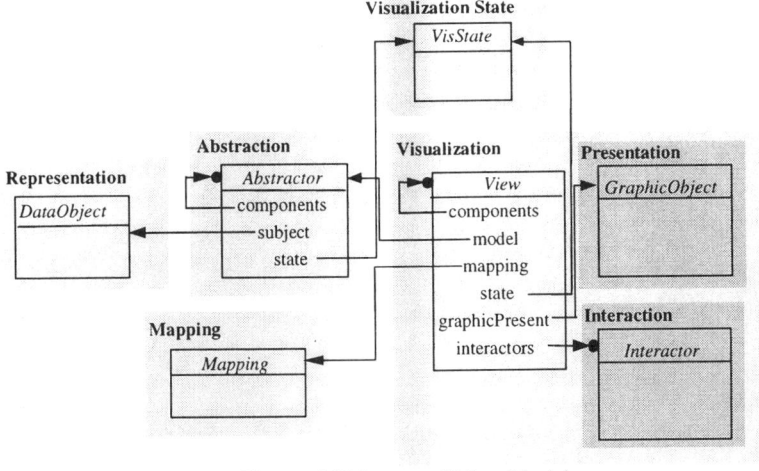

Figure. 3. Telescope Object Model

subclass), and an interactor for each allowed operation on it (for example, a *SelectInteractor* is used to perform item selections).

Views have an associated *Mapping* that performs the conversion between data objects and graphical objects. These mappings can be customized by the user at run-time or modified by the system according to changes in the visualization state. The *Mapping* class can be specialized through subclasses, for example to implement distortion-based visualization techniques.

Additionally, each view gets the information to be displayed through an associated model. This model consists of an abstractor (instances of an *Abstractor* subclass), which determines objects and properties to be effectively visualized. This abstractor has a reference to the data object, which contains its source data.

The visualization state component is mainly implemented by means of a *VizState* class, which manages all the information related to the current state of the visualization process.

6.   ABSTRACTORS USAGE

In this section, some of the main visualization features that can be implemented by designers are shown, by defining different kinds of abstractors that can be used in *Telescope*, as well as a hierarchy of abstractors that defines a complex data abstraction policy. The *Telescope* framework includes a predefined set of general purpose abstractors that can be used or adapted for the application designer in order to implement his visualization applications.

In the general way, views requests to the abstractor the items to be visualized, through interface methods provided by the abstractor. For example, in most visualization techniques implemented in *CityVis* and *WarVis*, the communication between views and abstractors consists on a *getItems* method, that provides to the view the data items to be visualized. Other visualization techniques can require a different interface; for example, graphs ask for their nodes and links through *getNodes*

251

and *getLinks* methods. Thus, views do not need to worry about how to determine which data will be presented to the user; they only need to manage the presentation aspects, such as the construction and rendering of presentations.

6.1   Filters

The simplest and most frequently used kind of abstractor is a filter. A filter simply selects a set of items from the application data model according to a given condition. The filtering condition can be fixed or it can be determined dynamically, for example depending on the users' requirements during the visualization process. The general form of a filter is

```
getItems
    items := subject selectItems: #objectType
    filtered_items:=items select: [:it | it satisfies: condition ].
    ^filtered_items
```

This code shows the typical form (in a very simplified way) of an abstractor interface, which generally consists on a method returning the items to be visualized. Here, the method *selectItems* retrieves the data from the storage, and then selects those items that satisfy a given condition (through the method *select*); finally, selected items are returned (to its associated views).

A particular kind of dynamic filters that is worth remarking is characterized by the fact that the filtering condition is parameterized and the values of the corresponding parameters are determined by actions of the user, like selecting items belonging to a particular topic (see *CityVis* below, section .7.1)

6.2   Derivation of new information

A second type of abstractors corresponds to the addition of new information to the visualization data. This information can be of several kinds, among which some examples are:

- *Derived information*: this kind of information is usually the product of an analysis algorithm or some other similar mechanism, as the use of statistics about the available data,

```
getItems
    items := subject selectItems: #conflicts.
    stats := StatisticsInfo computeDistributionOf: #fatalityLevel in: items.
    ^stats.
```

Here, *getItems* computes the distribution of the variable *#fatalityLevel* in a set of objects representing military conflicts. This computation is performed by the *StatisticsInfo* class, through the method *computeDistributionOf:in:*. *Telescope* provides a wide set of classes and methods for the calculation of statistics, metrics or similar measures, from which *StatisticsInfo* is only an example. In a similar way, the user may implement specific classes and methods for deriving new data, according to application needs.

- *Data enrichment*: Algorithms for data enrichment or enhancement, like data interpolation, can also be included in abstractors. They can include domain

252

information to avoid undesired facts like misrepresentation, although this can reduce their reusability.

```
getItems
    discrete_data := subject selectItems: #discreteTemperatureMeasures.
    continuum_data    :=    self    interpolateData:    items    withConstraints:    (self
domainConstraints).
    ^ continuum_data.
```

Here, the abstractor retrieves a set of values for temperature measures, for certain discrete locations. These data are then interpolated to obtain a set with continuous values, which are adequate for some visualization techniques, such as plots. The interpolation process takes into account some constraints imposed by the domain (e.g. temperature values cannot be higher than 100°C), to avoid incorrect measures.

- *Data aggregation (composition/decomposition)*: very often the desired visualization is based on groups of data more than on individual pieces of data. For example, we might want to be able to show a world map, containing only information about continents and not about countries. If the data available is only about countries, it is necessary to aggregate the information of countries belonging to the same continent in one object.

```
getItems
    countries := subject selectItems: #countries.
    continents := self deriveContinentInformationWith: countries.
    ^ continents.
```

This aggregation process can also be controlled by the user during his interaction, allowing different ways to build groups of data, different kinds of objects to which the accumulation process is applied, etc.

6.3   Abstraction Level Management

Abstractors allows the automatic management of abstraction levels through the usage of abstraction scales. An abstraction scale is an ordered tuple naming the order in which information, like a city map for example, should be visualized. An scale can have its own user-interface control (e.g. a slider) through which the user can interactively vary the level of abstraction of the visualization (i.e. showing or hiding dynamically details). Visualizations, in turn, only have to worry about what must be shown according to the data that abstractors pass to them, in the current abstraction level. For example, the scale below can be used to define the different detail levels in which a city map can be shown.:

(regionalView, globalView, detailedView, streetView)

A selection of a level in this scale will define which information the visualization will receive to be graphically presented. That is, if the selected abstraction level is *globalView* the visualization will only receive the information about roads, main streets and main interesting points in the city. After that if the user selects *detailedView*, the same visualization will receive the same information plus the information about other minor city streets.

To implement abstraction scales, each abstractor can have associated one instance of *AbstractionLevel,* which defines its current abstraction level and implements the abstraction scale mechanism. Subclasses of this class provide the support for comparing symbolic levels of abstraction according to the type of scale (i.e. discrete scale, inclusive scale, continuous scale, etc.). This scale can be interactively manipulated by the user to dynamically increase or decrease the detail level of the visualization, through the use of controls such as sliders or radio buttons.

6.4   Hierarchies of Abstractors

Atomic abstractors like the ones described up to here do not suffice for usual applications. The usual situation is that several simpler abstractors have to be composed to allow the accumulation of their corresponding data or the composition of their functionality. A mechanism for the hierarchical composition of abstractors can be used for this, and also to achieve other complex effects. For example, an abstractor that is responsible to give the information needed for the visualization of a graph can delegate the computation of this information into several component subabstractors. A *GraphAbstractor* exemplifies a simplified version of this situation:

getNodes
   "first subabstractor computes nodes of the graph"
   ^(components at: 1) getItems
getLinks
   "second subabstractor computes links of the graph"
   ^(components at: 2) getItems

This allows to change dynamically the configuration of the *GraphAbstractor* at execution time, by just changing its component subabstractors. A common use of this feature is to change one subabstractor when the user produces a change in the current abstraction level. This allows the visualization of a graph with different abstraction levels, where, in each level, the nodes and links are computed in a different way. Thus, the designer can implement particular abstractors for computing nodes or links in each abstraction level. Upon each level change, the root abstractor can change some of its subabstractors, replacing the old subabstractors by the abstractors that compute the items in the new abstraction level. An additional advantage of implementing specific abstractors for each level, is that the abstractors can be independent of the abstraction scale used; that is, the same abstractor, representing a particular level, can be used in different scales containing this level.

6.5   Assistance Techniques

In the last years, several visualization techniques providing some degree of user assistance in the visualization process have been developed (e.g. *Galaxy of News* (Rennison 94)). *AnkA*P*A*HN *(ORASCO 97U)* is an example of assistance technique whose goal is to assist the user in the exploration process, providing help in the focus specification and using 3D presentations conveying more information. The assistance in the focus specification is implemented by a statistical inference mechanism, that attempts to detect the criteria used by the user in item selections. Once these criteria have been estimated by the system, item presentations are updated accordingly to them, reflecting the relevance of each item with respect to the currently defined focus (using an item opacity proportional to the item importance). In this way, a quick approximation to the desired final focus is obtained, facilitating the task and reducing the user workload. Particularly, *CityVis* uses *AutoFocus* to assist the user in the searching of apartments on sale. This kind of techniques can be implemented through the incorporation of specialized abstractors, that perform the inference process and calculate each item relevance.

7. APPLICATIONS

In this section, two applications developed with *Telescope* are briefly described: *CityVis* (Orosco 97a), a system for the visualization of city data, and *WarVis* (Orosco 98), a system for the visualization of information about military conflicts. *Telescope* was also used in the development of other applications, such as *Luthier* (Campo 97a), an object-oriented software visualization system, and MetaExplorer (Campo 97b), a system for three-dimensional visualization of design patterns. All of these systems were implemented in *Visual Works - Smalltalk*, using *OpenGL* as 3D graphics platform.

7.1   CityVis

CityVis is an information visualization system for city data, with the goal to support the exploration of city information, providing techniques to assist the user in this process. The tool provides 3D visualizations of the city information. These 3D views can be converted into 2D views, by constraining the user navigation capabilities.

CityVis makes an extensive use of abstractors to provide powerful filtering mechanisms for semantic zoom based on inclusive abstraction scales. These mechanisms allows the user for the continuous zooming of city maps, showing or hiding pertinent information at each level of abstraction.

Interactive filtering of information through query capabilities is provided as an additional mechanism to reduce the complexity of visualizations. This capability is implemented by an abstractor that provides the views with those data resulting of the query evaluation. In this way, any visualization can reuse the generic query management mechanisms.

The information is organized in layers, allowing the differentiation of several topics in the visualization. The system visualizes different kinds of information associated to the city (hotels, apartments, restaurants, transportation, statistics, etc.), that may be combined by the user to build the desired visualization. These topics are managed by a hierarchy of abstractors, which is dynamically reorganized during user exploration.

The system provides several functions for the administration and management of information revealed during the exploration process, such as the definition of new topics or the computation of statistics about the visualized data. In both cases, specialized abstractors compute this new information, making it available for further explorations of the same city data.

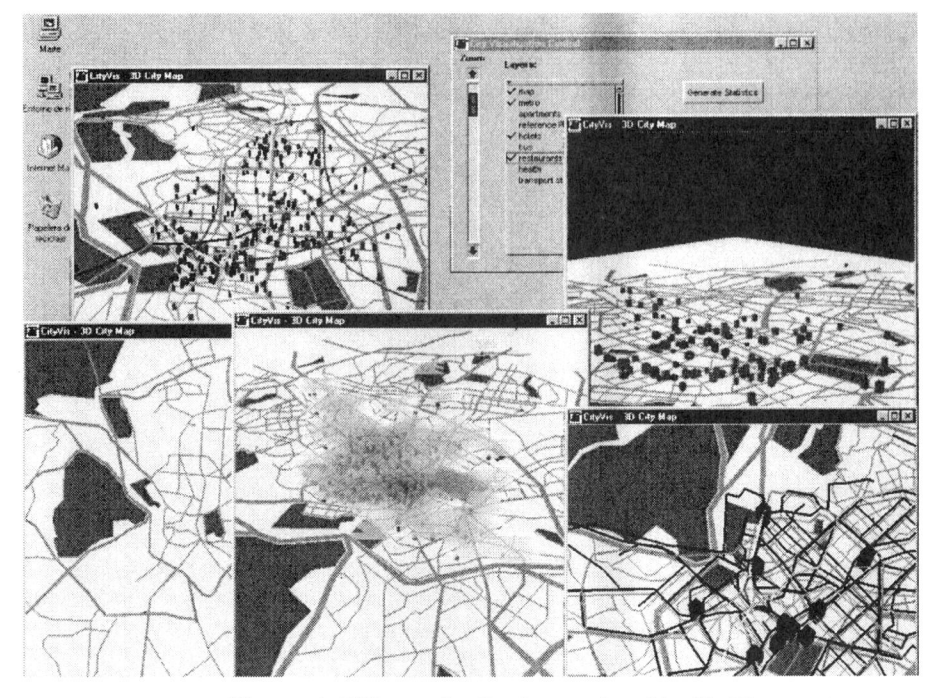

Figure. 4- Different visualizations produced by *CityVis*

Finally, CityVis implements assistance techniques, attempting to alleviate the user's work in the exploration. AutoFocus is one of these assistance techniques, which is implemented as described in previous section.

Fig. 4 shows an snapshot of *CityVis*. This picture shows several visualization techniques available in the system: layered organization of presentations, management of abstraction scale (semantic zoom), different abstraction levels and statistics about the concentration of data items in the map.

7.2   WarVis

WarVis is another visualization system developed with *Telescope*. This system provides visualizations of data about military conflicts among countries, from year 1800 to the present. It contains similar features to *CityVis*, such as the provision of 2D and 3D presentations, and the immersive navigation capabilities. The system consists on a set of different visualization techniques (such as plots or graphics), which the analyzer may use to visualize the data. He can dynamically create new views of the data, through the selection of an appropriate visualization technique. These presentations can share some abstractors (or subabstractors), because *WarVis* allows to provide several visualizations of the same data (provided by the same abstractor).

WarVis also has several abstraction scales, which can be interactively managed by the user. These scales control the information presented to the user and the way this information is calculated. In this case, a dynamic hierarchy of abstractors is used;

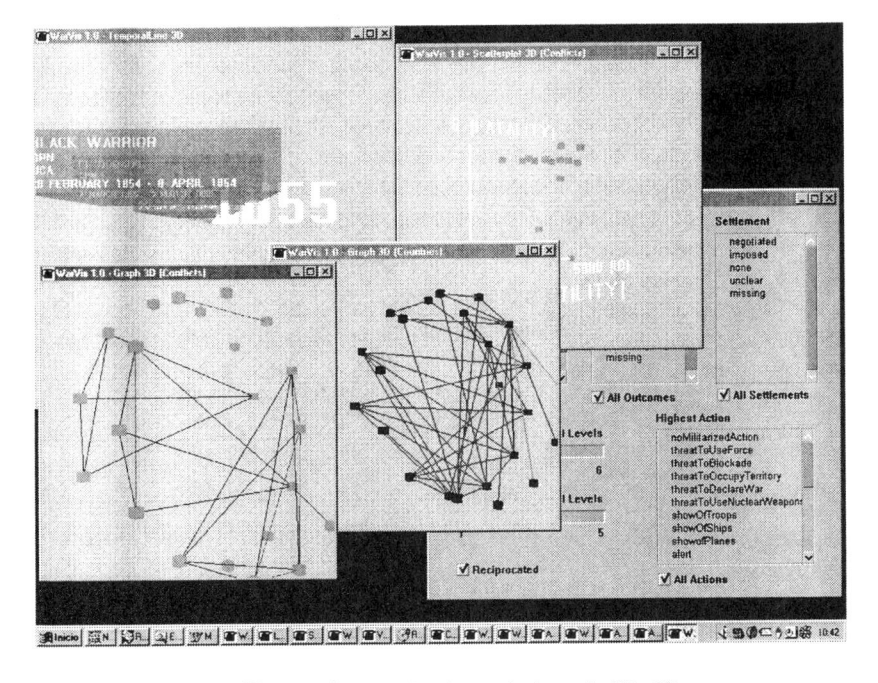

Figure. 5. Visualization techniques in *WarVis*

upon each abstraction level change, the hierarchy is modified to reflect the new abstraction level.

This system also provides non-conventional visualization techniques, such as *Abstract 3D Information Spaces*, which can be tailored by the system designer to the application needs. In this case, a particular version of this paradigm, Temporal 3D Lines was implemented, to visualize the location of each military conflict in the time.

Fig. 5 shows several visualization techniques used in *WarVis*: 3D plots, 3D graphs, and temporal 3D lines. The information presented in each case is determined by the user, through the use of device controls, as it is shown in the same picture.

8.   CONCLUSIONS

MAMP, a design model for object-oriented visualization systems was presented, along with a *Telescope*, an application framework based on it. Their suitability to the construction of visualization systems was demonstrated through the development of several applications for different domains and purposes: *CityVis*, for the visualization of geographical data (physical data with a given physical form); and *WarVis* for the visualization of military conflicts (combining data of abstract and physical nature); and *MetaExplorer* for the visualization of object oriented software (data without a physical form, with an abstract nature)

The inclusion of an explicit abstraction component, implemented by means of abstractor objects, enable the construction by composition of complex filtering mechanisms that greatly simply the implementation of visualizations, which is often the more time-consuming task in the development of visualization systems. Using *Telescope*, the development of new visualizations is simplified, due to the high reusability degree of the main components of the system. In our case, the development of *WarVis* was relatively fast, due to the previous components developed in *CityVis*. Additionally, the extensibility of these systems is high, due to the clear localization of possible changes and extensions. As another feature, *Telescope* allows the quick prototyping of new visualizations or techniques, due to its high flexibility.

The architecture preserves the modularity of dataflow systems, allowing the user to compose modules (abstractors) and views (visualization techniques), conforming a network. The produced network has a dynamic nature, allowing the addition and removal of new modules and/or visualization techniques at runtime.

Future work with *Telescope* includes development of an environment for visualization applications construction. This environment should automate part of the construction task, and guide the system-designer in the development of new applications or components. Also, the development of new visualization applications, particularly for WWW-based visualization and for numerical data domains are programmed.

9. REFERENCES

Campo, M. Orosco, R. Teyseyre, A. (1997) Automatic Abstraction Management in Information Visualization Systems. Proc. Intl. Conf. IV '97, London, 08/97.

Campo, M. (1997a) Compreensao Visual de Frameworks atraves da Introspecao de Exemplos. Phd. Thesis, UFRGS, Brasil (in Portuguese).

Campo, M. Orosco, R. Teyseyre, A. (1997b) Interactive Abstraction Control in Visualization Applications. Proc. SCCC '97, Valparaiso, Chile, 10/97.

Casner, S.M. (1991) A Task-analytic approach to the automated design of graphic presentations. ACM Transactions on Graphics. 10(3), 111-151.

Chuah, M. Roth, S. (1991) On the Semantics of Interactive Visualizations. Proc. InfoViz '96, IEEE CS Press.

Coutaz, J. (1987) PAC, An Implementation Model for Dialog Design. Proc. Of Interact '87, Stuttgart, September 1987, 431-436.

Duce, D. A. (1991) Visualization. Proc. Visualization '93 Conf.

Green, Mark (1985) Report on Dialogue Specification Tools. in G. Pfaff (ed) User Interface Management Systems, New York, Springer Verlag, 9-20.

Haber, R.B., McNabb. R. (1990) Visualization Idioms: A Conceptual Model for Scientific Visualization Systems. Visualization in Scientific Comp., 74-93.

Kazman, Rick. Carriere, Jeromy. (1996) Rapid Prototyping of Information Visualizations Using VANISH. Proc. IEEE InfoViz'96, San Francisco, CA.

Krasner, G. Pope, S. (1988) A cookbook for Using Model-View-Controller interface paradigm in Smalltalk 80. Journal of O. O. Programming, 08-09/1988, 26-49

Mackinlay, J. (1986) Automating the design of Graphical Presentations of Relational Information. ACM Trans. on Graphics, 5(2), ACM Press, 110-141.

Neider, J. Davis. T. Woo, M. (1993) OpenGL Programming Guide. Addison-Wesley.

Orosco, R. (1997) User Assistance in Information Visualization. Hypertext, Information Retrieval and Multimedia '97 Conf., Dortmund, Germany.

Orosco, R. (1997a) Telescope: A Software Architecture for Visualization Systems Construction. Proc. ASOO '97, Buenos Aires, Argentina, 08/97.

Orosco, R. Moriyon, R. (1998) Reducing the Effort of Building Object-Oriented Visualizations, 22th. Intl. COMPSAC'98 Conference, Viena, Austria, 08/98.

Rennison, Earl. (1994) Galaxy of News: An Approach to Visualizing and Understanding Expansive News Landscapes Proc. UIST '94, 11/94, 3-12.

Roth, S. Kolojejchick, J. Mattis, J. Goldstein, J. (1994) Interactive Graphic Design using Automatic Presentation Knowledge. Proc. CHI '94, 04/94, 112-117.

Schroeder, W. Martin, K. Lorensen, B. (1993) The Visualization Toolkit, An Object Oriented Approach to 3D Graphics. Prentice hall, 1996.

UIMS Tool Developers Workshop. (1991) A Metamodel for the Runtime Architecture of an Interactive System. SIGCHI Bulletin, 24(1), 1991, 32-37.

Upson, C. (1989) The Application Visualization System: a computational environment for scientific visualization. IEEE CG&A, 07/1989

BIOGRAPHIES

Ricardo Orosco received a PhD degree in Computer Science by the Universidad Autónoma de Madrid (Spain). He is a research staff member at the Systems Research Institute, Tandil, Argentina, in the Objects and Visualization Group. His research interests include user interfaces, information visualization, and three-dimensional interactions.

Marcelo Campo received a PhD degree in Computer Science by the Universidade Federal do Rio Grande do Sul (UFRGS, Porto Alegre, Brazil). Currently is the leader of the Objects and Visualization Group, at the Systems Research Institute, Tandil, Argentina. His research interests include object oriented application frameworks, software architectures, design patterns and information visualization.

Discussion

Henrik Christensen: Implementation arrows point from GUI to Model. Does this imply that visualization is static with respect to the 'on the fly' changes in underlying data?

Ricardo Orosco: We currently assume that data are static. In the future we must consider this possibility. Future work must be done to cope with dynamic data.

Prasun Dewan: How is your work different from the Mastermind project of Pedro Szekely?

Ricardo Orosco: Several ideas from Mastermind were used in this project. Some of our colleagues were part of the Mastermind team. We got the idea of a mapping from his team.

John Grundy: Lots of 'difficult' problems to 'automate': interface to raw data/tools, abstraction of raw data, mappings between abstractions, specifying graphical form, translating interaction to a visual form. Which aspects are you trying to automate?

Ricardo Orosco: The goal of our work is to automate parts of the process. It is not possible to automate all. We try to provide guidelines for each reusable part.

An architecture model for the hypermedia engineering process

J. NANARD and M. NANARD
LIRMM, CNRS/Université de Montpellier
161 Rue Ada, 34392 Montpellier Cedex 5, FRANCE
Tel.: (33) 4 67 41 85 17, Fax: (33) 4 67 41 85 00
nanard@lirmm.fr

Abstract: We propose an architecture model for the hypermedia design and engineering process that combines incremental design of specifications and automatic generation in an experimental feedback loop. We have developed PageJockey a hypermedia design environment on this model. The designer may incrementally capture hypermedia specifications into templates by graphically interacting with the automatically produced target hypermedia and evaluate and refine the design. We introduce HLHSL, an object-oriented language which internally captures these high level specifications. We argue that the quick feedback between usage and design concerns makes it possible to address early and continuingly their mutual constraints in the development process, thereby leading to improve hypermedia quality at low cost.

Keywords: Hypermedia design, design process, specifications, prototypes, hypermedia generation, templates, architecture, reuse.

1.   INTRODUCTION

Hypermedia is a highly intensive human-computer interaction technique to access documents. Designing good quality and cost effective hypermedia products for users implies to help the design process from early stage of design to full scale production.

As pointed out by the IFIPWG 2.7 (13.4), architecture is an important factor for such a purpose. In most cases, architecture concerns software or data. In this paper, we adopt a general view of architecture, as explained in (Shaw, 1995), including

Process models that focus on construction of target architecture. In this paper we present a model of the hypermedia design and engineering process that supports iterative refinement and abstraction, incremental design and reuse while allowing automatic generation from specifications. We have developed PageJockey, a hypermedia design environment based on this model and experienced its interest through several full scale hypermedia designs and developments. We describe also HLHSL (High Level Hypermedia Specification Language), an object-oriented specification language we have developed to internally support the process.

The paper starts by analyzing current results on architectural aspects of hypermedia design and development: no support is provided to the whole design process, especially to enable incremental design and development associated to a rigorous process based on specifications. We outline the principle of an architecture model of the hypermedia design and development process we designed to overcome this problem. We explain how PageJockey allows incremental design that benefits from an experimental feedback loop based on full-scale target product being designed and automatically produced from specifications. We detailed both the components of the design process architecture and automatic hypermedia generation from specifications. The main part of the paper describes HSHSL features.

Based on several applications designed and produced with PageJockey, we argue in the discussion on the interest of the proposed model on quality factors, such as consistency, reuse, maintainability, inclusion of good design patterns for hypermedia usability. These quality factors are important for managing high quality human computer interaction and decreasing design and development cost.

2. ARCHITECTURAL ASPECTS OF HYPERMEDIA DESIGN

Two classic architecture components are concerned during hypermedia browsing: the hypermedia "engine" (called also navigator) and the structured set of data accessed through the navigator, the hypermedia document called simply hypermedia in the following.

Works (Halasz, 1994) have introduced significant abstractions shared by typical hypermedia systems and powerful architectural principles for developing hypermedia engines and open hypermedia systems including systems relying on the web (Gronback, 1997). But they do not help building specific target hypermedia document structure, nor support the design process.

Tooling and effective manufacturing and high quality products for hypermedia presentations represent two major challenges for multimedia industry. Thus, studying the design process of hypermedia document is highly important.

The development of hypermedia documents by domain professionals is usually a sequence of two main independent steps: design and production (Figure 1). The design is done as a preliminary task which leads to a specification book. Some small scale sketching is usually performed. It is used to illustrate the specification rather than to produce an evaluable prototype.

The production steps are oriented towards intensive production without rigorous support. Very few changes are done on the final version. So, very little feedback takes place in the design process. Furthermore, most of production tools provides only low level abstractions with very poor support for incremental work. Late changes thus lead often to inconsistency.

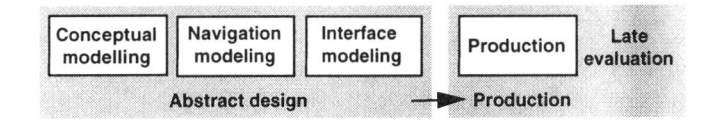

Figure 1 Approaches based on separation of design and production.

A great difficulty of hypermedia design is to produce in a straightforward manner a good design without feedback from end-users testing a full scale version of the product. But the production step of a hypermedia document is a very costly task, thereby the full scale evaluation step takes place only when the production is complete. Only very minor changes in the design can be done at this point. Very little feedback is used. To overcome this difficulty two directions are possible.

The first one consists in improving design methods and using rigorous formalisms and principles that have already proven their interest in software engineering. The stepping consists in elaborating a *conceptual data model*, an *abstract navigation model* and a *presentation and interaction model*. Object-orientation with OOHDM [Schwabe, 1996] or the Entity-Relationship Model in RMM [Isakowitz, 1995] add some interesting features but the overall underlying design stepping is globally similar to HDM [Garzotto, 1995]. In all cases the design deliverable is not a hypermedia document, but a specification book.

The second one consists in drastically reducing the production cost. Automatic structure transformation have been proposed (Kuikka, 1993, O2Web, 1996). Unfortunately they primarily rely on source document logical structure or database structure and do not take into account the reader's task to produce the hypermedia structure. Moreover, associated approaches do not take advantage of explicit evaluation and user feedback to improve design.

In this paper, we propose an architecture model for structuring the hypermedia design and engineering process that efficiently supports incremental design with user feedback loop and automatic production of target hypermedia from hypermedia specifications. This architecture is embodied in the PageJockey design environment that we have developed (Fraïssé, 1996) and used for producing several hypermedia documents (Nanard, 1998). This architecture relies on the feedback loop between the designer and an automatic production tool which spares the effort of production for the designer and enables her to focus on the incremental improvement of the work. It bridges the gap between the abstract design and the actual production.

The paper explains the architecture model of the design and engineering process, details the architecture of the automated production mechanism. The paper ends with a discussion on the main interests of the model for software quality factors directly related to usability.

3.   AN ARCHITECTURE MODEL OF THE DESIGN PROCESS

The key idea of our work is to consider a design and production environment as an interface between the *designer* and the *design process* rather than as a tool to describe, edit and directly produce a target object. See Figure 2.

The model relies on three major points:

a) supporting incremental design based on full scale evaluation of the target hypermedia with real users,

b) providing a rigorous framework to specify design in order to enable automated generation for boosting the feedback loop and to make updating at full scale easy and cost effective,

c) keeping the interaction between the designer and its work as close as possible to his usual way of working.

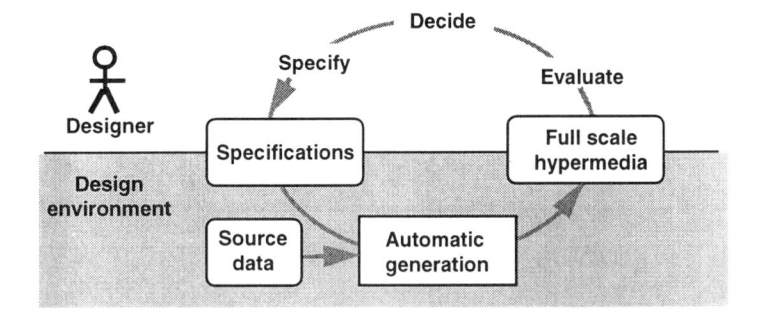

Figure 2 Cooperation between the designer and the design environment.

The design process is organized as a loop. To enable running the cycle as many times as suitable to achieve the wished quality, the cost of full scale production is made low enough so that most of the designer's effort for running a cycle only concerns the design. A *specification driven* automatic generation tool is responsible of full scale hypermedia production . Specifications are incrementally produced: the designer graphically sketches multimedia templates (Fraïssé, 1996) and the system produces their textual form and generates the target hypermedia.

Thus the designer can focus on its own expertise: create, evaluate and improve design without being hampered and slowed down by the burden of the production task. In this paper we no more develop the graphical aspect of the environment

3.1   A rigorous framework for automated production

A rigorous framework is needed to enable specification driven automatic generation. Producing the hypermedia is specified and performed as a structure transform. The architecture of the production process relies on distinguishing three components:

264

- what the designer starts from: *the source data,*
- what the designer intends to produce: *the target hypermedia,*
- how the source data are turned into the target hypermedia: *the generation specifications.*

The *source data* consist in all of the raw material such as images, texts, movies and so on, that the designer uses to produce the target hypermedia. They have their own structure independently of their context of use in the target hypermedia. This structure is elicited in two parts. The *conceptual data model* and the *actual data structure*. The conceptual data model often already exists, for instance as a database schema when data are stored in a database or as a DTD (Document Type definition) when the actual data structure is elicited by a SGML markup.

The *target hypermedia* is the result of the design and production process. Its structure is organized in an object-oriented manner and relies on the well-known concepts of hypermedia: the navigation model (pages and links), the presentation (abstract contents and layout) and the behavior (animation, choreography, interaction with the user).

The *specification of the target hypermedia structure* is described in a generic manner as classes with the high level hypermedia specification language HLHSL. Any component of the target hypermedia is considered as an instance of a class whose structure is specified in a *template*. Libraries of templates and contextual libraries make it easier.

The triple (*source data modeling, generation rules, target hypermedia specification*) defines a mapping between the source data and the target hypermedia (Figure 3). It specifies how the target hypermedia is populated. A *trigger* associated to each class of the target hypermedia specification defines its generation rules. It specifies which properties, defined on the source data model, any of the instances of a given hypermedia component class must match. Thereby a parser automatically fires the class instantiation whenever the specified property occurs in source data.

Once the target hypermedia specification and the generation rules are made available in HLHSL, a generator transforms the source data into the specified hypermedia.

265

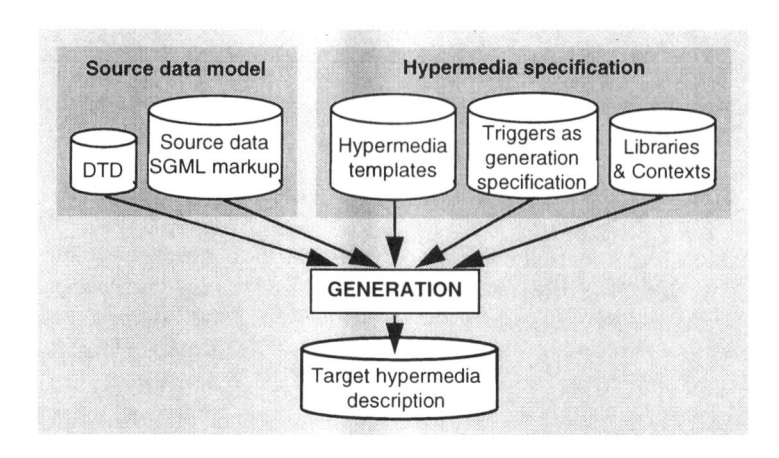

Figure 3 The architecture of the generation process.

3.2 Evaluation driven incremental design

The design process architecture is given in Figure 4. Evaluation operates on full scale generated versions of the hypermedia considered as drafts during an experimental feedback loop. According to evaluation, incremental improvements are introduced in the specifications or in the data or in their description. Since the incremental elaboration of the product is driven by its evaluation it is possible to iteratively refine the design. The speed and the extremely low cost of the automated generation process enables to check and evaluate as many design choices as needed. The designer may observe and evaluate -if needed with real users- the produced hypermedia at any stage of the design.

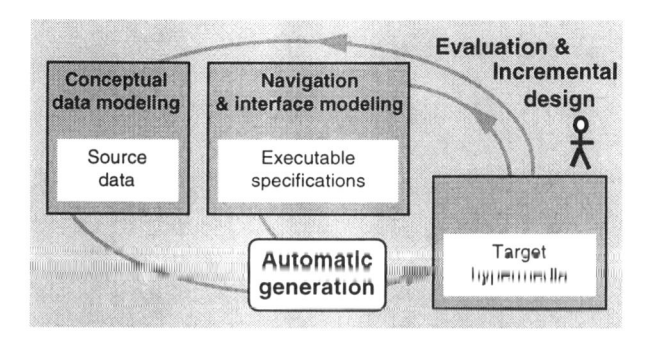

Figure 4 Generation from specifications with an experimental feedback loop.

3.3　Friendly interface for incremental template specification

The purpose of this architecture is to help the designer work at a high level of abstraction. Refining the design by simply updating specifications or data spares updating each target hypermedia component.

Nevertheless, elaborating textual specifications is often considered a tedious task for a designer. Thus, the architecture of the design environment is organized to:

- support the mainly graphical and incremental style of work of designers,
- provide the set of operations to step back and forth between graphical instances and their textual specification and to update either description,
- help capture as specifications the abstractions used by the designer.

We preserve the designer's natural way of working in the environment architecture. The approach for elaborating specifications relies on a visual description: the designer draws, the system helps him abstract, structure and reuse parts of the drawing. Specifying does not precede drawing, but results from the abstraction of the drafts which sketch the intended work.

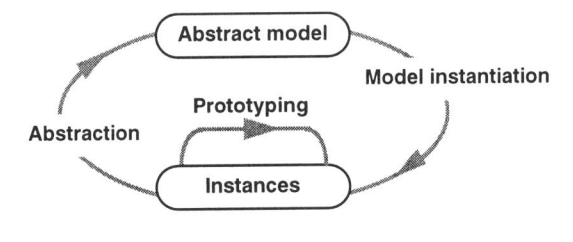

Figure 5 The interaction model for elaborating the specifications.

The formal mechanism used here relies on a visual prototype-based language. As shown on Figure 5, the designer can freely draw any object or structure, for instance some pages of the target hypermedia which are representative of the design. Such objects can be reused as prototypes by cloning[1] to build new ones. The system also helps turning any drafted objects into *templates* that are used for specifying the hypermedia structure and the generation rules. The selected object is turned (by the system with the help of the designer) into the model of a class which is later instantiated whenever needed in the design, improving by this way the overall consistency. For more details see (Fraïssé, 1996) and (Nanard, 1998).

The design environment provides the designer with the necessary operations for running the incremental abstraction / specialization cycle and to edit or reuse the graphical instances as well as their textual specifications (Nanard, 1995). The specification of the target hypermedia is a set of templates that the designer has abstracted from drafted objects produced to make the ideas emerge. Although

---

[1] Cloning is more than copy and paste: it induces inheritance between objects and thus makes consistency within the design explicit.

templates are stored as text for readability the environment helps to graphically specify a large part of them in order to minimize the programming effort.

The template mechanism offers a modular approach to encapsulate all of the information needed to specify and handle each abstraction of the design. A template captures the specification of reusable structures and components during design and rules for populating the target hypermedia. Thus changes are made easier since they can be done locally.

4.   THE ARCHITECTURE OF THE GENERATION PROCESS

PageJockey internally uses HLHSL, a hypermedia description language. Owing to object orientation, HLHSL is both a language for describing a target hypermedia structure and a language for specifying it. HLHSL enables inheritance, and by the way, reuse. A classless approach (prototype-based) is also supported. Furthermore some hypermedia specific notions such as choreography are supported by the language.

Although HLHSL descriptions of either target hypermedia or hypermedia specifications are more often generated and interpreted by the machine rather than handwritten by the designer, the HLHSL syntax is easily understandable by humans.

A design issue in HLHSL was to provide support for expressing the structural relationships that are graphically sketched by the designer. Thus most of the constructs reflect how the designer graphically builds objects. The language elicits the dependencies between objects, supports incremental design and enforces reuse.

We explain how architectural concepts of the different components of the generation process are expressed in HLHSL and processed.

4.1   Target hypermedia description in HLHSL

The target hypermedia description produced by the generator is expressed in HLHSL. It is further interpreted to display the generated hypermedia.

4.1.1   Creation of pages and actors

In PageJockey a hypermedia is structured as a set of "pages". Each page represents a scene like in a theater play. A page is a dynamic and interactive document. Its components are *actors* which are texts, sounds, graphics, images, movies, and so on. Pages as well as actors are objects in the sense of object-oriented languages. Each page has a *Choreography* which specifies the behavior of the actors during the scene and the navigation or the sequencing of the scenes. The notion of choreography allows to group as a single entity all of the behavior of a page rather than disseminating it in many scripts.

```
<Page Named = Pg1>
  <Circle Named = C1>
```

```
<Label Named = T1;  Hidden > This is a circle
<Choreography>
   <When entering C1 do T1 appears during 3>
   <When Clicks T1 do LoadPage "Demonstration" during 3>
</Choreography>
</Page>
```
The page named Pg1 contains a circle, when the mouse rolls over it,
a label displaying "This is circle" pops up during 3 seconds. if
the user clicks in the label, a link to page demonstration is
fired.

Any object, page as well as actor, is produced in one of the following ways:

- as an instance of a given class,
- as a clone of any other object used as a prototype,
- by grouping as a single entity several objects.

A set of primitive objects and classes are provided in the environment libraries to bootstrap the development. Thus a simple graphic object such as a circle simply is a clone of a primitive model of circle. An actor may be specified as a clone:

```
<Circle; Named = GlassLens;
LineSize = 3; LineColor = GoldenMetal;
FillColor = TransparentGlass;
>
```
The actor named GlassLens is specified as a clone of circle -a
primitive object in the libraries- overridden with specific color
attributes.

As soon as the designer names an object or an object property in the graphic window, the object or the property becomes an abstract prototype that can be reused and handled anywhere else. *Cloning* and *instantiating* are the key operations since they enable overall consistency and make specification simpler and more generic. They also better fit the designer's way of working.

Grouping allows to describe compound objects and to keep their structure visible. So, a compound object is described in terms of its components.

```
<group named = Glasses> <LeftLens><RightLens><Arms> </group>
```
A new actor called glasses is defined in an abstract manner.

4.1.2   Incremental design of objects

Any compound object can be modified in the following ways:
- *adding* new actors,
- *discarding* some inherited actors (they no longer belong to the new one),
- *overriding* some inherited actors to change their attributes,
- *substituting* an inherited actor by a new one which replaces it but still plays its role in the scene (basically this enables dubbing: the substituted item may even belong to a different class, but it keeps the links and the behavior of the initial one; this makes it simple to define place holders with specified behaviors. Substituting is not discarding plus adding!).

269

For instance:

```
<Glasses named = monocle ; group>
<Discard Arms> <Handle>
</group>
```
Discarding enables to define the notion of monocle. A monocle is a kind of glasses without arms but with a single handle.

```
<Page Pg1 named Pg2>
<Substitute C1 Diamond>
<Override T1> This is a diamond
</Page>
```
The page Pg2 is simply a clone of the page Pg1 in which the circle C1 is substituted by a diamond which have the same behavior as the circle in Pg1. Overriding the text T1 enables to change the label contents.

The features described above provide a simple, clearly readable, but expressive language to describe an actual hypermedia document. An important aspect of the language in terms of human computer interaction is its ability to preserve the intentions of the author in the structure description itself.

4.1.3   Behavior of actors

Another important point is the choreography section of pages which differs from most of other approaches. In many hypermedia production tools, the interactions are specified in scripts which are directly attached to objects and thus distributed in the whole document. Especially in Macromedia director, scripts are attached to movies, to frames, to cast members, to sprites…, making harder for the designer to remind why some sprite has a given behavior. In PageJockey, the explicit definition of page choreography enables the designer to catch at a glance the dynamic aspects of a page, like a choreographer does. The choreography is performed by individual on the stage but planned in a centralized manner by the choreographer.

4.2   Hypermedia templates specification in HLHSL

HLHSL contains features suitable to capture abstractions during design: for instance class specification, symbolic names for values, variable expressions to represent the values of attributes, and so on.

4.2.1   Attributes specification

Simple values for attributes often are represented by names:
```
<define GoldenMetal RGB% ( , , )>
```
The abstract notion of GoldenMetal color becomes available just by assigning it a name and adding it in the palette. Changing this color specification updates all of the objects which use this abstract color, not those who had the same RGB color. Remark that the designer does not write this sentence, she just operates on the palette representation.

270

4.2.2   Page template specification

The most important aspect concerns class specification. For instance:
```
<Page Named = Pg1>
...
</Page>
is the description of an actual page.
```

Conversely,
```
<Template Page Pg1; Parms =(&x, &surname, &dest)>
  <&x Named = C1>
  <Label Named = T1;  Hidden > This is a &surname
  <Choreography>
     <When entering C1 do T1 appears during 3>
     <When Clicks T1 do LoadPage &Dest during 3>
  </Choreography>
</Page>
is the specification of a page template which can be instantiated
by assigning actual values to the parameters &x, &surname, &dest of
its constructor.

<Instance Pg1,  Named = MyPg; Parms =(&x=Circle, &surname="Big
round", &dest="Pg12")>
is a page instance of that class.
```

Turning a prototype description into a template is done with the help of the designer who is the only one to know where are the variable parts of sketch. The designer graphically sketches a prototype of the object and then defines the variable parts.

The use of variable expressions in the specification of classes templates makes them play the same role as the constructors in O.O. programming languages. HLHSL also includes most of familiar notions such as iteration, alternative, dynamic arrays, and so on, which provides with the same power of expression as any programming language, though this language is especially shaped to describing hypermedia structures.

4.2.3   Generic navigation model in HLHSL

HLHSL uses the HTML like HRef tag to denote links. Defining expressions in a link description within a template provides with a powerful means to specify the abstract behavior part of the navigation model. The expression is elaborated according to the context in each instance.

4.3   Source data model and description

The source data consists of all of the raw material used by the designer and the producer to build a hypermedia document. By essence, the structure of these data is different from the target hypermedia structure, otherwise the hypermedia document would already exist. Most of the data which are present in a hypermedia document exist before being included in the hypermedia structure. Often, even when data are prepared especially for the document, they also exist as external data, for instance as

Photoshop images, or Adobe Premiere Movies. In order to define how to map this set of data into a hypermedia structure we need to describe the available data.

4.3.1 Source data conceptual modeling

Regardless to any presentation purpose, a semantic description of available data is needed in order to identify which role these data play in the communication process, and thus to be able to place them at the relevant place in the target hypermedia. The source data structure description elicits the logical and semantic modeling of data, it is not a description of the target hypermedia document like done in HTML. It is a detailed description of the relationships between the data. Descriptors of non textual objects such as images, video and sound files are also built in order to make their semantic available and handle them in the data model.

4.3.2 SGML-based Data description in PageJockey

We have chosen to use SGML for its flexibility. This enables at lower cost evolution of the source data during the design process. The readability of the markup language is an important advantage for the designers who are rarely computer scientists. It is easier to add tags into a marked up description than to write a program to fill up or update a database. On the other hand defining a SGML DTD or a database schema remains tasks which require some help from specialists.

Unlike HTML tags, the SGML tags used in the description have no presentation role nor hypermedia structure description function. No links are expressed in the source data description. For instance, here is a sample of a data file used for describing the data we used to produce a kiosk for the Musée National des Technologies in Paris.

```
<PERSON IMG =Lavoiser.face.Jpeg SHORTNAME=Lavoisier>
Antoine Laurent de LAVOISIER
<FUNCTION> French chemist .
<BIRTHDATE>1743 (Paris)<DEATH> 1794 (Paris)
<INSTRUMENT IMG ="Lavoisier.Gazo.Jpeg"
SHORTNAME=gasometer> Lavoisier's "gasometer"
<DESCR> This device, developed by Lavoisier,
can be used to precisely measure quantities of gas.
<EXPERIMENT >By isolating mercury and oxidizing it through heating,
Lavoisier noticed that some of the air disappeared, and that the
oxidization process then stopped. What remained was a gas that was
unable to support life: nitrogen. In contrast, when the mercury
oxide was taken and broken down, the initial quantity of gas
reappeared and the air recovered its usual properties. The gas in
question was oxygen, which can oxidize mercury and maintain
combustion.
<APPARATUS NAME-gasometer> Lavoisier brought the problem down to
measuring the volume of a variable cavity filled with a gas at a
pre-determined pressure and temperature. The variable cavity is a
bell jar filled with water, which is kept upside-down above a tank
by a balance. The water ensures that the variable cavity is
airtight and plays a role in the measuring process. The gas
introduced into the gasometer expels the water from the bell jar
until the pressures are balanced, thus altering the volume of
confinement.
```

272

Let us remark the semantic role of the tags in the description. The items above take place in several pages of the hypermedia document and some of them are reused in several places.

4.4 Generation specification

To better fit the designer's mental scheme, the generation specification is associated to the target hypermedia specification rather than to the source data description. This architecture choice is rather unusual since most of generation tools usually attach the generation actions directly to the grammar that defines the structure of the source data. As a consequence, the actions concerning a specific target item often are distributed in the code, making their maintenance more complex.

At the opposite, in HLHSL, a template encapsulates all information needed to produce and manage any instance of the described class. Generation rules are directly described as a specific part within the templates, improving maintainability.

Expressing generation specification from the target side is an architecture choice that has the same purpose as most of PageJockey's features: be an interface to the designer's work. The designer expresses any thing on the closest side and the environment acts as a functional core which converts the designer's intentions into the needed actions.

4.4.1 Specifying generation rules in HLHSL

To each template is associated one or several triggers which are a specification of the conditions in the source data files that lead a page of the class defined by the template to exist. A trigger specifies:

- an activation condition which expresses the invariant properties that the set of variables of the template must match in any of its instances,
- a rule for computing a unique identifier (UID) for each node instance according to the data,
- the way to compute the actual values of the template parameters.

```
For instance,
<Template page PGAboutScientist>
<Trigger Cond=&PERSON,   UID = &("Scientist-".&Shortname)>
<Attrib &ScientPortrait=&Img>
<Attrib &ScientLabel=&(&PERSON , \n,
&BIRTHDATE, &DEATH, /n, &FUNCTION>
...
</Trigger >
is a trigger in a page template.
```

Figure 6 shows a generated page with different user interactions.

Figure 6 Page generation example.

4.4.2   Generation rules processing

As shown in Figure 7, the source data SGML description is first parsed in order to build a derivation tree. The values of each attribute are referenced by their path name along the derivation tree. The generator explores the tree and checks for each node if a triggering condition fires in the current context. If so, the template attributes are assigned as specified from the actual values collected in the context of that node in the derivation tree. Then the template class is instantiated. The instance name is computed as declared in the template UID. If an instance with this name already exists, its attributes are just updated accordingly. This allows the designer to declare several triggers for a single template, or to fire a given trigger several times for the same page. For instance, indexes are incrementally filled-up in this way whenever relevant information is found in the source file.

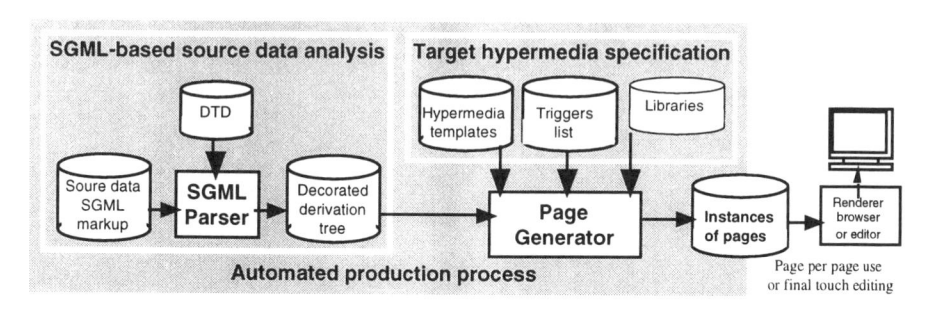

Figure 7 The internal production stages of the template-based generator.

5.   DISCUSSION

The architecture choices of PageJockey design rely on the following ideas:

- A designer's task is to design, not to produce, but often a designer sketches drafts for designing.
- A good design needs validation and improvement by evaluation feedback.
- A design environment is an interface between a designer and the designed work. Very few systems take these simple and obvious ideas into account.

274

5.1   Generating: from source data to target structure

A trend in software engineering is to consider that the designer should focus on design, not on final code production (Budinsky, 1995, Winograd, 1995). For this purpose, PageJockey strongly dissociates design and generation. Generation is only the environment concern. Moreover this enables the designer to take advantage of automated generation to support incremental design.

Some systems (Kuikka, 1993, Feng, 1993) also propose automated generation approaches but they directly associate generation specification to the source data, thus making difficult to follow a task-centered design (Paterno, 1997). In PageJockey, templates result from user's task elicitation. Other systems enable to produce target documents for different platforms or to adapt cosmetic aspects to the end users taste. For instance, style sheets enable a separation between the contents and the presentation (Rutledge, 1997). But the hypermedia structure remains the same and is often already made explicit in the data description. Work by (Kristensen 98) uses the current servlet mechanism (Sun 97) to implement specific kernel for controlling dynamic page production in response to http request. They introduce TML, a template markup language, but it does not support object-orientation. Furthermore their notion of template only concerns documents and there is no environnement for designing high level abstractions such as navigation structure. Thus, such techniques are helpful only to the back end of the production process and not to the design step.

At the opposite, PageJockey fully separates source data from the target hypermedia specification and claims that these structures are independent. Generation specifications, as an intermediate layer, make the separation clearer. PageJockey generates any level of structure. Moreover, one may produce several hypermedia from the same data, or reuse a subset of hypermedia structure specification to turn other data into a hypermedia which shares the same structure. This enables incremental design. The fast generation tool enables the designer to update at will either the data or the hypermedia structure specification and evaluate her design. A real application of 500 nodes is generated in one minute on a G3.

5.2   Elaborating specifications

Bottom up approaches in design are suitable as well as top down ones (Nanard, 1995). PageJockey supports both. The designer can work at the level of instances and use them as clonable prototypes without needing to define abstract classes. Conversely, the system helps turning prototypes into templates. Once classes are defined as templates, top-down design becomes easier. Alternating between both is simple and supported by the system. This enables to reduce the gap between expression of specifications and production: the designer expresses abstract specifications but directly observes their real effect at full scale.

5.3 Maintainability, consistency, reuse

Templates is an efficient mechanism to capture and express at a high level of abstraction shared structure, look and behavior that a designer sketches on the early drafts. It enables to evaluate them at a larger scale and thus improves the efficiency of the evaluation process, by providing earlier feedback.

Separation between source data, templates and their generation rules promotes reuse and solves the problem of information reuse context (Garzotto, 1996) since source data modeling does not include specification of use in the target hypermedia. The templates mechanism and the underlying object-oriented approach helps improve consistency by reuse. Inheritance is responsible for vertical consistency. Inherited elements have the same presentation rules and the same behavior whatever be the context in which they appear. Instantiation is responsible for horizontal consistency. All instances of a class share the same structure. Consistency is needed in hypermedia design in order to help the reader build up a mental model of the explored structure. This is an important factor for usability [Nielsen 89].

Templates provide good and reliable maintainability conditions. Any change done in a template is propagated wherever the template is used. So consistency is preserved. This clearly is a key factor for improving quality of the target hypermedia. Systems which do not provide with mechanisms to automatically propagate changes, raise the risk of introducing inconsistencies and require a heavy maintenance effort which is incompatible with incremental design.

6. CONCLUSION

A design and production environment is not simply a tool for recording the result of a design that a designer elaborates only in his mind. It must support the design activity (Winograd, 1995), especially the evaluation feedback which is a characteristic of all human creative activities, and relieve the designer from the burden of producing for evaluating the design choices. The described architecture is used in the PageJockey environment and has proven its usefulness in several real scale developments: "The computer science pioneers" (Fraïssé, 1996), "From the laboratory to the home" for the National Museum of Technology in Paris (Nanard, 1998). Beyond the currently available features, many issues are open:

- Use directly the components of the design process loop as a support for design rationale (Bœhm, 1995): it is possible to use the same technique to manage both the product and external information used during the design process and to organize information about the design as a hypermedia easy to explore.
- Generate features for recording users behavior and analyzing it during the evaluation steps directly into the generated target hypermedia. This enables evaluation to rely upon objectified data. The template mechanism makes it possible to specify control and record users actions wherever suitable.
- Extend the template mechanism in order to use it at a higher level of abstraction to handle design patterns (Gamma, 1995). Many hypermedia share the same

design patterns. Beyond identifying these patterns (Rossi, 1997) providing a simple mechanism to efficiently implement them (Nanard, 1998) is a very promising topic. Templates constitute one of the ways to study for promoting reuse and developing frameworks (Schmidt, 1997).

7.   REFERENCES

Bœhm, B., Bose, P., Horowitz, E., Lee, M.J. (1995) Software Requirements Negotiation and Renegotiation Aids: A Theory-W Based Spiral Approach. *Proc. ICSE'95.*

Budinsky, F.J., Finnie, M.A., Vlissides, J.M., and Yu, P.S. (1996) Automatic code generation from design patterns. *IBM Systems Journal*, Vol. 35, N°2.

A. Feng & T. Wakayama. Simon: a Grammar-based transformation system for structured documents (1993). *Electronic Publishing 6(4)*, 361-372.

Fraïssé, S., Nanard, M., Nanard, J. (1996) Generating hypermedia from specifications by sketching multimedia templates. *Proc. Multimedia'96*, ACM Press, 120-124.

Gamma, E., Helm, R., Johnson, R., Vlissides, J. (1995) Design Patterns: Elements of Reusable Object-Oriented Software. Addison-Wesley, Reading.

Garzotto, F., Mainetti, L., Paolini, P. (1995) Hypermedia design, analysis and evaluation issues. *CACM 38(8)*, 74-86.

Garzotto, F., Mainetti, L. Paolini, P. (1996) Information reuse in hypermedia applications. *Proc. Hypertext'96*, ACM Press, 93-104.

Gronbæk, K. (1997) Designing Dexter-based hypermedia services for World-Wide Web. *Proc. Hypertext'97*, 146-156.

Halasz, F. & Schwartz, M. (1994) The Dexter Hypertext Reference Model. *CACM 37(2)*.

Kristensen, A. (1998) Template resolution in XML/HTML. *WWW7*, Elsevier Publisher.

Kuikka, E. & Penttonen, M. (1993) Transformation of Structured Documents with the Use of Grammar. *Electronic PublishingVol. 6(4)*, 373-383.

Nanard, J. & Nanard, M. (1995) Hypertext Design Environments and the Hypertext Design Process. *CACM 38(8)*, 49-56.

Nanard, M., Nanard, J., Kahn, P. (1998) Pushing Reuse in Hypermedia Design: Golden Rules, Design Patterns and Generic Templates,*Proc. HT'98,* ACM Press, 11-20.

Nielsen, J. (1989) Tools for generating consistent user interfaces in Coordinating User Interfaces for Consistency, Academic Press, 107-130.

O2Web (1997) *User Manual.* O2 Technology.

Paterno, F., Bucca, M.F. (1997) Task-oriented Design for Interactive User Interface in Museum Systems. *Proc. ICHIM'97*, Le Louvre, 271-279.

Rossi, G., Schwabe, D., Garrido A. (1997) Design Reuse in Hypermedia Applications Development. *Proc. Hypertext'97*, ACM Press, 57-66.

Rutledge, L., van Ossenbruggen, J., Hardman, L., Bulterman, D. (1997) A Framework for Generating Adaptable Hypermedia Documents. *Proc. Multimedia'97*, ACM Press.

Schmidt, D.(1997) Object-Oriented Application Frameworks,*CACM 40(10)*,32-38.

Schwabe, D., Rossi, G., Barbosa, S.D.J. (1996) Systematic Hypermedia Application Design with OOHDM. *Proc. Hypertext'96*, ACM Press, 116-128.

Shaw, M. (1995) Abstractions for Software Architecture and Tools to Support Them. *Proc. of the 1st Int. Workshop on Architectures for Software Systems.*

Sun (1997), The Servlet API, Sun MicroSystems, *http://jserv.javasoft.com/products/java-server/servlets/*

Winograd, T. (1995) From programming environments to environments for designing, *CACM* *38(6)*, 65-74.

8.   BIOGRAPHY

Jocelyne Nanard is professor at Universite' de Montpellier (France). Her research interest covers HCI aspects of Hypermedia design, Hypermedia modelling, and design patterns. Marc Nanard is professor at Centre National des Arts et Me'tiers of Paris and Universite' de Montpellier. His research is in Interaction with documents, Hypermedia design methodology and development tools. He is chair of the ACM SigWeb, Special Interest Group on Hypermedia and the Web.

Discussion

Fabio Patterno: What assumptions do you make to build a page, because, for example, I don't think your environment can work with applets.

Jocelyne Nanard: The environment works with SGML implementation only.

Joelle Coutaz: What happens if the source data does not match the constraints expressed in the template?

Jocelyne Nanard: We must look at consequences of design decisions. We can modify data descriptions or the data.

Joelle Coutaz: Do you support temporal constraints such as Allen's operations?

Jocelyne Nanard: Yes. We can specify them by visual programming on concrete objects and then replace references to concrete instance objects in the generated code by variable names when abstracting the template.

Franck Tarpin-Bernard: For the moment, designers explicitly decide to view a page or an item as a pattern. Is it possible for the system to automatically identify patterns?

Jocelyne Nanard: No, but it is a future issue.

Stephane Chatty: Have you given thought to the extent of the systems your language can describe; in other words, what would you need in addition to your language to describe an interactive system?

Jocelyne Nanard: We don't handle computation properly. Apart from that, we handle user actions pretty well.

Towards a Framework and Procedure for Specifying User Interfaces

Paul Chesson, Lorraine Johnston, Philip Dart
Department of Computer Science, The University of Melbourne, Parkville, Australia, 3052
{chesson,ljj,philip}@cs.mu.OZ.AU

Abstract: This paper presents a framework for specifying user interface dialogue. The framework supports the integration of a dialogue specification with external environments such as the application core. Some results are presented concerning the development of a procedure for constructing a dialogue specification within the framework. This procedure considers meaningful pieces of work in the application environment, and relates the user interface design requirements to the various layers in the framework.

Keywords: dialogue specification, user interface model, development process

1. INTRODUCTION

User interface dialogue specification is concerned with describing the structure of dialogue between an interactive system and its users. The process and result of formally specifying a user interface is aimed at facilitating the understanding and communication of the design between the participants in software development. Specifications can also enable developers to analyse features related to the usability of an interface.

When applying languages to particular specification problems, procedural guidance is rarely given. Such guidance would reduce the time needed to learn the language, and avoid the language being used inappropriately (Monk et al., 1993). There is a need for representation techniques to be closely tied to, and interleaved with, the mental design process. Control over complexity can be achieved with carefully applied methods and sound principles (for example, abstraction and stepwise refinement) which have been successfully applied in other design environments (Hartson and Boehm-Davis, 1993).

This paper presents some results concerning the development of a framework and procedure for specifying the dialogue of user interfaces. User interface specification languages differ widely in the types of components used, and in the way in which these components are combined to form a complete description of the interface (Gray and Johnson, 1995). For this reason, no single procedure can hope to be applicable to all languages. Although the ideas presented here have been developed for use with the user interface specification language FLUID (Chesson and Johnston, 1996) in mind, they should be applicable to other languages which possess similar characteristics in their underlying model.

Section 2 introduces the high level model and concepts used for the specification of interactive systems. Section 3 presents a framework for specifying user interface dialogue, based on the level of abstraction of its requirements. Section 4 addresses the issue of specifying the interface between user interface dialogue and the external environments needed to provide application and computational functionality. Finally, work towards the development of a procedure for specifying the behaviour of an interactive system using the given framework is outlined in section 5.

2. MODELLING INTERACTIVE SYSTEMS

FLUID (Formal Language for User Interface Dialogue) is a language for describing the interactive dialogue between a user and an application. The model upon which FLUID is based (see Figure 1) treats the user interface as a processing unit which regulates the flow of control and data between the user and application environments. The user environment consists of one or more users, the physical devices which they use, and any information presented to them. The application environment provides the underlying functionality required by the users in order to perform their tasks.

Events are initiated by changes in the user or application environments. Actions describe the effects of these changes on the corresponding environment. Events and actions are modelled using a name and a list of parameters which describe the data associated with the event or action, for example, **move_cursor(POS1, POS2)**. Distinct instances of events which have the same name (regardless of whether they have matching data values) are said to be of the same *type*. Event types may be represented by using descriptive variable names to represent its data elements. To differentiate constant data values from variable names, variable names begin with a lower case letter, for example, **move_cursor(from_position, to_position)**.

The mapping from events to actions is defined by the dialogue specification and the state of the interface at the time when it receives its events.

The conceptual model of FLUID corresponds to the Seeheim model (Pfaff, 1985) for User Interface Management Systems (UIMS) in the following manner: the set of user events and presentation actions required by a user interface defines the logical units of the presentation component of the Seeheim model. Similarly, the set of application events and application actions correspond to the application interface component of the Seeheim model. Lastly, the FLUID dialogue specification corresponds to the dialogue control component of the Seeheim model. The dialogue control component will be further decomposed in section 3.

Since a user interface can be viewed as a unit which reacts to its environments, it seems natural to also model the internal components of a user interface in the same manner. The idea of scaling down a user interface model into its components has also

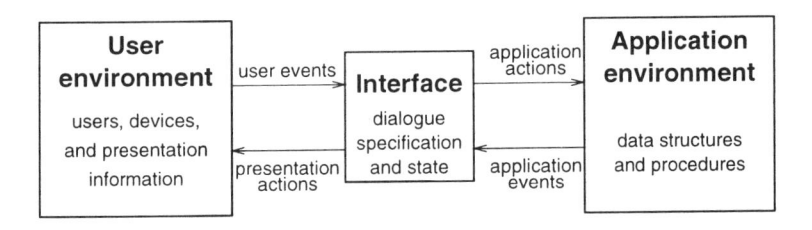

Figure 1: The conceptual model of FLUID

been applied by Palanque and Bastide who used the Seeheim model as a basis for specifying Interactive Co-operative Objects (ICOs) (Palanque and Bastide, 1994).

In the case of FLUID, a specification is divided into units called *sub-dialogues* which receive incoming events and can produce outgoing events and actions. This abstraction results in components that resemble instances of Paternó's LOTOS inter-actor model (Paternó and Faconti, 1992) which reacts to events via its input and output gates. In Paternó's model, each interactor represents a user interface element which transfers data across multiple levels of abstraction. However, the FLUID sub-dialogue represents a simple design requirement describing part of the behaviour of the system. Such a requirement is modelled by a constraint or rule, similar to those used in ERL (Hill, 1986) or PPS (Olsen, 1990), without any explicit object modelling.

Sub-dialogues are expressed using a combination of tables and simple Coloured Petri nets, allowing for more expressive rules to be formulated than could otherwise be obtained by using simple production rules. The sub-dialogue components process events according to particular aspects of the state of the user interface relating to the requirement being specified. As a result of processing, a sub-dialogue may produce new events called *contextual events*. In some cases, contextual events can be thought of as the same occurrences in a different context. For example, if a cursor is inside an icon, then the event of pressing a mouse button produces a new event indicating an icon is selected. In other cases, the new events being produced can be thought of as new occurrences. For example, if an icon is selected, then the event of selecting another icon produces a new event indicating that the first icon becomes unselected.

The method by which requirements are specified as sub-dialogues is an important issue, but is not addressed in this paper. Instead, these details are abstracted by treating sub-dialogues as black boxes which react to, and produce, events. The rule governing each sub-dialogue are expressed here using natural language.

3. THE THREE-LAYER DIALOGUE SPECIFICATION MODEL

Requirements for interactive systems can cover a wide range of conceptual levels from low-level user events such as mouse movements and key presses, to high-level application tasks. Sub-dialogues provide a way of abstracting the details of individual requirements, but sub-dialogues themselves may need to be hidden when dealing with other requirements at a higher level. The three-layer model proposed in this section aims to provide a framework for the classification and organisation of sub-dialogues. This framework promotes internal consistency by restricting the types of events and actions, and the ways in which they are used.

The use of layers representing different levels of abstraction is similar to the language stage concept (Hoffner et al., 1989). Hoffner et al. claims that the use of language stages, if carried out wisely, offers a number of benefits of modular design. In their model, the divisions (called language stages) are specifically defined for each system, rather than having precise boundaries which are applicable to all systems. In our three-layer model, sub-dialogues within the layer are responsible for the translation and interpretation steps that would be needed between the language stages.

3.1 Overview

Figure 2 presents the division of the user interface component in figure 1 into three layers: symbolic, semantic, and pragmatic. In addition, each layer can be divided into input and output streams. All sub-dialogues must be classifiable into one of these streams, in one of the layers.

Each layer can be thought of as a scaled-down version of the model of the user interface in figure 1. Actions are treated in the same manner as events, and are only differentiated from events because they happen to terminate at either the user or application environments and are not processed by the user interface.

Each layer in the model consists of sub-dialogues which are responsible for processing and producing events between two levels of abstraction. Consider the semantic layer which specifies the transformations required between symbolic events and semantic events. Sub-dialogues in the input stream take symbolic and/or semantic events as inputs, and can produce semantic events as outputs. Sub-dialogues in the output stream take semantic events as inputs and can produce semantic and/or symbolic events as outputs.

3.2 Symbolic layer

The symbolic layer deals exclusively with the specification of the user interface behaviour, without any reference to the domain of the application. The layer has two

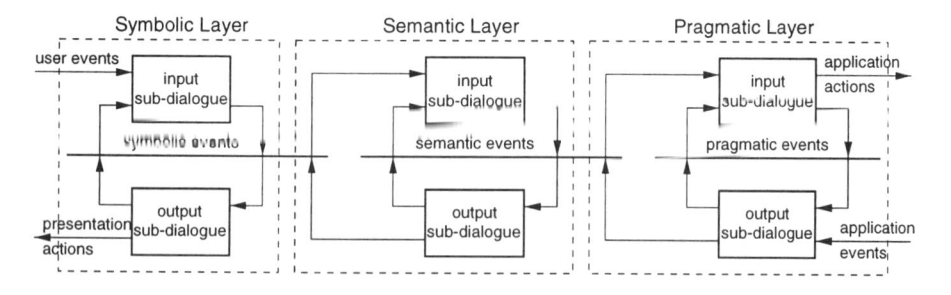

Figure 2: The three-layer dialogue specification model

284

main purposes. The first purpose is to provide a means of establishing a well-defined set of events which can be used to describe interaction with the user interface. This has a similar role to the set of subroutines used to describe the programming interface to a user interface toolkit.

The second purpose is to allow the specification of the behaviour of the user interface platform, itself. For example, the behaviour of a scrollbar widget can be specified in terms of clicking on its arrow buttons and dragging a slider. This level of specification is similar to that provided by Interaction Object Graphs (IOG) (Carr et al., 1994). In fact, since IOGs interact with external environments via event and data arcs and FLUID events have a data value attached to them, it is possible to incorporate the IOG formalism into the three-layer model by treating IOGs as one large sub-dialogue (with no separation of input and output streams).

In cases where a standard user interface platform has been specified, the symbolic layer will not need to be redefined when the same platform is re-used in other systems. In other circumstances, it may be acceptable to abstract the entire layer to a set of symbolic events, without detailed consideration of their underlying behaviour.

3.3   Semantic layer

The semantic layer deals with the relationship between the user interface and the meaning of its components and dynamic behaviour. Sub-dialogues in the input stream of the semantic layer typically take symbolic events representing user interactions with the interface, and describe their meaning in terms of the application domain. However, semantic events still convey some meaning in relation to the interface itself. Two alternative interfaces for the same application may vary in how their tasks are performed, or how they present information. Each interface is likely to employ a different set of semantic events. For example, a text editor may allow a user to delete a number of consecutive lines in a number of ways. A command line interface may use a semantic event such as **delete_lines(first_line, last_line)**. A graphical interface may use a set of semantic commands to delete an arbitrary block of text, such as: **mark_start_block(pos)**, **mark_end_block(pos)**, and **delete_marked_block()**.

Sub-dialogues in the output stream of the semantic layer are typically responsible for rendering the information conveyed by semantic events to the user. These semantic events may be generated by sub-dialogues in the input stream of the semantic layer (for example, highlighting the marked text when a block is selected), or from the results produced at a higher level (for example, deleting a block of marked text after it has been established that the document can be changed).

3.4   Pragmatic layer

The pragmatic layer deals with the relationship between the meaning of the information conveyed in the user interface, and the work being performed in the application domain, i.e. the practical significance of the information. Sub-dialogues in the input stream of the pragmatic layer typically take semantic events representing operations performed by the user, and specify how they are used to perform meaningful operations (pragmatic events) and tasks (application actions) in the application domain. Pragmatic events and application actions express interaction purely in terms of the application domain, independent of the user interface.

The set of application events and actions provides a similar role to the programming interface to the core functionality of the application. The definition of these events and actions should be exactly the same for any user interface which provides access to the same functionality and presents the same information to the user.

Sub-dialogues in the output stream of the pragmatic layer are typically responsible for determining how high level output from an application is visualised with respect to the user interface components. For example, the application event used to indicate that the request to move a block of text was successful, may produce two semantic events to handle this: **copy_document_text(start_pos, end_pos, new_pos)** copies a block of text in the document presented in the user interface, while **delete_document_text(start_pos, end_pos)** is used to delete the original block of text.

4. MODELLING INTERFACES WITH THEIR ENVIRONMENTS

There are a number of environments which are external to the user interface component of the dialogue specification model. In addition to the user and application environments in the conceptual model of FLUID, a computational environment may be required to perform generic computations which are not possible using a particular dialogue specification language. An overview of the interactions between the user interface and its external environments is presented in section 4.1.

Although the full details concerning the behaviour of external environments are not part of the user interface dialogue specification, the boundary between the two should be well defined. Each piece of functionality (typically, a single computation or procedure) supported by an environment is specified as a distinct unit called an *environment interface*. An environment interface is defined by the set of event types passed between the interface and the environment, and the constraints between them.

The nature of the data passed from an environment interface can be classified according to a number of characteristics which it may possess. Section 4.2 discusses some common features found in such data and suggests how the transfer of this data can be modelled by discrete events. Finally, section 4.3 examines the issue of specifying constraints in the sequencing of events in an environment interface.

4.1 Types of interface environments

Dialogue specification languages are typically designed to be expressive enough to accommodate a significant proportion of situations that may be encountered when describing the behaviour of user interfaces. There is usually some tradeoff between the expressiveness (or computational power) of a language, its simplicity of use, its readability, and its formality. For situations when the specification language is unable to describe the computational processing required by the interface, there needs to be some way of abstracting this functionality. Even in cases where the language can express such functionality, it may still be desirable to abstract these details.

Computations may be performed in any of the three layers in the dialogue specification model. The processing of computations is modelled by interaction with a computational environment. The computational environment represents some external entity which responds to queries. Although the computational environment may be implemented as part of the application code, unlike the application environment, it has no perceivable state and any interaction should be purely functional. In most cases, this can be thought of as occurring by the sub-dialogue sending a *computational query event* to the computational environment, and the computational environment returning one or more *computation response events*. The exchange of data involved in a computation is localised to a single sub-dialogue and as such, is not shown in figure 2.

In addition to generic computations, semantic and pragmatic sub-dialogues may require application-specific information. If this information is not required to perform work directly, but is used within the interface to assist the user in completing tasks, then an *application query* is required. An example of an application query is obtaining a list of files currently open in an application so that one of them may be selected for some purpose. This information is contained within the state of the application, and thus requires the application environment to be queried. Such a query is modelled in the same fashion as a computation, using *application query events* and *application response events*.

Finally, application actions which indicate requests for some action to occur in the application environment, are sent from the pragmatic input sub-dialogues to the application environment. Any subsequently related responses from the application environment are sent to pragmatic output sub-dialogues.

For the purposes of specifying the interface between a sub-dialogue and an environment, all three cases will be modelled in the same manner. Computation query events, application query events, and application actions, will be classified as instances of *stimulus events*. Computation response events, application response events, and application events responding to application actions, will be classified as instances of *response events*.

4.2 Characteristics of environment interface responses

After a stimulus event has been sent to an environment interface, the response of the environment depends on the data sent with the stimulus event and the state of the environment. In many cases, the response can be modelled using a single response event to represent the final result. However, in other cases, a sequence of several response events may be required to model the response accurately. In this section, three such cases will be examined. No claim is made that these cases cover all instances where the transfer of data cannot be represented by a single event, but it is expected that the solutions offered will serve as a useful guide for handling a number of common cases in a consistent manner. Lastly, the proposed use of standardised event types will be briefly discussed.

4.2.1 Case 1: Delayed response

In many interactive systems, some operations will involve periods where the user will be waiting for the application to provide a response. This delay can be caused by factors such as a complex computation being performed, or information having to be transferred over a network. In such cases, a response event should be returned by the environment to indicate that the subsequent response may be delayed. This initial response event can be handled by the dialogue specification which indicates to the user that a certain piece of data is awaited.

For example, the application environment of a web browser may not be able to respond with the contents of a requested page immediately, so a response event **start_page_contents**() should precede the delayed event **send_page_contents(data)**. The **start_page_contents**() event may be subsequently rendered to indicate to the user that a page contents transfer is in progress.

4.2.2 Case 2: Segmented response

In addition to being delayed, the actual response from the application environment can be spread over a period of time. This can occur when a large unit of data is progressively transferred, and it is useful to specify the behaviour of the interface as each segment of data is received, or to allow pre-emptive interaction to be modelled. Each segment of data is represented by a separate event, along with additional information regarding the state of the response (for example, time elapsed, time remaining, or percentage complete). The complete set of data segment events should occur between start and end events to indicate when the data is being sent, and when all the data has been sent. Once again, these events can be used to provide cues to the user regarding the progress.

Continuing with the web browser example, the progressive transfer of a web page can be treated as a segmented response using the set of event types: **start_page_contents**(), **send_page_contents(data, percent_trans)**, and **end_page_contents**(), where **data** refers to the segment of the page contents being transferred, and **percent_trans** refers to the total percentage of the page which has been transferred including the current segment.

4.2.3 Case 3: Multiple response

An environment may respond with several pieces of data, each of which are independent from each another. In such cases, start and end events are useful in indicating the commencement and termination of the complete response. If the instances of data themselves are delayed or segmented, then each instance will have its own start and end (in the case of segmented data) events.

When instances of data are of the same type, their corresponding events will also be of the same type. If each instance of data needs to be referred to at a later time, then it requires a unique identifier. One case where this is necessary is when the data from each instance is segmented. A unique identifier is required by the user interface to be able to associate the segment with the correct piece of data.

Once again using the web browser example, a request for a web page may result in a number of components being transmitted such as images, sounds and applets. Using the URL of each of these components as a unique identifier, the set event of event types needed to model multiple, segmented response is. **start_page contents**() and **end_page_contents**() for the response, and **start_url_contents(url)**, **send_url_contents(url, data, percent_trans)**, and **end_url_contents(url)** for each of the components.

4.2.4 Standardised event types

The use of standardised event types appears to be a useful approach in dealing with particular classes of specification problems. When modelling response characteristics for environment interfaces, events representing the transfer of data can be enclosed within "start" and "end" events to model delays in response and the termination of segmented data. Similar uses of standard events for dealing with specification problems has been found in other ongoing work related to the specification of sub-dialogues. Different types of states (for example, single values, sets, and mappings) may have their values changed via "change", "set" and "unset" event types, whose behaviours depend on the particular types of states to which they are applied.

4.3   Temporal constraints

In addition to defining the events required to formulate an environment interface, it is necessary to define the constraints between response events in cases where a sequence of more than one event may be used in response to a stimulus event. These constraints enable software developers to understand the possible behaviours which can be expected of an environment. In turn, this information can be used to devise scenarios for test cases, and verify properties of the interface based on the specified behaviour of its environment.

The possible set of responses in an environment interface can be defined by a grammar. This grammar may be represented using any number of formalisms, including BNF, LOTOS, temporal logic, or Petri nets.

Consider the example of a web browser with an environment interface for the process of requesting and serving the contents of a web page, using a multiple, segmented response. The stimulus event type representing the request for a page by the user is **request_page(url)**. In addition to the response events introduced in section 4.2.3, two error event types will be introduced: **connection_error(url)** to represent errors which occur before data from a URL is sent, and **transfer_error(url)** to represent errors which occur while data from a URL is being sent.

Figure 3 specifies the temporal constraints on the responses from the application environment using a Coloured Petri net (Jensen, 1992). When the stimulus event is received (1), the start event for the transfer of page contents is produced (2). A token is created to represent the URL of the page to be retrieved (3). Next, either a connection error occurs (4), or the contents of the URL start being retrieved (5). Then, the application can either indicate that a transfer error has occurred (6) or that the contents of the URL have been completely sent (7), or it can send some of the contents (8). The variables **data** and **percent_trans** represent data which is produced by the application and passed to the user interface. If the application sends some contents, additional URLs may be found in the new content which will commence being retrieved (9). These URLs are handled in the same way as the initial one (10). The double-headed arc indicates that multiple tokens may be created, each representing a reference to a new URL. Lastly, the application indicates that the retrieval of the contents of the page has been completed when no further URLs are pending (11).

5.   A SPECIFICATION PROCEDURE

The purpose of this section is to present work undertaken towards a structured approach to specifying user interfaces within the framework presented in section 3. The procedure to be presented focuses only on the activity of dialogue specification (i.e. the three layers of the model in section 3), and as such, requires that the developer

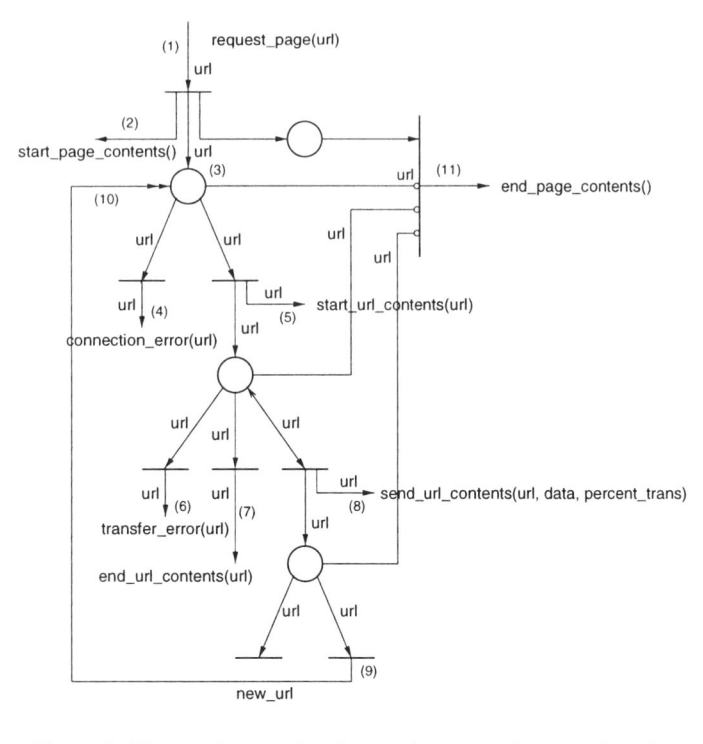

Figure 3: Temporal constraints for a web page environment interface

specifying the user-interface has an understanding of the section of the design being represented. However, this does not mean that the entire design needs to be completed before dialogue specification can commence, nor does it mean those parts that have been specified cannot be changed. Specification is organised around pieces of functionality called *work units* which are progressively refined and related to the user environment. The developer may chose to postpone specification of part or all of a work unit at any point, and then resume or begin specification of another work unit.

Two constraints are imposed on the development activity. First, any new requirement must either correspond to a new work unit, or be needed as a consequence of the requirements already in the specification. Second, any requirements which depend on a modified requirement and are no longer correct or consistent, must either be immediately updated or deleted.

5.1 Work decomposition

Since the proposed framework uses rule-based sub-dialogues as its primary unit of abstraction, it is more appropriate to approach the specification process in terms of functionality rather than objects. A starting point for dialogue specification which is commonly recommended is task analysis. One example of this is Dialogue Specification Notation (DSN) (Curry and Monk, 1995) which advocates the use of a task model to identify those parts of the model suitable for dialogue specification. While task ana-

290

lysis techniques can be useful in driving the high level dialogue of an interface, we will begin at an even higher level by examining the pieces of work which need to be performed by the system. In other words, we begin with the question, "What is the user supposed to be able to do with the system?", rather than, "How is the user supposed to use the system to do it?" This is similar to the distinction between the goal and task levels of Nielsen's virtual protocol model for HCI (Nielsen, 1986).

Specification commences with the designation of a piece of work which the system is required to perform. This piece of work is referred to as a work unit. The motivation in using work units is to promote a well-defined separation between the user interface and the application, and to help determine whether support for the users' access to the underlying functionality has subsequently been specified.

The functionality represented by a work unit should require some action to be performed in the application environment, and be independent of the user interface used to perform or control the work. The performance of a work unit will not necessarily have some perceivable effect on the user interface. This is similar to the distinction between the Result and Display components of the PIE model (Dix, 1991). Work unit functionality can be modelled by one or more stimulus and response events at the application environment interface (section 5.2).

In the web browser example, work units include: retrieving a web page, printing a web page, and locating a text pattern in a web page. Clearing and adjusting the cache would also be included if the browser makes these facilities available to the user, since they affect the application.

Examples of functionality which would not be considered work units include changing preferences, scrolling around a page, and interrupting the loading of a page. Changing preferences (such as whether images should be displayed) affect the work of retrieving and viewing a page, but do not achieve any results by themselves. Scrolling around a page is another way of controlling the results of work – in this case, how it is viewed. Interrupting the loading of a page controls the work of retrieving the page, and can be thought of as a *user exception* (Curry and Monk, 1995) which would be treated as a stimulus event for the page retrieval work unit.

Functionality related to bookmarks and history is less clear, as it may not be apparent whether it should be treated as part of the interface or the application. We judge that these mechanisms are a means of performing the work or retrieving a page, and as such, should be treated as part of the interface. Events representing the use of such mechanisms to retrieve pages would be classified as semantic events, and not part of a work unit. Dialogue relating to the manipulation of bookmarks would be specified in the semantic layer. The possible use of an external environment to support the loading and saving of the bookmarks without using the application environment, is briefly discussed in section 6. Nevertheless, even if a different division between the interface and application is chosen, the method is still applicable as long as consistency is maintained.

5.2 Application environment interfaces

After a work unit has been identified, an environment interface is used to specify the communication between the pragmatic layer of the user interface and the application environment. The developer firstly determines what information is required to be returned to the user upon successful completion of the work. For example, the result of locating a pattern in a web page can be represented by the application event **found_pattern(start_pos, end_pos, num)** where **start_pos** and **end_pos** represent the start and end locations of the pattern found in the web page, and **num** indicates the total number of times the pattern is found.

Next, each piece of information required to be provided by the user in order to complete the work, needs to be identified. Typically, only one set of information is needed to complete the work, and this can be represented by a single application event type which combines pieces of information. However, in some cases where the information is significantly disjoint, it may be more convenient to use multiple application events. For example, the act of locating a text pattern in a web page may be initiated by the application event **find_external_pattern(pattern, case, pos)** or **find_internal_pattern(start_pos, end_pos)**. In the first case, the search for **pattern** is commenced from the position **pos** in the web page. In the second case, the pattern to be searched for is defined by the text in the web page itself between **start_pos** and **end_pos**.

Next, any possible system errors or exceptions resulting from the work being performed are considered and represented by application events. Consideration should be paid to the complete set of application actions. Any irregular inputs should either be handled directly, or assumptions that they will not occur should be explicitly documented for later verification. For example, one assumption relating to **find_internal_pattern** might be that **start_pos** occurs before **end_pos** in the web page. The final set of application events are derived by considering their characteristics, and any temporal constraints between the application events should be documented (see section 4).

5.3   Pragmatic layer specification

Having defined the application environment interface, specification of the related pragmatic layer sub-dialogues is commenced in order to describe in abstract terms how the data associated with the work unit will be sent to the application and presented to the user.

The process of specifying the input stream of the pragmatic layer will involve defining how the user is able to provide the information required by the application actions and then invoke them. The developer will need to consider the final state that the user interface needs to invoke the application event, and then specify how each of its sub-states is reached. This refinement continues until the events involved are no longer completely independent of the user interface, and further consideration of the user interface platform is required (section 5.4). In the internal pattern searching example, the following pragmatic input sub-dialogue may be defined:

Example 1
If a request to find a pattern is made (semantic event **find_pattern()**) by designating a pattern on the web page from **start_pos** to **end_pos**, a request to find the pattern is sent (application action **find_internal_pattern(start_pos, end_pos)**).

The sub-state regarding a pattern being designated is defined as follows:

> **Example 2**
> If a pattern is designated from **start_pos** to **end_pos** in the web page (semantic event **designate_pattern(start_pos, end_pos)**), then a pattern has been designated until the pattern in cleared (semantic event **clear_pattern()**).

The process of specifying the output stream of the pragmatic layer will involve defining the operations to be performed by the user interface to present the information provided by the application environment to the user. In doing this, the developer should begin with the application events and refine them until the operations required to be performed are no longer completely independent of the user interface.

In the pattern searching example, the following pragmatic output sub-dialogue may be defined to specify how text patterns found in a web page are indicated:

> **Example 3**
> If a text pattern is found (application event **found_pattern(start_pos, end_pos, num)**) then indicate the pattern to the user (semantic event **indicate_pattern(VIEWING_WINDOW, start_pos, end_pos)**) and indicate the total number of times the pattern occurs (semantic event **indicate_num_patterns(num)**).

5.4 Symbolic layer specification

Before associating semantic events with their presentation components, it is helpful to define these components without reference to the application domain. Each type of presentation component should be identified along with the operations which can be performed on them. The specification process for the symbolic layer is similar in method to that for the pragmatic layer. Each operation on a presentation component should be classified into either the input or the output stream, where it can be progressively refined in a similar manner to application events and actions. Unless a developer is attempting to specify an entire user environment, the operations required can be specified as needed. The level of detail to which the symbolic layer should be specified (in other words, what constitutes a user event or presentation action) can be decided by the specification writer (see section 3.2).

An example of the operation of selecting text with a mouse is shown below:

> **Example 4**
> If the user releases the left mouse button (symbolic event **release_left_mouse()**) at position **pos2** while the mouse is being dragged from position **pos1**, then the text from **pos1** to **pos2** is selected (symbolic event **select_text(pos1, pos2)**).

5.5 Semantic layer specification

The semantic layer is defined last of all, linking the high level tasks and application information from the pragmatic layer, to the low level user interface operations and presentation data from the symbolic layer. Specification of the input stream requires the consideration of the semantic events defined in section 5.3, and defining the conditions under which which such events can occur. The following example demonstrates the mapping between the selection of text and its use in designating a search pattern:

293

> **Example 5**
> If a segment of text from **start_pos** to **end_pos** in the web page **VIEW-ING_WINDOW** is selected (symbolic event **select_text(start_pos, end_pos, VIEWING_WINDOW)**), then a pattern is designated between these two positions (semantic event **designate_pattern(start_pos, end_pos)**).

In the output stream, similar mappings can be specified to show how semantic events are mapped to presentation concepts. For example, **indicate_pattern** maps to highlighting of text, and **send_url_contents** maps to cumulatively creating and displaying new presentation objects.

6. CONCLUSIONS AND FURTHER WORK

This paper presented a model which provides a framework for the specification of user interface dialogue. The model consists of three layers (symbolic, semantic, and pragmatic) which constrain requirements to well-defined levels of abstraction. Environment interfaces are used to specify communication with the application core, and to support generic computations.

Work towards the development of a procedure for constructing a user interface dialogue specification within this model was presented. Use of the model aims to promote the construction of a specification which possesses a consistent structure across multiple levels of abstraction. The procedure aims to allow flexibility in the level of detail to be specified for various sections, and allow the writer to postpone and resume specification of any section, at any time.

The procedure should serve as a useful guide as to how to progress, to ensure that the writer knows how to begin or what to do next. While providing guidance, it should remain flexible enough to allow refinement to progress in the manner chosen by the writer. For each step performed, the amount of information required from outside the scope of what is being immediately specified should be minimised.

The procedure outlined is driven by work units which represent meaningful pieces of work in the application environment. The interface for each work unit is defined, and related requirements are specified for the three layers, in the following order: pragmatic, symbolic, then semantic.

Specification of individual requirements is outside the scope of the procedure presented and is dependent on the actual language used. Two omissions from the procedure are noted here. First, not all user interface functionality can be derived from work units. Operations which relate purely to the user interface, such as changing its configuration, must be specified separately in the semantic layer. Data related to this functionality which is stored or retrieved from external sources (for example, files) may need to be modelled using an additional environment accessible to the semantic layer. We are currently considering the use of work units for user interface tasks.

The second recognised omission is that the process does not have provision for semantic feedback for events which are not part of the dialogue required to perform a work unit. The strategy we are currently using to detect likely instances of such cases is to check where symbolic events are used to change the state of a sub-dialogue in the semantic layer, and to consider if additional semantic feedback is appropriate.

Acknowledgements

The authors wish to thank the anonymous referees for their valuable comments on an earlier draft of this paper.

REFERENCES

Carr, D., Jog, N., Kumar, H., Teittinen, M., and Alberg, C. (1994). Using Interaction Object Graphs to specify and develop graphical widgets. Technical Report CAR-TR-734, University of Maryland, College Park, MD.

Chesson, P. and Johnston, L. (1996). FLUID: Specifying data flow and control for user interfaces. In Yong, L., Herman, L., Leung, Y., and Moyes, J., editors, *Proceedings of the First Asia-Pacific Conference on Computer Human Interaction*, pages 171–180, Singapore. Information Technology Institute.

Curry, M. and Monk, A. (1995). Dialogue modelling of graphical user interfaces with a production system. *Behaviour and Information Technology*, 14(1):41–55.

Dix, A. (1991). *Formal Methods for Interactive Systems*. Academic Press, London.

Gray, P. and Johnson, C. (1995). Requirements for the next generation of user interface specification languages. In Palanque, P. and Bastide, R., editors, *Proceedings of The Design, Specification And Verification Of Interactive Systems*, pages 113–133, Toulouse. Springer-Verlag.

Hartson, H. and Boehm-Davis, D. (1993). User interface development processes and methodologies. *Behaviour and Information Technology*, 12(2):98–114.

Hill, R. (1986). Supporting concurrency, communication, and synchronization in human-computer interaction - the Sassafras UIMS. *ACM Transactions on Graphics*, 5(3):179–210.

Hoffner, Y., Dobson, J., and Iggulden, D. (1989). A new user interface architecture. In Sutcliffe, A. and Macaulay, L., editors, *People and Computers V, Proceedings of HCI'89*, pages 169–189, Nottingham. Cambridge University Press.

Jensen, K. (1992). *Coloured Petri Nets, Volume 1: Basic Concepts*. Springer-Verlag, Berlin.

Monk, A., Curry, M., and Wright, P. (1993). Why industry doesn't use the wonderful notations we researchers have given them to reason about their designs. In Gilmore, D., editor, *User-centred requirements for software engineering*, pages 253–261, Berlin. Springer-Verlag.

Nielsen, J. (1986). A virtual protocol for computer-human interaction. *International Journal of Man-Machine Studies*, 24:301–312.

Olsen, D. (1990). Propositional production systems for dialog description. In Chew, J. and Whiteside, J., editors, *ACM Annual conference on Human Factors in Computing Systems*, pages 57–63, New York.

Palanque, P. and Bastide, R. (1994). Petri net based design of user-driven interfaces using the interactive cooperative objects formalism. In Paternó, F., editor, *Design, Specification and Verification of Interactive Systems*. Springer-Verlag.

Paternó, F. and Faconti, G. (1992). On the use of LOTOS to describe graphical interaction. In Monk, A., Diaper, D., and Harrison, M., editors, *HCI'92, People and Computers VII*, pages 155–173, London. Cambridge University Press.

Pfaff, G., editor (1985). *User Interface Management Systems, Proceedings of IFIP/EG Workshop on UIMS*, Seeheim, Federal Republic of Germany. Springer-Verlag.

Biographies

Paul Chesson is completing a Ph.D. at the University of Melbourne, Australia, in the area of formal methods in HCI. His research involves the development of a dialogue specification language for interactive systems, and a supporting method and tools for its use. He holds a B.E. from Melbourne in software engineering.

Lorraine Johnston is a Lecturer at the University of Melbourne, Australia. Her research interests include usability engineering and software engineering education. She holds a BSc(Hons) and a PhD in quantum chemistry from the University of Queensland, and a DipComp from the University of Melbourne.

Philip Dart is a Senior Lecturer and the software engineering program coordinator at the University of Melbourne, Australia. His research interests include requirements engineering and formal methods. He received a BSc(Hons) from the University of Queensland and a PhD from the University of Melbourne.

Discussion

Gilbert Cockton: Is the line in the middle of the diagram a bus?

Lorraine Johnston: Yes

Len Bass: How does this notation "enable" usability evaluation of specified interfaces?

Lorraine Johnston: Some properties of usability such as deadlock detection or reachability can be analyzed via this approach. The model itself does not specifically support the production of a usable system, but a clear understanding of the design is more likely to minimize defects.

Ken Fishkin: Can you help me understand what information is known at what level of your pipeline? E.g. if I have a CAD application, and the user says, "show me parts of the circuit that aren't grounded," what does the symbolic layer know about this request? Does it know about "ground" and "circuits"

Lorraine Johnston: No, it knows about buttons and coloured rectangles. The input event is passed on to the semantics layer, which is responsible for mapping user's actions into meaningful input to the application.

Christian Gram: Is your work-unit the same as a task? How does one identify work units/tasks?

Lorraine Johnston: No. A work unit is a sub-task, a small task requiring only little interaction, being short and simple. One can choose whatever level of work unit seems appropriate for the functionality required.

Laurence Nigay: Your approach is pragmatic to symbolic to semantic. Why not pragmatic to semantic to symbolic, or vice versa?

Lorraine Johnston: The pragmatic layer can easily be defined, as we know what the application requires. The user interface elements can easily be defined, or may already have been defined (reuse). The semantic layer does the mapping between the two, so it seems reasonable and logical to treat them in this order.

Morten Harning: How does this scale to large complex systems? It seems very detailed.

Lorraine Johnston: It would not be used for all systems. However, it does promote reuse of user interface components. One would normally expect to use it only in mission-critical situation.

John Grundy: How does this architecture compare to MAMP? Is semantics mapping, or mapping and abstraction?

Lorraine Johnston: Maybe there is some similarity: pragmatic = model, semantics = abstraction/mapping, symbolic = presentation. MAMP's basis is objects; the basis of this architecture is requirements or rules.

Prasun Dewan: Could there not be an arbitrary number of semantic layers between the symbolic and pragmatic layers?

Lorraine Johnston: Three layers are found to be natural and sufficient. It would be possible to provide more structure within the layers, but three are necessary and sufficient.

Support for Iterative User Interface Prototyping: The Sherlock Guideline Management System

D. Grammenos, D. Akoumianakis, C. Stephanidis
Institute of Computer Science,
Foundation for Research and Technology - Hellas
Science and Technology Park of Crete,
Heraklion, Crete, GR-71110 GREECE

Abstract: This paper is about supporting the difficult and non-trivial task of user interface design by providing effective human factors input to early stages of system development. The work presented in this paper is motivated by the normative perspective that tools for working with guidelines should provide a collaborative, extensible and evolutionary medium, offering more than mere access to guideline reference manuals or hypertext retrieval, for early human factors design input. To this effect, this paper presents a novel method for working with guidelines and a supporting tool environment, namely the Sherlock Guideline Management System. Sherlock provides an integrated environment for articulating and depositing guidelines, accessing past experience and propagating guidelines in the form of recommendations, to the user interface development life-cycle. In this manner, persistency of organisational knowledge on guidelines and evolution of the accumulated wisdom are supported. Moreover, Sherlock provides facilities for the automatic usability inspection of tentative designs. Finally, the paper describes the results of a preliminary evaluation of Sherlock.

Key words: Design support, Usability, Guideline Management Systems

1.　INTRODUCTION

The proliferation of information technology products and services in everyday life, has created a compelling need for more usable and friendly user interaction. User-centred design (ISO, 1997) has emerged as a process for matching technological characteristics to user needs away from the technology-centred practices of the past. Usability engineering (Bevan et al., 1994) is at the core of the user-centred design process, focusing on the development of highly usable user interfaces of interactive products and telematic services, providing the necessary methods and techniques and emphasising iteration between the design and evaluation stages.

The adoption of user-centred design and usability engineering gave rise to an increasing need for methods and tools that bridge the gap between design and evaluation by offering practical, comprehensive, and, most of all, cost-effective support, during the early phases of design. Tools for working with guidelines (Cohen et al., 1995) is a methodological approach supporting an iterative development life-cycle and providing early and direct evaluation feedback. This paper reviews currently available systems and identifies their shortcomings; and describes the development and evaluation of a new software tool that overcomes existing problems highlighted by recent practice and experience and takes into account the results of previous research efforts.

For a number of years, the primary medium for propagating guidelines-based input to interactive system development has been paper-based guidelines reference manuals (Lim et al., 1994). However, in the recent past, a number of tools for working with guidelines have emerged to ease the tasks of accessing and retrieving guidelines, applying recommendations to design prototypes and allowing more effective human factors input to early stages of system development. The current generation of tools for working with guidelines exhibits several shortcomings which impede their wider use and adoption by practitioners (e.g., designers or developers of interactive software components).

The lack of adequate tools for supporting design, as well as the reported shortcomings and obstacles of previous research efforts, motivated the development of a new method for working with guidelines and a supporting tool environment, namely the **Sherlock** Guideline Management System. **Sherlock** provides an integrated environment for articulating and depositing guidelines, accessing past experience and propagating guidelines / recommendations to the user interface development life-cycle, thus supporting persistency of organisational knowledge on guidelines and evolution of the accumulated wisdom. Moreover, **Sherlock** provides facilities for the automatic usability inspection of tentative design.

2. COMPUTER-AIDED USER INTERFACE EVALUATION

2.1 Related work

A growing number of systems have addressed the issue of guideline management during design activities. Their underlying assumption is that the prevailing paper-based medium for propagating human factors knowledge (i.e., guidelines) to user interface design is insufficient and ineffective to provide the type and level of support designers require. In response, a number of systems have been developed to provide on-line hypertext access to guideline reference manuals, integrate a subset of relevant guidelines into knowledge bases that could subsequently augment the design phase, or to automate the evaluation of certain components of a user interface according to recommendations resulting from general or context specific guidelines.

Indicative systems which have been developed to pursue this line of work include Reisner's work (Reisner, 1981) on assessing simplicity and consistency of commands represented in a BNF grammar, the work by Blesser and Foley (Blesser et al., 1982), the EXPOSE system (Gorny, 1995), SIERRA (Vanderdonckt, 1995), GuideBook (Ogawa, 1994), HyperSAM (Iannella, 1994).

A more recent development within this line of work is the effort to develop tools for experience-based usability guidelines. This approach extends the scope of tools for working with guidelines to facilitate depositing and retrieval of design experiences and the construction of "living" design repositories. Though such a concept is still in its infancy, there have been some examples demonstrating the basic principles of the approach in selected application domains, such as software engineering (Terveen et al., 1995; Henninger et al., 1995) and accessible user interface design (Stephanidis et al., 1997).

2.2 Shortcomings of the current generation of tools

The current generation of tools for working with guidelines exhibits several shortcomings which impede their wider use and adoption by practitioners (designers or developers of interactive software components). These shortcomings, some of which have been identified in the relevant literature, are briefly discussed below.

Context specificity and guidelines customisation
One well-known shortcoming of the current generation of tools for working with guidelines is their insufficiency to cope with context parameters and customisation issues (Cohen et al., 1995). Specifically, existing tools do not account for context-specific variables that frequently differentiate the implications of a guideline on a particular design, while their support for interpreting and customising the guideline reference manual is limited (if any).

Loose coupling / integration with user interface development systems

Tools for working with guidelines have traditionally not been integrated with popular user interface development systems. This means that the effect of guidelines on a specific design can rarely be automatically articulated (Stephanidis et al., 1997). Instead, the vast majority of the existing tools provide support for hypertext access and retrieval of guidelines, which, though useful, does not provide a sufficient means for augmenting design practices.

Extensibility, maintenance and versioning of guideline knowledge
In currently available tools, guidelines are typically encoded as collections of ergonomic design rules which are subsequently integrated with a user interface management system. These efforts, however, offer no computer-aided support for: (a) maintaining the guideline rule base (e.g., identifying competing guidelines, conflicting recommendations, automatic updates); (b) extending its scope with new rules (e.g., dedicated programming functions for implementing new guidelines; (c) versioning of guideline reference manuals, so as to depict specific requirements of particular design cases.

Design augmentation is beyond guideline access
As already pointed out, tools for working with guidelines can be classified either into systems for access to electronically encoded guidelines, or rule bases that can be integrated with a user interface management environment. In both cases, the level of design augmentation that may be effectively supported is primitive and limited to posterior identification, and sometimes automatic correction of faults in the design, that can be traced through the available rules. There is no way to capitalise on, and reuse past experience, explore alternatives before committing to a particular design option, document problems and design deficiencies, so that they can be referred to by future activities.

Corporate support
Another important shortcoming of existing tools, is their lack for supporting corporate practices. This does not only relate to customising a guidelines reference manual, but also to developing domain-specific styleguides and offering organisation-wide support for appropriating the recommendations of these styleguides. In other words, it is not possible for an organisation to encode a corporate style guide into the representation supported by an existing tool and subsequently provide this representation as an internal company standard to be observed by different business units and development sections. As a result, it is practically impossible to support persistency in the use and application of human factors knowledge.

Reporting
Reporting design defects and alternative solutions is another important issue that needs to be supported by tools for working with guidelines, if they are to provide an effective and efficient medium for integrating human factors knowledge into software design and management. To this end, designers need to be able to effectively document and report the results of their assessments so that they can be communicated to developers, management and other stakeholders.

302

2.3   Rationale for **Sherlock**

The above shortcomings provide the motivating rationale for the development of Sherlock, as described in the current paper. Moreover, our prime concern in developing Sherlock has been to provide designers and developers with comprehensive support for iterative prototyping and user interface design. To this effect, we have tried to build upon specific properties of the tools reviewed in section 2.1 and integrate them within one extensible framework for managing guidelines and other interpretable usability heuristics and design principles.

3.   THE **SHERLOCK** GUIDELINE MANAGEMENT SYSTEM

3.1   Overview

Sherlock was implemented as a client/server application. Taking advantage of ActiveX technology (Appleman, 1997), the server and client modules, as well as the extension components, can reside on the same or different computers that are connected through the Internet. The server module runs under Microsoft Windows 95 and the client module is an add-in to the Visual Basic 5.0 Integrated Development Environment (IDE) (Microsoft, 1997).

3.1.1   The Server

The server's role is the inspection of user interfaces according to specific rules and the resulting report of possible rule violations. The rules and the corresponding inspection routines are not embedded in the server module, but they reside in external modules that can be created by any programming language that has the ability of creating ActiveX DLLs. Additionally, the server is also responsible for keeping the clients up-to-date, whenever the rule base is updated, keeping track of guideline violations encountered, as well as for consolidating knowledge about users' solutions to usability problems. Potential users of the server are usability experts and 'programmers' of new rules.

The Sherlock server comprises five basic components (Figure 1):

The User Interface Composer. This component parses a textual user interface description received by a client and converts it to a user interface hierarchical data structure, that will be later used by the inspection routines. The controls and properties recognised by this component can be easily updated and augmented.

The Client / Server Communication Module. This module is built using Window Sockets and is responsible for the communication between the client(s) and the server.

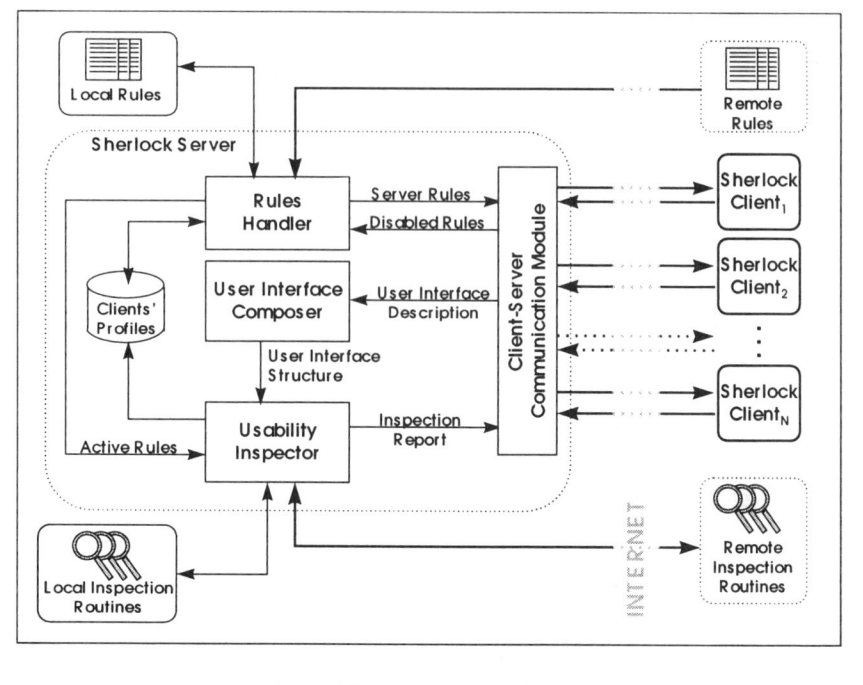

*Figure 1.*Sherlock server architecture

The Clients' Profiles Database. A repository of client-related information, such as identification details, but also rules preferences and evaluation history.

The Rules Handler Module. The *Rules Handler Module* is responsible for handling and integrating rules and inspection routines from a variety of sources. Additionally, this module offers tools for maintaining and extending the rule base and the relevant set of inspection routines.

The Usability Inspector Module. During the evaluation phase of a particular user interface, the *Usability Inspector Module* activates inspection routines based on: (a) which rules are active, and (b) user preferences. This module collects instances of rule violations detected. Upon the end of an evaluation, a comprehensive report of usability problems is compiled and sent to the client.

3.1.2   The Client

The client's main role is to compile a textual description of a user interface created in the Visual Basic 5.0 Integrated Development Environment (VB 5.0 IDE), send it to the server for inspection and then report the inspection results to the user.

Sherlock clients can be used by designers, developers and usability evaluators. The main characteristic of the client's design is simplicity, since Sherlock is intended to be as easy to use as a common spell checker.

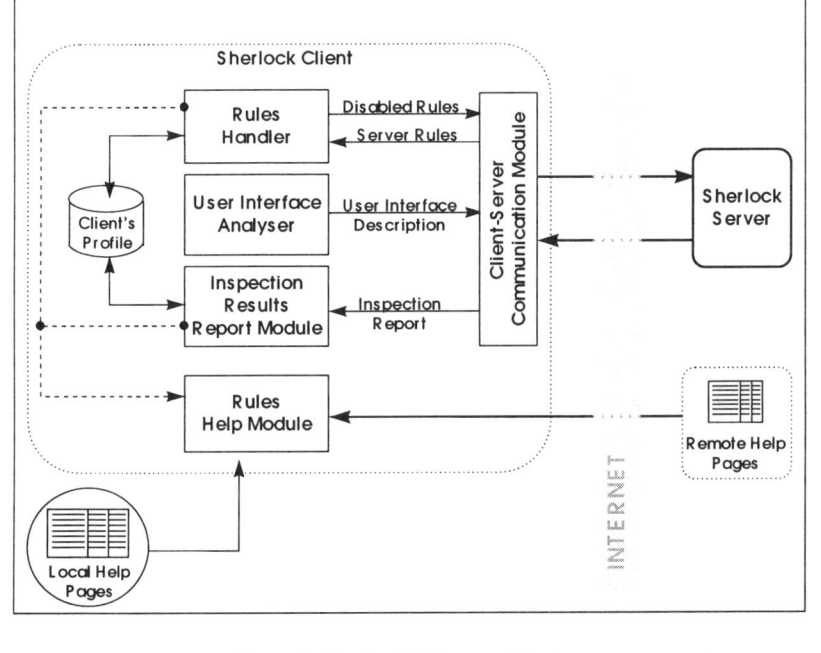

Figure 2. Sherlock Client architecture

The Sherlock client comprises six basic components (Figure 2):

The Client / Server Communication Module. This module is responsible for the communication and exchange of information between the client and the server.

The Client's Profile database. A database used to store information about the rules known to the client, user preferences and information about frequently encountered usability problems and corrections provided by the user.

The Rules Handler. This part of the system is responsible for the visualisation and handling of the rules hierarchy. Rules are presented in tree or list form. Through these visualisations the user has the ability to activate or deactivate rules and classes of rules, as well as to get a short description of each rule or rule class.

The User Interface Analyser. This is a non-interactive module of the client. Its function is to create a textual description of a user interface that was created in the VB 5.0 IDE in a predefined format and send it to the server for evaluation. In order to minimise the descriptions created, a mechanism for assigning default values is used.

Stages	Activities
PREPARATION PHASE	⇨ Identification of relevant design input materials ⇨ Development of the rules ⇨ Integration of the rules into the server
EVALUATION PHASE	⇨ Use of the guidelines server to assess tentative designs and identify design defects ⇨ Presentation of the problems detected ⇨ Problem analysis
PROPAGATION PHASE	⇨ Problem classification ⇨ Problem correction ⇨ Provision of information about the correction of each problem

Figure 3. Stages during iterative prototyping with Sherlock

The Inspection Results Report Module. This module is responsible for presenting the evaluation results. The user can have an overview of the rule violations that were detected by the system, and browse and sort them according to a set of different attributes, such as rule name, severity, class, etc. Furthermore, an in-depth analysis of each rule violation is provided along with background information (such as related theory and examples) and a history of previous solutions to the same problem. Finally, a classification mechanism is provided for separating problems that were fixed, or were not applicable to the specific interface, from those that are still pending.

The Rules Help Module. A customised web browser that presents rule-related information to the user. Each rule can be associated with a web page, or even a whole web site, that contains relevant information, such as, theoretical background, in-depth description, violation and correction examples. The main problem with this type of information is that, since it comes from different sources, it does not have a specific structure or format. The format can be "homogenised" through the use of common web page design guidelines, but there is no way for creating an explicit structure, since the related data is changing dynamically and may be distributed over the Internet. This is why, this module creates 'on the fly' a *"table of contents page"*, based upon the *Class* information in the rules' profiles, which presents the underlying (implicit) structure of the information.

3.2   Phased process model

Sherlock follows an iterative prototyping paradigm (Grammenos et al., 1999) and supports a phased process model for assessing tentative designs and propagating the results back to user interface development. The phased approach comprises three main stages which are depicted in the diagram of Figure 3 and which can be initiated from the basic toolbar of the system (see Figure 4). It is important to mention that these stages may be performed more than once, thus leading to design-evaluation cycles and a user-centred perspective to the overall design approach. This tight evaluation feedback loop, which is further discussed in the following sections, ensures that design defects are identified early enough, when their cost of repair is minimal.

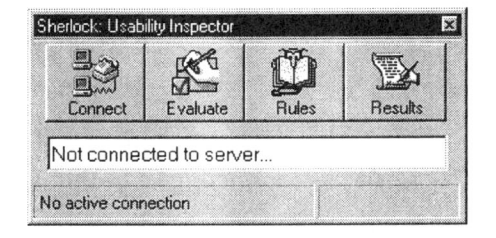

Figure 4. The Sherlock usability inspector

Preparation phase
This is a critical step in the use of Sherlock and an important determinant of the quality of the results. During this phase, two alternatives may be pursued, depending on the availability and sufficiency of the usability knowledge accumulated within the guidelines server. For purposes of simplicity, we assume that the guidelines server contains a sufficient set of guidelines, reflecting the organisation's accumulated wisdom and that the only preparatory activity that is needed is that of selecting the parts within this knowledge component that are relevant to the current design step. The illustration of Figure 5 depicts the dialogue through which the designer may activate or deactivate a relevant subset of the rules. Such rules are classified into clusters of related content and may be represented either through a tree or a list view.

Evaluation Phase
The evaluation phase entails use of the guidelines server to assess tentative designs, identify design defects and support the developers in correcting them. It is important to mention that the same guidelines server may be used by different developers in a project, thus guaranteeing consistency of the designs produced. In order to make use of the evaluation module, a developer should produce a tentative design and should activate the corresponding inspection module of Sherlock (see Figure 4).

An evaluation step entails the assessment of an internal textual description of the object hierarchy against the current version of the guidelines server. The evaluation module per se acts as a passive critic, which collects usability errors and presents

307

them to the developer. A typical example of the dialogue used to report a usability problem is depicted in Figure 6. The *Inspection Results Report* window comprises three parts. In the upper part, a single problem is presented using all the available information. In the middle of the window, a set of push buttons allows the user to: (a) move to the next/previous problem; (b) access background information about the problem (such as related theory and examples); (c) view a history of previous solutions to the same problem (Figure 7); and (d) classify the current problem as *'Fixed'* or *'Not Applicable'*.

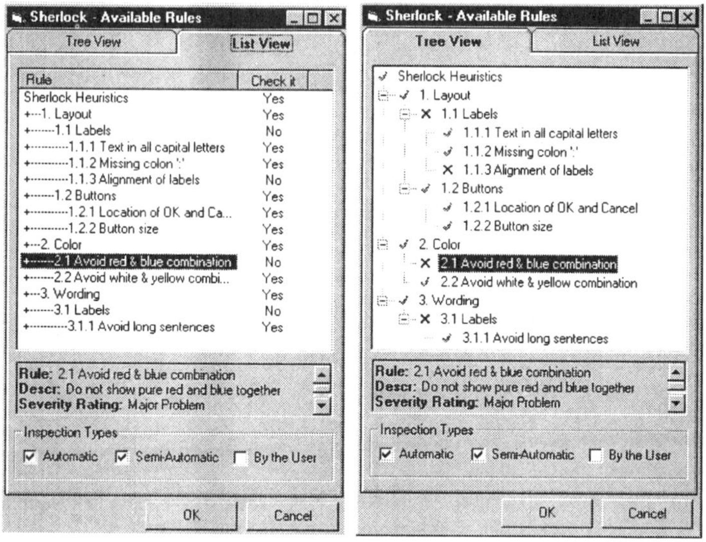

Figure 5. Alternative views for rule handling

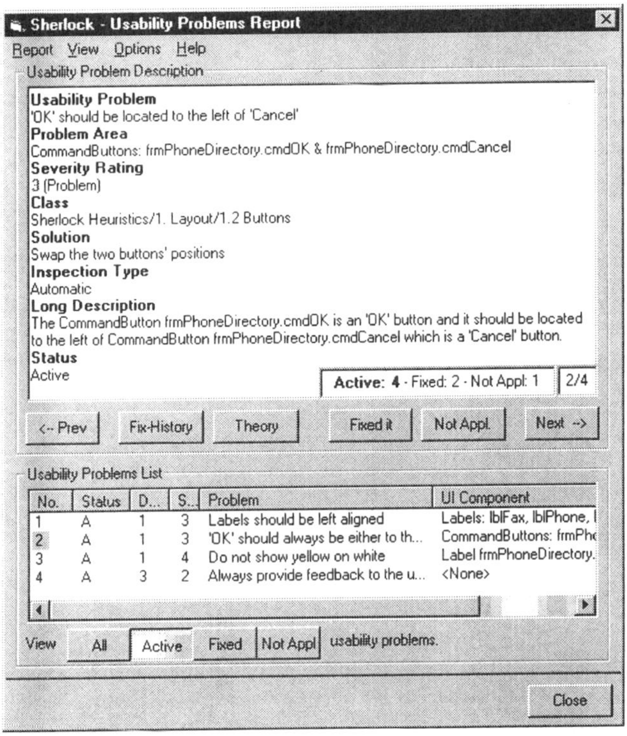

Figure 6. Inspection Results Report

The lower part of the *Inspection Results Report* window is a list (titled *Usability Problems List*) that contains one of the following, depending on the user's choice: (a) all the problems found; (b) the *'Active'* problems; (c) the *'Fixed'* problems; (d) the *'Not Applicable'* problems. Each list entry represents a single problem detected, and contains a short description of the problem, its status, diagnosis type and severity and the user interface component(s) related to the violation. The list can be sorted by any one of these attributes. The user can retrieve more details about a specific usability problem simply by clicking on it.

Propagation Phase
When a rule violation is detected, a usability problem is reported that is automatically classified as *'Active'*. Browsing through the inspection report, the user can explicitly declare a problem *'Fixed'* and optionally provide information on the actual steps taken to tackle the problem (Figure 8); alternatively, the user may decide that the violation reported was *'Not Applicable'* to the specific interface.

309

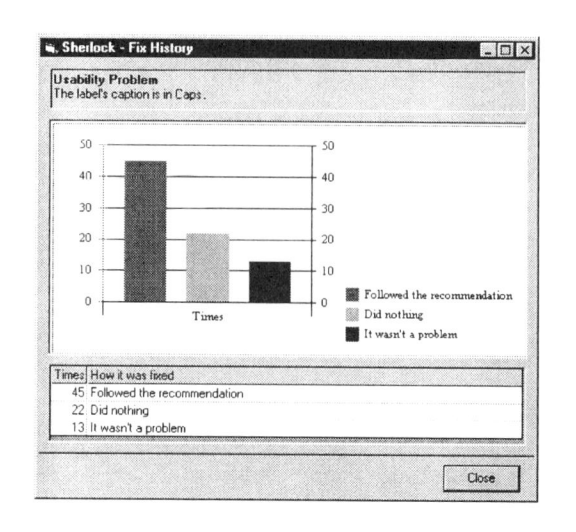

Figure 7. Reviewing deposited information

This classification data is stored in the user's profile, as part of the inspection history. All the classification actions are reversible. The above approach to problem classification was selected in order to assist the developer in organising the task at hand, by providing a quick overview of the problems found, the ones which have been taken care of, and those ignored.

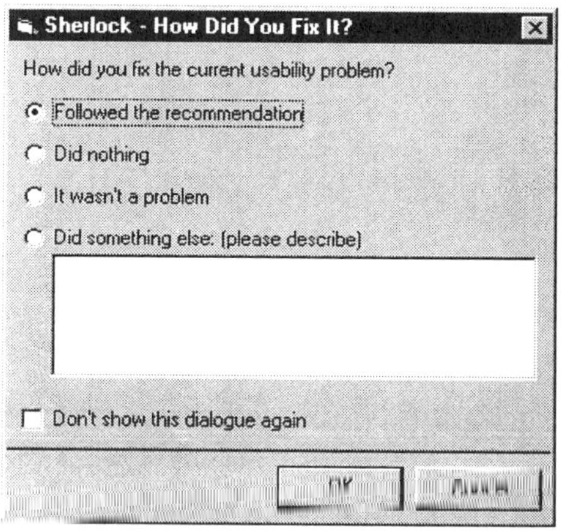

Figure 8. Depositing information about fixing a problem

310

4.   SHERLOCK EVALUATION

Sherlock was evaluated using the thinking aloud method in combination with a widely used questionnaire measuring user satisfaction. The rationale of this decision is as follows: first of all, there are no available heuristics or guidelines, in the available literature, for evaluating a design support system from the perspective of the designer. Additionally, Sherlock is a unique tool, i.e., there are no other existing systems depicting equivalent functionality that can be used for comparative assessments. These two facts have ruled out the use of a non-empirical evaluation method. The existence of a high fidelity prototype made feasible the use of a user-based method. The available options were two: (a) measure user performance, or (b) assess the users' subjective opinion. Given the intention of the current effort (to demonstrate the technical feasibility for such a tool, as opposed to developing a commercial product), the subjective measurement was selected, as this would be more informative of the opinion of designers.

Thinking aloud would be used to observe the user interacting with the system, asking vocalisation of thoughts, opinions and feelings while working with the interface, in order to understand the user's mental model, the way he thinks and performs tasks and find out any mismatches between the mental model and the system model. The questionnaire would be used in order to assess the users' opinion in a more formal way about the perceived usability of the system.

Two questionnaires were used (*IBM Computer Usability Satisfaction Questionnaires* (Lewis, 1995)); the first, namely *After-Scenario Questionnaire* (ASQ), is filled in by each participant at the end of each scenario (so it may be used several times during an evaluation session), while the other one, namely *Computer System Usability Questionnaire* (CSUQ) is filled in at the end of the evaluation (one questionnaire per participant). The result of the subjective evaluation with the IBM Computer Usability Satisfaction Questionnaires is a set of metrics which can be summarised as follows:

- ASQ metric provides an indication of a participant's satisfaction with the system for a given scenario;
- OVERALL metric provides an indication of the overall satisfaction score;
- SYSUSE metric provides an indication of the system's usefulness;
- INFOQUAL metric is the score for information quality;
- INTERQUAL metric is the score for interface quality.

Sherlock was evaluated by eight expert users with substantial experience in user interface design. All users had a University degree in Computer Science or related subject and some of them postgraduate education; all of them had at least a few years experience (typically, four to six years) in the field of human-computer interaction. The user group consisted of five males and three females, whose age ranged from twenty-five to forty years.

Each subject had to execute two scenarios. The first scenario required minimal interaction with the system, and included the evaluation of a very simple interface, as well as the correction (by the user) of the usability problems detected. The second scenario required the interaction of the subject with most parts of the system. The subject had to configure the rules used for the evaluation, to retrieve background information about the usability problems detected, to classify those problems in the categories supported by Sherlock and finally to record the way he/she had corrected them.

During the execution of each scenario, users were prompted to vocalise their thoughts, pinpoint any problems encountered and express suggestions for improving the tool. After the execution of each scenario, each subject filled in the ASQ questionnaire, while at the end of the evaluation session each subject filled in the CSUQ questionnaire.

The results of the subjective assessment of the users' opinion are summarised in Table 1 and Table 2. The lower the score, the better the quality being assessed; this is a property of the instrument used for the evaluation which follows a 7-point scale (1; strongly agree - 7; strongly disagree). The slight increase in the scores observed between the two scenarios in Table 1, reflects their difference in required user interaction load.

Table 1. After-Scenario Questionnaire (ASQ) Results

	U_1	U_2	U_3	U_4	U_5	U_6	U_7	U_8
Scenario 1	2,00	3,00	3,33	1,33	2,33	3,00	3,67	2,67
Scenario 2	2,00	3,33	3,67	2,00	3,00	3,00	4,00	3,33

Table 2. Computer System Usability Questionnaire (CSUQ) Results

	U_1	U_2	U_3	U_4	U_5	U_6	U_7	U_8
SYSUSE	2,00	2,75	2,63	1,38	1,63	2,13	2,63	2,25
INFOQUAL	2,86	4,00	4,43	1,86	3,14	3,57	4,00	3,23
INTERQUAL	2,00	3,00	2,00	2,33	2,00	4,00	3,00	2,67
OVERALL	2,3	3,21	3,16	1,74	2,26	3,00	3,05	2,58

As shown, the overall score, as well as the specific metrics, illustrate a very positive user attitude towards the system. The thinking aloud protocol verified the quantitative assessment and provided valuable insight as to how the prototype could be improved. Some of the recommendations that were collected reflected the requirement for better documentation, on-line help facilities and design examples, so as to help users become accustomed to the system. In addition, users raised the request to provide undo facilities at various steps of the computer-aided assessment.

In general, this preliminary evaluation of Sherlock, by designers and usability experts working in the field, has confirmed the initial hypotheses of an existing real need for such a tool, and in particular, the actual usefulness of Sherlock in supporting the user-centred design process and its potential in contributing to higher quality of human computer interaction.

5. SUMMARY & FUTURE WORK

This paper has highlighted the importance of providing adequate and timely user-centred support during the process of designing the user interface of interactive applications. In particular, it described a new methodological approach and a tool

(Sherlock) intended to provide a means for improving current HCI design practices and potentially enhancing the quality of the resulting interactive software products and services. The results of the evaluation of Sherlock, have confirmed the initial hypotheses of an existing real need for such a tool, and in particular, the actual usefulness of Sherlock in supporting the user-centred design process as well as its potential in contributing to higher quality of human-computer interaction.

Future work is seeking to extend the current capabilities of the tool to include support for group collaboration and design rationale. This is in line with available evidence suggesting a pressing need for further work in this research direction. In particular, developments under way concern not only enhancements of the present functional characteristics of Sherlock, but also the identification and development of additional means (methods, techniques and tools) to automate different types and levels of support for designers and usability experts.

6.   REFERENCES

Appleman D., (1997). Developing ActiveX Components with Visual Basic 5.0 - A Guide to the Perplexed, Emeryville: Ziff-Davis Press.

Bevan, N., Macleod, N., (1994). Usability measurement in Context, *Behaviour and Information Technology*, vol. 13(1&2), pp. 132-145.

Blesser, T., Foley, J., (1982). Towards specifying and evaluating the Human Factors of User-centered Interfaces, Proceedings of ACM Conference on Human Factors in Computing systems (CHI'82), ACM Press, pp. 309-314.

Cohen, A., Crow, D., Dilli, I., Gorny, P., Hoffman, H.-J., Iannella, R., Ogawa, K. Reiterer, H., Ueno, K., Vanderdonckt, J., (1995). Tools for Working With Guidelines, SIGCHI Bulletin 27(2), pp. 30-32.

Gorny, P., (1995). EXPOSE: An HCI-Counselling tool for User Interface Design, INTERACT'95, pp. 297-304.

Grammenos, D., Akoumianakis and D., Stephanidis, C., (1999). Integrated Support for Working with Guidelines : The Sherlock Guideline Management System, accepted for publication in the International Journal of Interacting with Computers, Special Issue: Tools for Working with Guidelines, vol. 11(2), May.

Henninger, S., Heynes, K., Reith, M., (1995). A Framework for Developing Experience-Based Usability Guidelines, Conference Proceedings of DIS'95, University of Michigan, ACM Press, pp. 43-53.

Iannella, R., (1995). HyperSAM: A management tool for large user interface guideline sets, SIGCHI, vol. 27(2), pp. 42-43.

ISO/DIS 13407, (1997). Human-centred design processes for interactive systems, International Organisation for Standardisation, Geneva, Switzerland.

Lewis, R. J., (1995). IBM Computer Usability Satisfaction Questionnaires: Psychometric Evaluation and Instructions for Use, International Journal of Human-Computer Interaction, vol. 7(1), pp. 57-78.

Lim, K. Y., Long, J., (1994). The MUSE Method for Usability Engineering, Cambridge University Press.

Microsoft, (1997). Microsoft Visual Basic 5.0 Programmer's Guide, Microsoft Press.

Ogawa, K., Useno, K. (1995). GuideBook: Design Guidelines database for assisting the interface design task, SIGCHI, vol. 27(2), pp. 38-39.

Reisner, P., (1981). Formal grammar and human factors design of an interactive graphics system, IEEE Transactions on Software Engineering, SE-7(2), pp. 229-240.

Stephanidis, C. Akoumianakis, D, (1997). Preference-based Human Factors Knowledge Repository for Designing User Interfaces, International Journal of Human Computer Interaction, vol. 9(3), pp. 283-318.

Terveen, L., G., Selfridge, P., G., Long, M., D., (1995). "Living Design Memory" - Framework, Implementation, Lessons Learned, Human-Computer Interaction, vol. 10(1), pp. 1-37.

Vanderdonckt, J., (1995). Accessing guidelines information with SIERRA, Proceedings of IFIP Conference on Human Computer Interaction (Interact'95), London: Chapman & Hall, pp. 311-316.

7.   BIOGRAPHY

Constantine Stephanidis, Ph.D, leads the Assistive Technology and Human-Computer Interaction Laboratory at the Institute of Computer Science, Foundation for Research and Technology - Hellas (ICS-FORTH), Heraklion, Crete, Greece. He is a Visiting Professor at the University of Crete, Department of Computer Science, teaching Human-Computer Interaction. He is the Founding Chairman of the Working Group "User Interfaces for All" of the European Research Consortium on Informatics and Mathematics (ERCIM), and the Founding Chairman of the International Scientific Forum "Towards an Information Society for All".

Demosthenes Akoumianakis is on the research staff at the Assistive Technology and Human-Computer Interaction Laboratory, ICS-FORTH, Greece, with extensive experience in computer-aided user interface design.

Dimitrios Grammenos is on the research staff at the Assistive Technology and Human-Computer Interaction Laboratory, ICS-FORTH, Greece, with expertise in user interface design and usability evaluation.

Discussion

Laurence Nigay: Where does the UI description come from?

Dimitris Grammenos: It is automatically generated by Visual Basic.

Laurence Nigay: What is the control of the UI description? How do you describe the dynamic aspects of the dialogue?

Dimitris Grammenos: SHERLOCK is not a remedy for everything but it can assess many important aspects. Many of the usability problems can be automatically detected by SHERLOCK.

Claus Unger: In your presentation, you give some examples for simple rules. To get an idea of the sophistication and complexity of your system, could you please give an example of a complex rule.

Dimitris Grammenos: The provision of rules is not a major goal of the system. The system mainly serves as an umbrella for embedding user provided evaluation rules. Rules can be expressed in terms of programs and thus can be of arbitrary sophistication and complexity.

Ken Fishkin: Does the system support tools to correct errors rather than just report them.

Dimitris Grammenos: Yes, an earlier version of the system had this feature. In the current version, we had to drop this feature due to time constraints but we plan to re-introduce it in the next version.

Jean Scholtz: Can designers utilise SHERLOCK for partial designs or must the design be complete?

Dimitris Grammenos: Designers can work with it as objects are added to the design. This is the preferred mode for using SHERLOCK.

Jean Scholtz: Can designers input usability problems manually?

Dimitris Grammenos: Problems are kept in the data base and can be managed (or added) through database management tools.

Joelle Coutaz: How is information about context embodied?

Dimitris Grammenos: By customising the rules.

Joelle Coutaz: How do you cope with conflicting rules?

Dimitris Grammenos: There are two cases:

a) Two rules refer to the same guideline. This is identified when the rules are specified.

b) Each rule has a detailed profile. In the profile is a field labelled "conflict". In this field is a message for the user in the case of conflicting rules. The user can then specify which rule should be used.

Helmut Stiegler: What are the technical prerequisites for your tool? How much effort needs to be invested to adapt it to a new environment? How close are you to a product?

Dimitris Grammenos: It is now based on the Visual Basic environment. Adaptation to a different environment may cost a couple of months of work but the textual description is stored in the server and any environment could use this server. In order to turn SHERLOCK into a product, more rules need to be developed. Right now we have integrated a small set of rules for demonstration purposes.

Deriving Presentations from Task Models

Fabio Paternò (*), Ilse Breedvelt-Schouten (+) & Nicole de Koning (+)
(*)CNUCE-C.N.R., Via S.Maria 36, 56126 Pisa, Italy, f.paterno@cnuce.cnr.it

(+)BAAN Labs, BAAN Company N.V., P.O. Box 250, 6710 BG, Ede, The Netherlands, {ibreedvelt, ndkoning}@baan.nl

Abstract: Most task-based approaches have been used to analyse and design the dialogue part of interactive applications. There has been less focus on how a task model can be used to derive systematically indications for the design of the presentation of a user interface. This paper presents a solution to this problem which is based on identifying the sets of tasks that are active during the same period of time, and rules that take into account the semantics of the tasks considered and their relationships.

Key words: Task models, Design of presentations, Systematic methods for supporting design and development

1. INTRODUCTION

The design of the presentation of modern interactive user interfaces is often complex and requires in-depth design knowledge. It is thus important to identify declarative models and inference mechanisms that significantly reduce the demands on the interface developer. Many aspects of design knowledge are domain-independent so that it only needs to be stated once and then can be applied to many different domains.

Task models (Diaper, 1989) have been recognised as an important element in user interface design (Johnson et al., 1993) as they incorporate knowledge of the user's intentions and activities. However most of the work on task-based design has focused on how to support the design of the structure of the dialogue. Less attention has been paid to supporting the presentation design. A few exceptions, such as the declarative presentation structures in Mastermind (Castells et al., 1997), and the layout rules developed by Vanderdonckt and others (1994), have attempted to provide more structured and declarative approaches to the design of presentations. Another interesting type of approach is in (Zhou and Feiner, 1997) where the generation of a presentation is considered as the development of a visual discourse which is developed top-down with the design constraints incrementally specified at each level.

Some work has been developed following a different approach: considering the data to be presented and their semantic features to identify effective presentations (Mackinlay, 1986) (Roth et al., 1994). We believe these are useful contributions though we assume that effective presentations can only be generated after an integrated analysis of data semantics and possible user tasks.

In the TLIM method (Paternò, 1997) a task model can be designed and then a corresponding architectural model produced so that it complies with the same temporal and semantic constraints indicated by the task model. The method is supported by a tool which automatically supports the transformation of a task model into an architectural model. Further, designers can still interactively customise the transformation for specific aspects of the application considered. This method has raised the interest of industrial developers who are tailoring it for the design and development of Enterprise Resource Planning applications (Breedvelt et al., 1997).

In the current version of the method the problem of designing the presentation of the user interface is addressed only after the architectural model has been defined. This may be too late for those designers who want to have a preliminary view of the user interface presentation.

This paper presents a proposal that uses the ConcurTaskTrees notation as a starting-point for expressing task models. These models implicitly contain design knowledge which can be used for the design of the presentation of the user interface. We thus need a systematic method that can analyse them, derive this knowledge, and use it for the design of the presentation of the application.

We first give an overview of our approach and then we discuss each individual phase. Finally, we give an example of an application, followed by some concluding remarks and areas for future work.

2.   OUR APPROACH

Our approach takes a task model expressed using the ConcurTaskTrees notation (Paternò et al., 1997) and indicates how to design the presentation. These indications are generated by a visit of the task tree. This visit is top-down and it identifies the set of tasks that are enabled in the same period of time and thus can be presented at the same time. These sets of tasks are called "activation sets".

Next we take the tasks that are in the same activation set and indicate how to group them in the presentation of the user interface. These indications are derived from the temporal operators among tasks, and the structure of the task model.

For example, tasks that have to communicate information with each other should be placed in close proximity. If there is a choice among tasks to perform then we know that the possible presentation should highlight what the various choices available are. If there is a disabling task then we know that we have a control task, which may be placed in a predefined location, whose purpose is to disable one or more other tasks. We try to identify whether the group of tasks corresponds to some predefined task pattern. Then we apply specific layout policies in order to define the structure of the overall presentation.

Finally for each basic task we identify the related specific presentation using some predefined task-oriented presentation templates which take into account the semantics of the task. Basic tasks are those tasks which are not further decomposed in the task model. Thus they correspond to the leaves of the task tree.

At this level we consider only application tasks (which can be classified into Overview, Comparison, Locate, Grouping of data, Calculate, Application control types of tasks, depending on the type of use expected for the data presented by the application) or interaction tasks (which can be classified into Select, Control, and Edit).

We also consider the properties of the data that have to be presented (data type, cardinality, presentation type) in order to understand the type of presentation that they require.

We decided not to take information from the task model for the design of the presentation by a bottom-up analysis because this may generate a non-consistent design which would require many modifications later on. In bottom-up approaches designers associate a possible presentation to each basic task and then they have the problem to compose these basic presentations to obtain the overall presentation of the user interface of the application. We soon realised that associating a presentation to a basic task in isolation with respect to the design of the other basic tasks can conduct to low effective presentations which conflict for the type of design choices and generate bad overall presentations whereas with top-down approaches it is possible first to make the overall design decisions and then refine each basic presentation within a common framework.

3. IDENTIFYING ACTIVATION SETS OF TASKS

We can define a task in terms of its subtasks and related operators. For example, the Printing task can be decomposed into the sequential composition of Selecting a file, Selecting parameters, and Print subtasks.

Since the semantics of many temporal relationships depends on the first action (in our case the first subtask) of the task considered we need to introduce two functions:

First, which takes a task and provides a set of subtasks where each of them can be the first one to be accomplished. In the Printing example it would return the Selecting a file subtask. In this example the First function returns only one subtask but there are examples where it can return multiple tasks.

Body, which takes a task and provides all the subtasks that cannot be the first one to be performed. In the Printing example it would return the Selecting parameters and Print subtasks.

With the support of these two functions we can analyse the task tree to identify the set of tasks which are active at the same time. We have defined some rules to identify the Activation sets which depend on the temporal operator we use:

- independent concurrent tasks (tasks composed by the ||| operator) and communicating concurrent tasks (|[]| operator) belong to the same activation set;
- sequential tasks (>> operator), where the task on the left (when it terminates) enables the task on the right, belong to different activation sets;
- choice tasks ([] operator) belong to different activation sets except their first subtasks which all belong to the same activation set;
- when there is a disabling task ([> operator) its first action belongs to all the activation sets associated with the tasks which can be disabled and its body belongs to another activation set.

We introduce our approach with a short example (Figure 1) where we consider a simplified task model for managing files. The abstract tasks (indicated by a cloud icon) are tasks whose performance cannot be allocated uniquely as they have subtasks that, in this case, are user interactions (indicated by a human/computer icon) or application-only tasks (indicated by a computer icon). At the beginning we have an alternative choice among *Editing*, *Printing* and *Deleting* tasks. Their performance can be disabled by the *Close* task. In the case of editing we decompose the task into opening a file followed by the parallel execution of multiple tasks (*Insert*, *Cut* and *Scroll* tasks). The *Printing* task is decomposed into a different structure as we first have the *Select print* activity (which activates a dialogue box for specifying the print parameters), followed in this case by three sequential tasks:

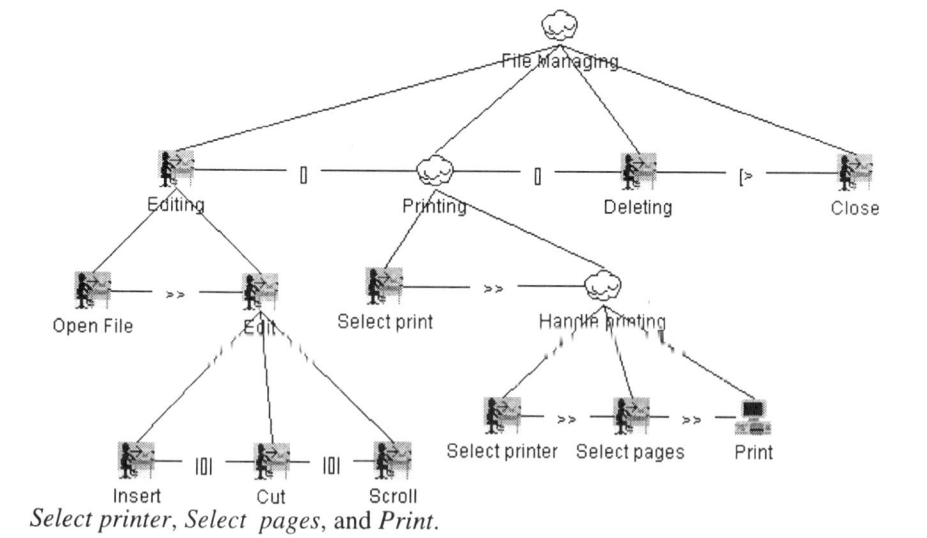

Select printer, *Select pages*, and *Print*.

Figure 1: An example of a simplified task model

If we analyse the tree top-down we have to identify the activation sets for each level of the tree. At the first level we find three tasks which are composed by the choice operator ([]) and finally they are composed with another task (by a disabling operator [>). The semantics of the choice operator indicates that at the beginning the first action of each task is available, and as soon as one of them is performed the other tasks are no longer available. On the other hand, the semantics of the disabling operator indicates that the first action of the disabling task is always available and when it occurs it activates the performance of the body of the disabling task, if any. Thus there are five activation sets: one with the first actions of the tasks, and then one for the body of each task along with the first action of the disabling task and, finally, one with the body of the disabling task.

More precisely, we have:

Activation task sets (Level 1) = {first(Editing), first (Printing), first(Deleting), first(Close)}, {Body(Editing), first(Close)}, {Body(Printing), first(Close)}, {Body(Deleting), first(Close)}, {Body(Close)}.

If we consider the next level the temporal operators that we find do not need any new activation sets. However, we find information that can be used to give more precise definitions of the activation sets identified. For example, we know that the Delete task is considered as a single action task, thus first(Deleting) = Deleting and Body(Deleting) is empty. The same holds for the Close task. Similarly, we know that Body(Editing) = Edit and Body(Printing) = Handle Printing. Thus we obtain:

Activation task sets (Level 2) = {Open file, Select print, Deleting, Close}, {Edit, Close}, {Handle Printing, Close}.

Finally, if we consider the third and last level we see that both Edit and Handle Printing are further decomposed, but Edit is decomposed into subtasks which are active during the same period of time and are thus still part of the same activation set, whereas the subtasks of Handle Printing have to be performed sequentially and thus each needs one activation set. The final definition of the activation sets is therefore:

Activation task sets (Level 3) = {Open file, Select print, Deleting, Close}, {Insert, Cut, Scroll, Close}, {Select printer, Close}, {Select pages, Close}, {Print, Close}.

We can note that one task can belong to multiple activation sets.

In Figure 2 we can see the result of our tool for calculating activation sets according to the rules that we have introduced in this section. The tool has been integrated with the editor of the task models. It is also possible to update the activation sets in case the designer changes the task model and to save the activation sets, and then to activate the second part of the design method which concerns the support for the design of the presentations associated with each activation set.

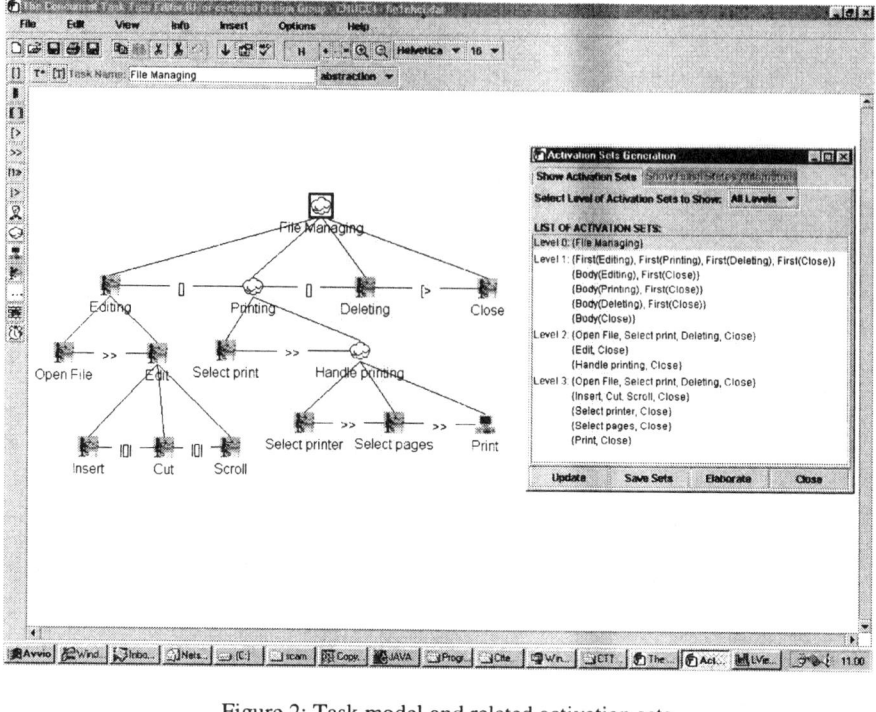

Figure 2: Task model and related activation sets

4. GATHERING INFORMATION FOR PRESENTATION DESIGN FROM THE TASK MODEL

In the activation sets associated with the lowest level of the task tree, only the basic tasks of the task model are involved. The amount of basic tasks per activation set can differ substantially. If there are multiple basic tasks in one activation set we need to determine rules to indicate the most effective structures of presentations taking into account the temporal operators and the structure of the task tree. A *structure for presentation* gives an overall indication of the presentation which can be obtained leaving the definition of some details for the next phase. These structures of presentation can be represented with the support of an automatic tool so that the designer has an idea of the possible impact of the task model on the final presentation.

4.1   Gathering information from the task model structure

An important aspect within an activation set is the structure of the task tree which has generated the set. The tasks which are part of an activation set can be composed by all the operators except the enabling one. One element is the possibility to identify both groups and subgroups, depending on whether tasks which belong to the same activation set share the same ancestor or parent task. If we consider the task tree at bottom levels, we find that the groups of tasks which share the same parent task are semantically closer to each other than the groups of tasks which share an ancestor at a higher level in the task tree. Figure 3 shows an example of a task model along with the related structure of presentation. The subtasks of the Enter Date task are one group of tightly related tasks. One level higher, the Show Calendar task and the Enter Date task are also grouped in close proximity, since they share the same parent. Again one level higher, the Enter Calendar task and the Enter Project Team task are grouped together.

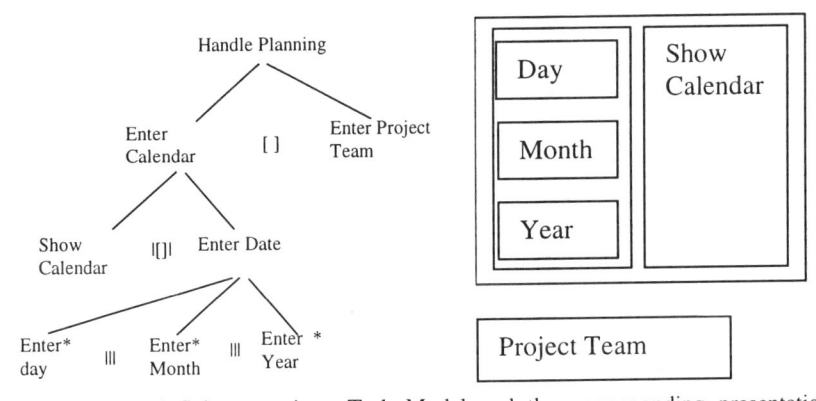

Figure 3: Groups and Subgroups in a Task Model and the corresponding presentation structure

The tasks at one sibling level combined by a synchronisation operator (|[]|) have to exchange information and are thus semantically closer to each other than the tasks combined by a choice ([]) or interleaving (|||) operator where the performances of the tasks are more independent.

4.2   Gathering information from temporal relations among tasks for structuring presentations

Temporal relationships among tasks can give useful information for structuring presentations other than the dialogues of the concrete user interface.

First of all, the temporal relation called enabling (>>) always indicates the border between two activation sets. Thus within an activation set, there will never be tasks composed by an *enabling* operator which indicates that when a task terminates it activates another task.

Different presentations can be used to present two activation sets where the transition among them is determined by an enabling operator (Figure 4 shows an example where the user first specifies a query and next receives the related result):

- Both activation sets can be shown in the same presentation unit, this is suggested when we have sequential tasks with information exchange ([]>>) because this can mean that they are tightly related, especially when such sequential tasks have to be performed multiple times.
- The first activation set is presented in one presentation unit, and the second activation set is shown in a separate unit. The first presentation unit is no longer visible when the second presentation unit is shown. This is suggested when there are sequential tasks that are strongly unrelated to each other or the tasks require a high amount of information to be presented.
- An intermediate solution is that both activation sets are presented in separate presentation units, as in point 2, but here the first presentation unit is still visible but not reactive, while the second presentation unit is shown in a modal state. When the task associated with the second presentation unit is being performed the first presentation unit cannot be manipulated. However, if it is possible to perform multiple iterations of the two tasks then when the second task is terminated it is possible to activate again the first presentation unit.

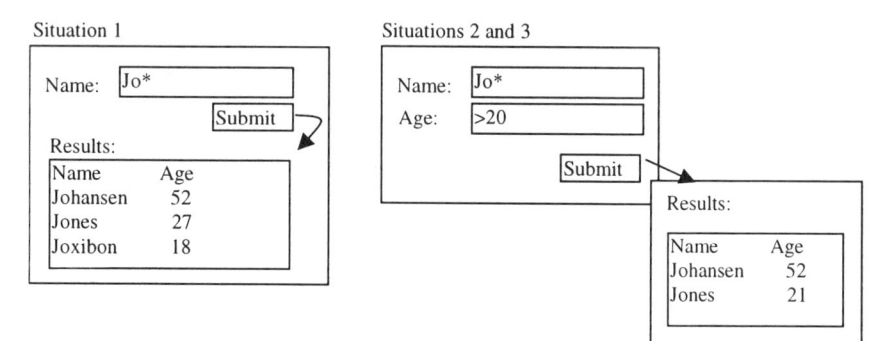

Figure 4: The three possible displays of two activation sets divided by an enabling operator

The disabling ([>) operator does not generate a division between the presentation of the tasks of the two activation sets, but they suggest how to structure the presentations of the tasks belonging to one activation set. They indicate a kind of group division within an activation set.

The tasks before the disabling operator can generally be considered as one group and thus be presented closer to each other. The control tasks, which perform the disabling, can be located so that they highlight their function of controlling the tasks which can be disabled and belong to the same activation set.

In the example of task specification in Figure 5 we can find one activation set {Enter Name, Enter Department, Submit} whose tasks are composed by one disabling operator and one interleaving operator. The Submit task applies to both the Enter Name and the Enter Department task.

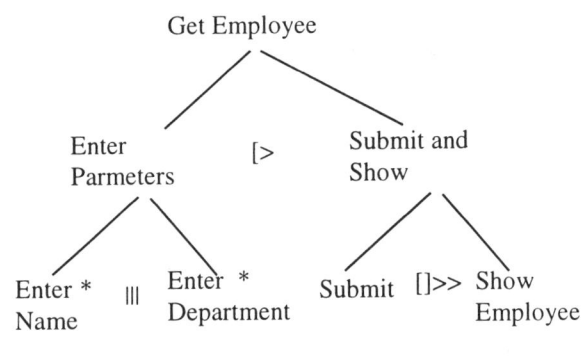

Figure 5: A task model containing a disabling and an interleaving operator

Figure 6 shows an example of a corresponding presentation structure. The advantage of this rule is that some control tasks can be automatically identified and then placed in a part of the presentation following the designer's choice.

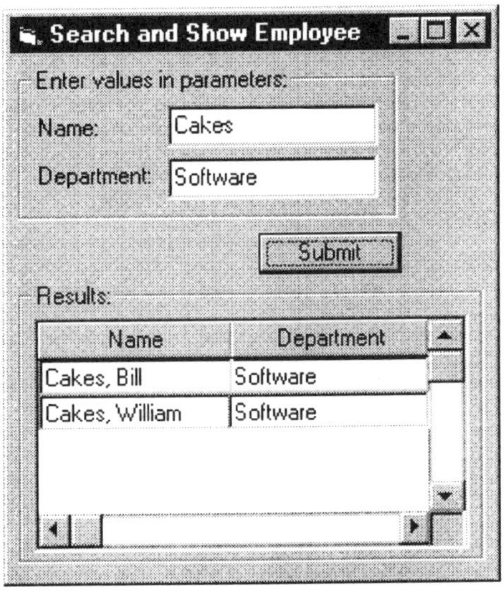

Figure 6: Division into an activation set by the disabling operator

The interleaving operator (|||) does not provide any particular indication, whereas the use of the synchronisation (|[]|) operator shows that we have tasks that communicate with each other and thus need to be presented close together. This often happens when there are multiple tasks that allow the user to modify the same data.

When the choice operator ([]) occurs at the lowest level of the task tree it indicates choices that are strictly connected as they are grouped by some parent tasks, whereas if it occurs at the highest levels it indicates activities which are not too semantically related.

4.3 Relationships among Activation sets

Once we have identified activation sets and their main presentation structure, we have to take into account the problem of the transition between the presentations of two activation sets.

If we find that there is an intersection among the tasks belonging to the two activation sets then we can have a rule indicating that the presentation of the tasks included in both activation sets should be the same in order to keep consistency across different presentations. For example, the usual tasks allowing users to close or cancel an application should be placed in the same position with the same interaction technique. For the tasks which are no longer available, in the next activation set the related presentation resources can be reallocated for the new tasks introduced in the next activation set.

5. TASK TYPES AND DATA TYPES FOR PRESENTATION SELECTION

Once we have defined the structure of the presentation we have to define the type of presentation to associate with each basic task in the structure. In this case our approach is to create an environment where for each task, depending on its type, there is a set of predefined Presentation Templates which are suitable for supporting its semantics.

We now consider the basic tasks and we try to indicate their possible presentation, depending on their semantics and the type of data involved. Here we only consider single leaf tasks, and thus the related presentations are not particularly structured.

For the choice of the most suitable presentation some additional information might be needed about data cardinality.

5.1 Task Types

In the ConcurTaskTrees notation, four categories of tasks are recognised: *Abstract, User, Interaction* and *Application* task types. The *Abstract* task is used to indicate that it has subtasks of different types. The *Abstract task* is not directly applicable as an indicator for what type of presentation should be chosen for a specific task. This is because the abstract task is never a basic task.

The *User task* is a task type that does not require direct interactions with the user interface because the actions of this task type are cognitive actions which do not require the manipulation of any device such as identifying a strategy to solve a problem or looking at the screen or speaking with a colleague.

The two remaining task categories directly involve interactions with the presentation of the user interface. The *Interaction task* requires the user's initiative in interacting with the presentation objects.

The *Application task* is used to indicate activities completely performed by the application. The application task is often a system reaction to a user's action. There are also situations in the interaction where the application itself initiates actions, for example by giving the user an instruction or a suggestion for some action.

In the activation sets at the lowest level of the task tree only interaction and application basic tasks are included. The task classification needs to be further subdivided in order to give clearer indications of the semantics of the task, for this purpose we introduce a set of task types for each task category. Other specific information is also needed for the design of the presentation related to the task tree: the data types manipulated to perform the tasks.

The data type is an indicator of what type of presentation to choose. In Interaction tasks we want to consider the type of data that is the input to the application. For example, an "enter name" interaction basic task will be connected with the data type *string*. In Application tasks we want to consider the type of data which have to be presented.

For this selection of presentations, rules can be defined to (semi-)automatically choose the most suitable presentation for that specific task.

5.2   Interaction Tasks

In interaction tasks, the user takes the initiative in the interaction: s/he gives input to the application. In combination with the data types and cardinality, some basic presentation rules can be determined.

We can classify interaction tasks into Selection, Edit and Control task types.

A *Selection* task is very common in many applications. The user can select one or more items from a set or range of items. We can further classify this type of task depending on whether single or multiple selections are supported, and whether the selectable items are of the same type.

The presentation rules for selection take the data cardinality into consideration. In this case the data cardinality indicates the amount of data the user can select from. For example, if we consider a range of Integer value(s) then if it is a single selection with a small amount of data then a spin button is preferable, if a large amount of data is considered, then a data slider would be better. For multiple selections from a small amount of data, check boxes are preferred, while for multiple selections from a large amount of data, a listbox allowing the selection of multiple items is the best presentation.

Edit tasks are tasks that allow users to specify input data and this information can be modified before being definitively sent to the application. The presentation for editing is very simple to determine, since it depends on the data types associated with the information which has to be given as input to the application.

In *Control* tasks the user triggers actions explicitly. This means that this type of interaction task needs to be presented very clearly in the user interface, since triggers have important effects on the total task of the user. There is no data type involved in the trigger task, since the purpose of the control task is to generate a control event indicating when something should happen.

Several presentations can be used to trigger an action. Buttons, toolbar buttons, icons, hyperlinks and menu items can all be used to perform control tasks, directly needed by the user. Actions can also be activated by voice and gesture-based techniques.

The presentation of a control technique should attract the user's attention. Colour, size and font determine the appeal of the presentation. Another option is the use of colour to indicate that the user has already performed a certain trigger action, as with hyperlinks.

5.3 Application Tasks

Application tasks are used to indicate that the application performs an activity. In combination with the purpose of the presentation and the data types, some presentation rules can be defined.

There are various types of application tasks:

- *Overview*: the application shows a summary of a set of data, for example giving the minimum, average, and maximum values of the data considered.
- *Comparison*: the purpose of the presentation is to facilitate the user in comparing the values of some quantities of the same type, for example the revenues of different years.
- *Locate*: the application gives detailed information on a set of data so as to allow the user to rapidly find the desired information, for example emails received by name of sender, date or topic.
- *Grouping*: there is a one-to-many relationship among two data attributes which have to be presented at the same time and this relation has to be highlighted in the presentation (Aloia et al., 1998). For example, if the application has to present clients and sales orders the presentation should group the orders by clients.
- *Calculation*: the application performs some internal processing and gives feedback on the partial results; for example, when the application is searching for data that satisfy some criteria and it dynamically indicates the number of data found.
- *Application control*: a control event has to be generated after a predefined time and the application dynamically gives feedback on the time left before generating the control. For example, in computer-based training there may be an indication of the time available for completing an exercise.

6.   PRESENTATION PATTERNS

Once the task types of the leaf tasks of the activation sets have been determined and the task model structure from which the activation set is generated is known, we can identify patterns of presentations. We can identify structures of presentations which can be considered task-oriented presentation patterns. In some cases combinations of these patterns can be used in a task model. The patterns that we have identified until now are:

- *Form*: contains combinations of Edit and Select tasks following indications from the structure of the task model such as possible groupings of tasks.
- *Control*: concerns the tasks that control the main current activities. These tasks can be triggered either by the user or the application, and they usually are in mutual choice.
- *Multiple Views*: tasks communicate with each other. There are some data which can be modified, either by the user or the application, and two or more representations of such data are updated and given to the end user.
- *Process&Present*: occurs when there are some sequential tasks that are semantically strictly connected. In this situation there is an application with some processing and results presentation. The user may want to perform these tasks several times, so s/he prefers to have them presented continuously even if they belong to different activation sets.

7.   AN EXAMPLE

This section gives an example of a task model, and uses the proposed approach to determine the final presentation. The example chosen is taken from an application for Enterprise Resource Planning. We consider the possibility to search for some employees from a data base, and then select and edit the data of a particular employee.

In the task model we can first identify an iterative handling task which can be disabled by a close task. Then we can search for employees by entering parameters such as name and department. Once these parameters have been submitted, the application can calculate them and show the list of employees satisfying the criteria given. The user can select one of them. Both searching and selecting can occur many times without constraints until the user decides to edit either one selected item of information about an employee or some new information. During editing various items of information can be given until the user saves or cancels the modification.

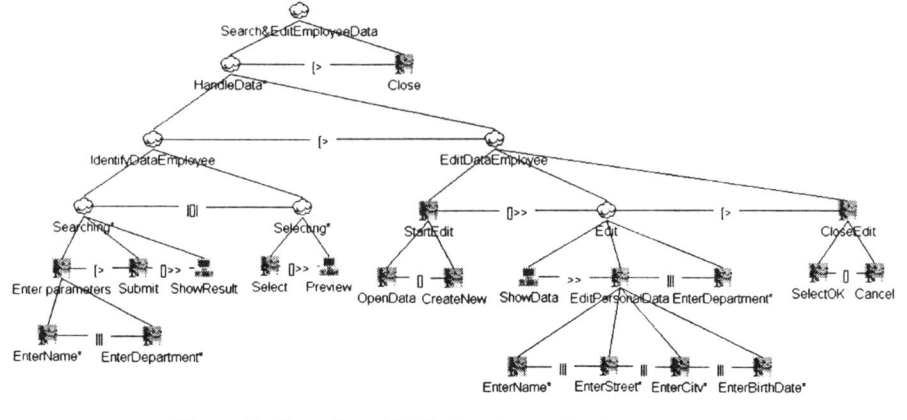

Figure 7: Search and Edit Employee Task Model Example

Once the activation sets of the example are identified by applying our algorithm we can start to consider how to design the presentation.

Activation Sets Generation

Show Activation Sets   Show Finish States Automation

Select Level of Activation Sets to Show: All Levels ▼

LIST OF ACTIVATION SETS:

Level 0: {Search&EditEmployeeData}
Level 1: {HandleData, First(Close)}
        {Body(Close)}
Level 2: {IdentifyDataEmployee, First(EditDataEmployee), Close}
        {Body(EditDataEmployee), Close}
Level 3: {Searching, Selecting, StartEdit, Close}
        {Edit, First(CloseEdit), Close}
        {Body(CloseEdit), Close}
Level 4: {Enter parameters, First(Submit), Select, First(OpenData), First(CreateNew), Close}
        {Enter parameters, First(Submit), Preview, First(OpenData), First(CreateNew), Close}
        {Body(Submit), Select, First(OpenData), First(CreateNew), Close}
        {Body(Submit), Preview, First(OpenData), First(CreateNew), Close}
        {ShowResult, Select, First(OpenData), First(CreateNew), Close}
        {ShowResult, Preview, First(OpenData), First(CreateNew), Close}
        {Body(OpenData), Close}
        {Body(CreateNew), Close}
        {ShowData, First(SelectOK), First(Cancel), Close}
        {EditPersonalData, EnterDepartment, First(SelectOK), First(Cancel), Close}
        {Body(SelectOK), Close}
        {Body(Cancel), Close}
Level 5: {EnterName, EnterDepartment, Submit, Select, OpenData, CreateNew, Close}
        {EnterName, EnterDepartment, Submit, Preview, OpenData, CreateNew, Close}
        {ShowResult, Select, OpenData, CreateNew, Close}
        {ShowResult, Preview, OpenData, CreateNew, Close}
        {ShowData, SelectOK, Cancel, Close}
        {EnterName, EnterStreet, EnterCity, EnterBirthDate, EnterDepartment, SelectOK, Cancel, Close}

Update   Save Sets   Elaborate   Close

Figure 8: The activation sets of the example

332

The structure of the task tree highlights that there is an initial main grouping of tasks at the second level (those related to Search and Select employee and those related to Edit employee). In the first group of tasks we can further decompose it into two activation sets. Since these activation sets are tightly semantically related we are in the case of Process&Present, and we present them all together in the same presentation structure. In this structure there are couples of tasks which have to be presented in close proximity because they often communicate with each other, such as Select and Preview.

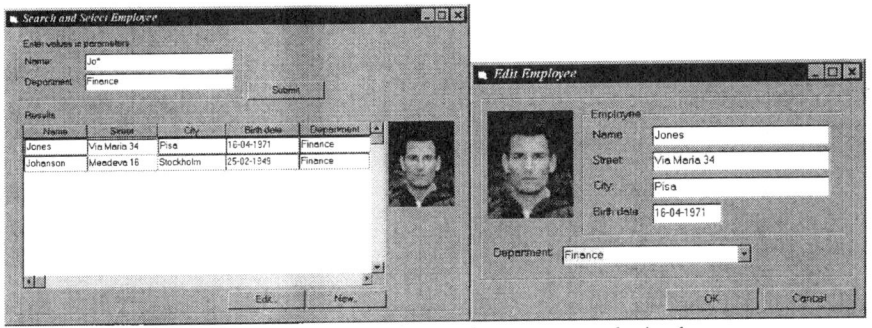

Figure 9: The two presentation structures obtained

In the second main structure there are two patterns: one Form which involves Editing tasks which can be logically grouped, and one Control which allows the user to determine whether or not to save the modifications.

8.   CONCLUSIONS

In this paper we have shown the first results of an approach which aims to give systematic support for deriving information from task models which are useful for the design of presentations.

The proposed approach starts with a top-down analysis of the task model to define the activation sets of basic tasks. These activation sets give an indication of what basic tasks should be enabled during the same period of time and thus be supported by the same presentation. The second part of the approach is to determine the combined presentation of the basic tasks. We consider possible grouping of basic tasks identified using information in the task model itself. This grouping can be derived from the temporal relations involved in the task tree of the activation set and from the structure of the task model. The temporal relations can be useful to determine the design of possible presentations. Finally, how the basic tasks are presented depends also on their type.

We plan to further refine our approach in order to identify an extended set of rules which can be incorporated into an automatic tool which we have started to

333

implement with the initial rules. This tool will be integrated with our current tool for task modelling (http://giove.cnuce.cnr.it/ctte.html). The purpose of the new tool is to exploit the knowledge of the information in the task model which for designing presentations. Such information will be given to designers in order to support their work while allowing them to tailor it for their specific application.

Further work will be dedicated to extend the taxonomy especially to take more into account the possibility of multimedia support of task performance.

9. REFERENCES

Aloia, N. Bendini, T. Paternò, F. Santoro, C. (1998) Design of Multimedia Semantic Presentation Templates: Options, Problems and Criteria of Use, Proceedings ACM AVI'98

Breedvelt, I. Paternò, F. Severijns, C. (1997) Reusable Structures in Task Models, Proceedings Design, Specification, Verification of Interactive Systems '97, Granada, June 97, Springer Verlag, pp.251-265.

Casner, S. (1991) A Task-Analytic Approach to the Automated Design of Graphic Presentations, ACM Trans. on Graphics, Vol. 10, N. 2, April 1991.

Castells, P. Szekely, P. Salcher, E. (1997) Declarative Models of Presentation, Proceedings ACM IUI'97, pp.137-144

Diaper, D. (1989) Task Analysis for Human Computer Interaction, Ellis Horwood, Books in Information Technology, 1989.

Johnson, P., Wilson, S. Markopoulos, P. and Pycock, J. (1993) "ADEPT, Advanced Design Environment for Prototyping with Task Models", Proceedings of INTERCHI'93, ACM Press, 56-57.

Mackinlay, J. (1986) Automating the Design of Graphical Presentations of Relational Information, ACM Transactions on Graphics, Vol.5, N.2, April 1986, pp.110-141.

Marcus, A. (1992) Graphic Design for Electronic Documents and user Interfaces, ACM Press, 1992.

Paternò, F. (1997) Understanding Task Model and User Interface Architecture Relationships, CNUCE Internal Report, December 1997.

Paterno', F. Mancini, C. Meniconi, S. (1997) ConcurTaskTrees: A Diagrammatic Notation for Specifying Task Models, Proceedings Interact'97, Chapman&Hall, July'97. pp.362-369.

Roth, S. Kolojejchick, J. Mattis, J. Goldstein, J. (1994) Interactive Graphic Design Using Automatic Presentation Knowledge. Proceedings of ACM CHI'94 Conference, Boston, USA, April, 1994, pp.112-117.

Vanderdonckt, J. (1993) A Corpus of Selection Rules for Choosing Interaction Objects, Technical report 93/3, August 1993.

Vanderdonckt, J. Gillo, X. (1994) Visual Techniques for Traditional and Multimedia Layouts Proceedings AVI'94, pp.95-104

Zhou, M. Feiner, S. (1997) Top-Down Hierarchical Planning of Coherent Visual Discourse, Proceedings IUI'97, pp.129-136

10.   BIOGRAPHY

Fabio Paternò

Fabio Paternò received Laurea Degree in Computer Science from University of Pisa (Italy) and Ph.D. in Computer Science from University of York (UK).

Since 1986 he has been researcher at CNUCE-C.N.R., Pisa, where he is head of the HCI group. He has worked in various national and international projects on user interfaces-related topics. He is the coordinator of the MEFISTO (Modelling Evaluating and Formalising Interactive Systems Using Tasks and Interaction Objects) Long Term Esprit European Project.

He has developed the ConcurTaskTrees notation for specifying task models, which has been used in various industries and universities, and related methods for supporting the design of user interfaces. His current research interests include Methods and Tools for User Interface Design and Usability Evaluation, Formal Methods for Interactive Systems, and Design of User Interfaces for Safety Critical Interactive Systems. He has published more than sixty papers in refereed international conferences or journals.

He is co-editor of the book on Formal Methods in Human-Computer Interaction and author of the book on Model-Based Design and Evaluation of Interactive Applications. He has been member of the Programme Committee of the main international HCI conferences.

Ilse Breedvelt-Schouten

Ilse Breedvelt-Schouten works for Baan Company since 1995, where she is a Human-Computer Interaction Architect in the Task Modelling project at Baan Labs. Based on the work of and in co-operation with CNUCE, she started this project in 1996 in order to develop a task modelling environment for (semi-) automatically generating user interfaces for ERP applications of Baan. In this project she specialized in designing task models, finding task patterns and designing user interfaces according to these task models. Next to that she has written a white paper for the future user interface development of Baan Company.

In 1998, she became a technical manager of the ESPRIT project called GUITARE, which is started to further develop the task modelling environment, but in this case for multi-user applications.

Nicole de Koning

Nicole de Koning works for Baan Company since 1997. She is a Human-Computer Interaction Designer at the Task Modelling project of Baan Labs where a task modelling environment for (semi-) automatically generating user interfaces for ERP applications of Baan is under development. The project is based on the work of CNUCE. Within the Task Modelling project Nicole focused on designing task models and designing presentation rules for the automatic generation of user interfaces.

Discussion

Robert Spence: Often it is difficult - sometimes impossible - to elicit task descriptions from users. Usually they are not tree-structured and often are of the form "I want to improve my mental model of ..." and "what actions should I take next?" To what extent is your work relevant to the design problems I am faced with?

Fabio Paterno: We consider task models as a logical description of the activities required to reach a user goal that can be either to modify the state of the application or to get some information from it. They should be the result of the discussion among various people such as the designer, the application domain expert and the end user. Often this discussion is useful to clarify what the possible user tasks are and what the effect ways to perform them are.

Nick Graham: How do you avoid the problem of cumbersome sequential screens?
Fabio Paterno: The use of activation sets enables the identification of concurrent tasks that can be supported by the same presentation without using sequential screens.

Joelle Coutaz: This work assumes WIMP style interfaces. What about other interface styles such as the ones developed by Ken Fishkin

Fabio Paterno: We are thinking about this problem and will address them in future work.

Philippe Palanque: How do you handle tasks dependent on data such as: ask maiden name if female?

Fabio Paterno: The task model allows optional tasks.

Jean Scholtz: Is it feasible in your system to be able to prioritise tasks - those that should be more visible, for example?

Fabio Paterno: Task models can be useful for giving this type of design recommendation.

Morton Borup Harning: Do you distinguish between tasks that are performed frequently and those that are performed less often and how does this influence the design of the presentation units?

Fabio Paterno. We do model these aspects, and in terms of design we highlight frequent tasks in the presentation and locate interaction techniques so to better support the need to switch between related tasks often performed in sequence.

Lorraine Johnston: You are dealing with business process modelling. Presumably your proposed tool will support reuse of component tasks.

Fabio Paterno: Yes, we have recognised that there are a number of common tasks and are already working on mechanisms to support this. We have developed some patterns and given them to the programmers.

Claus Unger: If the layout of your UI does not fit into a single window, how do you split the UI into different windows?

Fabio Paterno: Our concept of activation sets gives some advice how to build such an interface, for example tasks belonging to different activation sets should be supported by different presentations that should be available for the user according to the temporal relationships indicates in the task model.

Workshop on Technical Feasibility: Initial Lessons from an IFIP WG2.7 Virtual University Case Study

Gilbert Cockton
School of Computing, Engineering and Technology, The Informatics Centre, University of Sunderland, PO Box 299, Sunderland, SR6 0YN, UK
Tel/Fax: +44 191 515 3394/2781   Email: Gilbert.Cockton@sunderland.ac.uk

Abstract: IFIP Working Group 2.7 (13.4) on User Interface Engineering has a specific interest in the software engineering of interactive systems, especially its interaction with other design activities. In 1997 and 1998, the Working Group (WG) used a Virtual University case study to track the emergence and discussion of implementation issues across a simulated development life cycle. The case study provided examples of requirements and design decisions that had to be formulated in an implementation-dependent manner, since available implementation options would constrain the viability of specified requirements or preferred design features. Only some options were technically feasible. This should be recognised when forming requirements. Technical feasibility needs to be addressed early in development.

This report summarises the results of a workshop held during the 1998 EHCI conference. The workshop concluded that technical feasibility cannot be fully addressed unless a mature and stable IT strategy exists for the commissioning organisation. It found that simple process models provided a better framework for analysis than narrative scenarios. A framework for identifying technical issues, technical options and option inter-dependencies was developed. The workshop reinforced the frustrating nature of technical feasibility studies using current methods. There is a clear need for further in-depth research.

Key words: IT strategy, software engineering, requirements engineering, technical feasibility, scenarios, virtual university.

1.   EARLY ASSESSMENT OF FEASIBILITY

Arguments for delaying commitment and abstracting away from implementation issues have been regularly articulated within the structured and formal methods communities. The argument is that design is eased by hiding complexity to focus on the critical aspects of the design, trapping errors early in development when the cost of correcting them is still low. There is however a presumption here that neglected complexities can be trickled back into a design in a smooth process of refinement, and indeed that these complicating factors *are not the critical aspects of the design!*

All aspects of software development — requirements, design and implementation — have potentially equal status. Structured and formal methods originally addressed a once ubiquitous neglect of careful requirements and design formation. However, they carry with them the danger that implementation issues will not be given due weight during early development, even though studies of developers reveal a shifting focus between requirements, design and implementation during initial activities (Guindon 1992).

Given the neglect of implementation issues, it is no surprise that software developers regularly encounter feasibility problems late in development (e.g., van Vliet (1993, p.142) cites Baber (1982), which examines projects that have failed due to technical infeasibility). Idealised decisions may ignore whether a feature can be implemented for a chosen platform (hardware, communications, system software, development tools). Current development methods provide insufficient direction on how to avoid implementation crises. They could be extended by older systems analysis approaches to feasibility studies (although relatively few feasibility studies do result in projects being cancelled!) Yet interestingly, a standard Software Engineering text only offers a simple description of a feasibility study:

An estimate is made of whether the identified user needs may be satisfied using current software and hardware technologies. The study will decide if the proposed system will be cost-effective from a business point of view and if it can be developed given existing budgetary constraints. A feasibility study should be relatively quick and cheap. The result should inform the decision of whether to go ahead with a more detailed analysis (Sommerville 1995, p. 67)

This description is incompatible with a seasoned practitioner's view:

The functional specification stage is the earliest (in life cycle terms) at which ... feasibility questions — technical and economic — can be answered with any degree of confidence, in general (Macro 1990, p. 175)

The difficulty of technical feasibility is noted in another standard text, which in turn contradicts the expert opinion above:

Technical feasibility is frequently the most difficult area to assess at this [requirements] stage of the system development process. Because objectives, functions and performance are somewhat hazy, anything seems possible if the right assumptions are made. It is essential that the process of [requirements] analysis and definition be conducted in parallel with an assessment of technical feasibility (Pressman 1992, pp. 148-49)

So, three experts offer three different opinions on when technical feasibility should be assessed: before any formal requirements analysis (Sommerville), alongside formal requirements analysis and definition (Pressman), alongside functional specification (Macro, but with an first feasibility study during concept development, p. 106). This confusion is compounded by the view that "the matter of major concern ... is the *economic* feasibility" (Macro 1990 p.185). Furthermore, anecdotal evidence suggests that current feasibility studies tend to focus almost exclusively on *business feasibility*. Thus commercial structured methods give far more attention to business and IT strategy than to technical issues, for example:

A Feasibility Study is a short assessment of an information system to determine whether the system can meet the specified business requirements of the organisation, and whether a business case exists for developing such a system.

... The SSADM techniques primarily assist the identification of information requirements and the assessment of technical feasibility. Feasibility activities do not describe the other aspects of feasibility in detail, ...

The current and required environments are studied and only in sufficient detail to enable a Problem Definition Statement to be developed ... and for Business System Options and Technical System Options to be identified.

Objectives

— To establish whether a proposed information system meet the specified business requirements of the organisation.
— To establish the business case for the proposed system and enable the project board to decide whether to commit resources to a more detailed study.
— To determine whether to proceed in a different direction than that envisaged in the IS [IT] Strategy.
— To enable the project board to select from a range of business and technical options and to identify the necessary to implement the chosen option.

(Sandhill 1998)

Technical issues are given limited attention in this process, and much is left to the role of *Specialist Advisor,* who is (Sandhill 1998)

responsible for providing input to a Feasibility Study on specific areas concern to the Study, e.g., technical feasibility, security specialists, database designers.

From the above it is clear that there is no consensus on:
a) When to carry out technical feasibility studies
b) How many such studies to carry out
c) Their relative importance in relation to economic/business feasibility studies

This is of little help to a software project team who want to address technical feasibility as early and effectively as possible. There is a pressing need to address technical feasibility early and systematically in the development process. Realistic software development methods must support opportunistic shifts in focus and should not obstruct opportunities to explore key implementation scenarios during requirements and design.

The software development lifecycle can be structured in many ways (Royce 1970, Boehm 1988, Gram and Cockton 1996) with respect to the number and nature of development phases and the relationships between them. However, all idealised development lifecycles begin with problems to be addressed and end with operational software, which has an internal structure, or software architecture. This architecture comprises a set of components and a set of links between them A software architecture represents an allocation of function to structure (Kazman et al. 1994), in that separate functions are achieved by individual components or some linked combination. Software developers rarely have freedom of choice in the design of software architectures, as they can rarely provide optimal support for all requirements. Compromises and trade-offs are generally unavoidable.

IFIP Working Group 2.7 (WG 2.7) sought to develop an understanding of implementation-dependencies during development by following through a case study. One aim of the case study was to explore the identification and formation of compromises and trade-offs The EHCI'98 workshop reported here concludes this case study by addressing how technical feasibility could be studied early in development.

2. THE VIRTUAL UNIVERSITY AS A CASE STUDY

The topic of the case study was *the Virtual University*. Unlike traditional universities, the activities for a virtual university are not restricted to fixed times in fixed places. Instead, activities can be distributed in space and/or time by combining the storage and editing facilities of computer systems with the multimedia communication capabilities of broadband digital networks.

The systems architecture of a Virtual University (VU) is critical to its success. The functions of the university must be allocated to appropriate software and hardware components, which in turn must be linked by appropriate communication channels. In addition, this architecture problem for a VU has to be addressed at least three levels (individual, group and corporate).

This section outlines work at three WG2.7 meetings before the EHCI 98 workshop. Notes on the results of each meeting are reported elsewhere (Cockton 1998). The first meeting focussed on requirements, and was held in combination with some members of IFIP WG2 9 (Requirements Engineering) at Stone Mountain Inn, Georgia, USA (1th-?nd March 1997). The second meeting at Certosa di Pontignano, Italy (13-15th September 1997) focussed on design and was attended by the chair of IFIP WG13.2 (User Interface Design). The third meeting focussed on implementation and was held at ISI, California, USA (16-18th April 1998). Most members of WG2.7 attended at least one meeting. Observers and guests also contributed to working group discussions (see Cockton 1998 for lists of contributors).

With between 1.5 and 2.5 days work on the case study at each WG meeting, there was little time for tutorial material on specific methods and techniques. Further complications arose from the fact that all methods and techniques need to be tailored to the context of development, and it was not clear how to tailor for the unusual context of WG2.7!

Existing methods were used at the ISI meeting (see Cockton 1998), when WG members used methods and approaches that were familiar to them, although a novel approach to scenarios emerged in the process. Rather than vary the human scenario details of who, what, where, when and why, *technical variation points* were altered within the same core scenario. This appeared to offer a way to address technical feasibility early in software development. A core scenario forms the basis for initial discussions. Implementation issues associated with the scenario can then be discussed, and the effects of selected technical variations (e.g., 28K line) and some social changes (e.g., no late joiners, fewer/more questions) can also be explored.

The scenarios in this new approach are called *Technical Envisionment Scenarios* (TEnS). TEnS could become a useful tool for feasibility studies by increasing the chances of revealing implementation difficulties. To avoid missing some critical technical variation points (e.g., issues known from the European Virtual Summer School were missed during the Spring 1997 requirements meeting — Cockton 1998), focused prototyping needs to be carried out to complement scenario-based analyses. Where prototypes cannot resolve uncertainties, a project should almost certainly be abandoned. However, technical prototypes "often take years to do, and cost millions — in any currency — before they demonstrate their virtues" (Macro 1990 p.186). There is clearly a challenge in focusing the prototyping effort. One possible approach is to simulate software architectures.

Some argue that architecture should be examined as part of the requirements process (e.g., McDermid 1994). It is not clear from our case study that this is so. Software architecture made no contribution during the exercise. Implementation constraints are certainly central to the analysis of technical feasibility, but they tend to arise in a piecemeal manner rather than arising from complete and coherent architectural models. If TEnS and prototyping are sufficient for feasibility studies, then software architectures have no separate role in early technical feasibility. Choices of concrete architecture, especially for component integration and inter-operation will arise as simple technical variation points. The role and value of software architectures needs to be further explored to establish whether it does have any role in early technical feasibility studies. This matches the findings of the SAMSA project, which explored architecture simulation for feasibility analysis. SAMSA identified further research issues rather than developed proven architecture based approaches to technical feasibility (Boehm and Scaachi 1996).

3.   THE EHCI'98 WORKSHOP

Technical feasibility is an important issue. The approach taken by WG2.7 overlaps with recent leading work on 'buildability'. This section reports the framework developed within the EHCI 98 workshop.

3.1   The Plan

A range of issues had been identified for the workshop:

– Where are good technical feasibility (TF) methods documented? Are there best industrial practices that could be formalised?
– Are Technical Envisionment Scenarios well defined as a technique? Are they credible? What needs to be done to improve them?
– How should TF studies (i) present and (ii) defend conclusions?
– What, if anything, is the role for architectural analysis in a TF studies?
– How does prototyping fit into TF studies?
– Can methods from requirements engineering be simplified for rapid use in the early stages of feasibility analysis (which? how?)
– How can TFS influence further development (e.g., stop it, phase it, scope the initial functionality, or provide input to later development stages)?
– Can previously published research be used to defend TF decisions?

3.2   The Reality

Only the first two issues were explored, with most of the emphasis on the second. On the first issue, Len Bass reported that scenario-based approaches to technical feasibility and similar issues (e.g., security) were used on SEI projects. Although the third issue was not addressed, there are useful structures for feasibility reports (e.g., Pressman 1992, p.150).

At the first session *Technical Envisionment Scenarios* (TEnS) were presented, using the remote synchronous lecture example from the ISI meeting (Cockton 1998). A new example, based on a student enrolment scenario, was developed at the first workshop session. The aims were to establish how well TEnS were defined as a technique, whether they were credible and what needed to be done to improve them.

It soon became apparent that the narrative format used for TEnS at the ISI meeting was too detailed. Simple process models were a better starting point. Thus the main activities within the enrolment process were identified as:

1. Student: Expressing an interest in a course
2. Student: Supplying information about oneself
3. Student, Advisor: Discussing possible options and identifying best choices
4. Student: Making final choice of course
5. Student: Paying for course.

We could see different ways of composing these activities within a temporal framework. For example, would a student pay (4) before making a final choice (3)? Would expressing an interest (1) and supplying full relevant information (2) be a pre-requisite for proceeding to discussing possible options and identifying best choices (3)? How long could a student spend on discussion before being forced to make up their mind (the 'permanent student' could be replaced by even more frustrating 'permanent enrolee')? Such uncertainties exposed a point that would dominate the workshop.

Policy decisions must be in place before technical feasibility can be assessed

This is consistent with the model for feasibility studies within SSADM (Sandhill 1998) where an IT strategy has to be in place before feasibility can be assessed. However, many of the necessary policy decisions only arose because technical issues were under consideration. This would suggest that technical envisionment should be used to assess the stability of an IT strategy. A stable IT strategy would thus be defined as one that would not require revision when any previously unaddressed technical issues are examined. To some extent, this addresses the issue of when technical feasibility can be assessed. If system's development occurs within the context of an organisation's IT/IS strategy, then technical feasibility can be addressed before requirements definition (Sommerville's preference). When no stable strategy exists, Macro's preference for feasibility studies alongside outline system design seems to be more realistic.

It was possible to continue the analysis in the absence of Virtual University policies on time limits on enrolment processes and payment points (Pay for a year? Pay for a module? Pay for a module without committing to a course[†]?) For each activity it was possible to identify a set of technical/strategy concerns as follows:

1. Expressing interest: fixed set of programmes or free student choice of modules? Full or part programmes (individual modules)?
2. Supplying information: authentication (use trusted third parties such as national examination boards?), hardware/software needs (digital photos? security mechanisms, private keys?)
3. Discussing options: format for course requirements, ability to automatically check pre-requisites, evidence/audit of student qualifications, special cases, timing (synchronous/asynchronous, fixed times in year?), modalities (phone, video, email), agent (single human, help-desk team, software agent), availability of agent (24 hours a day 7 days a week?), impact of and information about a course's schedule, access to previous and current students as part of an applicant's 'due diligence'
4. Making final choice of course: how does the student 'sign'? What is the nature of the contract? What about later changes (is a course change a re-enrolment?)
5. Paying: different costs of courses? Module costs for flexible and partial courses? Identification of student? Fund transfer? Receipts? Relationship to contract issues? Manual system as an alternative? Currency?

Technical options and policy decisions are inseparable. The level of requirement for secure payments and authentication depends on the Virtual University's policies e.g., payment schedules, contract details, course structure and flexibility, costing models, policy on pre-requisites. It was thus not possible to explore technical issues further unless we committed to specific policies. When developing TEnS, we had hoped to accommodate technical and policy variations simultaneously, but this quickly proved to be too ambitious. A clear problem statement is essential. Note however that for one existing structured method, the aim of a feasibility study is to allow "a Problem Definition Statement to be developed" (Sandhill 1998). Our experience is that technical feasibility requires a clear definition of organisational

[†] Note that British terminology is used above: a *Course* spans several years and leads to a degree (programme in North America). Courses are composed from *modules* in the UK (courses in North America!) Many European countries do not have modular courses. A course of study is often fixed with limited choice.

345

policy in order to proceed. Thus a feasibility study should begin with one form of problem statement (organisational policies and IT strategy), and end with a specific problem statement that scopes out the technology to be developed and the technical options that are acceptable and/or mandatory for a viable system.

One interesting example that clarifies the role of organisational policy was enrolment onto high demand courses. This gave rise to several questions:

- Will students and advisors be aware of courses that are 'filling up'?
- How and why can courses at a Virtual University 'fill up'? Do enrolments for parts of courses contribute to filling up? How?
- Do current manual systems cope well enough? Will they scale for higher student targets and lower course budgets?
- Would enrolment operate on a 'first-come first-served' basis for suitably qualified candidates (as in UK and USA)? If so, what would 'first come' mean? Earlier time of sending choice message? Earlier arrival at system of choice message? Any compensation for network delays and system failures (students', university's and intermediaries') or compensation for time-zone advantages? Process in single transactions or batch (when?)? When/how to confirm a place on a 'full' course ...
- Would enrolment be cut-off at a fixed time and then a ballot decide who would be given a place on a course (as in Denmark)?

Technical feasibility for managing courses that were 'filling up' could not be explored until these related policy issues were resolved. Similar issues arise for courses that are not 'full enough'? Do courses have to break even? Is there a business model for each course? At what point does a virtual university enter into a contract to run a course?

For the remainder of the workshop, we assumed that policy decisions and a stable IT strategy existed for a Virtual University. This strategy would commit to the use of IT or (part-)manual solutions for different activities (e.g., manual payments system, automatic advice agents). Technical options could then be identified. These options would not be orthogonal, since the choice of some options would entail or rule out some options for other choices. Options should thus be considered in groups before examining technical issues such as reliability in detail.

3.3   An Emerging Framework

The recognition of the need for mature and stable IT strategies (and in turn their dependence on some technical envisionment) was a key important insight at this stage. TEnS were thus quickly replaced by a new approach as follows:

1. Identify the main processes within an application domain e y for a Virtual University process lecture, enrol student ...
2. Iterate through steps 3 to 9 below for each process, merging outcomes into a single feasibility plan and noting needs for/securing necessary policy/strategy decisions/amendments.
3. Select a process within a Virtual University
4. Decompose the process into activities and identify temporal dependencies
5. Identify areas of technical concern (e.g., queuing for popular courses)
6. Identify values for requirements associated with each area

7. Isolate technical options for each activity
8. Group options on the basis of dependencies (option A for activity X requires option B for activity Y – or for some generic system property, e.g., security features such as digital watermarking of content may require high performance processors). Where possible, associate clusters of options with current implemented IT solutions as reference points.
9. Specify required expert technical studies or consultations.

The output of this procedure is thus a set of questions and identification of experts and/or studies that can answer them adequately. No example was developed in any depth beyond Step 4 above. Indeed, the above procedure was never followed through systematically. The workshop tended to gravitate towards brainstorming, and the actual relevance of an observation to a particular step of the procedure was often reverse-engineered on an ad-hoc basis. Thus for Steps 5 to 7 for enrolment, areas of technical concern included student authentication, accessibility and role of public enrolment statistics for popular courses, timing and time scales for specific activities (especially consultation and choice activities). These concerns gave rise to requirements for security, capacity, availability and performance, amongst others (again, we did not have time for thorough derivations). Options that could address technical concerns within the constraints of recognised requirements included a manual enrolment system, lotteries or complex queuing systems for popular courses, access to advisers via phone, email or videophone, appointments systems for consultations, and call-centres for consultations on demand.

The above framework was used to quickly re-analyse the remote lecture scenario from the ISI meeting. More of the framework was applied here than to the enrolment example (we were learning quickly!). The lecture process was decomposed into activities such as setting up (considered at the 1997 design meeting), starting the lecture, accommodating late joiners, taking and answering questions, requesting and responding to votes, conversations between students, and gauging the mood of the audience. Late joining was the main area of technical concern, followed by protecting property rights for digital content (see 4.2 below for further examples). For IS/IT strategy, some constraints for Step 6 had already been considered (requiring a specific web browser, restricting the use of pluggable applications to ones approved and supplied by the university). Further requirements could be expressed with reference to values for security, adaptability, performance and capacity, amongst others. Options that could address technical concerns within the constraints of recognised requirements video/audio buffering, slow scan video, stills-only, audio-only, digital watermarks and encryption.

4.   TOWARDS A METHODOLOGY

In the time available (and in the absence of a virtual vice-chancellor, president or principal!), we could not complete a methodology for technical feasibility. This was not surprising. The problem is pressing and has received sustained attention from highly experienced groupings of IT experts. Nevertheless, we feel that our human-centred approach based on organisational processes does provide a rapid way into an analysis of technical feasibility. In particular, the framework above could be used to 'shake down' an IT strategy. Consideration of processes and issues would continue until the strategy stabilised. After that, more detailed technical studies could proceed, perhaps using architectural analysis (e.g., Boehm and Scaachi 1996).

We hope that others can build on the insights we developed during the workshop. At the least, we hope that they confirm the thinking of other groups who have addressed technical feasibility. In addition, we have adopted some initial positions on some issues and hope that these too will be useful.

4.1   What is Technical Feasibility?

Technical feasibility is 'buildability'. It has to be *demonstrated* (but without actually building the system!) It is demonstrated by specifying a coherent set of technical options that are viable within known and mandated resources and requirements. These options should cover all areas of technical concern.

A proposed IT solution is *technically infeasible* when there is no possible option for a key feature, or no option that meets all specified constraints.

4.2   What Are Areas of Technical Concern?

Areas of technical concern are aspects of activities that cannot be addressed by basic implementation strategies, i.e., there is no stable solution, as e.g., for basic document editing (i.e., use off-the-shelf wordprocessor).

In the case study, some further areas of concern for the remote synchronous lecture were (see Cockton 1998 for more details):
– Functionality and inter-operability for pluggable applications, security for unauthorised applications
– Operability for instructor (avoid high cognitive load during lecture)
– Security of content and transmission
– Functionality of history/playback/re-wind mechanisms
– Accessibility for students
– Observability of network state

4.3   Why do Technical Concerns Arise?

Areas of technical concern arise because a requirement associated with an activity has a value that cannot be obviously met by current known options. As well as the requirements mentioned in 3.3 and 4.2 above, further requirements include maintainability, operability and modifiability.

Values for these requirements must be set in accordance with IT strategy and related organisational policies.

4.4   How do Requirements Guide Feasibility Studies?

High level requirements allow possible options to be identified once values and tolerances (allowable flexibility) are set for each of them (even if only in outline).

These options are then grouped according to the framework developed in Section 3.1. These structures and associated requirements form the basis for commissioning specialist studies or opinions from technical experts.

5.   CONCLUSIONS

The work reported here will hopefully be useful to future research on technical feasibility. In particular, the following positions appear to be robust and should form a reliable basis for further work:

–   Mature IT strategies and relevant organisational policies must be in place for technical feasibility studies to proceed effectively.
–   Opportunistic considerations of technical feasibility are a useful approach to checking the stability of an IT strategy and relevant organisational policies
–   Technical feasibility has to be re-visited in different ways at different points of the development process, especially during strategy formation, requirements analysis and architectural analysis
–   Processes of component activities provide a lightweight approach to identifying areas of technical concern and associated requirements
–   Options need to be related in terms of dependencies and incompatibilities before commissioning specialist studies and opinions
–   The output of an initial feasibility study should be a plan for commissioning specialist studies and opinions, which form the basis on which a final technical feasibility report can be based

Realistic tests of approaches to technical feasibility can only be carried out on real projects with real organisational policies, real IT strategies and real technical experts and studies. Technical feasibility cannot be effectively addressed in the abstract. However, brainstorming, envisionment and role playing activities such as those used during the WG2.7 case study are valuable in exposing the main activities and inter-dependencies in a structured approach to technical feasibility.

ACKNOWLEDGMENTS

Gilbert Cockton's participation in the first two WG meetings on the case study was funded by UK EPSRC grant GR/K82727. Workshop participants worked effectively over the four workshop sessions at EHCI98. I would like to thank them for their contributions to the work reported here. The participants were:
–   Margherita Antona, FORTH - Institute of Computer Science, Crete, Greece.
–   Len Bass, Software Engineering Institute, Carnegie-Mellon University, USA
–   Michael Freed, NASA Ames Research Centre, USA.
–   Christian Gram, Technical University of Denmark.
–   Dimitris Grammenos, FORTH - Institute of Computer Science, Crete, Greece.
–   Xiangshi Ren, Tokyo Denki University, Japan
–   Chris Roast, Sheffield-Hallam University, UK.

- Helmut Stiegler, STI-Consulting Gmbh, Munich, Germany.

REFERENCES

Baber R. (1982), *Software Reflected*, North-Holland.

Boehm, B.W.. (1988), 'A spiral model of software development and enhancement', *COMPUTER*, 21(5): 61-72.

Boehm, B.W. and W. Scacchi, (1996) Simulation and Modeling for Software Acquistion (SAMSA): Air Force Opportunities (Extended Report), http://sunset.usc.edu/SAMSA/samcover.html, Created March 1996, Accessed 28/10/98.

Cockton, G. (1998), *IFIP Virtual University Case Study*, http://osiris.sunderland.ac.uk/~cs0gco/IFIP/ifip_index.htm, Created August 1998

Gram, C. and G. Cockton (eds.) (1996), *Design Principles for Interactive Systems*, Chapman and Hall, 1996.

Guindon, R. (1992), 'Requirements and Design of DesignVision, An Object-Oriented Graphical Interface to an Intelligent Design Assistant', *Proc. CHI'92*, 499-506.

Kazman, R., L. Bass, G. Abowd and M. Webb (1994), 'SAAM: A method for analyzing the properties of user interface software architectures', *Proc. ICSE-16*, Sorrento, Italy, 81-90.

McDermid, J. (1994). "Requirements Analysis: Orthodoxy, Fundamentalism and Heresy", in Jirotka and Goguen (eds.), *Requirements Engineering: Social and Technical Issues*, Academic Press, London

Macro, A. (1990), *Software Engineering: Concepts and Management*, Prentice-Hall

Pressman, R. S. (1992), *Software Engineering: A Practitioner's Approach*, 3rd edition, McGraw-Hill.

Royce, W.W. (1970), 'Managing the development of large software systems', *Proc. WESTCON*, Ca., USA.

Sandhill Consultants Ltd, (1998) *Stage: Feasibility Study (Feasibility Study Module)*, http://www.sandhill.co.uk/pware/feas/ac06190.htm, Created 1/7/98, Accessed 28/10/98.

Sommerville, I. (1995), *Software Engineering*, 5th edition, Addison-Wesley.

Van Vliet, H. (1993), *Software Engineering: Principles and Practice*, Wiley.

BIOGRAPHY

Professor Gilbert Cockton FRSA, is Research Chair in Human-Computer Interaction in the School of Computing and Information Systems at the University of Sunderland in North-East England. During 15 years of HCI research, he has (co-) authored nearly 60 publications on several topics. He became a member of WG2.7 in 1988 and secretary in 1993. He co edited WG2 7's monograph on Interactive systems development with Christian Gram (Gram and Cockton 1996) His interest in early assessment of technical feasibility arises from seven years of commercial and government consultancy, including independent design and development work and as an expert project monitor and proposal evaluator for the European Commission. A Fellow of the Royal Society for Arts, Manufacture and Commerce, his user interface work has been exhibited at a Scottish design exhibition.

The Visualisation of Web Usage

R. Spence[1], S. Chatty[2], H. Christensen[3], K. Fishkin[4], L. Johnston[5], N. de Koning[6], S. Lu[7], L. Nigay[8], R. Orosco[9], J. Scholtz[10]

1 Imperial College, London
2 CENA, France
3 University of Aarhus, Denmark
4 Xerox PARC, USA
5 University of Melbourne, Australia
6 Baan Labs, The Netherlands
7 CSIRO, Australia
8 CLIPS-IMAG, University of Grenoble, France
9 University Autonoma de Madrid, Spain
10 NIST, USA

Abstract: In the course of a six-hour workshop, participants from a wide range of backgrounds considered the task of designing a visualisation tool on behalf of an investigator interested in the behaviour exhibited by users of a web site. The group identified the motivation behind the search for a tool as well as examples of the type of question the tool might have to answer. It then proposed a variety of potentially useful visualisation tools, techniques and concepts, and carried out a first evaluation, partly assisted by reference to an aide-memoire which had resulted from an earlier brainstorming session. The result was deemed to be useful for transmission to the problem-holder to act as a starting point for more intensive study, prototyping and evaluation.

Key words: Visualisation techniques, World Wide Web, Design Method.

1. THE SCENARIO

1.1 Motivation

The scenario selected for attention was the acquisition of insight into the behaviour of users of a web site. There are many motivations for acquiring such insight, especially if the site has commercial relevance. For example: to provide a more comprehensive interpretation of large amounts of data than more traditional interpretations of separate metrics; to allow exploration of data to see possible trends, perhaps by filtering data and grouping nodes; to facilitate comparisons of usage before and after a modification; to see the effect of different browsers and different cultural backgrounds; to examine an overview of use patterns, thereby helping to focus detailed user studies (for example on parts of sites not used, and short loops); and generally to compare expected use of the site with actual use to see if design objectives are being met. Particularly for the designer of a commercial web site (here, 'site' can be one page or a grouping of pages), it may be desirable for users to quickly find the data they seek, and to spend a reasonable time there. Alternatively, it might be desirable to allow users to find what they want quickly, but then to have a variety of tempting items on the way out. Sites that serve as reference or informational sites may profitably support rapid entrance and exit.

Current web usage statistics focus on hits per page, which has little to do with user paths. If a designer constructs a web site based on a model, then being able to view usage to see if it conforms with the model is essential.

1.2 Questions

A first evaluation of any proposed visualisation tool or technique benefits from a list of questions an investigator might pose. The list included:

- Are people entering my site as I thought?
- Are there *de facto* front pages?
- If I have 'goal' pages, how can I characterise users who do not get there?
- Are there 'poison' pages that scare people away from further exploration?
- Is a given user visiting a given node more than once per session (this could be desirable, or not)?
- How are people getting to my site?
  (referral from another site? web search engine? bookmark?)
- Are people coming to my site by mistake?
- Where do people go afterwards?
- What is the average path length to a node?
- How many nodes are visited per session?
- Does my search facility work?

Design of a visualisation tool should also acknowledge the possibility of questions that cannot be anticipated beforehand. As Cleveland (1985) has pointed out:

"Graphing data needs to be iterative because we often do not know what to expect of the data; a graph can help discover unknown aspects of the data, and once the unknown is known, we frequently find ourselves *formulating new questions about the data*" (our italics)

1.3   A Model

A natural model for discussion is the node-link directed graph (Figure 1). It reflects the essential *connectivity* of the Web while supporting consideration not only of the numeric aspects of Web usage (for example, the number of times a node is visited) but also temporal behaviour. As shown, it may be useful to indicate notional entry and exit points.

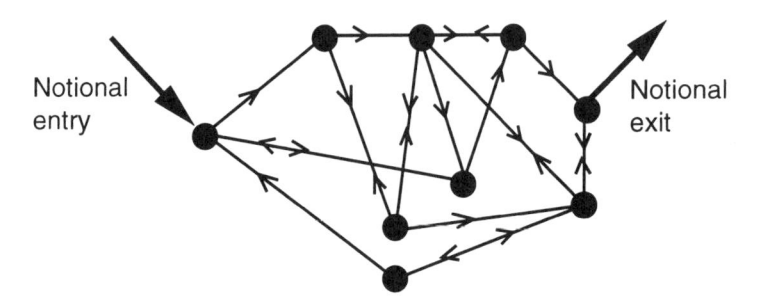

Figure 1. Node-Link representation of a web site

2.   REPRESENTATIONS

The selection of a representation for Web behaviour must bear in mind the meaning of visualisation:

"the formation of an internal mental model"

Visualisation is something a human being - here, the investigator - does, by viewing and interacting with some externalisation (i.e., display) of the data. The overall goal of the investigator is to be able to perform various tasks, supported by an internal mental model derived via a visualisation tool. Consequently we need to evaluate the various representations of web usage according to those tasks. To identify the tasks the list of questions of section 1.2 is used as a starting point.

2.1 Node-Link representation

It is reasonable to enquire whether the node-link model (Figure 1) provides a suitable representational basis. It was suggested that a disadvantage would be associated with the high data density, leading to a confusing display, though some amelioration may be obtained by means of distortion ('fisheye') techniques (see section 3). It was thought there would be some difficulty in grouping nodes, and probably some difficulty in interpreting temporal behaviour. A node-link diagram representing a Web site does not have the same spatial significance that is associated with the representation of many physical networks. Nevertheless, potentially it was thought to be worth investigating transformations such as those associated with node-link and node-loop duality (Seshu & Reed, 1961).

2.2 Landscape representation

Established work by Chalmers (1992, 1993) and others has illustrated the 2.5D 'landscape' metaphor, sometimes in the context of showing the extent of a relationship between a collection of items. In Chalmer's BEAD system, items in a database (the papers in two conferences) were compared on the basis of a selected set of keywords, and their location in multi-dimensional space determined by their overall similarity. A mathematical projection of that data into 2.5D space leads to a landscape presentation in which similar items are seen to be clustered together.

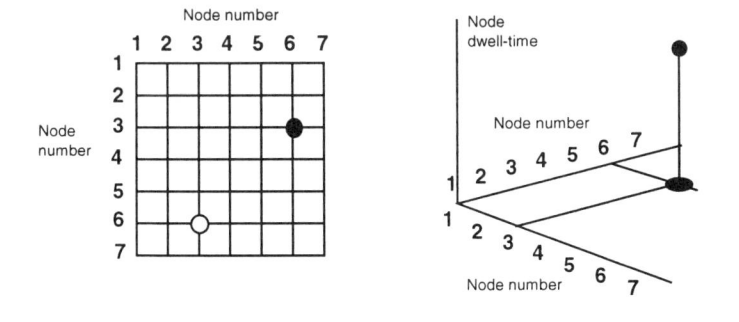

Figure 2. Node-to-node transition   *Figure 3.* Node dwell-time following a transition

A possibly novel landscape representation of Web usage can be introduced by first considering a plane having identical axes which contain the nodes, here represented by integers (Figure 2). A dot ([3,6] as shown) can then represent a transition from one node to another, in this case from node 3 to node 6. The associated point, here [6,3] would represent transition in the reverse direction. Now consider the addition of a third dimension (Figure 3) whose value can characterise any of a wide range of Web usage metrics such as node dwell-time. The result will be a number of points in 3-dimensional space that can be joined to form a surface (Figure 4). It is suggested that such a surface might reveal significant aspects of Web usage, particularly if transitions can be reordered interactively and if effective use is made of available encoding techniques (e.g., colour) to enrich the display. Exploration using prototypes, following a study of existing literature, will be needed to establish the value of such a landscape representation. The work of Andrews (1995) may well be relevant in this regard.

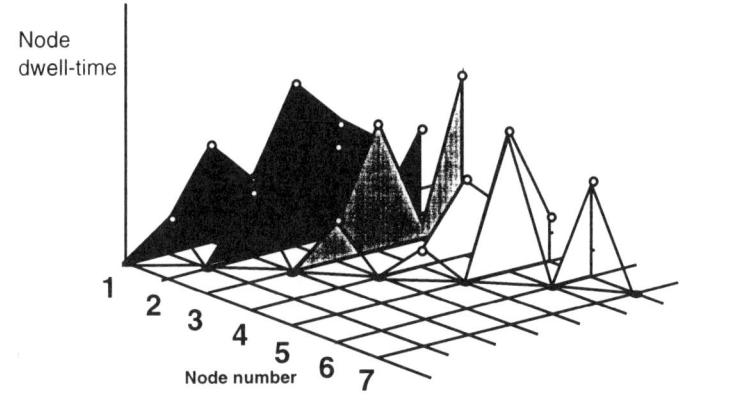

Figure 4. A surface of node dwell-times

2.3 Netmap™

Netmap™ (Westphal & Blaxton, 1998) is a proprietary information visualisation tool specifically developed for the study of data principally characterised by connectivity. Its facilities appeared to offer an attractive means for investigating many of the questions (section 1.2) pertinent to Web usage.

In the anticipated use of a product such as Netmap™, nodes would be associated, possibly in groups sharing some property, with radial segments of an annulus (Figure 5). Within the central circular area, a transition from one node to another - the essential connectivity data - would be represented by a straight line connecting those nodes. The complete history - or even some relatively limited time-slice - of Web usage could well result in such a high density of lines within the central circular area as to significantly impede interpretation. However, thresholding techniques can be employed to suppress lines incident on selected nodes (for example those visited less than x times) and thereby reveal patterns of usage. Many other enhancements to the underlying concept of Netmap™ (some already included) can easily be envisaged: they include radial bar charts (Figure 6) representing some node-specific behaviour such as number of visits (a feature offered by the Daisy visualisation tool (Westphal & Blaxton, 1998)); the clustering, in 'mini-maps', of nodes sharing a common feature; the encoding of lines by thickness and colour; the interactive ordering of groups of nodes; the creation of new segments; and algorithmic support of the kind that may carry out relevant calculations (say of total time through the web site).

At this stage no firm opinion as to the relative value of various representations could be offered: the further development of ideas and exploration of prototypes is the next step.

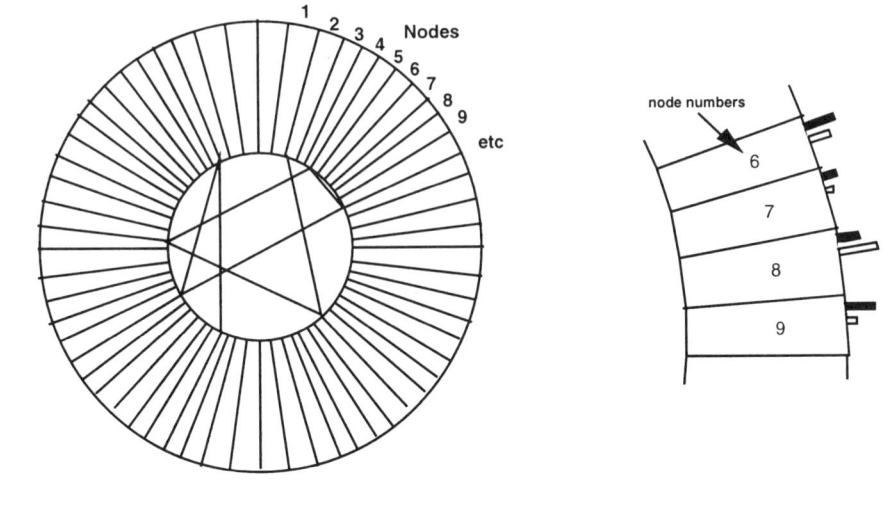

Figure 5. The main Netmap™ display   *Figure 6.* Bar charts associated with segments

2.4   Temporal behaviour

Temporal aspects of Web usage are of particular interest. The simple 2-dimensional representation of Figure 7 may be worth investigation as also might the animation of a Netmap™-style display and the representation of that display in a third dimension of time. Again, much remains to be discovered about the value of such representations and the way in which a useful visualisation tool might finally emerge.

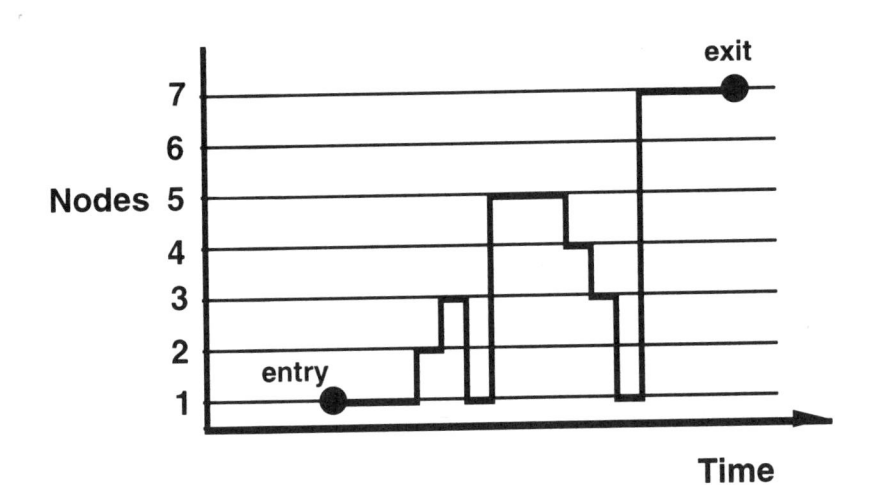

Figure 7. The temporal aspect of node traversal

3. DESIGN STEPS AND THE QOC TECHNIQUE

A classical and relevant design approach involving task identification, user interface concept selection and interface definition can benefit from the QOC (Questions, Options, Criteria) technique devised by MacLean et al (1989). Its application to the design of the visualisation tool is briefly illustrated here.

Some of the tasks the investigator will perform can be deduced from the questions of paragraph 1.2: an example is to establish how users reach a particular node.

The next step involves identifying the concepts to be embodied in the interface, an important one being the internal representation of web usage. A possible solution, as remarked in section 2.1, is to base the user interface on the web site's node-link representation (Figure 1): this can afford a direct mapping between the psychological variables of the web site designer and the physical variables manipulated in the user interface, thereby hopefully reducing the designer's cognitive load.

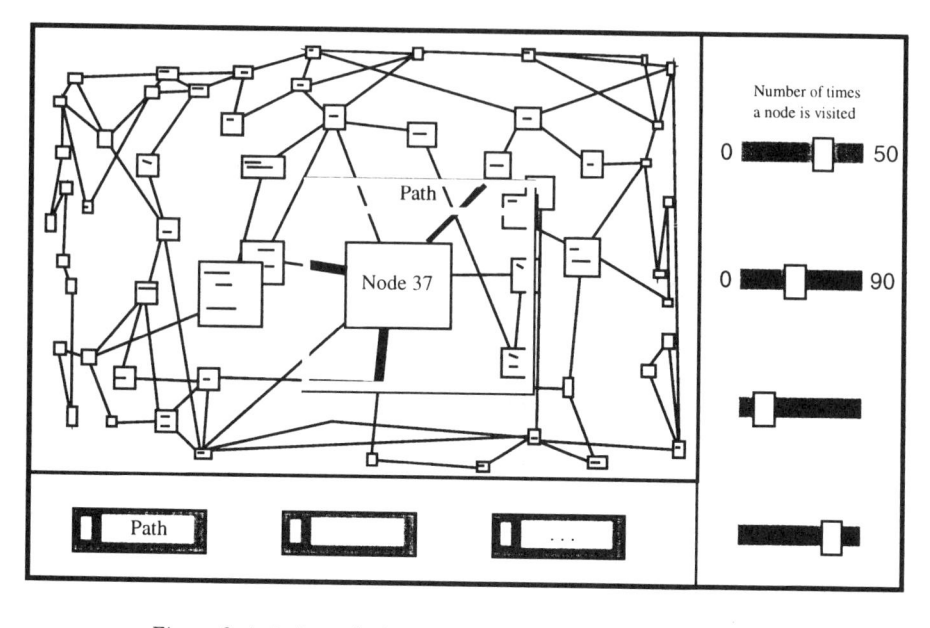

Figure 8. A design solution for the visualisation tool for web usage

The last step is to design the interaction techniques appropriate to the identified task and interface concept. Figure 8 shows one possible design which can be guided by ergonomic requirements using the QOC technique. On the right the palette of alphasliders (Ahlberg, 1994) is dedicated to tasks related to the global graph. On the other hand, each task related to a particular node or link is performed using a Magic Lens (Stone et al, 1994), of which a selection is available under the graph. Finally, the graph itself is displayed in the main part of the window by applying the bifocal/fisheye technique (Spence & Apperley, 1982; Furnas, 1986). Several views of the graph are possible by filtering it by means of the alphasliders or by investigating a particular node or link using one or more Magic Lens.

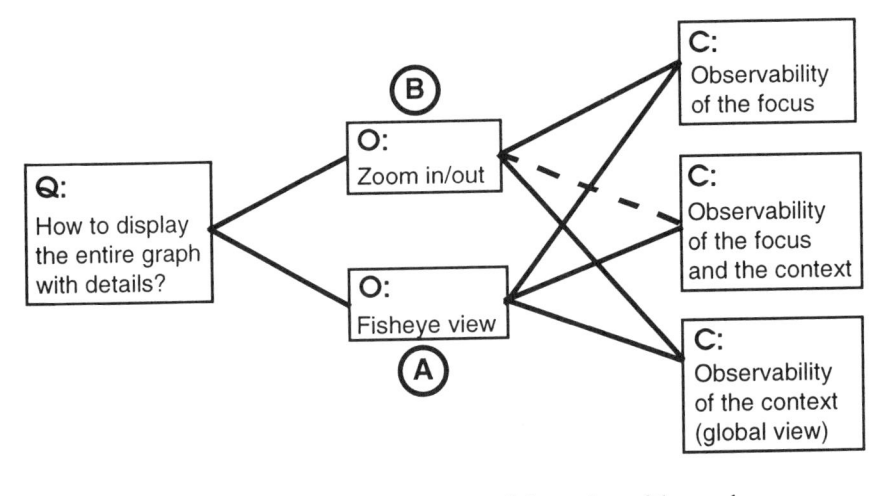

Figure 9. A QOC space to justify the fisheye view of the graph

The QOC technique can be used to rationalise the design in a number of ways. For example, one design issue arises from the need to view the entire graph, but also see enough detail to perform a task. Two options will be examined. In the first (labelled A in the QOC diagram of Figure 9), a subset of the elements of the graph can be observed in detail, while allowing the complete set to be observed without detail, by using 'compression' or 'distortion' procedures, an approach called 'Focus + Context'. The user can rely on global context to orient themselves and on the current focus to make sense of local information. A second option (B) is to provide zoom in/out functions. In this case the investigator can obtain details on demand but then loses global context. In this way the design of Figure 8 is justified using the QOC space shown in Figure 9.

The design solution illustrated in Figure 8 and discussed above may well be acceptable, but only combines already existing visualisation techniques. Nevertheless, under these conditions, the steps appear to provide a framework for design.

4. CHECKLISTS

The creation of an effective visualisation tool remains an essentially craft activity: there are no procedures leading directly from a knowledge of data characteristics and the tasks to be performed, to the description of an interactive tool. Moreover, and especially during the past decade, new representations, encoding techniques and interaction mechanisms - as well as new concepts (Tweedie, 1995) - are emerging at a rapid rate. The commissioning or design of a new visualisation tool is therefore very much a creative act requiring constant and iterative evaluation. One would therefore expect the person taking the ideas already presented, and developing them further, to be reaching for one or other of Tufte's (1990) books for possible inspiration. In fact, the further development of the ideas presented here would benefit from a checklist of some sort. In the limited time available to the authors such a (partial) checklist was generated by a brainstorming technique: following the identification of the representations discussed above, randomly selected items were used as a checklist. One was the concept of filtering by means of the Magic Lens.

5. CONCLUSION

The authors felt, after due consideration, that it would be inappropriate to offer a set of guidelines to the person or group given the task of developing the above ideas further, with the eventual intention of implementing an operational visualisation tool. Such a task calls for a considerably expanded study, ranging from the essential motivation and typical questions to a thorough study of available knowledge about information visualisation tools and, eventually, to a great deal of prototype studies and evaluation: the Task/Artefact cycle identified by Carroll (1991) will surely be much in evidence.

6. REFERENCES

Ahlberg, C., and Shneiderman, B. (1994) Visual Information Seeking: Tight coupling of dynamic query filters with Starfield displays, ACM, in *Proc. CHI'94*, pp.313-317.

Andrews, K. (1995) Visualising Cyberspace: Information Visualisation in the Harmony Internet Browser, IEEE, in *Proc. Information Visualisation'95*, pp.97-104.

Carroll, J., Kellogg, W.A., and Rosson, M.B. (1991) The Task-Artefact Cycle, in *Designing Interaction* (ed. Carroll), CUP.

Chalmers, M., and Chitson, P. (1992) BEAD: Explorations in Information Visualisation, ACM, in *Proc SIGIR*, pp.330-337.

Chalmers, M., (1993) Using a Landscape Metaphor to Represent a Corpus of Documents, in *Spatial Information Theory* (Frank & Campari, eds), Springer Verlag LNCS, 716, pp.377-390.

Cleveland, W.S. (1985) *The Elements of Graphing Data*, Monterey, Wadsworth.

Furnas, G. (1986) Generalised Fisheye Views, ACM, in *Proc. CHI'86*, pp.16-23.

MacLean, A., Young, R., and Moran, T. (1989) Design Rationale: the argument behind the artefact, ACM, in *Proc. CHI'89*, pp.247-252.

Seshu, S., and Reed, M.B (1961) *Linear Graphs and Electrical Networks*, Reading, Mass.: Addison Wesley.

Spence, R., and Apperley, M.D. (1982) Data base navigation: an office environment for the professional, *Behaviour and Information Technology*, 1, 1, pp.43-54.

Stone, M., Fishkin K., and Bier, E. (1994) The Movable Filter as a User Interface Tool, ACM, in *Proc. CHI'94*, pp.306-312.

Tufte, E.R. (1990) *The Visual Display of Quantitative Information*, Graphics Press, Cheshire, Conn.

Tweedie, L. (1995) Interactive Visualisation Artefacts: how can abstractions inform design? in *People and Computers X* (eds. Kirby, Dix and Finlay), Cambridge, CUP.

Westphal, C., and Blaxton, T. (1998) Data Mining Solutions, New York, John Wiley.

7. APPENDIX: AIDE MEMOIRE

Prior to the consideration of the visualisation of web usage, a brainstorming session generated a large number of terms relevant to visualisation tools. Following the generation of the terms they were assigned to groups, at the time classified as Means, Ends, Requirements, Abstract and Other. Means included Filters and Metaphors; Ends included interpretation time; Requirements included Semantic Zooming and Cognitive Overhead; and Abstract included Derivative Information.

8. BIOGRAPHY

Bob Spence is Professor of Information Engineering and Head of the Department of Electrical & Electronic Engineering at Imperial College, London. His research interests are in the fields of Engineering Design and Human-Computer Interaction. Bob is a Fellow of the Royal Academy of Engineering.

External Requirements of Groupware Development Tools

T.C. Nicholas Graham and John Grundy
Department of Computing and Information Science, Queen's University, Kingston, Ontario, Canada, K7L 3N6, graham@qucis.queensu.ca
Department of Computer Science, University of Waikato, Private Bag 3105, Hamilton, New Zealand, jgrundy@cs.waikato.ac.nz

Abstract: The EHCI'98 Workshop on Requirements of Groupware Development Tools examined six groupware applications in order to derive requirements for tools for developing groupware. We hope that these requirements will be useful to designers of new tools in motivating what features their tools should have.

Key words: Groupware Development Tools, Requirements

1.   INTRODUCTION

Recent research in tools for developing groupware applications has focused on increasing the range of applications that can be built using high-level tools. For example, significant advances have been made in:

- *Support for flexible coupling,* allowing users to configure the granularity of their interaction with other users (Dewan, 1992; Grundy in this volume);
- *Support for versioning/merging,* allowing users to dynamically migrate between shared and private work (Munson, 1994; Edwards, 1997);
- *Support for group awareness,* such as the provision of awareness widgets in a toolkit (Gutwin, 1998);
- *Support for combining synchronous and asynchronous styles,* such as rooms or web pages with synchronous applications (Roseman, 1996; Graham, 1997);
- *Support for making existing applications into groupware,* recognizing that many existing applications cannot be rewritten as custom groupware (Begole, 1997);
- *Support for sound and video,* to allow multimedia to be used in a multiuser context (Dewan, 1992; Graham, 1997);

– *Support for workflow,* to aid in the coordination of groups (Grundy, 1998).

While significant advances have been made in the range of interaction styles supported by groupware development tools, little effort has been made to systematically relate this support to the requirements of actual groupware applications. The goal of this workshop was therefore to examine a representative set of groupware applications and to draw from them a set of requirements for groupware development tools. This report focuses on the *external* requirements of groupware development tools, exploring the application functionality that the tools should support. An interesting further problem would be to consider the *internal* requirements of tools, considering how the tools support the development process.

In order to explore the external requirements of groupware development tools, we first described a set of six example groupware applications. These applications provide a wide range of interaction styles. From the applications, we drew a set of generic application features that groupware development tools should support. These features are structured using the Clover model (Calvary, 1997).

The report is organized as follows. Section 2 describes the six example groupware applications intended to motivate features of groupware. Section 3 summarizes the Clover model. Section 4 then presents the requirements of groupware development tools synthesized from the features of the six groupware applications.

2. APPLICATIONS

This section describes six applications illustrating features of modern groupware systems: a mediaspace, a visualization system, a virtual university, a metaCASE tool, a chess tutoring system and a software inspection tool. These applications cover a wide range of communication, coordination and media styles. Four of the six applications have been implemented while two are speculative, allowing features found in current groupware to be contrasted with features of future groupware systems.

2.1 CoMedi

CoMedi is a prototype mediaspace developed for exploring computer-mediated communication between the fifty members of a research laboratory (Coutaz, in this volume). The design of CoMedi is grounded on technical, functional and interaction requirements. CoMedi is implemented in Java to accommodate a wide range of hardware. The functional requirements were driven by a desire to support awareness, privacy, and scalability. The interaction requirements include that users should be able to perform frequent tasks with a minimum of explicit actions.

The functional and the interaction requirements result in a user interface based on the porthole metaphor enriched with an optional fisheye facility. To support privacy, CoMedi uses two orthogonal mechanisms: an accessibility matrix and the published observability of private state variables. These variables express, for example, the user's level of availability and the video scene. The user can export private state variables to the members of his/her choice. If exported, private state variables can optionally be filtered. CoMedi provides filters for video scenes such as Venetian blinds, the shadow, temporal difference images, replacing one's image with a poster, and the eigen space filter. The accessibility matrix allows users to specify permissions, such as allowing a user to authorize every member of the mediaspace to contact him/her using the V-Phone or the Chat facilities. In addition, the published observability mechanism allows the user to export his/her private video scene to selected friends, possibly filtered through one of the privacy filters.

Although perceptual bandwidth may be unimportant for loosely coupled activities, it becomes vital for real time communication such as V-phone connections and tele-explorations. CoMedi proposes Fovea and a face tracker as two interaction techniques to alleviate visual discontinuity. The video image presented to the distant user is a composition of a high-resolution fovea and a low-resolution periphery. The fovea is provided by a high-resolution steerable camera, while the periphery is given by a low resolution fixed camera. The fovea can be zoomed to provide the required level of detail.

2.2   The Manicoral Cooperative Visualization Tool

Manicoral is a prototype distributed cooperative visualization (DCV) tool. It allows geoscientists to work together on visualizations without having to share the same machine. The following scenario (Duce, 1998) illustrates the use of the tool:

A geoscientist (A) is examining a dataset of sea surface height readings from a satellite-borne altimeter. He is interested in a specific part of the Mediterranean. The original track data has now been gridded and this is what A is visualizing. The visualization mapping method could be quite straightforward - a set of solid contours with some parameters controlling the range of data values with an active colour mapping. He has experience of other more widely known data and something does not look right.

He phones or emails a colleague (B) elsewhere in Europe and proposes that they engage in a computer mediated cooperative session. A informs B at the start of the session how to find the data and the visualization processing network. A sets the scene for B showing some pregenerated visualizations on the shared whiteboard. Now that each participant has the visualization system and all the software necessary for cooperation, A guides B through his reasoning with the help of shared control of colour maps via the DCV. B then begins to have some ideas about the cause of the problem and guides A through these in turn, reversing the roles.

B then explains to A that the problem is the choice of dataset and explains where an alternative can be found. At this stage both need to see both datasets in order to compare them. Ideally, the shared control parameters would govern the visualization of both datasets. This does not require additional shared control capability per se, but does require flexibility in how each shared parameter is linked to the visualization system - a flexibility which a dataflow system is able to provide.

B guides A through his reasoning and demonstrates that the new dataset solves the problem. As a result of the discussion a better understanding of the data has been obtained and an opportunity to publish a joint paper has been generated!

In the scenario a shared whiteboard is used to present prepared material, in this case snapshots of visualizations. The shared whiteboard can be used both as a presentation tool, where the presenter controls what images are shown, and as a workspace where non-standardized material can be shared. Interaction devices like telepointers and annotations are also available.

Geoscientists can share data at any point in the visualization pipeline, ranging over the raw data, the pre-processed data, the analyzed data, and the visualization itself, including the attributes controlling the visualization. The DCV tool, similarly to the whiteboard, allows the use of telepointers and annotations.

The work with the visualization tool needs to be supplemented by some kind of communication device (in the scenario phone/email, but in the prototype this was achieved by using an existing audio and video communication tool).

When working with the visualization, it is important to allow the sharing of existing data and the use of existing software. It is important that the tools support flexible transition between local and collaborative work. In the DCV prototype, values may be local or shared in the session. Users may switch between local and shared values, and introduce new values or data sets that might later be shared.

Each researcher runs a copy of the visualization tool on his/her own machine. This can lead to problems if a researcher with a powerful machine experiments heavily with a shared value, causing slower machines to spend all available resources on keeping up with redrawing.

2.3   Virtual University

The Virtual University is a proposed tool for presenting remote real-time lectures (Cockton, 1998). Students attend class by opening a set of windows allowing them to view a lecture in progress. A video window may show the lecturer or other physical materials the lecturer chooses to show. Normally, video is broadcast in real time. However, students may enter a lecture up to ten minutes late, and review the video they missed in condensed form.

An application window contains prepared materials such as lecture slides. Students may view these materials in slaved mode, automatically following the lecturer, or may skip forwards or backwards privately. The application is pluggable, meaning that any existing application can be used.

Students may communicate with the lecturer by posing questions. Questions are typed off-line and sent to the lecturer, who may pause and respond at any time.

A number of *gestalt* views give students an overview of the virtual lecture room. A question queue shows how many people wish to pose a question to the lecturer. Students may indicate their current level of comprehension. A mood view synthesizes the general level of comprehension in the room into a single image. A position view shows what point the lecturer has reached in his/her materials, allowing students to retain context when they are privately reviewing the materials.

The virtual university is flexible with respect to the students' hardware. As networking or machine performance degrades, the presentation of the lecture also degrades. For example, video images may be replaced with portholes, and eventually with still images. Live sound may be replaced with chat windows.

2.4   JComposer

The JComposer Object-Oriented Analysis and Design metaCASE tool (Grundy, in this volume) supports flexible collaborative editing for OOA/D diagram views. JComposer has been built and used in an industrial setting. JComposer supports a wide range of collaborative editing styles. A collaboration menu allows users to specify which other users can collaboratively edit their views and the coupling level of these other users, ranging from asynchronous to fully synchronous editing. Asynchronous view editing allows users to independently modify private versions of a view, then exchange and incrementally merge sets of view edits. Presentation-level view editing distributes view edits to collaborators as they are made, and presents them as human-readable descriptions. Users can choose to incrementally merge selected changes into their version of the view. Synchronous view editing broadcasts edits as they are made and automatically merges them into the views of collaborators.

JComposer provides a range of awareness, coordination and communication facilities. Colouring of OOA/D iconic components indicates who last modified parts of a view. Human-readable change descriptions are annotated to indicate who made each view edit. Audio and/or chat facilities help to coordinate editing, especially when using the synchronous editing level. Email helps coordinate asynchronous editing. A workflow tool, Serendipity-II (Grundy, 1998), can be used with JComposer to coordinate or automate editing level usage, to automate notification of view edits, and to annotate change descriptions with workflow stage information.

2.5   Chess Collaborative Teaching Application

The Group for Interactive Tools and Applications (GHIA) at the Universidad Autónonoma de Madrid has specified a Chess tutoring application to motivate the requirements of teaching applications. The Chess application has not yet been built.

A chess tutoring application should allow interactive collaborative learning, reviewing, and analysis of chess rules and strategy. The application should allow one person to create a chess game or to review an existing one. When reviewing a game, a user should be able to explore alternative scenarios, by adding alternative moves and possible continuations from these moves. The resulting analysis would include attached notes and graphical comments, such as indications of weak and strong points and threatening aspects for the players. Both textual and graphical information could be created by authorized users and by an agent that has knowledge about relevant aspects of chess positions. Analysis would be available for other players to consult or further analyze, either individually or synchronously with others. Attached notes could become discussion threads on game issues.

In addition to discussions, the application should permit two players to play a game on distant screens or to continue an existing game where they left off. At any time they should be able to go back and analyze the game, either individually or collaboratively. Finally, a chess teacher should be able to access games as they are played or following their completion, analyze their history, and discuss them with any of the players. Agents may be used to advise the teacher of appropriate times to enter a game.

Users should also be able to filter chess analysis. Filtered analysis could be generated either by direct selection of the relevant snapshots or by automatic checking of positions and moves by agents that locate hot spots.

2.6   Collaborative Software Inspector (CSI)

John Riedl's group at Minnesota (Mashayekhi, 1993) has developed several versions of a tool for supporting collaborative inspection. The first version supported Humphrey's inspection process, where a group of *reviewers* asynchronously inspects a document, preparing a list of faults. These are handed to a *producer*, who correlates the faults into an integrated list. A *moderator* then guides a synchronous meeting in discussing the integrated fault list. A *recorder* takes minutes of the meeting. Thus, the meeting consists of an asynchronous fault detection phase and a synchronous fault discussion phase.

The first version supported both the asynchronous and synchronous phases of the meeting. During the asynchronous phase, users made annotations to the lines in which they found faults, incrementally publicising their annotations. During the synchronous phase, they used the same tool, but this time coupled the scrollbars, mouse positions and all other aspects of their user interface so that they could have a shared discussion thread. Consensus was reached through a talk window and audio conferencing.

Their experiments showed that users wished to work asynchronously during the fault discussion phase. In particular, they wished to privately review the faults made by them or others, and to enter new faults. The tool supported private reviewing by allowing users to dynamically uncouple their windows from the moderator's window. To support asynchronous addition of new faults, the tool was extended to permit asynchronous voting and to provide discussion threads allowing parallel groups to discuss unrelated faults (Stein, 1997).

3.   DEFINITIONS

The requirements presented in the next section are structured using the Clover model (Calvary, 1997). This model partitions the features of groupware applications into functions supporting *production, coordination* and *communication*.

The *production space* denotes shared artifacts that are collaboratively manipulated to perform some task. Example objects in the production space might include shared documents or drawings. Functions related to the production space include the viewing and manipulation of these shared artifacts.

The *coordination space* codifies the protocols governing how tasks are carried out by groups of people. Such protocols may be purely social (e.g., social rules specify that only one person should talk at a time) or may be formally specified through a workflow system.

The *communication space* supports person-to-person communication. Email and mediaspaces are examples of systems designed for supporting computer-mediated communication, either asynchronously or synchronously.

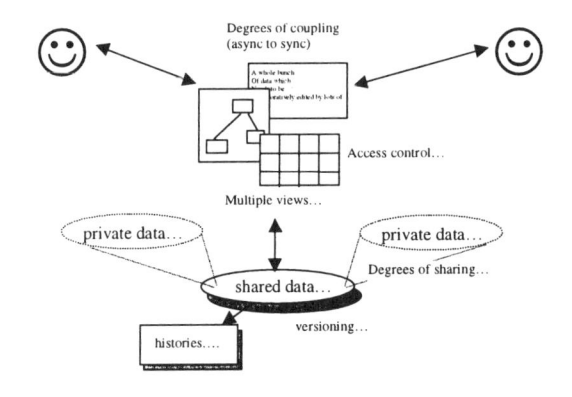

Figure 1. Production space continuum to be supported for groupware applications

4. EXTERNAL REQUIREMENTS

The example applications of section 2 allow us to derive a set of groupware features that development tools should support. In this section, we summarize the wide variety of external requirements of groupware development tools, using the Clover model. In addition, we list technological requirements of groupware relating to adaptability, integration and hardware issues.

4.1 Production Space Requirements

All groupware applications have some notion of data or information that has to be shared, exchanged and/or modified, as illustrated in Figure 1. The applications outlined in section 2 have a variety of requirements for how information is shared, viewed and edited, including flexible coupling of participants' views, flexible configuration of views and privacy settings, and support for production history.

4.1.1 Support for Flexible Coupling

The applications show that people work together at the same time or at different times, and that people smoothly move between these forms of work. For example, in the Virtual University, students may decouple from the lecture presentation, review material that was presented earlier in the lecture, and then later rejoin the presentation. In CSI, JComposer and Manicoral, users may at any time make a version of shared data for private use, work alone on the private data, and later merge their results with the shared data. In the Chess application, players smoothly move between reviewing and playing games A groupware development tool is required to support the creation of applications where users can seamlessly move between synchronous and asynchronous work, and where users have control over

369

the degree of coupling of views. More specifically, a groupware development tool should provide support for:

- *Seamless transition from shared to private use of data:* CoMedi, Manicoral, JComposer and CSI require that information be shared to various degrees. For example, in Manicoral some physics data is local while other is shared, while some shared data is updateable, and some read-only. In CoMedi and Manicoral, users need to be able to dynamically control the degree of sharing.
- *Versioning and merging:* As asynchronous editing must be supported by some views, and some view data may be copied, edited independently and then merged with old data, versioning and merging of views and data must be supported by groupware development tools. For example, JComposer allows users to control versioning and merging of views. Manicoral also requires such dynamic versioning and merging, but for both views and viewed data. The chess learning program requires versioning of game play histories.
- *Support for conflict resolution:* JComposer and Manicoral require conflict detection and resolution during version merging. This should be integrated with both the merging system supported by a groupware development tool and the general syntactic/semantic constraint system used by the application.

4.1.2   Support for User Configurability

The applications show that it is important for users to be able to configure the behaviour of groupware. The last section discussed the importance of user control over coupling. In addition, users should be able to customize the appearance of their views of shared artifacts, and control how much private information they reveal to others. Groupware development tools should support:

- *Customizable views.* JComposer and Manicoral support multiple views of shared (and local) information. In Manicoral, viewing filters and display mechanisms can be defined by users rather than being hard-coded into the environment; in JComposer, users control what information is placed in views and how the information is laid out. View filtering, rendering, composition and layout information should itself be sharable, as well as the data actually being viewed.
- *Customizable access control.* Some users may have the ability to edit some data and/or views, while others may only view information or not have access to it at all. CoMedi, Manicoral, and the Virtual University have such requirements, and CoMedi and Manicoral require users to have some control over access control rights. Access control rights may be applied to kinds of data, subsets of data, views and/or parts of views. All should be supported by groupware development tools, with appropriate end user control mechanisms.

4.1.3   Support for History

Many groupware applications require a history of work and/or discussions to be maintained, including JComposer (history of view edits), CSI (history of discussion), and Chess (history of game play). History items should be treated in much the same way as other sharable data, as the histories in all of these

370

environments may be edited and revised, annotated, undone/redone, filtered and versioned.

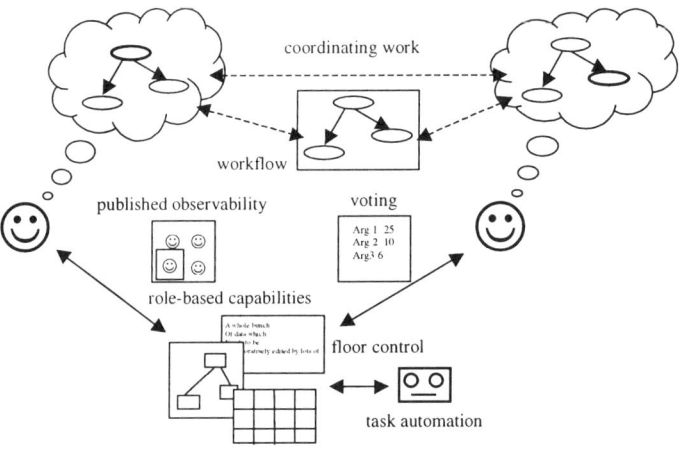

Figure 2. Coordination approaches to be supported for groupware applications.

4.2 Coordination Space Requirements

Groupware systems need to provide support for coordinating work, so that tasks done by different people are done in the correct order, peoples' work doesn't conflict, and negotiation and agreement is achieved in appropriate ways. The applications from section 2 support coordination in a wide variety of ways.

For example, in CoMedi and Manicoral, users coordinate the degree of coupling between their views and plan transitions between coupling levels using social protocols. In JComposer, users may coordinate coupling and sharing using social protocols, or via an integrated workflow system which guides or enforces work. The workflow views and artifacts can be treated as elements in the production space, and thus provide different access rights, coupling levels and histories. In the chess learning system, coordination may be guided by agents which watch the progress of the students' games. Figure 2 illustrates the various kinds of coordination present in the applications of section 2.

Groupware development tools should support:

— *Role-based coordination.* Participants in groupware applications may have different capabilities depending on the roles they fill. The Virtual University has a strong distinction between lecturers and students, with these different classes of user having very different sets of views, view editing ability, access control rights, and communication support. CSI differentiates between a moderator and reviewers, with the former having control over advancement of line inspection, controlling the overall inspection process. Chess differentiates between students and tutor, with the later able to review games, version the game history and suggest move changes.

— *Floor control.* Floor control coordinates production and communication aspects of groupware, giving one or more users control of audio/video channels, messaging, viewing and editing mechanisms, and coordination facilities. The Virtual University uses floor control to enable structured questions.

- *Task automation.* While cooperating users carry out many tasks, there is often a need for some automation in groupware environments. The Chess learning system requires the tutor to be able to specify a variety of notification and automatic annotation tasks, such as informing them when checkmate moves are missed via messaging and/or annotation. Agents may help in these tasks, and in notifying the instructor when students may require his/her attention. JComposer allows users to specify notification and simple task automation agents using a visual language, which can be enabled on the fly.

- *Published observability.* CoMedi allows users to view and hear other users and their offices. Users need control over what parts can be viewed and in what ways. Manicoral also needs to coordinate viewing of data, with some views at times invisible to others and at other times visible. In CoMedi, users publish the actions that they permit other users to perform. This published observability information allows users to coordinate what actions they may perform on another users data.

- *Voting.* Some applications require a formalised mechanism for reaching agreement. CSI uses voting to reach a consensus on whether or not a line has errors and on what action to take. Development tools should support facilities for negotiation and reaching agreement.

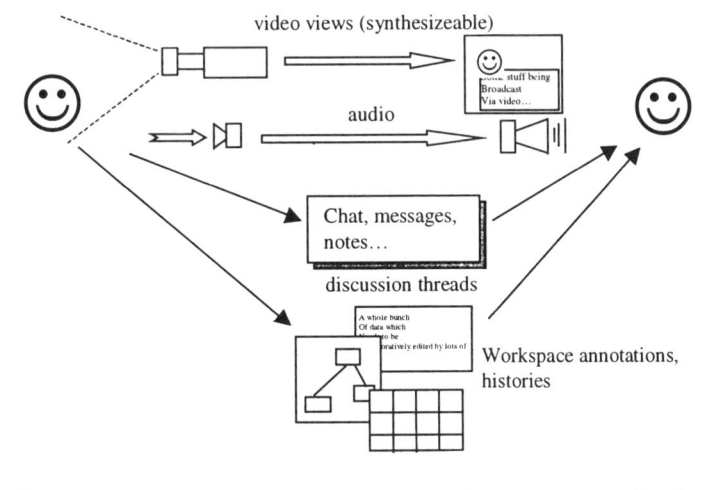

Figure 3. Communication approaches to be supported for groupware applications.

4.3   Communication and Awareness Requirements

In addition to the communication that is inherent through the manipulation of shared artifacts, groupware applications need to facilitate direct communication between distributed people. Communication techniques range over synchronous channels such as sound and video to asynchronous channels such notes and annotations. Figure 3 illustrates these communication mechanisms. Groupware development tools need to support communication through person-to-person messaging, annotations, and specialized awareness views.

4.3.1   Synchronous and Asynchronous Messaging

The most fundamental form of communication is through messages sent from one person to one or more others. Email asynchronous messaging and IRC-style synchronous messaging are two of the most common text-based messaging facilities available in groupware applications. All of the applications in section 2 make use of such messaging facilities, and some, such as Manicoral, JComposer and CSI assume users can easily switch from one mode to the other. In addition to these traditional mechanisms, groupware development tools should support:
- *Controllable video views.* Communication via video may not only include people's faces, but also views on whiteboards, office space, etc. For example, CoMedi provides a variety of video communications, including portholes indicating the presence of others, fovea views, and automated camera tracking.
- *Audio communication.* Many applications utilise audio communication, providing a synchronous, real-time chat system. Audio can also be used in voice-mail systems to provide asynchronous messages. CoMedi, the Virtual University, Manicoral and JComposer all utilize synchronous audio communications.

4.3.2   Annotation

Annotation is a useful asynchronous communication system which may take the form of textual "sticky notes", graphical items overlaying artefact views and history and message item textual annotation. Manicoral uses textual annotation of data views; the Virtual University textual and graphical annotations of slides and messages; JComposer uses textual annotation of editing histories and graphical and textual annotation of diagram views; CSI annotation of discussion threads and code lines; and Chess annotation of game histories. Tools for developing groupware should support annotation of all media and artifacts.

4.3.3   Gestalt Views

To collaborate effectively with a group, people require knowledge of the activities of other group members. A number of the applications make use of views synthesizing information about the group or its members to aid in communication. The virtual university uses several of these *gestalt* views: a timeline view showing the current location in the lecture, a question queue showing how many questions have been posed, and a mood view showing the general level of understanding of the class. CSI provides a view showing the results of the voting so far. Gestalt views synthesize information, both to provide a quick mechanism for summarizing information useful to group interaction, and as a mechanism for abstracting information that may be private. For example, the virtual university's mood view does not reveal the mood of individual students; CSI's voting view need not reveal the individual people's votes.

CoMedi provides synthesized views based on sophisticated image processing. For example, CoMedi provides gestalt views showing who is available in their office, and synthesized facial images filtering out non-facial data.

4.4 Technological Requirements

In addition to the requirements relating strictly to the functionality of groupware, the applications suggested a variety of technological requirements related to the use of available hardware, networks and software available to groupware applications. Groupware development tools should support:

- *Resource adaptivity:* At times groupware applications can be run by users with very different hardware and resources available. For example, CoMedi might be used with one user with a high-end workstation and high-resolution video camera, and another user with a Palm-top. The Virtual University has a lecturer with high-end workstation and I/O devices, some students with similar hardware and networking, and others with low-end PCs and modem connections. JComposer is often used by groups with one user on a PC with a fast LAN, and another a slow modem connection. Thus groupware toolkits should facilitate applications adapting to variable hardware in graceful ways.
- *User preferences:* Often users have different preferences as to what hardware resources should be used. For example, some Virtual University students want full-motion video and rich audio, while others just want low-resolution audio and sampled video stills. Groupware tools should allow such user requirements to be handled in seamless ways, and to be easily configured by end users.
- *Reusability of existing applications:* It is often far too difficult to replicate commercial software applications in order to make them group aware. Most groupware systems require existing applications to be integrated with their capabilities in appropriate ways. For example, Manicoral uses existing visualisation software; the Virtual University uses an existing pluggable application; JComposer uses existing workflow and programming environments.
- *Network state reporting:* Often it is important for users to be aware of whether or not others are seeing/hearing them and/or their modifications of work artifacts or messages and annotations. The Virtual University lecturer wants to be aware of the number of students engaged in the lecture and when students arrive/leave. JComposer users need to be informed when collaborators lose their connections.
- *Fault-tolerance:* All groupware systems use network connections and computer hardware which can fail unpredictably. Thus all need mechanisms for recovery from people going off-line or rejoining cooperative work sessions.

5. CONCLUSION

This report has summarized the conclusions of the EHCI Workshop on Requirements of Groupware Development Tools. We have outlined the general external requirements of groupware development tools, as driven by the features of the applications surveyed in section 2. We do not claim to have a complete coverage of all possible external requirements of groupware systems, but as illustrated above, many applications exhibit common requirements. Thus the workshop participants believe that developers of new CSCW architectures should endeavour to address all of the requirements outlined in this section, or at least ensure their architectures and implementations can be extended to accommodate them.

ACKNOWLEDGMENTS

This report is the result of a workshop held at EHCI'98. The report was edited from written contributions by Joëlle Coutaz, Prasun Dewan, Morten Borup Harning, Roberto Moriyon and the authors. Other participants contributing to the report were Remi Bastide, Patrick Girard, Jocelyne Nanard, Philippe Palanque, Fabio Paterno, Franck Tarpin-Bernard and Claus Unger.

REFERENCES

Begole, J., Struble, C.A., Shaffer, C.A. and Smith, R.B. Transparent Sharing of Java Applets: A Replicated Approach. In *Proc. ACM UIST '97,* pages 55-64. ACM Press, 1997.

Calvary, G., Coutaz, J. and Nigay, L., From Single-User Architectural Design to PAC*: a Generic Software Architecture Model for CSCW. In *Proc. CHI '97,* pages 242-249, 1997.

Cockton, G. *IFIP Virtual University Case Study.* http://osiris.sund.ac.uk/~cs0gco/IFIP/ifip_index.htm, 1998.

Dewan, P. and Choudhary, R. A High-Level and Flexible Framework for Implementing Multiuser User Interfaces. *ACM TOIS,* 10(4):345-380, October 1992.

Duce, D.A., Gallop, J.R., Johnson, I.J., Robinson, K., Seelig, C.D., and Cooper, C.S. Distributed Cooperative Visualization - The MANICORAL Approach. In *Proc. Eurographics UK,* pp. 69-85, 1998.

Graham, T.C.N., GroupScape: Integrating Synchronous Groupware and the World Wide Web, In *Proc. INTERACT '97,* pages 547-554. Chapman and Hall, 1997.

Graham, T.C.N. and Urnes, T., Integrating Support for Temporal Media into an Architecture for Graphical User Interfaces, In *Proc. ICSE '97.* IEEE Computer Society Press, 1997.

Grundy, J.C., Hosking, J.G., and Mugridge, W.B., Visual Specification of Multi-View Visual Environments, In *Proc. VL'98,* Halifax, Canada, Sept 4-7, IEEE CS Press, 1998.

Grundy, J.C., Hosking, J.G., Mugridge, W.B., Apperley, M.D. An architecture and environment for decentralised, internet-wide software process modelling and enactment. *IEEE Internet Computing* 2(5), IEEE CS Press, September/November, 1998.

Gutwin, C. and Greenberg, S. Effects of Awareness Support on Groupware Usability. In *Proc. CHI'98,* ACM Press, pp. 511-518, 1998.

Mashayekhi, V., Drake, J., Tsai, W.T. and Riedl, J. Distributed Collaborative Software Inspection. *IEEE Software,* pp. 66-75, Sept. 1993.

Munson, J., Dewan, P. A Flexible Object Merging Framework, *ACM CSCW,* pp. 231-242, Oct. 1994.

Roseman, M. and Greenberg, S. TeamRooms: Network Places for Collaboration. In Proc. *ACM CSCW,* pp. 325-333, 1996.

Stein, M.V, Riedl, J.T., Harner, S.J. and Mashayekhi, V., A Case Study of Distributed, Asynchronous Software Inspection, In *Proc. ICSE'97,* May 1997.

BIOGRAPHY

T.C. Nicholas Graham is an Associate Professor at Queen's University, in Kingston, Canada. His Doctorate of Engineering was granted by the Technical University of Berlin. His research interests include tools for groupware development, software architecture of interactive systems and the human factors of software design tools.

John Grundy is a Senior Lecturer in Computer Science at the University of Waikato, New Zealand. He holds the BSc(Hons), MSc and PhD degrees, all in Computer Science from the University of Auckland. His research interests include software engineering environments, software architectures and component-based software development, groupware systems, human-computer interaction and user interface technology, and object-oriented systems.

KEYWORD INDEX